THE SCOTS ABROAD

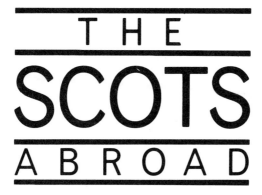

THE
SCOTS
ABROAD

LABOUR, CAPITAL, ENTERPRISE, 1750-1914

Edited by

R.A. CAGE

CROOM HELM
London • Sydney • Dover, New Hampshire

© 1985 R.A. Cage
Croom Helm Ltd, Provident House, Burrell Row,
Beckenham, Kent BR3 1AT

Croom Helm Australia Pty Ltd, First Floor,
139 King Street, Sydney, NSW 2001, Australia

British Library Cataloguing in Publication Data

The Scots abroad.
  1. Scotland—Emigration and immigration—History
  I. Cage, R.A.
  304.8'09411   JV7701
  ISBN 0-7099-0833-4

Croom Helm, 51 Washington Street, Dover,
New Hampshire 03820, USA

Library of Congress Catalog Card Number: 84-19985
Cataloging in Publication Data applied for.

The publishers acknowledge the financial assistance of the Scottish Arts Council
in the publication of this book

Printed and bound in Great Britain by
Biddles Ltd, Guildford and King's Lynn

CONTENTS

To F.M.

EDITOR'S INTRODUCTION

'The ubiquitous Scot' would be an apt description of the descendants of St Andrew, who left their native land for foreign shores. They have become a 'natural' feature of every corner of the world. In its recent advertisements for the 'Return to Glasgow' celebration, Glasgow Corporation estimated that ten million descendants of Glaswegians lived outside of Scotland! And that represents the result of movement from only one city. The Scots gained a reputation out of proportion to their numbers.

> When colonisation came into vogue, he [the Scot] was foremost among colonists . . . Invariably fortune attended his steps. He opened up new channels for trade; he wrestled with savage nature, and tamed her into a submissive servant; whenever money was to be made, the proverbial Scotchman had not long to be looked for.[1]

In its broadest sense the purpose of this book is to examine the extent of Scottish migration. In its narrowest sense the book presents case studies of Scottish involvement in the process of development. Numerous books have been written about the Scots abroad, yet this volume is unique in that it has a unifying theme; each contributor has concentrated on the role played by the Scots in the economic development of their relevant country or area. The list of countries is by no means comprehensive; selection was limited to the availability of interested and willing scholars.

Roy Campbell sets the scene. First he explains that the Scots movements overseas was an extension of movement within Scotland; that by 1750 the Scots were a mobile society. Therefore, the major factors in the decision to emigrate or move to another location within Scotland were based upon established links and expectations. Professor Campbell then briefly describes the economic development of Scotland, answering the paradox of why large-scale emigration occurred at a time of spectacular economic growth within Scotland. Finally, he describes the economic decline of Scotland and the demise of her overseas links. Thus, Professor Campbell's chapter provides not only background knowledge for Scottish emigration and development, but also a clear understanding as to why Scotland was not able to maintain her competitive economic position.

This is followed by Bob Cage's challenge to English economic historians. Dr Cage advances the hypothesis that the English Industrial Revolution owes much to Scottish involvement, and that this fact has been largely neglected in modern studies. His argument is not that England would not have developed without the Scots, but rather that perhaps the process would have been slower and less spectacular. Scottish banks were active in northern England, introducing the concept and practice of small banknotes; the course of English banking was directly influenced by the Scots. Many of the most successful engineers were Scots, who controlled the largest engineering firms in Britain. The development of the English road system owes much to two Scots, Telford and MacAdam. Many of the top industrial scientists were either Scots or trained in Scottish universities. The Scots even had an impact on England's political thinking. Hopefully, the Sassenachs will be sufficiently upset to broaden the scope of their research.

The scene then shifts to the New World. The first country examined is Canada. Professor Macmillan argues that of the countries examined in the book, Canada benefited the most from Scottish connections. He states that the links established between Scotland and the economies of British North America were strong and necessary for the rapid and sustained development of all parties concerned; the Scots were responsible for the establishment of crucial links not only between the Canadian provinces and Scotland, but also between the Canadian provinces and the United States. Not surprisingly, the first important commodities of trade were fish and timber. With the expansion of trading activities Scots merchants, especially from Glasgow and Greenock, established operation within Canada. To facilitate trade, Scots worked for development of improved systems of transport and finance. Professor Macmillan concludes by claiming that Glasgow was as important an influence upon early Canadian development as was London.

Bernard Aspinwall argues that the Scots viewed the United States as an escape valve, a place where they could mould the perfect society. As forms of transport improved, the Atlantic shrank, and America was less a foreign land and more an idealised Scotland. The 'new Scotland' was epitomised in geographical areas, such as Ohio, where there was a concentration of Scots. The Scots realised the importance of education and shaped the educational system in the United States, providing an intellectual base and influencing political thinking. The Scots changed the course of technological development in the United States by bringing new techniques in with them and teaching them to others.

Ironically, their contribution to technological advance caused less reliance on the relatively more expensive Scottish labour. Therefore, eventually the Scots became less important and they had less influence on the shape of American society; idealised Scotland was lost.

The North American continent enjoyed the largest influx of Scottish migrants. The next most important area for Scots immigration was the Antipodes, particularly Australia and New Zealand. In both these countries the Scots' impact was pre-eminent.

Australia's origin was as a penal colony for Britain. Eric Richards points out that few Scots were transported to the Australian continent, but most hardened criminals were Scots. The low proportion of Scots was not due to a more law-abiding nature, but rather to the character of the Scottish legal system. Major Scottish free migration to Australia occurred only after the 1820s and resulted from the organisational work of emigration societies creating an awareness of potential benefits; before that date, the Scots viewed North America as the major area. Professor Richards argues that the Scots were important for the development of Melbourne and that their impact on the new colonies of Victoria and South Australia was greater than on New South Wales and Van Dieman's Land. In terms of economic activity the Scots were particularly successful in the pastoral section, where they were major suppliers of capital and in the process there were numerous rags to riches stories, as they were willing to take risks. As in other countries, the Scots in Australia maintained a community spirit, preserving the observance of peculiar Scottish customs. Scotland was an important source of capital for Australia. Unlike the case for North America, Eastern Scotland was more important than Western Scotland as a source of investment funds. Professor Richards concludes that although the Scots made important contributions to the development of Australian society, it is not possible to state that the contributions were disproportionate to their numbers.

Tom Brooking is not as hesitant in his conclusions. He feels that New Zealand probably benefited more from Scottish migration than did Australia. In fact a number of Scots first went to Australia, where they made money and then moved on to New Zealand. Dr Brooking argues that the Scots made important and distinctive contributions in the areas of capital, enterprise and labour. Moreover, they influenced the nature of land tenure, so that New Zealand became a land of small holders. Scottish runholders were responsible for developing vast areas of country. Scots were prominent in the management level of banks and major firms, and featured in the establishment of such industries as woollen mills, paper mills and breweries. Even though Scottish capital, like labour, was important, it mainly supplemented that from England, though significant amounts of Scottish capital came to New Zealand via Australia. Finally, Dr Brooking concludes that the Scots influenced the nature of early New Zealand, as a disproportionate number of them were represented on boards of local government.

In assessing the Scots contribution to the economic development of India, James Parker argues that their initial impact was via the East India Company, hence the two cannot be separated. Because the Scots were able to establish influential connections within the Company, they were able to construct valuable links with India. Those Scots interested in the Indian trade who could not obtain positions within the Company could either enter by joining European companies or by becoming free merchants. A number of them attained dominant positions in the local economies as free merchants, almost entirely as members of family concerns. Ironically, these firms were frequent suppliers of cash to assist the Company in local administration. But the impact of the Scots in India was the greatest after the downfall of the Company and with the rise of the managing agents. During this period Scottish investment was the most pronounced in the areas of jute, tea, shipping and railways, and banking. Dr Parker examines each of these in detail, concluding that the Scots impact on India was largely transitional, as most viewed their stay in India as being only a temporary exile.

The final two chapters examine areas where the extent of Scottish involvement is surprising, and helped at least in some measure to shape the development of the societies concerned. This was the case even though the number of Scots present was extremely small, and in the case of Japan most were only temporary residents.

Manuel Fernandez begins with an explanation as to why the Scots were not attracted in large numbers to Latin America, though their absence in part may be due to the common practice of classifying all British subjects as 'English'. Deficiencies in numbers, however, were compensated for by some 'colourful' characters. A couple of these were active in the various wars of independence. Dr Fernandez argues that the Scots' involvement in the wars was not just for personal glory, but also for the development of economic intercourse between Scotland and the emerging new republics. To assist this desire, some Scottish settlement schemes were attempted, the results of which were nearly as disastrous as the ill-fated Darien Scheme. Argentina, perhaps because of vast resources, was the favourite destination for the Scots. Not surprisingly, the initial economic impact in Latin America was in sheep breeding and cattle raising. Yet, a sizeable mercantile community also developed, with tea and nitrate becoming two important commodities. Another area of importance was shipping, with the Scots being major suppliers of ships.

In the final chapter Olive Checkland traces the Scots contributions to Japanese economic development. Again, it is extremely difficult to separate the Scots from the British component. None the less, Mrs Checkland argues that the Scots played a role in creating the new Japan after 1868. But as early as 1858, it was a Scot, a representative of Jardine Matheson, who managed to surmount many of the barriers imposed against foreign traders, opening up Japanese trade. Thus began a strong contingent of Scots traders in Japan. A Scot is credited with influencing the early Japanese banking practices. Similarly, the course of technical education in Japan springs largely from Scottish involvement; this led to the formation of strong links in the engineering field between Japan and Scotland. The establishment of Japan's lighthouse network was also the result of Scottish efforts, permitting night-time navigation. This led to the strengthening of the ties that Scotland had with Japan, ties which remained until after the First World War.

An important underlying feature emerges from all the chapters: it is not possible to define 'Scottishness'; all eighteenth-and nineteenth-century attempts to enumerate essential Scottish characteristics were romantic and idealistic. The Scots' success cannot be explained in genetic terms. Indeed, it is even necessary to question the ethos of Scottish successfulness; were they proportionately more successful than other ethnic groups? Perhaps not, but it is not possible to state with certainty, for in none of the countries examined have there been detailed studies of the impact of other nationality groups on economic, social and political development.

Whether or not they were disproportionately successful is debatable. But they were frequently successful. Therefore, if genetic factors are discounted, what can account for this phenomenon? Perhaps the most realistic explanation can be found in the links which were maintained with Scotland. In all the countries examined the Scottish migrants established and maintained strong commercial connections with Scotland. These connections were valuable to both parties. Newly arrived emigrants benefited as well, for they could take advantage of introductions to established contacts. The Scots in their new homes formed networks, preserving and cultivating their 'Scottishness'. Many would employ only Scots, or buy only from Scottish firms. Yet, Scottish blood was not an automatic passport to employment or success; hard and productive work was expected.

Ironically, in spite of their clubbishness, the Scots easily assimilated into their new environment; most were used to moving and re-establishing themselves. This was probably a crucial factor in their success. They were willing to take risks to meet new sets of challenges. They were willing and able to adapt to new circumstances. For most the opportunities in their new home were greater than they ever would have been in Scotland. They set about the task of building their new land.

In editing this volume some debts have been incurred, which require special thanks. Edited volumes are a team effort, requiring co-operation from all parties. The contributors to this volume have made my job easy. They have met my deadlines and editorial comments without complaint, frequently displaying a wonderful sense of humour. To them I will always be grateful. Christopher Helm of Croom Helm has been an enthusiastic supporter of this volume ever since I first approached him in 1981; he has closely followed its progress. Finally, this book would not have been possible without the generations of Scots who have enriched this world with their presence.

Notes

1. Anon, 'Scottish Capital Abroad', *Blackwood's Edinburgh Magazine*, vol. CXXXVI (October, 1884) pp. 468-80.

1 SCOTLAND

R.H. Campbell

In discussing Scots abroad, an examination of the background from which they came must concentrate on the causes of their movement, or on the characteristics and qualities which the emigrants took to their new abodes. The general assertion that people moved because they felt — with or without justification — that opportunities overseas were relatively more attractive draws attention to the complexities involved, and shows that emigration could take place even when opportunities were available at home, which, at other times, might not have led to extensive emigration. In examining the determinants of such assessments made by many individuals, the influence of personal qualities of character may be distinguished from external changes in the environment. The former leads individuals or groups to be more ready to exchange their native land for life abroad; the latter renders life abroad more attractive at times. The influences of the two converge. Cultural factors, notably their religious and educational background, may have led Scots to seek self-advancement more readily than others, in which case any assessment of a relative absence of opportunity in Scotland was more likely to lead them to emigrate. While their character may have made the Scots more ready to move, its influence was to be seen in their lives abroad. Ways in which the Scots took with them their educational and religious practices, and translated Scottish institutions overseas, is more appropriately the concern of essays on Scots in the countries of their adoption. The emphasis in the essay on Scotland should stress the opportunities which were open at home, in the industrial Lowlands as well as in the rural Highlands, but which, when compared with the openings available elsewhere, were unable to retain the population at home. A study of the Scotland which many left to seek a new life overseas should then begin with a warning against regarding emigration as a spirited adventure. That it was often the reverse was pointed out with startling clarity in the most literate study of emigration ever made by a Scot, who himself died far from Scotland:

There is nothing more agreeable to picture and nothing more pathetic to behold [than emigration] . . . around me were for the most

1

part quiet, orderly, obedient citizens, family men broken by adversity, elderly youths who had failed to place themselves in life, and people who had seen better days . . . We were a company of the rejected; the drunken, the incompetent, the weak, the prodigal, all who had been unable to prevail against circumstances in one land, were now fleeing pitifully to another; and though one or two might still succeed, all had already failed. We were a shipful of failures . . . [1]

Whatever the successes and achievements of Scots abroad, their journey from Scotland often began with failure at home.

I

Whatever the many influences which forged links between Scotland and countries overseas one easily neglected cause was simply the existence of a tradition of movement even before 1750. The Scots pioneered several colonial schemes throughout the seventeenth century, though with indifferent success, before the major, and as it transpired, catastrophic colonial scheme of the Company of Scotland Trading to Africa and the Indies (the Darien Scheme).[2] These attempts were part of a general desire to build up a self-sufficient economy. The records of the Scottish parliament and privy council after the Restoration are replete with attempts to conserve bullion and promote internal economic growth, leading objectives which encompassed a number of subordinate aims: to try to stop importing goods which could easily be made at home; to prevent the export of domestically produced raw materials and semi-manufactures which might help competitors; to provide employment, especially of 'poore people and idle persones and vagabonds' whereby 'vertew will be increased and idlest curbed and restrained'.[3]

The policy of maintaining a closed economy and of exploiting its indigenous resources was dismissed contemptuously by later generations. The advocacy of protectionism in the twentieth century, especially for weaker economies liable to be affected adversely by large-scale importation of foreign goods, should lead to greater sympathy with its adoption in the seventeenth century in economies, such as Scotland, which were competitively weak. In addition, the diplomatic principle that political independence requires economic independence was as applicable as in other ages of international conflict. In most cases the policy could not easily achieve the ultimate objective of economic independence without establishing colonies as extensions of the domestic economy and so geared to its needs.

The numbers who went overseas in the early colonial schemes were few, many with no intention of settling, but planning to return with their fortunes made, which, of course, practically none did. Limited as these movements were, they established a tradition for Scots to go overseas in modern times, and basically for economic reasons. They also showed how central to many of these movements were the links with England. The resentful response of the Scots to the measures and actions of England confirms their reluctance to accept an incorporating union, and in many cases a union of any kind, while the weakness of any independent Scottish policy shows their inability to support continuing political independence with the economic power it required. In these circumstances both those present-day historians who argue that the parliamentary union of 1707 was inevitable, and those who argue the reverse, can cite the same evidence to prove their different cases.[4] They are at one, at any rate, in demonstrating that the parliamentary union of 1707 is critical in understanding Scottish history, including the position of Scots abroad.

The early colonial ventures, culminating in the fiasco of the Darien Scheme, confirmed the need for some form of union if the Scots were to gain from the growing opportunities England offered. The threats in the English Alien Act[5] reflected an astute awareness by the English of the weak economic position of the Scots, and the nature of the relationships between the two countries was then a major determinant of Scottish emigration. Even before the parliamentary union of 1707, Scots went to England and its colonies, encouraged by the regal union after 1603. After 1707 the removal of some of the impediments provided further encouragement, though the Scots were not thereby made any more acceptable or welcome. The closeness of the much richer neighbour induced a greater sense of relative deprivation among the Scots, which their urge for self-advancement led them to try to remedy by moving south or to the colonies. The well-recognised shift of the Scottish nobility to the London scene is an example of a more general response by lesser mortals. After the Union of 1707 the Scots were able to exploit the possibilities more effectively through the new political links and the political machine which accompanied it. They provided institutional means of making an existing desire more effective.[6] Even if few in number moved overseas in direct consequence, as through Dundas's later influence in appointments in India,[7] they could have great influence, and their movement can be attributed to the prospects opened up by the union. In that respect Dr Johnson's assertion was valid, that 'the noblest prospect which a Scotchman ever sees, is the high road that leads him to England!'.[8] The effects of the road to England, perhaps especially of the road to London, can easily be underestimated. The mercantilist attitudes of the time had an equivocal attitude to emigration, as is only to be expected of a way of thought which had many varied adherents over a long period. Overpopulation was not the fear it was to become later. National greatness was still thought to depend on retaining as many as possible in the country,[9] while radical critics saw attempts to prevent emigration as an example of feudal victimisation.[10] Even when the reluctance to countenance general loss of population was fading, the reluctance to see special skills go persisted in the nineteenth century, especially those which lay behind the country's international industrial success. The attempts at control were never completely successful, largely because of the attractiveness of gaining such skills overseas.[11] The restrictions did not apply in the movement to England.

II

In the later eighteenth century new forces which support Stevenson's interpretation that much emigration began in failure were added to the tradition of migration. They were most evident in the Highlands, though the intensity of distress and dispute which followed was caused as much by the response of the Highlanders as by their environment. In discussing the contribution of the Highlands to Scots abroad the historical analysis must be distinguished from the counterfactual evaluation of how the problems of the Highlands might have been tackled but were not. Confusion increases when historians accept the same evidence but deem it of different relevance.[12] Conflict is then often purely verbal and not on matters of substance.

A key to the difference lies in the failure of many to progress beyond a short-term analysis, that — at its simplest — the landlords cleared the people to make way for sheep, to a longer-term analysis of trends which may have determined some such outcome in any case. The latter suggests a revision both historically and counterfactually of some commonly-held views. The substance of the long-term evaluation is an interpretation of the relationship between changes in the structure of Highland society and of the consequences of demographic change. The evidence for both is widely accepted, but, providing confirmation that differences of opinion are often of methodology and not of historical fact, the assessment of its relevance varies. According to one interpretation: 'The commercialisation of the agricultural structure in response to the chieftains' financial necessitousness . . . is the great fact of eighteenth century Highland history. From it all else follows.'[13] A fundamental consequence which did follow from the older social structure was that 'In proportion as his clan was numerous and his estate covered with inhabitants, he [a Highland chieftain] felt himself great and respectable . . . '[14] All agree that this social structure crumbled. The timing of the change is less important, but had one major consequence. So long as medical deficiencies and physical limitations on subsistence ensured that the population never grew to an extent which exceeded the desire of the chief to have retainers, then in one sense it was not possible to have a demographic crisis. Before the eighteenth century the limitations on population growth were so effective that the resiliency of the social structure, and especially the response of the landowners to the strains of long-term population growth, were not put to the tests they had to face later.[15]

Since population changes have long-term effects, the demographic increase is often underestimated in a short-term analysis. It is also underestimated by many who stress the influence of the changing social structure, but who, once they recognise its influence, introduce into their historical discussion the unhistorical counterfactual suggestion that changes in the social structure, other than those which took place, could have led to an effective exploitation of the economic potential of the region, adequate to support the rising population.[16] Such an interpretation cannot be proved or disproved convincingly because it depends on an assessment of the economic potential of the region and on the possibility of an economic transformation following a change in the social structure or in social attitudes. Some historical evidence can be advanced in support, because the rise in population did not lead quickly, and without interruption, to a demographic crisis. Increased subsistence from the land and the growth of cash income enabled the rising population to be supported for a time within the framework of the increasingly commercial society which was evolving. Subsistence increased particularly through the cultivation of the potato; income grew notably through short-term migration to the Lowlands for seasonal employment. Coinciding fortuitously with the rise of population came an increase in price and consequential growth of production of a wide range of indigenous Highland goods for export from the region, especially cattle and kelp.

These developments hardly provide adequate evidence to support the counterfactual position that an economic transformation was possible in the Highlands and that it was impeded, perhaps prevented, by an inappropriate social structure dominated by the narrow and increasingly commercial interest of the landowner. The increases in subsistence, and in cash income, contributed little to solving the fundamentally long-term problem of how to accommodate the rising population. They merely postponed the catastrophe, and one by one the supports of the precariously balanced structure were removed: the opportunities for short-term migration began to falter as the new industrial structure sought full-time labour; the wartime inflation came to an end and prices for Highland products fell sharply; the potato failed with blight, especially in the 1840s. Then the region faced two grim alternatives: the maintenance of a demoralised population through imports of grain, provided, both physically and financially, from outside the area, or emigration. In reply a short-term analysis stresses the historical fact that emigration arose because many people were cleared by the landowners to enlarge holdings to make way for sheep, and so the landowners and sheep were at least the agents in the process. It can also be maintained – counterfactually in an even stronger criticism of the landowners – that they let slip opportunities to tackle the demographic problem by economic reform: by default if not deliberately, they removed the tacksmen, who might have provided the entrepreneurial talent for the new commercial society;[17] above all they used rising cash incomes, especially those generated by the inflation and the special and narrow opportunities of the Napoleonic Wars, to be dissipated in increased consumption, instead of being invested to provide a permanent and wider base for the maintenance of a larger but still prosperous population. It is then easy to suggest that – at best – the landowners left matters alone too long and – at worst – that they were interested only in short-term gain.

A case can be advanced against this persuasive short-term view on both historical and counterfactual grounds. Historically, in much of the eighteenth century, until the demographic crisis engulfed the Highlands, opposition to emigration was general. The actions which followed the developing demographic crisis were confusing, often haphazard and not the product of any design, whether benevolent or malevolent in intention. Sometimes emigration followed the introduction of sheep; sometimes it emerged independently; sometimes it was the consequence of deliberate clearance, sometimes it was not. 'Indeed, there is strong presumption that propinquity to the Lowlands makes more potently for depopulation than does internal agrarian change.'[18] Counterfactually, the loss of the tacksmen in the earliest waves of emigration, and the dissipation of financial resources in more ostentatious living, did not necessarily inhibit the more permanent transformation required to support the larger population in the Highlands. They were as tied to the old social structure as anyone, and their achievements when they left the Highlands and moved to a new environment are irrelevant to what they would have done if they had remained. Nor would the expenditure of capital on economic projects have guaranteed an economic transformation any more then than now. The major lesson to be learned from the experience of the Sutherland estates[19] – or, perhaps from the activities of the 1st Lord Leverhulme in more modern times[20] – is that schemes for the regeneration of the Highlands can easily absorb much capital to little effect.

These examples of failure suggest two propositions, which, if accepted, virtually prevent any attempt to entertain possibilities of ways of escape from the long-term catastrophe of rising population and so of emigration. First, the Highlands did not have the resources – of whatever kind –for the maintenance of an indigenous and independent connection with the rising industrial economy of the south, sufficiently strong and resilient to maintain the rising population. The problem is not unique to the Highlands and can be seen in other parts of rural Scotland, particularly in the south-west. Bluntly, but concisely, it was not easy for an area to make any substantial economic progress, adequate to support a rising population at an acceptable standard of living in the nineteenth century, without coal. For the Highlands the next best thing was probably sheep farming, perhaps the enterprise for which it was naturally best fitted.[21] Second, even if the proposition that economic resources were inadequate is rejected, another barrier lies in the way of a solution. The view that the problem was merely one of determining an appropriate social structure to maintain the rising population implies that any way of life would have been acceptable if it had realised that objective. In practice the only way of life which was acceptable may not have exploited effectively such resources as the Highlands had. In short, with the rising population the old social and agrarian structure could not be perpetuated, yet that old structure was the one still desired in the Highlands. To that assertion there is one qualification. If a successful transformation of the Highland economy was possible, the opportunity came early rather than late, before the demographic problem had become acute. Success on the Argyll lands was not only because of the power — entrepreneurial and financial — of Argyll, or of the proximity of much of his land to markets and opportunities for seasonal employment, but to early timing.[22] More important still, Argyll's success rested on authoritarian action, and the exercise of such power is perhaps the most critical issue of all in any evaluation of the clearances. Fundamentally the issue is moral not historical, and so it is hardly surprising that the same evidence is often interpreted differently. The Highlanders wished to retain as much of the old social order as possible; especially, they were attached to the land, but with population rising, and with the expectation of a higher standard of living as wealth increased generally, change was necessary. The maintenance of the old society would itself have meant the loss of the basis of economic survival.[23]

III

The distressing experiences of the Highlands should not be allowed to eclipse emigration from other areas. In the opinion of its residents, lowland industrial Scotland also had its own failures, which led them to assess opportunities overseas more favourably than those at home. Many left later in the nineteenth century, in the move which Stevenson recorded so graphically when he joined them. Given the contrasting demographic experiences of the areas, their move differed from the better-known one from the Highlands.

The opportunities of permanent support in lowland industries enabled the population of the whole of Scotland to grow from an estimated 1,265,380 in 1755 to 1,608,420 in 1801, to 2,888,742 in 1851, and to 4,472,103 in 1901.[24] There is then a paradox in Scottish experience at this time. While many Scots were leaving the country, more were being supported at home. The movement of many Scots overseas may have been accompanied by the depopulation of parts of Scotland, but not of the whole.

The economic opportunities which lay behind these developments came with the rise of the modern industrial structure from the late eighteenth century. The speed and extent of the change should not be overestimated. When information on the nature of employment became available in the census of 1841, almost a quarter of the workforce were still in agricultural and related employment. The proportion, which was always higher than for Great Britain as a whole, fell only slightly until the census of 1881, which recorded the first of several sharp drops which continued until 1911, when it was just over 10 per cent.[25] The Scottish figures mask considerable regional diversity.[26] Large areas were little affected by the change, but to stress even the quantitatively small beginnings of the industrial changes of the eighteenth century, which were slowly to engulf the whole, is appropriate when the objective is to isolate the emergence of the means of supporting the larger population. Though industrial enterprises, especially those associated with the overseas trade of Glasgow,[27] were notable by the mid-eighteenth century, the mechanisation of spinning in the last quarter of the century is recognised as the first major move to the industrial state. Its effects spread widely from the spinning mills — few in number — to the weavers, who worked domestically throughout the adjacent countryside until their activities were absorbed and concentrated in mechanised production in the second quarter of the nineteenth century. At the same time the structure of the Scottish economy changed as the increasingly successful exploitation of the country's natural resources of coal and iron supported the expansion of the iron industry, which was followed later in the nineteenth century by the manufacture of steel. The increased output of the semi-manufactured products of iron and steel accompanied and encouraged the growth of heavy engineering from the later years of the nineteenth century until 1914. From the mid-eighteenth century, but especially from the 1780s until 1914, Scotland offered increasing industrial opportunities. The story is well known and needs little repetition.[28]

Such opportunities lay behind the paradox that more Scots were able to live at home while many left for life overseas. The paradox is still more striking as the opportunities attracted immigrants into Scotland when Scots were moving out, chiefly, of course, from Ireland. The number of Irish-born, only slightly inflated by the inclusion of seasonal immigrants, was 126,321 or 4.8 per cent of the population when the information first became available in 1841; by 1851 the number had increased sharply to 207,367 or 7.2 per cent of the population. From 1861 until 1901 it ranged from 194,807 or 4.8 per cent in 1891 to 218,745, the highest recorded, or 5.9 per cent in 1881. In 1911 the number had fallen sharply to 174,715 or 3.7 per cent of the population. Even when the numbers were maintained, the proportion fell from its peak of 7.2 per cent in 1851.[29]

The number of Irish-born in Scotland is not great, much below what was required to offset the emigration from Scotland. From the census year of 1861, when it first becomes possible to calculate the changes, after the institution of civil registration in Scotland in 1855, a substantial net loss by migration was recorded, though always less than the natural increase until after the First World War. The decade from 1881 to 1891 recorded an increase in the net loss to over 217,000 or 43 per cent of the natural increase. It fell to only slightly over 53,000 or 11 per cent in the 1890s, rose sharply to 254,000 or 47 per cent of the natural increase between 1901 and 1911, and remained high after the war. How many of these emigrants went overseas and not only along Dr Johnson's road to England is uncertain. From 1825, and more reliably from 1853, the number of those who left Scotland for non-European destinations is known, though the figures are subject to qualifications.[30] Using them as the basis, one calculation[31] suggests that from 1861 to 1939, 43.7 per cent of the natural increase of these years was lost overseas against 54.5 per cent to destinations overseas and to other parts of the United Kingdom. The calculation is based on many assumptions but the magnitude is sufficiently great to show that Scotland was high among the countries which lost population to countries overseas and that was at a time when it was increasingly urban, industrial and prosperous.

An elucidation of this paradox may be found by examining in some detail the movements of the population within Scotland to draw attention to the fundamental fact — so obvious that its radical influence on the movement of Scots overseas can be neglected — that from the later eighteenth century the Scots were becoming a mobile people at home. A dramatic consequence of the industrial growth of the nineteenth century, now an accepted part of Scottish social life, was the redistribution of the bulk of the population towards the central belt. It is evident in the various censuses from 1801 and can be linked to Webster's census of 1755 (see Table 1.1). The population of the ten counties of Ayr, Clackmannan, Dunbarton, Fife, Lanark, Renfrew, Stirling, West, Mid- and East Lothian increased steadily from 1755 and came to represent a higher proportion of the total population. More than two-thirds of the total were living there in 1911. The proportion in the four west-central counties of Ayr, Dunbarton, Lanark and Renfrew, the heartland of industrial growth, grew from over one-half to almost two-thirds between 1801 and 1871, but increased only slightly thereafter. By contrast, rural counties recorded peak populations from the middle of the nineteenth century: in 1831 in Argyll, Kinross and Perth; in 1841 in Inverness; in 1851 in Kirkcudbright, Ross and Cromarty, Sutherland and Wigtown; in 1861 in Berwick, Caithness, Orkney, Roxburgh and Zetland. Depopulation was a rural and not simply a Highland problem.

Scotland

Table 1.1: Population of Scotland and Central Counties

	1755	1801	1871	1911
Total Population				
Scotland	1,265,380	1,608,420	3,360,018	4,760,904
Central Belt	445,774	656,963	1,931,767	3,258,680
West-Central Counties	181,237	331,110	1,241,952	2,167,754
Percentage of Population				
Central Belt Scotland	35.2	40.8	57.5	68.4
West Central Scotland	14.3	20.6	37.0	45.5
West Central Central Belt	40.7	50.4	64.3	66.5

Note: Central Belt: Ayr, Clackmannan, Dunbarton, Fife, Lanark, Renfrew, Stirling, West, Mid-, East Lothian.
West Central Counties: Ayr, Dunbarton, Lanark, Renfrew.
Source: Censuses.

More detailed information on the movement of Scots within Scotland can be derived from the information on places of birth in the various censuses. Obviously those counties which had the larger populations were likely to be the major contributors to, or recipients of, those who moved and so a way has to be devised of comparing their contributions to movement and reception of population with their share of the total. Doing so is an elaborate exercise, but a simple test reveals the main conclusions (see Table 1.2). The net balance of the population between those born in the county but living elsewhere in Scotland, and those not born in the county but now living in it, shows those counties which had the highest net movement in and those which had the highest net movement out. In the three census years of 1851, 1871 and 1891 Lanarkshire and Midlothian, especially the former, had a substantially greater net gain within their boundaries than any other county. Perth was one of the two with the greatest net loss in each year; Argyll was the other in 1851, and Ayr in 1871 and 1891. The positions of Lanark and Midlothian are not surprising; the positions of those with the greatest net losses are explained by their propinquity to the areas of greatest development.[32] Even such a county as Ayr, with important industrial development of its own, though less expansive in the later nineteenth century, still lost on balance. Such movement can be

Table 1.2: Movement of Scottish-born

	1	2 (%)	3 (%)
1851			
Lanark	+80,595	85.3	55.8
Midlothian	+37,992	79.1	58.7
Argyll	−24,099	70.0	87.2
Perth	−25,235	72.2	83.0
1871			
Lanark	+123,409	85.4	57.7
Midlothian	+58,092	79.7	57.6
Perth	−26,904	63.9	74.7
Ayr	−29,638	73.4	77.3
1891			
Lanark	+149,707	85.1	61.7
Midlothian	+69,250	79.8	59.6
Perth	−27,260	59.3	70.1
Ayr	−36,880	70.8	77.2

Note: Col. 1. Net movement of Scottish-born.
　　Col. 2. Percentage of county-born in Scotland still living in county.
　　Col. 3. Percentage of total population of county of county-born still living in county.
Source: Censuses.

illustrated further by determining the proportion of those born in the county who still lived in it and not in other parts of Scotland and also by expressing their number as a percentage of the entire population of the county. In the three census years examined, Lanarkshire had over 85 per cent of its native-born population living in Scotland still in the county, but they accounted for less than two-thirds of the total population. In Perth the proportion of natives to the total population was always higher than the population of the Perth-born in Scotland who still lived in the county. The high net movement of population into some counties reflected the opportunities for settlement in them. Their own native-born population did not move so readily to other areas, and so they recorded a high proportion still at home, but the movement of others into the area to take advantage of their opportunities meant that the native-born were still only a relatively small part of the total population. By contrast, those with the high net loss had a lesser proportion of their native-born still living in the county of their birth, but they were a higher proportion of the total.

As would be expected in these conditions the Irish moved into the central belt as much as the Scots. Three-quarters of the Irish-born lived in the four west-central counties in the later nineteenth century. Even in the counties in which they were a significant group, they were swamped by the natives. The concentration in the central belt was of Scots (see Table 1.3).

Table 1.3: Irish-born Living in Scotland

	1851		1871		1891	
	1	2 (%)	1	2 (%)	1	2 (%)
Ayr	20,969	11.0	15,684	7.8	11,074	4.9
Dunbarton	5,356	11.9	6,398	10.9	9,845	10.4
Lanark	89,330	16.8	104,656	13.7	107,863	10.3
Renfrew	25,678	15.9	28,179	13.0	24,668	8.5
Total of above	141,333	15.3	154,917	12.5	153,450	9.3
Scotland	207,367	7.2	207,770	6.2	194,807	4.8

Note: Col. 1. Total number of Irish-born.
      Col. 2. Irish-born as percentage of population of area.
Source: Censuses.

The concentration of the population involved more than a change of location. Most had also to change their way of earning a living. In the central belt the occupational structure changed much earlier and more extensively to non-agricultural occupations[33] (see Table 1.4). By 1841 the proportions employed in agriculture, forestry and fishing in Lanark of 7.2 per cent and Midlothian of 9.0 per cent were below the proportion for the whole of Scotland in 1911 of 10.6 per cent, while in the more remote parts, both north and south, half the population was in that category in 1841. In those counties near the central belt — for example in those which made the greatest net contribution to the movement of Scots within Scotland — the proportion fell steadily and more rapidly than on the perimeter where, in areas of agricultural success or not, the proportion engaged in agriculture remained high.

The Scots who availed themselves of the opportunities in the central belt had to accept geographical and occupational mobility. The population was on the move at home. Moving within Scotland did not eliminate the personal difficulties involved. To move or not was then the greater issue to be faced, and in those areas where the reluctance to move was most intense, social tensions and pressures emerged. Once the decision was made, movement might as easily be out of Scotland, especially for those to whom movement to the central belt gave rise to

Table 1.4: Employment in Agriculture, Forestry and Fishing as Percentage of Total Employment

	1841 (%)	1851 (%)	1861 (%)	1871 (%)	1881 (%)	1891 (%)	1901 (%)	1911 (%)
Ayr	19.0	21.1	17.6	17.1	14.1	11.9	9.7	9.4
Berwick	48.6	53.1	50.0	50.7	49.3	46.6	44.1	43.7
Inverness	48.3	55.1	48.6	58.0	44.9	38.0	35.4	34.5
Lanark	7.1	6.1	5.1	4.1	2.8	2.1	1.8	1.7
Midlothian	9.0	9.1	8.0	5.8	4.7	4.2	3.3	3.2
Perth	30.8	31.8	31.3	33.0	28.0	23.9	20.8	21.4
Sutherland	53.5	57.4	59.7	67.7	60.5	58.2	52.4	48.1
Wigtown	43.2	42.5	42.2	42.6	41.5	39.0	39.7	41.1
Scotland	24.3	24.9	22.2	22.2	16.7	14.0	11.5	10.6

Source: C.H. Lee, *British Regional Employment Statistics, 1841-1971* (Cambridge, 1979). I am grateful to Dr Lee for supplying me with a further breakdown of his statistics into counties.

changes in the environment as radical and permanent as going overseas, as it was to a Gaelic-speaking Highlander. The direction of movement was frequently the consequence of personal or family links with a particular area, and it could be as easy to go to a Highland settlement in Canada as into one in Kingston or Partick in Glasgow. The lack of opportunities in some parts of Scotland — indeed in the greater part spatially — encouraged the growth of a mobile population — both geographically and industrially — which contributed directly to the development of the modern Scottish economy, but which also spilled over into emigration overseas.

Unfortunately it is not possible to go much beyond general statements about the occupations or regional origins of the emigrants, of whether they were highland rural or lowland industrial migrants. The record of occupations begins only in 1912,[34] when almost half of those males who stated their occupations were in skilled trades and about one-third were labourers. Among those females who gave a gainful occupation almost three-quarters were in some form of domestic service, though one-half of the total were housewives or did not state an occupation. The skilled went mostly to South Africa and the United States, the unskilled to Australia and Canada. The geographical origins of the migrants are even less certain, though there is evidence of a switch from a preponderance of rural migrants, especially from the Highlands, in the later eighteenth century giving way to a preponderance of urban migrants in the later nineteenth century.[35] The shift, which reflects the balance of geographical location and industrial occupation in Scotland in the nineteenth century, came when emigration absorbed a large part of Scotland's natural increase of population. Much emigration from Scotland came then from a successful industrial country and not from a decaying rural one.

The structural changes which lay behind the success of the Scottish economy in the years from 1750 to 1914 provide a clue to an explanation. The emergence of new industries gave opportunities to those who remained in Scotland, notably the growth of the heavy industries to take the leading place from the textile industries, and, within the heavy industries, the supplanting of the older pig iron industry by steelmaking, shipbuilding and heavy engineering. The other aspect of industrial history, so easily submerged in the success, was the decline of some sectors. They encouraged lowland, industrial emigration in an already mobile society. Of these declining industries the best known example was handloom weaving, which experienced its protracted period of increasing extinction mostly in the second quarter of the nineteenth century. It provides a specific example of the more general phenomenon of some moving into an industry as others were moving out.[36] Those who moved in were generally the new arrivals in central Scotland, particularly Irish immigrants, who could easily acquire the minimum skills and capital required. Scottish weavers moved out, to go overseas in many cases. Official investigations of the nineteenth century agreed. Witnesses convinced the Select Committee on Emigration of 1827: ' . . . there can be no doubt that the space created by their [potential emigrants] removal would be instantaneously filled up . . . above all, the space would be instantaneously filled up by the resort of Irish to that part of the country'.[37] The analogy of the vacuum was cited by other witnesses.[38] A decade later, when the state of the handloom weavers was examined in detail in the 1830s, the Assistant Commissioner for the South of Scotland reported the same problem.[39] Given the identification of this tendency for the vacuum to be filled up by the Irish, it is easy to sympathise with the view of the Select Committee that it had been charged with a subsidiary issue, because

> . . . although the Scotch Emigrants are in most instances very valuable settlers, and although there is a strong disposition among its people to emigrate, yet, as a national measure, more effectual relief may be afforded by a reconsideration of the laws above alluded to, and by the diversion elsewhere of the influx of Irish paupers, than by any system of Emigration which might be applied to the removal of the Scotch population.[40]

Facilitating emigration as the means of alleviating pauperism may have been pointless, but there was no doubt that many weavers wanted to emigrate. Witnesses from the Glasgow Emigration Society maintained that of their member 'not all, but a great proportion' were weavers. Alexander Campbell, a member of the select committee, thought the societies were 'entirely' handloom weavers, and the list of Scottish applicants for help has large numbers of weavers among the Lowlanders, especially from Glasgow.[41] The influx of the Irish may have perpetuated the degradation of the handloom weavers, but the structural changes in weaving in the second quarter of the nineteenth century encouraged many of the Scots to go overseas. In these circumstances a cyclical downswing often provided the necessary final short-term impetus. The opportunities in the coalmines and in the ironworks were less attractive. If a break had to be made, the prospects overseas seemed preferable. The opportunities in Scotland were not for those who had once known better days.

The experience of the handloom weavers shows that all industrial sectors did not share in the general prosperity of the economy. An occupational group could then be in a position similar to those in a geographical area suffering from the demographic and social pressures of the Highlands. Since the extent of both contemporary and subsequent concern often reflects resistance to emigration, the handloom weavers have never received the same attention as the Highlanders, even though they also resisted leaving their occupations. Of course the bulk of emigrants were neither Highlanders nor handloom weavers and did not display the resistance to movement which guarantees attention from historians. The two examples have been examined, not to explain why all Scots emigrated, but to suggest that Stevenson's assessment that emigration began in failure is probably correct. In these two examples the failure is obvious. Failure also explains the movement of many others: a perception that Scotland was failing to offer opportunities comparable to those overseas. Sometimes — as in the Highlands and among the weavers — the failure was objective, though subjective assessments of it varied; for many others the failure was only in their subjective assessment of relative prospects at home and abroad, and they were often wrong. Perhaps the Scots were unusually dissatisfied with their lot at home, or unusually attracted by the openings overseas: they were pessimists at home and optimists abroad. To explain such psychological propensities requires an investigation of personal characteristics which this essay avoids. When a population is mobile at home, as it was in Scotland in the nineteenth century, it is a short step for such psychological propensities to drive it overseas as the facilities to travel there improved rapidly.

IV

When many Scots sailed overseas for whatever reason, any links which remained provided personal but no less potent encouragements to others to follow, and even more so to go to a specific location. The effects of reports of life overseas are difficult to judge. Some were blatant propaganda aimed at encouraging emigration for the benefit of the propagandist. As has been pointed out,[42] they could meet with resistance, especially in the eighteenth century. Opposition did not vanish quickly or completely in the nineteenth century, not even when Malthusian fears of population pressure were accepted increasingly.

Generally, however, by the nineteenth century an emigration agent had an easier task, when few were anxious to retain what was regarded as surplus population, even if not all were willing to finance emigration. A good account of how agents went about their business is in a description of recruitment of Nova Scotia in the 1820s.

> A Scotchman who has got habituated to the country came home as an adventurer, to bring out passengers; he travelled through the north of Scotland, and engaged as many passengers as pleased to go with him, and when he had got two to three hundred to go, he then hired a vessel, and agreed to take them out, and by such trade he generally made something handsome for his trouble. In that way the people were carried out in great numbers and at small expense.[43]

Letters from those who had gone before encouraging friends and relations to follow were probably less prejudiced than the propaganda of the agents. They were certainly directed more specifically to the personal needs and aspirations of the recipients and often held out the incalculable incentive of a known face at the end of the long journey. Such letters have tended to disappear, but one study,[44] based on a number received from the United States between 1815 and 1861, shows that the letters shared the economic emphasis of the propagandists and the agents. Since the study concluded that the emigration was 'largely economic, with comparatively few Scots leaving their homeland for political or religious reasons after 1851', it is hardly surprising that the letters used as evidence showed little interest in educational or religious facilities. Instead the writers 'emphasised the land as the greatest attraction — it was fertile, easily available, and cheap and the climate was good'. The bait held out was that there was 'work for all and high wages'.[45] Though not all who emigrated settled on the land, such a message was obviously seductive to those in rural Scotland, who were faced, less with the choice of whether to move or not, as that was inevitable for many, but with the subordinate question of where to go, whether to the horrors of urban Glasgow or overseas. Nor was the availability of land without its attractions to others, even to those leaving industrial occupations, since many of them were of rural origin. It certainly attracted the weavers, many of whom lived in agricultural villages and were often accustomed to agricultural labour.[46]

Those who were attracted out of Scotland made their mark overseas. A direct effect on Scotland came when sectors of the Scottish economy were geared to activities overseas. It is useful to distinguish three categories into which such contacts may be classified. The first, which attracts much attention, should be handled with care. In this case the source of the contact came from Scotland, but its influence was felt almost entirely elsewhere. The category includes many of the merchants and traders who are cited so often as representatives of the Scot abroad, but whose activities, exceptionally influential as they could be overseas, were of little consequence in Scotland.

The potentially limited nature of this connection was evident in the trade with the American colonies in the eighteenth century, in which re-exports accounted for about one-third of the total before 1776. The limited ability of the Scottish economy to respond to all the demands made was evident when Scottish merchants had to obtain supplies of goods they required from elsewhere. Exports of Scottish domestic production were more important in the West Indian trade after the American Revolution, but grew to dominate foreign trade only with the modern industrial growth of the late eighteenth, and especially of the nineteenth century. Even if the early overseas trade encouraged industrial ventures in Scotland — the sugar houses and other activities in the west of Scotland — it is less certain that it contributed to the more substantial industrial growth which spread from around the 1780s and which relied for a large measure of its success on favourable indigenous causes.[47] Many of the Scots who made their mark throughout the world as great merchants and traders had then often very little lasting link, if any at all, with Scotland. A good example is the firm of Jardine, Matheson and Company, in discussing which the historian of the China trade rightly commented: ' . . . it was not unimportant that in this period the Eastern trade was so largely developed by Scotsmen, with family connections in every port east of the Cape, not to speak of relatives in the neighbourhood of Lombard Street'.[48] The importance lay in their influence on the development of the China trade and not on events in Scotland, except as a vehicle for yet more Scots to go overseas.

The second category into which the contacts fell arose from activities which were usually directed from Scotland, at least in their early days. They can be subdivided into three groups: financial, shipping and industrial connections. Around 1840 a number of Aberdeen financiers launched real estate companies chiefly to invest in the United States. The pioneer was the Illinois Investment Company in 1837. At the same time, and again in Aberdeen, the Scottish Australian Company was founded to carry on business in New South Wales.

The pioneers were not emulated immediately, perhaps simply because investment in the Scottish economy was absorbing much of the available risk capital. Conditions changed from the 1870s. More capital was available for investment overseas, though not to the detriment of Scottish industry in the years which witnessed the establishment of modern steelmaking and shipbuilding. Robert Fleming was the pioneer of this phase when he formed his Scottish American Trust in 1873, chiefly to invest in railway mortgage bonds. The Fleming group of trusts spread in number and in the range of their investments. Others followed. In the 1880s a number of land mortgage companies were formed, though some of them had earlier roots, again to invest chiefly in the United States.[49] At much the same time, in 1873-4, the Scottish American Investment Company Ltd and the Scottish American Mortgage Company Ltd were registered in Edinburgh to concentrate respectively on stock market securities and on real estate.[50] Edinburgh and Dundee provided eight of the eleven British joint-stock ventures formed between 1880 and 1885 for cattle ranching in Texas. Dundee provided its capital locally but the Edinburgh-based concerns had to be supported financially from Dundee.[51] Glasgow's apparent backwardness in this field was evident by 1914. Twenty-five investment trusts were then based in Edinburgh, eight in Dundee, but only three in Glasgow.[52] The difference does not necessarily reflect an absence of financial enterprise in Glasgow, but the availability of alternative opportunities. Dundee had a prosperous jute industry by the later nineteenth century, but was isolated from the mainstream of Scottish industry and so not as able as Glasgow to exploit by personal contact the major industrial openings of the time. Dundee found that its overseas commitments soon made investment overseas as easy as at home. In one, perhaps unfortunate, overseas investment Glasgow led. Both the Western and the City of Glasgow Banks invested overseas. At its failure in 1878 the City of Glasgow Bank had considerable property interests in Australia and in New Zealand and had financed much of the Western Union Railroad, which ran from Lake Michigan to the Mississippi.[53]

Shipping connections were as widespread as financial. The Clyde had a number of shipping lines offering world-wide services which conveyed many emigrants to their new homes. Five first emerged from the 1850s to provide the major passenger services until 1914. They merged into larger units thereafter. The Allan, Anchor, and Donaldson Lines sailed mainly on various routes across the Atlantic; the City Line plied to India and the Clan Line of Cayzer, Irvine to South Africa as well.

Even shipping lines operating chiefly or entirely from English or overseas ports owed much to Scottish initiative and capital. The Cunard Company's origins were in Glasgow. The Peninsular and Oriental Steam Navigation Company emerged from the activities of a group of Scotsmen who had emigrated to London, while the British India Steam Navigation Company, with which the P & O amalgamated, originated in Mckinnon and Mackenzie and Company, Indian merchants of Scottish origins, from whose service James Mackay, 1st Earl of Inchcape, rose to dominate the P & O and much else. Even if the headquarters of a shipping line remained in Scotland, its influence there was limited. A good example is in the activities of P. Henderson and Company, founded by four brothers, whose personal migration took them from Pittenweem to Glasgow. The firm's chartering and shipbroking department was a clearing house for the Glasgow tramp owners in the years before 1914. More interesting in the present context were the firm's efforts to provide new shipping services in a complex system of shared ownership. Attempts to enter the Australian trade in the 1850s or of the River Plate in the 1880s did not succeed, but three notable ventures did: the trade to New Zealand, carried out by the Albion Line from 1864 until its amalgamation with the Shaw Savill in 1881; the service to Burma by the British and Burmah Steam Navigation Company and the Burmah Steam Ship Company; and the trade on the Irrawaddy by the Irrawaddy Flotilla Company.[54] The one direct influence on the Scottish economy was the demand of the shipping lines for ships. Proximity of head office to the shipbuilding yard did not mean the assurance of orders, but proximity helped. It did so to William Denny and Brothers of Dumbarton, which built many ships for Burma and the east because of their interests in shipping firms and especially in P. Henderson and Company.[55]

Industrial investment had more direct effects on the Scottish economy, both beneficial and harmful. The most obviously beneficial, indeed necessary, investment overseas was to obtain raw materials which the Scots needed to support their industrial production, but which they could not obtain at home, either because they had exhausted local supplies or did not possess them at all. The pyritic ore mines at Tharsis[56] and the mining of hematite ore in Spain and Scandinavia are examples.[57] In other instances the industrial investment overseas was an extension of activities for which there was only limited potential at home and so the overseas investment soon achieved such a degree of independence that its links with Scotland quickly became comparable to those of the great merchant houses or shipping lines. The early

Scottish shale oil industry suffered from American competition but revived on the basis of new technology, particularly the Pumpherston Oil Company. More lasting success came later in the 1880s when David Cargill, a Glasgow merchant in the East Indian trade, formed the Burmah Oil Company, which retained its head office in Glasgow when its main activities were far away. In such cases there was no alternative but to exploit the resources overseas. The outcome was very different when future competition was encouraged directly, though it was not always evident at the time that such would be the case. Investment by Dundee jute interests in mills in India is one example. Less obvious where the eventual consequences for Paisley of J. & P. Coats' extension of thread production throughout the world, less obviously immediately because of the comprehensive selling network of which all their production was part and which was based in Glasgow. In many cases the switch of investment overseas represented a gradual progression of interests, essential to the growth of the firm even if leading to the ultimate eclipse of its Scottish interest. The origins of James Finlay and Company[58] lay in the early phase of the modern cotton industry in Scotland. It expanded to manufacture nearer its sources of supply of raw materials in India and increased its range of interests. Cotton manufacture in Scotland came to an end after a protracted demise, though unlike many similar concerns the head office remained in Scotland.

In retaining its administrative headquarters in Glasgow, James Finlay was unusual. Unfortunately for Scotland the move of head offices to London, if not overseas, became common among the various enterprises which had their origins in Scotland, but operated mainly overseas. The headquarters of merchant houses could be retained least easily. They needed the assurance of sources of supply and of points of export. As Scotland ceased to offer these as in the past, the firms left. Their needs and problems were probably not appreciated as they might have been. A study of the work of Glasgow firms in Africa revealed little concern over their activities in the city of their origin.[59] The home-based industrialist, not the overseas merchant, was the central figure of the city's life in the nineteenth century. The trend for the direction of the overseas enterprises which had started in Scotland to move to London was particularly obvious in the rationalisation of much of British industry and commerce after 1918. The most striking example was in shipping, which led to the loss from Glasgow of many of the offices which had once been a leading part of the commercial life of the city and had helped to justify its designation as the second city of the empire. As a consequence, Glasgow lost much of its cosmopolitan character.

The third category into which the overseas contacts of Scotland may be classified had a greater effect on Scotland than any discussed so far. It was the direct demand from overseas customers for Scottish industrial production. The demand grew but changed its form with the expansion of the Scottish economy from the late eighteenth century to 1914.

The textile industries, the growth of which marked the beginnings of the modern industrial structure, required overseas territories both to supply raw materials and to take the finished products.[60] The heavy industries found their raw materials at home, at least until later in the nineteenth century, when the exhaustion of some sources and the lack of others — particularly for steelmaking — led to the need to import. When the special skills of heavy engineering were developed, the indigenous basis of the Scottish economy was strengthened. As with the textile industries, the heavy industries needed markets overseas. Because of the difficulty of giving adequate recognition to Scottish production exported through English ports, the compilation of comprehensive figures of Scottish exports is not possible,[61] but the experience of the two heavy industries of coal and iron provide adequate illustration of the dependence on the export trade. In the first half of the nineteenth century the expansion of the iron industry contributed to the expansion of the coal industry, especially in the west of Scotland, and consequently a large part of the production was consumed at home. The major exporter was the iron industry, which by the mid-nineteenth century sent about one-third of its pig iron overseas, another third coastwise to England and Wales, and only the remaining third to customers in Scotland. By the later nineteenth century the iron industry's demand for an increasing quantity of coal was stagnant, forcing the coal industry to rely more on export markets, particularly from such areas as Fife. At the end of the century, from 1895 to 1900, 18.95 per cent of Scottish output was exported, greater than the 17.84 per cent exported from the entire United Kingdom, and accounted for 18.2 per cent of the value of all exports through Scottish ports in 1900.[62]

It has been suggested in this chapter that many of the links Scotland had with countries overseas had little direct economic effect in Scotland. In the years before 1914 overseas demand for the products of Scottish industry was very different. Industrial prosperity depended heavily on it.[63] The vital link became less secure even before 1914, either because of the imposition of such artificial trade barriers as tariffs or because the Scots were no longer competitive. Even firms which had skills not easily rivalled found that traditional markets in the empire or less developed areas were being invaded by German and American producers. In the first year of the twentieth century the locomotive manufacturers were concerned about the loss of Indian and South American orders. In 1909 their trade association complained that the Imperial Chinese Railways were showing preference for German products. A month before the war began its chairman reported that 'German competition in the Colonies and elsewhere was being strongly felt and likely to continue, worst of all perhaps in India and South Africa'.[64] After 1918 the dependence remained, but the links were broken. In 1922 the North British Locomotive Company reported deliveries to India, New Zealand, Rhodesia, Chile and 'some heavy tank engines to the Glasgow and South Western Railway'. Orders for 48 engines for India were on hand, for the mechanical portions of electric locomotives for Japan and some work for the Caledonian Railway. The continued dependence on overseas demand was obvious, but there was also a significant warning:

> . . . India, on which the prosperity of our locomotive builders has so largely depended in the past, is now, in furtherance of the policy of 'India for the Indians', desirous of having the work done within her own borders, and is ready to give preference to the native production. Even in the case of contracts which she is prepared to place outside she is advertising her requirements and inviting offers for the work from foreign builders, and orders for our own Indian Empire have recently been placed with Continental builders.[65]

As was almost traditional, the response to such failure was emigration. Apart from a decline in the 1890s, the level of emigration seemed so high from the 1880s that the prospect of a high rate of natural increase being no longer able to make good the loss was in prospect. Between 1921 and 1931 such was the case and, for the first time since modern demographic records began, the population fell. Some evidence of a reversal of the trend appeared in the early 1930s, but there were fears that it was not being sustained on the outbreak of war. The 1930s marked another change. In 1923 the number of emigrants of Scottish origin bound for non-European destinations touched the pre-war peak of 1911, but it was an exceptional year and throughout the 1920s the annual totals were high but usually less than for the pre-war years. Ih the 1930s they collapsed, as prospects overseas darkened and barriers to immigrants went up. The emigration of the years after 1918 was then often along Dr Johnson's road to England.

The links of all kinds which Scotland had with countries overseas were dying, and new ones had to be forged. When Scotland most needed markets pioneered by Scots abroad they became less available, and those Scots who had gone overseas in earlier days, or their descendants, seemed no more ready to share whatever prosperity they had with new arrivals. The emigrant Scot may have succeeded because his affection for his native land was never allowed to interfere with his own commercial judgement.

Notes

1. Robert Louis Stevenson, *The Amateur Emigrant: Part I, From the Clyde to Sandy Hook* (written 1879, published 1895), Tusitala edn (1924), pp. 8-10. For an excellent exposition of the issues raised in the present volume, see Gordon Donaldson, *The Scots Overseas* (London, 1966).

2. F.R. Hart, *The Disaster of Darien* (London, 1929); G.P. Insh, *Scottish Colonial Schemes, 1620-1686* (Glasgow, 1922) and *The Company of Scotland Trading to Africa and the Indies* (London, 1932).

3. *Acts of the Parliaments of Scotland*, vii, p. 261.

4. A representative sample of views is: I.B. Cowan, 'The Inevitability of Union — A Historical Fallacy?' in *Scotia*, v, pp. 1-8; Gordon Donaldson, *Scotland: the Shaping of a Nation* (Newton Abbot, 1974), Chapter 2; William Ferguson, *Scotland's Relations with England: A Survey to 1707* (Edinburgh, 1977); P.W.J. Riley, *The Union of England and Scotland* (Manchester, 1978); T.C. Smout, 'The Road to Union' in G.S. Holmes, *Britain after the Glorious Revolution* (London, 1969).

5. 3 and 4 Anne, c. 6 threatened to ban Scottish cattle, linen and coal from English markets. See T.C. Smout, 'The Anglo-Scottish Union of 1707. I: The Economic Background' in *Economic History Review*, xvi (1964), pp. 464-6.

6. A Murdoch, *The People Above* (Edinburgh, 1980); J.M. Simpson, 'Who Steered the Gravy Train, 1707-1766?' in N.T. Phillipson and R. Mitchison (eds.), *Scotland in the Age of Improvement* (Edinburgh, 1970), p. 47.

7. H. Furber, *Henry Dundas, First Viscount Melville* (London, 1931); C. Matheson, *The Life of Henry Dundas, First Viscount Melville* (London, 1933); John Dwyer and Alexander Murdoch, 'Paradigms and Politics: Manners, Morals and the Rise in Henry Dundas, 1770-1784' in John Dwyer, Roger A. Mason and Alexander Murdoch, *New Perspectives in the Politics and Culture of Early Modern Scotland* (Edinburgh, 1982).

8. James Boswell, *Life of Johnson* (1791) Chapman (ed.), corrected Fleeman (London, 1976), p. 302.

9. A.J. Youngson, *After the Forty-Five* (Edinburgh, 1973), pp. 44, 66; M.M. McArthur (ed.), *Survey of Lochtayside, 1769* (Scottish History Society, Edinburgh, 1936), pp. lxxii-lxxiii.

10. For example in Robert Burns, *Address to Beelzebub;* or from a different time and standpoint, K. Marx, *Capital*, Book I, Everyman edn (London, 1930), ii, p. 808.

11. Details are in six reports from the Select Committee on Artizans leaving

the Country, Exportation of Tools and Machinery . . . British Parliamentary Papers, BPP, 1824, V; Report from Select Committee on . . . Machinery, BPP, 1825, V; two reports from the Select Committee on . . . Machinery, BPP, 1841, VII. For details of interesting Scottish cases, *Calendar of Home Office Papers, 1760-1765* (London, 1878), pp. 606, 620, 637-8 and *Calendar of Home Office Papers, 1766-69* (London, 1879), pp. 41-2, 57, 68-9, 87-8, 88-9. An example of the effects of emigration is in R.P. Bartlett, 'Scottish Cannon-Founders and the Russian Navy, 1768-1785', *Oxford Slavonic Papers*, new series, X (1977), pp. 51-72.

12. M.M. Postan, 'Fact and Relevance in Historical Study', *Historical Studies*, 13 (1968).

13. James Hunter, *The Making of the Crofting Community* (Edinburgh, 1976), p. 9. From an extensive literature on the Highlands the following also provide essential background from different standpoints: M.I. Adam, 'The Highland Emigration of 1770', *Scottish Historical Review*, 16 (1919), 'Causes of the Highland Emigration, 1783-1803', *Scottish Historical Review*, 17 (1920), 'Eighteenth Century Landlords and the Poverty Problem', *Scottish Historical Review*, 19 (1922); Philip Gaskell, *Morvern Transformed* (Cambridge, 1968, 1980); Malcolm Gray, *The Highland Economy, 1750-1850* (Edinburgh, 1957); Rosalind Mitchison, 'The Highland Clearances', *Scottish Economic and Social History*, vol. 1, no. 1 (1981); Eric Richards, *A History of the Highland Clearances* (London, 1982).

14. Henry Dundas to William Eden, 5 September 1775. Auckland papers. BM.34.412.

15. M.W. Flinn, 'Malthus, Emigration and Potatoes in the Scottish North-west, 1770-1870' in L.M. Cullen and T.C. Smout, *Comparative Aspects of Scottish and Irish Economic and Social History, 1600-1900* (Edinburgh, 1977), p. 49.

16. Hunter, *Making of the Crofting Community*, p. 11.

17. T.C. Smout, *A History of the Scottish People, 1560-1830* (London, 1969), pp. 358-9.

18. Gray, *Highland Economy*, p. 99.

19. R.J. Adam (ed.), *Papers on Sutherland Estate Management, 1802-1816*, 2 vols. (Scottish History Society, Edinburgh, 1972); E. Richards, *The Leviathan of Wealth* (London, 1973), 'An Anatomy of the Sutherland Fortune: Income, Consumption, Investments and Returns, 1780-1880' in *Business History*, xxi (January 1979), p. 45.

20. Nigel Nicolson, *Lord of the Isles* (London, 1960).

21. M.L. Ryder, 'Sheep and the Clearances in the Scottish Highlands: A Biologist's View' in *Agricultural History Review*, 16 (1968), p. 155.

22. E. Cregeen, 'The Changing Role of the House of Argyll in the Scottish Highlands' in Phillipson and Mitchison, *Scotland in the Age of Improvement* and *Argyll Estate Instructions, 1771-1805* (Scottish History Society, Edinburgh, 1964).

23. S.R. Sutherland 'Ethics and Economics in the Sutherland Clearances' in *Northern Scotland*, 2 (1974-5), p. 81.

24. Alexander Webster's enumeration of 1755 is available in J.G. Kyd, *Scottish Population Statistics* (Scottish History Society, Edinburgh, 1952). A useful analysis of annual population gains and losses by counties is in Appendix IX (pp. 79-137) of the 100th Report of the Registrar-General of Scotland, 1954.

25. C.H. Lee, *British Regional Employment Statistics, 1841-1971* (Cambridge, 1979).

26. See below, p. 13.

27. T.C. Smout, 'The Early Scottish Sugar Houses, 1660-1720' in *Economic History Review*, XIV, p. 240.

28. Some useful recent studies which provide a general account are: Christopher Harvie, *No Gods and Precious Few Heroes: Scotland 1914-1980* (London, 1981); Bruce Lenman, *An Economic History of Modern Scotland* (London, 1977) and *Integration, Enlightenment and Industrialization: Scotland, 1746-1832* (London, 1981); Anthony Slaven, *The Development of the West of Scotland, 1750-1960* (London, 1975); David Turnock, *The Historical Geography of Scotland since 1707* (Cambridge, 1982).

29. J.E. Handley, *The Irish in Scotland, 1798-1845* (Cork, 1945) and *The Irish in Modern Scotland* (Cork, 1947); J.A. Jackson, *The Irish in Britain* (London, 1963); R.D. Lobban, 'The Irish Community in Greenock in the Nineteenth Century' in *Irish Geography*, 6 (1971).

30. N.H. Carrier and J.R. Jeffrey, *External Migration. A Study of the Available Statistics, 1815-1950* (General Register Office. Studies on Medical and Population Subjects, No. 6, 1953), pp. 92-3, 138-9.

31. M.W. Flinn, *et al., Scottish Population History* (Cambridge, 1977), p. 448.

32. See above note 18.

33. Lee, *Employment Statistics.*

34. Carrier and Jeffrey, *External Migration*, pp. 116-25.

35. Charlotte J. Erickson, 'Who were the English and Scots Immigrants to the United States in the Late Nineteenth Century?' in D.V. Glass and Roger Revelle, *Population and Social Change* (London, 1972), pp. 347-81.

36. Norman Murray, *The Scottish Hand Loom Weavers, 1790-1850: A Social History* (Edinburgh, 1978), esp. pp. 142-7.

37. Second and Third Reports to the Select Committee on Emigration, 1827. BPP, 1826-7, V. Evidence of T.F. Kennedy, Q. 228.

38. Ibid., Evidence of Archibald Campbell, Q. 219, and others.

39. Select Committee on Hand-loom Weavers. Report of Assistant Commissioner on South of Scotland, 1839, p. 19. BPP, XLII, 13.

40. Third Report of the Select Committee on Emigration, 1827, pp. 14-5.

41. Ibid. Q.10,176, and section 3 to Appendix 1 to Third Report, pp. 500-8.

42. See above notes 9 and 10.

43. Select Committee on Emigration from the United Kingdom, 1826, BPP, 1826, V. Evidence of R.J. Uniacke, Q. 598.

44. Dallas L. Jones III, 'The Background and Motives of Scottish Emigration to the United States of America in the period 1815-1861, with Special Reference to Emigrant Correspondence', unpublished PhD thesis, University of Edinburgh, 1970; also Roderick A.C.S. Balfour, 'Emigration from the Highlands and Western Isles of Scotland to Australia during the Nineteenth Century', unpublished M. Litt. thesis, University of Edinburgh, 1973.

45. Ibid., pp. 21, 131, 405, 406.

46. Third Report of the Select Committee on Emigration, 1827, p. 15, and Evidence of Henry Home Drummond, Qs. 287-90.

47. A good summary of the state of the debate on this issue is in T.M. Devine, 'The Colonial Trades and Industrial Investment in Scotland, C. 1700-1815' in *Economic History Review*, XXIX (1976). A comparison may be made with Smith's views on the 'carrying trade' in the *Wealth of Nations* (1776), Glasgow edn (Oxford, 1976), II.v.19,30-1.

48. Michael Greenberg, *British Trade and the Opening of China, 1800-1842* (Cambridge, 1951), p. 38.

49. J.C. Gilbert, *The History of Investment Trusts in Dundee, 1873-1938* (London, 1939); J.M. Jackson, 'Finance', Chapter 9 in J.M. Jackson (ed.), *The City of Dundee*, Third Statistical Account of Scotland (Arbroath, 1979); R.C. Michie, *Money, Mania and Markets* (Edinburgh, 1981), pp. 154-60.

50. W. Turrentine Jackson, *The Enterprising Scot* (Edinburgh, 1968), p. 13.

51. W.G. Kerr, 'Scottish Investment and Enterprise in Texas' in P.L. Payne,

Studies in Scottish Business History (London, 1967), pp. 368-9, and *Scottish Capital on the American Credit Frontier* (Austin, 1976).

52. M. Gaskin, 'Finance', Chapter 12 in J. Cunnison and J.B.S. Gilfillan, *Glasgow. Third Statistical Account of Scotland* (Glasgow, 1958), p. 408.

53. R.E. Tyson, 'Scottish Investment in American Railways: the Case of the City of Glasgow Bank, 1856-1881' in P.L. Payne, *Scottish Business History*, p. 387.

54. Hector Bolitho, *James Lyle Mackay, First Earl of Inchcape* (London, 1936), pp. 25-30, 119; F.E. Hyde, *Cunard and the North Atlantic, 1840-1973* (London, 1975), Chapter 1; Dorothy Laird, *Paddy Henderson* (Glasgow, 1961); Alister McCrae and Alan Prentice, *Irrawaddy Flotilla* (Paisley, 1978); Alister McCrae, 'The Irrawaddy Flotilla Company' in *Business History*, XXII (January, 1980), pp. 87-99; John Orbell, *From Cape to Cape: A History of the Lyle Shipping Company* (Edinburgh, 1978).

55. P.L. Robertson, *Shipping and Shipbuilding*, The Johns Hopkins University School of Advanced International Studies, Discussion Paper No. 7 (February, 1974) and 'Shipping and Shipbuilding. The Case of William Denny and Brothers' in *Business History*, XVI (1974), p. 36.

56. S.G. Checkland, *The Mines of Tharsis* (London, 1967).

57. Michael Flinn, 'Scandinavian Iron Ore Mining and the British Steel Industry, 1870-1914' in *Scandinavian Economic History Review*, ii (1954), p. 31.

58. *James Finlay and Company, 1750-1950* (Glasgow, 1951).

59. William Thompson, 'Glasgow and Africa: Connexions and Attitudes, 1870-1900', unpublished PhD thesis, University of Strathclyde, 1970, pp. 156, 272.

60. A. Slaven, 'A Glasgow Firm in the Indian Market: John Lean and Sons, Muslin Weavers' in *Business History Review*, xliii (Winter, 1969), p. 496.

61. M.W. Flinn, 'The Overseas Trade of Scottish Ports, 1900-1960' in *Scottish Journal of Political Economy*, XIII, p. 220, and 'Exports and the Scottish economy in the depression of the 1930s' in W.H. Chaloner and B.M. Ratcliffe, *Trade and Transport* (Manchester, 1977), Chapter 11.

62. Ibid., p. 234.

63. Michael S. Moss and John R. Hume, *Workshop of the British Empire* (London, 1977).

64. See letters to *The Times* and leading article, 19 October 1901 and minute books of the Locomotive Manufacturers' Association, 6 August 1909 and 1 July 1914. I am grateful to the Association for permission to consult their records.

65. *Glasgow Herald Trade Review*, 1930, p. 30.

2 THE SCOTS IN ENGLAND

R.A. Cage

Certainly, without the Scottish virtues, England would not have stood by 1800 — as she did — and even more by 1851, at the head of the nations of the world in industrial prowess. (Charles Wilson and William Reader, *Men and Machines*, p. 10.)

It has been said that England was built by coal, iron, and Scotsmen; but in view of the facts, we think the statement is much too broad. All things considered — and nothing would induce us to look at the matter from the purely Scottish angle — we are firmly of the opinion that, in the interests of accuracy, the reference to coal and iron might be quietly dropped! (McCulloch, *The Scots in England*, pp. 187-88.)

This chapter is unashamedly *pro* Scots. Its chief aim is to illustrate that the economic development of England was in part a Scottish phenomenon. Much has been written about the Industrial Revolution in Britain. Today it frequently is viewed as an English phenomenon; indeed, most writers limit their discussion to England. Even general works with 'British' in their title contain few references to Scotland. However, few authors go as far as Crouzet, who states, that ' . . . England, as the pioneer country, industrialised without any outside help.'[1] Though most authors recognise numerous factors responsible for British industrial growth, little mention is made of the significant role played by the Scots. The Border is not only a line on the map, but also a psychological barrier. Its existence is perpetuated by English economic historians, who tend to view Scotland as an isolated case study worthy of only brief mention, rather than as an integral part of the Industrial Revolution. In reality, there were three main centres of industrial development within Britain: the London area, the Liverpool-Manchester-Newcastle belt, and the Glasgow-Edinburgh belt. These were interdependent, relying on each other for manpower, finance, raw materials, and markets.

An assessment of the Scots impact on England is extremely difficult for a number of reasons, not the least of which is a scarcity of readily available information. The topic is too vast to undertake a detailed study of primary source material. Recourse to secondary sources provides some information, albeit sketchy. Most researchers apparently have neither thought it necessary to try to isolate Scottish contributions, or, even had they wanted to, be able to address this topic because of data limitations. The major purpose of this chapter is to present the limited evidence available in support of the hypothesis that the Scots made significant contributions to the English Industrial Revolution, and indeed played an instrumental role.

The Scots contribution to English social and economic history began long before the advent of the Industrial Revolution. Even before the Union of Parliaments in 1707, London had a sizeable Scottish community of merchants, bankers, bakers, doctors, and writers. The Scots did not always receive a warm welcome, both because the English resented the migrants' successes and considered them to possess certain obnoxious traits, such as drunkenness, boastfulness, and cunningness. Indeed, many astute Scots in England changed their names to avoid being discriminated against.[2]

London was not the only area to experience an influx of Scots; the northern counties were another important centre of concentration. Some of this movement was due to seasonal migration of agricultural labourers. However, permanent settlement also occurred, especially in the English coal fields. As early as 1582, the partners of Winlaton colliery in Durham solved labour shortages by importing Scottish workers. By 1640 it was reported that many Scottish families had settled in Newcastle and that about 300 Scots were working in the coal mines.[3] The flow of Scots into England intensified with the accession of James VI/I to the English throne in 1603, and then again with the Union of Parliaments in 1707.

Scotland was able to make pre-industrial revolution contributions because her economy possessed several manufacturing industries, such as woollen, linen, and coal, as well as an active commercial sector engaged in colonial, European, and English trade.

The introduction of the manufactures so far discussed into Scotland during the eotechnic age show that Scotland was ripening for industrial capitalism before her merger with England. At the beginning of the seventeenth century, nine-tenths of Scottish exports had been either raw materials or manufactured articles in the unfinished state: by the end of the century the foundations of an economy had been laid which help to bring about the second English

Industrial Revolution.[4]

One important factor which enabled Scotland to make these contributions was its educational system. Scotland's parish schools have long been famous for both their extensive coverage and their departure from a classic education. Even before 1800, the curriculum in these schools included English, bookkeeping, natural science, and home science, as well as the classics. But even more important than the parish schools were the Scottish universities, and in particular Glasgow and Edinburgh. Both reached their zenith in the eighteenth century, attracting students and professors from Europe and England. The universities stressed a science-based curriculum: chemistry, mechanical engineering, natural philosophy, and medicine. Many graduates eventually found their way to England, where the opportunities were greater. Scottish physicians, scientists and publishers were an accepted fact in England by 1750.

I

The Scots have always been wanderlusts, migrating to all parts of the world. Hence it is not surprising to learn that large numbers of them migrated south to England. Indeed, before 1800 England was the major benefactor of Scottish emigration. Unfortunately it is not possible to determine the exact numbers involved until the second half of the nineteenth century. None the less, some observations can be made regarding the scale of migration before 1850, the areas where migrants concentrated, and the type of employment pursued.

Migration patterns were firmly established by the middle of the eighteenth century. These movements were strengthened by periodic bad harvests in Scotland. Migration was also encouraged by the opportunities for employment and advancement that existed in England. The 'manufacturing towns and villages of Lancashire were then [1780-90] developing very rapidly' and were attracting Scottish settlement.[5] Concentrations of Scots subsequently arose in Lancashire, Liverpool, and Manchester. Not surprisingly, substantial movement also occurred from Scotland's border counties into the counties of northern England, as well as long-distance migration to East Anglia, Norfolk, Norwich, and of course, London. Part of this was due to Scottish entrepreneurs importing Scottish labour for their textile mills and machinery works in England.[6]

Redford argues that the relative lack of information about Scottish migration is perhaps because the Scots resorted to poor relief only infrequently during this period. 'This was noticed both at Manchester and at Liverpool, though in each town there was a considerable Scots colony. In London, also, there were very few Scottish beggars compared with the number of Irish, few Scottish families in distress, and few Scottish paupers brought before the City magistrates.'[7] The explanation for this low demand for relief perhaps can be found in the Scottish character, and as some have argued, in their strict Protestant upbringing. These features were recognised by contemporaries. 'Scotsmen are in demand not merely when accidents happen, but at all times, in order that they may be ready against emergencies. We are referring, it will at once be seen, to the commonplace of life; but it is especially in mediocrity that the Scotch are great.'[8] But not all Scots were forthright members of society. At Eccleston Crown Glass Company, excessive drinking at the works on New Years Eve, 1828, led to a fight and the killing of one workman. The drinking habits of the Scottish work force were blamed.[9]

The demand for Scots in the English labour force was such that some enterprising individuals made their living by recruiting Scottish labourers. One such entrepreneur was the Scot, Adam Douglas, who enticed mill workers from established mills in larger urban areas to go to new mills in sparsely populated regions during the last quarter of the eighteenth century. He was particularly successful at encouraging Scots to migrate to England.[10]

While Scots were sometimes used as strike breakers, they also were responsible for causing strikes. For example a strike resulted at Bridgewater Foundry in November 1836, because three men imported from Scotland refused to join the mechanics' club. 'Nasmyth succeeded, however, in breaking the strike by importing sixty-four men from Scotland . . . Relatives followed them, so that the majority of workers in the Bridgewater Foundry became Scottish.'[11]

Besides going into mining and the textile mills, the Scots also concentrated on glassworks,[12] soap manufacturing,[13] engineering,[14] London bakeries,[15] and banking.[16] As a contemporary describes, they did not avoid the more tedious occupations, either. 'They swarm in countinghouses and engineer-shops — in the subordinate departments of government- offices — in the India-house, and so forth: their triumphs are over the commonplace and narrow-minded of society — the class most alive to the dislike of successful rivals.'[17] In all cases England received a bargain. The vast majority of Scots had been trained in Scotland, at

Scottish expense, and possibly possessed higher levels of skill than their English counterparts.

Post-1850 census data provides information regarding the areas of concentration of Scottish settlement. Highest concentration, in terms of both absolute numbers and percentage values, occurred in the northern counties, followed by the northwestern counties, and then London (See Table 2.1). This pattern is identical to the traditional one. The counties adjacent to the Border had the greatest attraction, with the work force mainly engaged in agriculture and mining. The other two areas were predominantly industrial, allowing employment in diverse occupations.

II

The impact of Scottish finance on the industrialisation of England is very difficult to assess. Given the nature of capital investment during the initial stages of industrialisation, it is likely that in quantity terms this was the area of least significant impact. Yet it would be foolish to suggest that Scottish finance had no role to play in the English Industrial Revolution. The Scots were actively involved in banking, especially in the northern counties, and invested capital directly in industries as well as supplying technical expertise.

In September 1717, Andrew Drummond of Perthshire established a bank at Charing Cross. The Drummond Bank was the first private bank founded by a Scot to become a major bank in England. In fact it handled the accounts of royalty and still survives as the Drummond Branch of the Royal Bank of Scotland.[18] It is not known how many other private banks were founded by Scots in England. However, it is clear that Scottish banks had numerous agents in England by the late 1700s, especially in the north-west. The principal duty of these agents was to issue Scottish bank notes, which received such general use that they were preferred to local notes. In Carlisle four out of the six private banks established before 1810 issued Scottish notes. Between 1788 and 1836 the financial arrangements of Cumberland rested upon the banks of Scotland, such as the Leith Banking Company, East Lothian Bank, Paisley Banking Company, and the Paisley Union Bank.[19] Cumberland was not the only county dependent upon Scottish notes, for the principal currency of Westmoreland was also Scottish notes.[20] Rondo Cameron argues that Scottish banks generalised banknotes in practice.[21] The extensive use of Scottish small notes in northern England

Table 2.1: Total Population, Total Scots-born and Proportion of Scots-born, for England, by Division, 1851-91

	1851			1861			1871			1881			1891		
	Total	Scots	(%)	Total	Scots	(%)	Total	Scots	(%)	Total	Scots	(%)	Total	Scots	(%)
London	2,362,236	30,401	1.29	2,803,989	35,733	1.27	3,254,260	41,029	1.30	3,816,483	49,554	1.30	4,211,743	53,390	1.27
South-Eastern	1,628,386	7,568	.46	1,847,661	20,505	1.11	NA	NA	NA	2,487,076	18,068	.73	2,867,538	23,182	.81
South-Midland	1,234,332	3,112	.25	NA	NA	NA	NA	NA	NA	1,596,259	7,375	.46	1,863,469	10,835	.58
Eastern	1,113,982	1,998	.18	1,142,580	2,599	.23	1,253,961	3,860	.31	1,343,524	6,360	.47	1,575,311	10,014	.64
South-Western	1,803,291	3,495	.19	1,835,714	4,847	.26	1,879,914	4,664	.25	1,859,013	5,994	.32	1,908,998	7,040	.37
West-Midland	2,132,930	6,536	.31	2,436,568	8,868	.36	2,739,473	10,016	.36	3,029,504	10,944	.36	3,244,717	12,028	.37
North-Midland	1,214,538	2,627	.22	1,288,928	3,040	.24	1,427,135	3,919	.27	1,637,865	5,327	.33	1,806,415	6,446	.36
North-Western	2,490,827	31,061	1.25	2,935,540	42,656	1.45	3,380,696	52,585	1.56	4,108,184	63,701	1.55	4,665,884	65,056	1.39
Yorkshire	1,789,047	7,947	.44	2,015,541	10,376	.90	2,436,355	15,423	.63	2,894,759	19,386	.67	3,218,882	21,387	.66
Northern	969,126	33,034	3.41	1,151,372	42,852	3.72	1,356,998	56,000	4.13	1,624,213	61,379	3.78	1,863,163	65,952	3.54
Totals	16,738,695	127,779	.76	NA	NA	NA	NA	NA	NA	24,396,880	253,528	1.04	27,226,120	282,271	1.04

Note:
London: Intro-Metropolitan areas of Middlesex, Surrey, Kent
South-Eastern: Extra-Metropolitan areas of Surrey and Kent, plus Sussex, Hampshire, Berkshire
South-Midland: Middlesex (Extra-Metropolitan), Hertford, Buckingham, Oxford, Northampton, Huntingdon, Bedford, Cambridge
Eastern: Essex, Suffolk, Norfolk
South-Western: Wiltshire, Dorset, Devon, Cornwall, Somerset
West-Midland: Gloucester, Hereford, Shropshire, Worcester, Warwick
North-Midland: Leicester, Rutland, Lincoln, Nottingham, Derby
North-Western: Cheshire, Lancashire,
Yorkshire
Northern: Durham, Northumberland, Cumberland, Westmoreland
Source: Computed from Census material.

was such that a bill was passed in 1818 that prohibited the circulation of Scottish notes in England. This Act quickly led to the development and growth of joint-stock banking in England, and it has been suggested that the Scottish system was the model and inspiration for this development.[22] Thus, it can be seen that banking legislation in England was directly influenced by Scottish banking practice.

As a result of restrictive legislation, Scottish banks were eventually forced to establish branch offices, as opposed to only having agents, in England. The first Scottish bank opened a branch in London in 1864. In 1874 the Clydesdale Bank opened three offices in Cumberland: at Carlisle, Whitehaven, and Workington. These branches supported the already strong commercial connections between Cumberland and the west of Scotland, particularly with respect to the iron trade.[23]

Scottish banks were important sources of currency and credit in northern England. Scottish bank notes were in demand mainly because of a scarcity of English currency. McConnel & Kennedy sought coins from their Glasgow agent in 1812, which indicates that this shortage was not just confined to notes, but also included coins.[24] As well as supplying currency, Scottish banks were also a major source of funds for investment. Cumberland banks made liberal use of the surplus funds of Scottish banks. 'At one time, for example, the Cumberland Union Bank was enabled to make heavy loans to steel companies by virtue of a large credit from the London office of a Scottish bank.'[25] Besides being invested directly in industrial operations, Scottish funds were also invested in government securities. The Bank of Scotland first ventured into government securities in 1766. The purchase of government bonds increased dramatically after 1792, when American investment opportunities were temporarily curtailed. The Bank of Scotland also held shares in the Bank of England (founded by a Scot, William Paterson!) and the East India Company.[26] The National Bank of Scotland and the Commercial Bank of Scotland were frequent suppliers of finance to the Lancashire & Yorkshire Railway. 'Loans were usually for three and never less than two years, and varied from £400 to £17,500. At least twenty-one loans totalling more than £98,000 were repaid to the bank between 1851 and 1873.'[27] The Scottish Equitable Life Assurance Company also loaned money to the Lancashire & Yorkshire Railway between 1858 and 1873. In 1884 it was claimed that,

Three-quarters of the foreign and colonial Investment Companies are of Scottish origin. If not actually located in Scotland, they have been hatched by Scotchmen and Work on Scottish models. Quite as many of them have their headquarters in Edinburgh as in London and even the English ones find it necessary to come to Scotland for the debenture money and the deposits with which high dividends are conjured up.[28]

Although not much evidence is available regarding the extent of private investment by Scots in English industrial activities, it must have been considerable. The direct evidence which is available indicates that the amount of funds invested by Scots increased as the industrialisation process continued. For example in the early years of railway construction Scottish holdings in English companies were a small proportion of total capital. However,

> During the 1840s substantial Scottish holdings of the securities of English railways were built up. The Liverpool and Manchester Railway had only 10 Scottish shareholders in 1838, but 29 by 1845, while the Grand Junction Railway had 4 in 1835 and 122 in 1845. Scots had invested only £2,000 in the Newcastle and Carlisle Railway in 1838, but £9,300 in 1844, while they held £94,000 of the stock of the Great North of England Railway in 1845 compared to a mere £4,700 in 1838.[29]

Large numbers of Scots established firms in England. George Robinson of Scotland built six mills along the River Leem in Nottinghamshire between 1776 and 1791.[30] J. and H. Hadden moved from Aberdeen to Nottingham in 1787 to supply the Midlands with Scottish yarn.[31] Modern St Helens largely owes its existence to John Mackay from Inverness, who '. . . was ahead of his contemporaries in that, while they only saw the St Helens coalfield as a centre of supply for the saltfields and for Liverpool, his greater vision foresaw its future as a site for coal-burning furnace industries'.[32] Even when not establishing their own firms, the Scots invested in English industrial activities. Archibald Cochrane, the 9th Earl of Dundonald, invested heavily in the Tyneside chemical industry and in soda and alkali production.[33] George Burns, a Glasgow shipowner, and 32 other Glasgow businessmen provided £270,000 to Cunard to start the Cunard Line.[34] In 1869 the British & African Steam Navigation Company was formed in Glasgow, but used Liverpool as its main port. This further strengthened Liverpool's connections in the growing African trade.[35] John Mackay invested heavily in the St Helens glass-making industry, as did a number of other

Scots.[36] From material contained in the following chapters of this book it is clear that numerous Scottish merchants based in London established extensive world-wide trade networks; this would have been of great benefit to English trade statistics, besides causing a flow of funds into England. As David Macmillan points out, in the second half of the nineteenth century England attracted the best of Scottish talent and the most profitable Scottish companies.

III

Although Scots established numerous firms in England, the number of Scottish-owned firms as a proportion of the total number of firms in England was small. Yet Scottish enterprise was important, as Scottish entrepreneurs were leaders in English business development and organisation, besides frequently controlling the largest firm in their type of activity. Four areas were particularly noteworthy: textiles, science, engineering, and transportation.

Even though Scots involvement in textile manufacturing in England was substantial long before the advent of cotton textiles, it is in the cotton textile industry that the Scots are best known. Since the amount of capital needed to establish a cotton textile firm was relatively small, at least in the initial stages of industrialisation, thousands of small firms came into existence. Most of the markets for these firms were local, and individual firms thus had little impact on the industrialisation process. However, some firms stand out because of their size, impact on markets, and the development and adoption of new technology. Two such firms were McConnel & Kennedy and A. & G. Murray. Both were located in Manchester and were owned by men from Kirkcudbrightshire and were initially listed as machinery makers and cotton spinners, a commonplace practice at the time. In 1816 Murray's was the largest employer in Manchester, employing 1,215 workers; McConnel & Kennedy was the second largest, with 1,020 employees.[37] Both firms developed in a similar fashion. James McConnel, John Kennedy, Adam and George Murray all were apprenticed to William Cannan and James Smith (both also from Scotland) in the machine-making business at Chowbent in Lancashire in the 1780s. All four men made their way to Manchester in the 1790s, eventually setting up their own businesses, which were to become the largest cotton spinning firms in Britain.[38] They were major suppliers of yarn to the Manchester area, Nottingham, Glasgow, Paisley, Belfast, and foreign markets. As well as supplying yarn, McConnel & Kennedy played another crucial role in the textile industry. Applying their training as machine makers, they improved existing machinery and developed new equipment for use in the textile mills. The Manchester cotton textile mills also benefited from the work of another Scot, William Fairbairn, who became a leading architect for cotton mills.

The Scottish scientific contribution to the Industrial Revolution was paramount. Scottish universities led development of production technology for such goods as alkali, soap, glass, bleaches, dyes, and others.[39] Thus, little wonder that the Clows state,

> a galaxy of Scotsmen (Joseph Black, Francis Home, James Watt, James Keir, Patrick Copland, the Earl of Dundonald, James Hutton, William Murdock, George and Charles Macintosh, Charles Tennant, James B. Neilson, David Mushet, George and Cuthbert Gordon) gave scientific direction to the Industrial Revolution, particularly to its hitherto neglected non-mechanical aspects. The vital contributions of these men were made for the most part between 1750 and 1830.[40]

James Keir, a Scottish graduate, founded the chemical works at Tipton, Staffordshire and wrote a *Dictionary of Chemistry*. Alexander Chisholm, also a Scottish graduate, was a leading research chemist for Wedgwood. Charles Macintosh studied at Glasgow and Edinburgh universities and went on to a pioneering role in textile-chemical manufacturing, as well as to found the rubber industry in Manchester.[41] William Murdoch, another Scot, invented gas lighting. James Beaumont Neilson of Glasgow developed the hot blast in 1829, thus permitting the use of uncoked coal and appreciably reducing the amount of coal required to smelt a ton of iron.[42] 'At the University of Glasgow, Professor John Black was teaching the theory of latent heat. Scotland was at the beginning of its most distinguished phase of intellectual and scientific development. Many of those who, directly or indirectly, were affected by the intellectual and scientific ferment of the times followed Watt along the road to England.'[43]

Probably the most significant contribution from the chemical industry was the development by Charles Tennant of a method to produce a chemical bleach in powder form using lime. This revolutionised the bleaching industry. The success of this development led the Earl of Dundonald, a Scot, to send a Newcastle manufacturer, William Losh, to Paris to study chemistry. Losh's later experiments in the production of soda eventually led to the establishment of chemical works in New-castle.[44]

Besides the chemists, other members of the theoretical sciences made important contributions towards enhancing the efficiency of new machinery. 'Professors such as Black and Robison in Scottish universities were in close contact with industrialists, giving scientific advice on chemical or engineering matters, and, in return, themselves acquiring much knowledge of industrial techniques.'[45] Another outstanding example is Lord Kelvin, whose work in thermodynamics, electricity, and instrument design had many industrial applications. As a result of Kelvin's experiments, the trans-Atlantic telegraph cable was able to become a reality.

The work of the non-mechanical scientists allowed greater utilisation of the work of the mechanical engineers. Benefits were derived from '. . . the work of industrial chemists trained in Scottish universities. . . to the stream of Scottish immigrants, particularly engineers, who brought their superior education and habits of application as the form of capital which was likely to yield the highest returns in the English revolution'.[46] The role of the mechanical engineer has been well described; without him, the Industrial Revolution could not have occurred. The engineers were more than builders of machines. They also were entrepreneurs in the true sense of the word, for in the initial stages they had to supply their own finance, develop their own markets, and bear their own risks. Their ability to provide technical services depended as much on their entrepreneurial success as on their inventive genius. And in this realm,

> a disproportionate number of their successors [mechanical engineers] were Scotsmen: John and George Rennie, designers of bridges, docks, canals, later of railways and machinery; William Fairbairn, founder of a famous machine shop at Manchester, and his brother Peter who founded another at Leeds; Henry Bell, builder of the first steamship, the *Comet*; David Napier who contributed to mechanical printing and became the founder of an engineering dynasty; William Murdock and James Nasmyth, not to mention Thomas Telford and John Macadam. They came down to England to finish their training and they made up for their lack of capital by a native endowment of character as well as of skill which reflected their Scottish background of poverty, piety, and learning.[47]

A colony of Scottish engineers had existed in London from the eighteenth century. From this group came many important developments and inventions. Three of the most important are David Napier, James Nasmyth, and John Rennie. David Napier was the founder of one of the largest and most important engineering firms in Britain. Nasmyth invented the steam hammer, and Rennie designed Albion Mills, using steam engines for the first time to drive mills. He also developed the centrifugal governor for the steam engine. Rennie has been described as

> one of the principal architects of the first phase of that [technological] revolution. He helped to make Great Britain the workshop of the world, initiated a number of advances in structural science, played a big part in designing the transport system which enabled industry to develop, and with the light touch of genius, graced the country with a whole series of beautiful bridges.[48]

It has been claimed that the largest proportion of engineers working in England were Scots.[49] The major reason for this must be the superior Scottish school system and universities. Even English born engineers benefited, as many were trained by Scottish engineers. Even though 'Many of the ideas that came to fruition in the nineteenth century were the discovery of eighteenth-century Englishmen and Frenchmen, their industrial development was often due to Scottish tenacity. The debt which England owes in these matters of research and development to Scotland is quite incalculable.'[50]

The above list of important Scottish engineers is not exhaustive. Even if John Rennie's sons, John and George, Peter Fairbairn, and Alexander Galloway are included, the list is far from complete. And of course there was James Watt, who some would credit with starting the industrialisation process with his work on the steam engine.

As important as the textile industry, chemicals, and engineering were, the Industrial Revolution would not have been possible without the development of an adequate transportation system. England's pre-industrial road network could only be described as barbaric. The roads were rough, in poor repair, and impassable in wet weather. Vast improvements were necessary in order to link markets. Two Scots figured prominently in the transportation revolution, namely Thomas Telford and John MacAdam. Telford was responsible for the design, construction or improvement of hundreds of bridges and roads, a number of major canals, tunnels and several docks. Few areas in England lack examples of his work. MacAdam is best known for developing techniques of building smooth, all-weather roads. But W. J.

Reader argues that MacAdam's major impact was the efficient organisation and management of turnpike trusts, putting them on a paying
basis. This encouraged larger-scale investment in road building. John
MacAdam started a family dynasty in road surveyorship. Besides himself, his two sons, four grandsons, and a nephew also held surveyorships
in road trusts. These numbered 144 in all, covering 3,699 miles
throughout Britain.[51]

Advances also were being made in ship design. The first passenger
steamship was the *Comet*, built by Henry Bell and first sailed on the
Clyde in 1812. The Clyde basin became an important shipbuilding
centre, supplying quality ships not to just England, but also to the rest
of the world. John Elder invented the compound engine in 1854, which
reduced the fuel consumption of the steam engine by nearly 50 per
cent, allowing more efficient ship designs.

IV

The English industrialisation process relied not only on Scottish labour,
entrepreneurship, and scientific knowledge, but also on Scottish raw
materials and processed goods. For example, all the pigskins for saddle-
making in Birmingham came from Scotland, '. . . as pigs were not flayed
there as they were in England'.[52] In addition, the English wrought-iron
industry depended on pig iron imported from Scotland.[53] By the 1840s
25 per cent of the pig iron was supplied by Scotland.[54] Furthermore,
Cunard purchased most of his vessels from the Clyde shipyards; the first
Cunard ship was built by Wood and Napier.[55] McConnel & Kennedy
purchased raw cotton from Glasgow.[56] Even as early as 1700 the trade
of cloth and yarn was important. In 1736 a complaint was made that so
much yarn was going to Manchester and other ports of Northern
England that there was a shortage in Scotland, causing a price rise.[57]
Scotland was also a major supplier of food products, such as grain and
meat. In fact, cattle were one of Scotland's major exports to England.
These are just a few examples of a long list of products that flowed
from Scotland to England. As one would expect, this flow was not one-
way.[58] McConnel & Kennedy and A. & G. Murray were major suppliers
of yarn to the Glasgow market. 'The Scottish trade not only provided a
market for their fine yarn greater than any other for the first thirty
years of the firm's existence, but made possible the building up of
strong financial reserves and enabled McConnel & Kennedy to expand
their efforts into the export market.'[59] By 1815 most of the fine yarn

exported by McConnel & Kennedy seems to have been going from Glasgow, illustrating the continuing re-export function served by the Glasgow merchants, a function established by that city's tobacco merchants. The increase and intensity of trade between Scotland and England meant the 'Progressive Scottish firms, like William Stirling and Company [calico printers], Carron Company and the Dumbarton Glassworks, opened warehouses in important English markets – London, Hull and Liverpool'.[60]

An examination of the establishment and maintenance of links between Scotland and England should include not only the exchange of goods and services, but also the interaction of ideas. The role of the Scottish universities in English industrialisation has already been emphasised. These were the first institutions of advanced learning in Britain to stress practical, rather than classical, education. As a result, most of the ablest scientists of the nineteenth century were Scots or were trained in Scotland. The Scots also were leaders in mechanic's institutes, the most famous being the Andersonian Institution, founded in Glasgow to spread technical knowledge to the working classes. In turn, the Birkbeck Institution in London was founded by a former lecturer at the Andersonian. J. L. Gamble's son, David, was sent to the Andersonian, which reflects the importance that this major English-based entrepreneur placed on a technical education.[61] 'Edinburgh and Glasgow also had philosophical and chemical societies and academies in which science was taught outside the universities.'[62] All these were means of educating the masses to the ways of the industrialisation process.

Scottish publishers in England, such as Millar, Strachan, Black, Unwin, Blackwoods, and Macmillan, also helped to fashion the thinking of the period. Johnson's dictionary was published by Andrew Millar, with William Strachan providing financial support and with five of the six compilers being Scots.[63] William Strachan published Gibbon's *Rise and Fall* and Smith's *Wealth of Nations*. Even that traditional English song 'Rule Britannia' was an ode written by James Thomson from Roxburghshire and first read on 1 August 1740.[64]

So far no mention has been made of the Scots role in agriculture, medicine, religion, and politics. This chapter would not be complete without a few words on each of these topics.

Agricultural improvements in England and Scotland occurred simultaneously, with both areas making important contributions toward more efficient and profitable agricultural operations, supplying capital and raw materials to industry and food to the growing urban populations. The Scots are probably best noted for animal husbandry, and especially for improving breeds of cattle, such as the Galloway and the Aberdeen-Angus, and for developing that magnificent draught horse, the Clydesdale. Their horticultural work also was important, and especially that of William Paterson of Dundee, who developed many new varieties of potatoes between 1850 and 1870. In addition James Smith of Deanston improved the techniques of under-drainage and deep ploughing, while John Small of Dalkeith invented the swing plough. The list goes on.

The medical schools at Edinburgh and Glasgow produced excellent doctors, many of whom made their way to England. These medicos had an impact in London, as well as further afield. Scots founded medical schools, infirmaries and hospitals in Liverpool, Manchester, Birmingham, and Sheffield. In London the St Bartholomew's Hospital Medical School was founded by David Pitcairn and John Abernathy, while the Royal Society of Medicine was co-founded by John Yellowly. London's first eye hospital was co-founded by John Richard Farre. Robert Ferguson established the *Medical Gazette* and John Hunter was a co-founder of the London Veterinary College. Scots such as William Hunter, Charles Bell, and William Smellie, pioneered work in surgery. James Simpson discovered the use of chloroform. These are just a few examples of the Scottish medico's influence on the state of England's health.

Although the Church of Scotland did not have a significant impact on religious practices in England, a few individual Scots did. For example, the Revd Dr Thomas Chalmers' views were widely followed in England; the 1834 English Poor Law was based on some of his arguments.

In the realm of English politics the Scottish experience has been mixed. The Scots have had their share of Prime Ministers, not all of whom have been well-suited for the job. The first, and no doubt one of Britain's worst Prime Ministers, was John Stuart, 3rd Earl of Bute, who assumed office in 1762. Gladstone, the most famous, was of direct Scots descent, although he himself was born in Liverpool. His father, John (a former MP), came from Leith. Gladstone's Scottish background no doubt influenced his policies. Even though the Scots may have held few political offices in England, their thoughts were pervasive. The writings of Hume, Smith, and Hodgskin, to name a few, had a profound impact on economic and social policies in England.

A canny Scots would never unequivocally claim that the English Industrial Revolution would not have occurred without Scottish assistance. Even a responsible non-Scots would not be so brash as to make such a claim. Yet both would no doubt be willing to state that the

Scots played an integral part, if for no other reason than that industrialisation occurred simultaneously in Scotland and England — it was truly a British experience. Moreover, English involvement in Scotland is less apparent than Scottish involvement south of the Border.

The Scots role in the English industrialisation process has been largely ignored. This chapter has attempted to rectify this, for the Scots were an important factor in the economic development of England. Perhaps the English could have industrialised on their own, but the process would probably have taken longer. The contributions made by Scottish scientists, engineers, financiers, and labour cannot be ignored. The Scots were in England; they were a force to be reckoned with; they were successful; they were an integral part of the English Industrial Revolution.

Notes

1. F. Crouzet, 'Capital Formation in Great Britain during the Industrial Revolution' in Crouzet, *Capital Formation in the Industrial Revolution* (London, 1955), p. 162.

2. J.H. McCulloch, *The Scots in England* (London, 1935), pp. 88-9.

3. J.U. Nef, *The Rise of the British Coal Industry* (London, 1966), vol. II, p. 148.

4. A. and N.L. Clow, *The Chemical Revolution* (London, 1952), pp. 36-7.

5. A. Redford, *Labour Migration in England*, 3rd edn (Manchester, 1976), p. 134.

6. Ibid., pp. 136-7.

7. Ibid., p. 137.

8. James McTurk, [Anon], 'Scotsmen in London' in Charles Knight (ed.), *London* (London, 1842), vol. III, p. 325.

9. T.C. Barker and J.R. Harris, *A Merseyside Town in the Industrial Revolution* (Liverpool, 1954), p.287.

10. Redford, *Labour Migration*, p. 22.

11. A.E. Musson and E. Robinson, *Science and Technology* (Manchester, 1969), pp. 505-6.

12. Barker and Harris, *Merseyside Town*, p. 206.

13. Ibid., p. 223.

14. Charles Wilson and William Reader, *Men and Machines: A History of D. Napier and Son, Engineers Ltd., 1808-1958* (London, 1958), p. 6.

15. McTurk, *London*, p. 322.

16. McCulloch, *Scots in England*, p. 201.

17. McTurk, *London*, p. 325.

18. See Hector Bolitho and Derek Peel, *The Drummonds of Charing Cross* (London, 1967).

19. W.F. Crick and J.E. Wadsworth, *A Hundred Years of Joint Stock Banking* (London, 1936), 4th impression, 1964, pp. 112-3.

20. Ibid., p. 113.

21. Rondo Cameron, *et al.*, *Banking in the Early Stages of Industrialization* (New York, 1967), p. 315.

22. See S. Evelyn Thomas, *The Rise and Growth of Joint Stock Banking* (London, 1934).

23. M. Gaskin, 'Anglo-Scottish Banking Conflicts, 1874-1881' in *EHR*, vol. XII (1959-60), p. 447.

24. S. Shapiro, *Capital and the Cotton Industry* (Ithaca, 1967), p. 117.

25. Crick and Wadsworth, *Joint Stock Banking*, p. 134.

26. Cameron, *Banking*, p. 81.

27. Seymour Broadbridge, *Studies in Railway Expansion and the Capital Market in England, 1825-1873* (London, 1970), p. 96.

28. Anon, 'Scottish Capital Abroad', *Blackwood's Edinburgh Magazine*, vol. CXXXVI (October 1884), p. 469.

29. R.C. Michie, *Money, Mania and Markets* (Edinburgh, 1981), pp. 117-18.

30. S.D. Chapman, *The Early Factory Masters* (Newton Abbot, 1967), p. 80.

31. Ibid., p. 101

32. Barker and Harris, *Merseyside Town*, p. 36.

33. Norman McCord, *North East England* (London, 1979), p. 42.

34. Francis E. Hyde, *Liverpool and the Mersey* (London, 1975), p. 55.

35. Ibid., p. 61.

36. Barker and Harris, *Merseyside Town*, p. 113.

37. C.H. Lee, *A Cotton Enterprise* (Manchester, 1972), pp. 79-80.

38. For a detailed history of McConnel & Kennedy, see C.H. Lee, *Cotton*, and G.W. Daniels, 'The Early Records of a Great Manchester Cotton-Spinning Firm' in *EJ*, June, 1915.

39. A.E. Musson, 'The Diffusion of Technology in Great Britain during the Industrial Revolution' in A.E. Musson (ed.), *Science, Technology, and Economic Growth in the Eighteenth Century* (London, 1972), p. 99.

40. Clow, *Chemical Revolution*, p. xii.

41. See A.E. Musson, 'Editor's Introduction' in Musson (ed.), *Science*, pp. 63-4.

42. P.J. Riden, 'The Iron Industry' in Roy Church (ed.), *The Dynamics of Victorian Business* (London, 1980), p. 74.

43. Wilson and Reader, *Men and Machines*, pp. 6-7.

44. Clow, *Chemical Revolution*, p. 100.

45. Musson and Robinson, *Science and Technology*, p. 182.

46. J.D. Chambers, *The Workshop of the World*, 2nd edn (Oxford, 1961), p. 8.

47. Ibid., p. 19.

48. C.T.G. Boucher, *John Rennie, The Life and Work of a Great Engineer* (Manchester, 1963), p. x.

49. Lee, *Cotton*, pp. 15-6.

50. Wilson and Reader, *Men and Machines*, p. 10.

51. See W.J. Reader, *Macadam, The McAdam Family and the Turnpike Roads, 1798-1861* (London, 1980).

52. G.C. Allen, *The Industrial Development of Birmingham and the Black Country* (London, 1966), p. 102.

53. McCord, *North East England*, p. 123.

54. Riden, 'The Iron Industry', p. 66.

55. Francis E. Hyde, *Cunard and the North Atlantic* (London, 1975), p. 6.

56. Lee, *Cotton*, pp. 10-91.

57. S.G.E. Lythe and J. Butt, *An Economic History of Scotland, 1100-1939* (Glasgow, 1975), pp. 144-5.

58. For an excellent discussion of trade between Scotland and England, see T.C. Smout, 'Scotland and England: Is Dependency a Symptom or a Cause of Underdevelopment', *Review*, vol. III, 4 (Spring 1980), pp. 601-30.

59. Lee, *Cotton*, p. 44.

60. Lythe and Butt, *Scotland*, p. 146.

61. Barker and Harris, *Merseyside Town*, p. 237.

62. Musson and Robinson, *Science*, p. 179.

63. McCulloch, *Scots in England*, p. 91.

64. Ibid., p. 62.

3 SCOTTISH ENTERPRISE AND INFLUENCES IN CANADA, 1620-1900

David S. Macmillan

Of all the areas affected by Scottish emigration and enterprise in the last three centuries, Canada stands out as that where the impact has been greatest and the cultural and psychological side-effects the most pronounced. With the possible exception of India under the Dundas establishment, no field of activity attracted more Scottish attention, and the Canadian scene was to provide opportunities for a much longer period than the Asian sub-continent. It can in fact be argued, using recent (1945-82) emigration figures for Scottish immigrants of all occupations, that the process still continues, and in the field of business enterprise, particularly in the exercise of managerial, investment and higher technology skills, the movement is still significant.[1]

From the abortive, vain and underfunded attempt of Sir William Alexander and Lord Ochiltree to establish settlements, 'feudal domains and Scots baronies or Stewartries' in Nova Scotia and Cape Breton Island (New Galloway) in the 1620s, to the successful projects of later colonisers such as Sir James Montgomery, Lord Selkirk, Archibald MacMillan and many other successful entrepreneurs and emigration leaders and organisers in the eighteenth and early nineteenth centuries, Canada was an obvious and appealing field for economic development and settlement. Unlike Australia, where plans such as those of the Revd Dr John Dunmore Lang for purely Scottish settlements in Cooksland and Phillipsland failed to materialise, Canada did, in its early phase, have areas of concentrated Scottish settlement, such as Glengarry County, with its disbanded MacDonald soldiers, MacMillan's Grenville, Lochaber and Templeton Townships on the Ottawa River, Lord Selkirk's settlement of Highlanders in Prince Edward Island, and the earlier settlements of Lowlanders sent out by Sir James Montgomery to his lands in that island in the 1770s.[2] Yet, as with the Australian connection, the emigration drive was linked to the quest for export markets, to the creation of a demand for Scottish manufactures. Just as the Australian Company of Edinburgh and Leith deliberately sponsored the settlement of Scots in Van Diemen's Land and New South Wales in the 1820s and early 1830s, and encouraged a traffic through its Sydney and Hobart warehouses in Scottish exports in return for colonial produce, so did the Glasgow, Greenock, Kilmarnock and Leith entrepreneurs in the earlier period of 1760-1820 establish their agencies in Halifax, Montreal, St John and other Canadian centres as outlets for the home exports for which Scottish emigrants, shipped out under their indenture and other systems, would help to stimulate and maintain a steady demand.[3] Especially after 1780, as Scotland's industrial capacity developed rapidly, did this process become more obvious; but as early as 1761, Scottish entrepreneurs were utilising the experience of working indenture and other emigration processes gained in the previous century in the West India, New York, the Carolinas, Maryland and Virginia trades to supply contracted servants from the much sought after craftsmen and labourers and domestic servants to schoolmasters and tutors on the professional level, as well as providing passages for fare-paying emigrants of types ranging from Highland tacksmen to Lowland farmers and such superior professional people as surgeons, physicians and ministers of religion.[4]

Between 1760 and 1825 there is record of no fewer than 279 Scottish mercantile houses and shipowners, on both sides of the Atlantic active in the trade to Canada and the emigrant traffic to the colonies. Others probably existed, for whom the records have disappeared, individuals and firms employing single ships and operating out of small ports and outports. Apart from these figures, there were other firms engaged in the timber trade after 1800 (at least 100 in the years up to 1830), which were not concerned with the shipping out of emigrants.[5]

The basic reasons for the diaspora of the Scots have already been considered with care by several writers. The increase in rents, the pressure of agricultural improvement on small Lowland tenants and Highland tacksmen are among them. Bruce Lenman has probably pinpointed the main driving force in his recent book, *Integration, Enlightenment and Industrialization: Scotland, 1746-1832*, where he shows that the cycle of expansion and contraction in the population due to periodic dearth was 'decisively broken in 1739-41'. Thereafter there was a demographic surge, and the total population estimated in 1755 by Dr Alexander Webster at 1,265,000 increased to 1,608,000 by 1801. Similarly, the changing pattern in landownership in the 1670-1750 period, with larger estates replacing many smaller ones in the Lowlands, helped to produce the very class of entrepreneurs, many of them the lesser gentry, who were to alleviate the effects of the driving out of lesser tenants, kindly tenants and cottars, through providing emigration facilities by indenture systems and the keeping of registers of potential and aspiring emigrants and of immigrants required by colonial employers.[6] The concurrence of these two effects of the changes in the Scottish economy, changing landownership pattern and displacement of the lesser gentry, were to have crucially important results in the field of Scottish emigration to Canada and in the development of Scottish trade, especially after 1783, with Britain's remaining North American colonies. Good times and high production at home brought the need to seek expanding markets in Canada, and bad times led to the quest for emigration outlets and new fields for enterprise across the Atlantic. In the years 1815-20 more than 20,000 Scots sailed for Canada.

Between 1750 and 1800 Scotland's overseas commerce grew by nearly 300 per cent, as compared with England's remarkable growth rate of 200 per cent in the same period. Such rapid change from a largely agricultural country in the first half of the century was bound to shatter the old structure of Scottish society, and the new men who came to the fore in commerce and industry bore the marks of the changed economic and social environment. From their ranks were drawn the great majority of the entrepreneurs who came near between 1775 and 1850 to making British North America into a sort of Scottish commercial preserve, almost an informal empire. To their new colonial environment they brought the characteristics that had been moulded by the changes they had known at home, and these were to condition their conduct, their outlook, and their aspirations in the very different setting of Newfoundland, Nova Scotia, New Brunswick, Canada, and the other colonies.

These features may be summed up as an attachment to the idea of free trade and an impatience with the mercantile pretensions of England, especially the dominating role of London; a tendency towards secession as anti-Burghers or under various dissenting labels from their own established moderate Kirk, dominated by the gentry and the nobility with their powers of patronage; a belief in Parliamentary and Burgh reform, in both of which Scotland stood in much greater need of change than any part of the United Kingdom; and a belief in the efficacy of education as an improver of mankind (which seems rather touching now in retrospect, but which was perhaps a natural enough belief to hold at the time when Scotland's educational system was distinctly superior to that of England, and Henry Brougham and many another beat their way north across the Border to grace the benches at Edinburgh and other Scottish universities). They also held strongly to the conviction that 'Scotland's time had come at last', as Kirkman Finlay of Glasgow put it, and that no opportunity must be lost to bring their country's commerce and prosperity up to par with that of England. Apart from these five characteristics, which might be considered progressive, if not entirely admirable, there were other possibly less attractive features of the new mercantile men of Scotland, which they were to display to the full in the colonial settings of British North America. One was their intense localism. Scotland, for all the rapid rate of industrial change, was still a country of regions within which population movement was as yet slight. This bred a clannishness and, sometimes, a narrowness of viewpoint. Scottish merchants and shipowners in the colonies tended to trade with their home ports, to recruit their partners, clerks, shipmasters and other associates from their own home districts, especially from among their own kinfolk, if suitable candidates were available. In colonial centres like Halifax and Saint John and Montreal, it led them to form cliques and coteries and rings among themselves, sometimes to promote such worthy ventures as the building of churches, but occasionally for such questionable purposes as the virtual defrauding of the authorities through rigged sales of prize ships and cargoes.[7] This latter activity, which reached its peak in Halifax during the War of 1812, was probably the most lucrative type of venture in which Scottish merchants during the period are found to be acting in collusion. There was also the illicit sale of Nova Scotia and New Brunswick gypsum, used as a fertiliser in the Southern States, to American vessels during the War of 1812. Yet it must be remembered that Scottish overseas trade in its earliest phase could only have existed, far less grown, through the exercise of a calculated indifference to the law as laid down in London.[8]

After 1783 many Scots, especially those who had been engaged in the profitable tobacco trade, were even more resentful against the vested monopoly interests of London, for they felt that the final breach with the 13 insurgent colonies had been largely occasioned through the pressures brought to bear by shipowning and mercantile groups in London and Bristol. In their determination to make the best of a changed situation, by expanding their commerce with the remaining North American colonies, the Scots merchants were resolved that their trade should not be trammelled by restrictions, that it should be immediately profitable, and that the contacts already established in Newfoundland, the Maritimes and Canada should be utilized to the full. In this they were helped by the commercial activities of their countrymen in these areas, which had begun in 1759-60, and by the flow of Scottish emigration at an increasing rate after 1770.

By 1793 Greenock, with a population of 15,000, had become the recognised port and outlet for the booming city of Glasgow. Greenock's shipyards, especially that conducted by the family of Scott, were already achieving a reputation throughout Britain. Between 1784 and 1791, according to a 'View of the Situation and Trade of Greenock' in the *Scots Magazine* of January 1805, inward shipping rose from 2,600 tons to 43,400 tons. 'By 1800', claimed David Macpherson, 'Greenock owned 377 ships employing some 4,000 men.' Its merchants, and those of Glasgow, had established trading connections with the West Indies and the Americas as early as the 1670s.[9] The result of the American War of 1776-83 was to make the merchants of Greenock and Glasgow look very closely at the more northern parts of the Americas, and in this field they were no novices. As early as 1620, a small group of Glasgow merchants had given financial assistance to the Newfoundland Company, founded and chartered in 1610 in Bristol and London.[10] This was the time when many Scots fondly believed that they would be allowed to share the fruits of empire and trade with the English, who shared their king; when Sir William Alexander was forming his feudal domain of 'New Scotland' and Lord Ochiltree was forming his 'Scots Barony or Stewardry' in Cape Breton Island. The schemes for Scottish settlements in Acadia to rival the English colonies of Virginia and New England broke down in the confusion and financial turmoil that beset the first two Stuart kings of Great Britain, but the Glasgow merchants maintained their interest in the area, because it provided some useful subterfuges in the increasingly popular national sport of evading the English Navigation Acts.

Edward Randolph, Surveyor-General of Customs for the American Plantations in the last 20 years of the seventeenth century, plaintively reported to the Commissioners of the Customs in June 1680, that 'many ships full laden with tobacco' gave bonds at the Naval Office in Boston that they were bound to Newfoundland, but proceeded in fact to 'Scotland, Canada and other foreign countries'.[11] This useful pretext, in addition to the trick of registering their vessels at Whitehaven, helped the Glasgow merchants to get established in the tobacco and plantation trades long before the Act of Union of 1707 gave them legal entitlement to participate. By 1699 the traffic in tobacco, carted north through Pennsylvania, and shipped in the ports of that colony, or of Massachusetts, to Newfoundland and thence to the Clyde, was considerable enough to cause grave concern to the Board of Trade. In this dubious trade the Scots made full use of the legal questions and uncertainty that surrounded the status of Newfoundland, for some English legal authorities contended that it was 'no true plantation' but rather 'a part, nay an extension of His Majesty's realm of England' with which the Scots were in fact allowed to trade openly, since the Acts of Trade did not apply in such areas. In March 1701, Randolph reported to the Board of Trade the further enormity that a combine of Scottish merchants had shown the audacity to establish a 'factory' on the coast of Newfoundland, and that through this warehouse, set up purportedly as a fishing station, they were sending large quantities of enumerated commodities, especially tobacco and sugar, back to Scotland, Holland and other places.[12] After 1707 the Scots were not slow to engage fully in such trades, and they developed further their skills in breaching the Navigation Laws and the trade regulations. By 1725 Greenock had three sizeable vessels at the Newfoundland fisheries, and the number increased steadily as the years passed.

This may seem surprising, in view of Scotland's own natural wealth in fish resources, which were exploited increasingly in the eighteenth century. But it is less surprising when one considers that Newfoundland and its fisheries were being used increasingly as a cover not only for the shipping out of colonial produce from the Southern plantation colonies and the West Indies to foreign European ports, but also as a blind for importing large quantities of European goods, such as French brandy, laces, silks, Dutch spirits and German Osnaburgh linens into all the British colonies of the North American seaboard and the West Indies.[13] The nature of the Newfoundland fishery conducted from Greenock in the eighteenth century, and even into the early 1800s, is perhaps revealed by the fact that the Greenock vessels participating by 1807 were, with those from Liverpool, the largest of the entire fleet. They were also the most heavily gunned.[14] The records of Johnstone and Co., of Lang and Co., of the Greenock-connected firm of Hamilton, Graham and Co., all operating in Newfoundland in the 1770-1810 period, leave no doubt that there was much more concern in the Newfoundland trade than codfish, sealskins, and the provisioning of the scattered settlements.[15] The absence of any effective government authority for most of the year, or of any naval patrol, rendered the area a natural *point d'appui* for smuggling and illegal trade activities, and the naval officers who performed their annual tours of duty as justices had little interest in checking the traffic.

After 1776 there was a noticeable increase in Scottish trade with the island (see Table 3.1), though it is difficult to know how to interpret the figures in view of the wholesale illicit trade which was obviously being transacted on its shores and in the waters about it. A list of

Table 3.1: Scottish Trade with Newfoundland, 1764-1801

Year	Scottish Imports from Newfoundland (in pounds sterling)	Scottish Exports to Newfoundland (in pounds sterling)
1764	—	340
1765	—	2,453
1769	4,984	962
1775	2,783	4,053
1778	5,668	14,077
1781	3,720	17,836
1786	1,292	13,784
1790	5,499	11,991
1793	3,098	18,498
1797	18,846	13,745
1798	6,125	27,683
1799	13,953	23,291
1801	18,830	46,888

Source: Glasgow Chamber of Commerce Abstracts.

exports from Scotland to the island in the years 1770-85, sent from the headquarters of the Scottish Customs at the order of the 'Lords of the Committee of Council for Trade and Foreign Plantations' in January 1786, showed the principal items sent out as meal flour, fresh pork, linens, leather goods, barrelled beef, and sailcloth, totalling in value for the fifteen year period no less than £133,000.[16] It is difficult in the light of these figures to avoid the conclusion that the wars of 1776-83 and 1793-1801 gave a considerable stimulus to the trade, and that the export figures are much higher than can be accounted for by the returns from the fisheries, even allowing for direct shipments of fish to foreign ports. Obviously the illicit trade was plied with particular vigour in wartime, and it is worth noting that when Chief Justice Reeves made his third report on the state of the island in 1793, several Greenock and Port Glasgow firms had recently established Newfoundland agencies; these were the four important houses of Messrs Andrew Thomson and Co., Crawford and Co., Stevensons and Co., and Stuart and Rennie.[17] The predominance of Scots in the trades masked by the fisheries and in the fish-trade itself was noticeable to several observers, and the Scots operated not only in St John's and other island settlements and from Greenock, but from other colonial centres as well. When war came in 1776, the thriving firm of Messrs Cochrans, at Halifax, took over the Newfoundland trade in fish to Bermuda from the Boston concern of Russell and Co. It is significant that it was a Scot, Nathaniel Atcheson of London, holding such large Nova Scotian and Newfoundland interests that he was regarded as mercantile agent for these colonies, who secured the exclusion of foreign fish from the West Indies in 1813, earning for himself the title of 'saviour of our livelihood' from the islanders.[18]

The Early Phase of Operations in Continental Canada, 1759-76

Apart from the Scottish troops who served in the campaigns in North America, there were Scottish merchants active on the fringes of mainland Canada — a few at Halifax, and some in the Albany and Schenectady areas, where profits in the fur trade were already proving attractive. Some of these Scots received concessions to operate in certain French areas in North America between 1748 and 1756, but little is known of their background or activities. Unlike the Hudson Bay and North West Company venturers, the men of the dark age of free enterprise and endeavour in the North American fur trade have been sadly neglected. There were also Scots among the 'four hundred and fifty contemptible sutlers and traders' to whom General Murray made scathing reference as being an embarrassment to him in the new conquest of Canada.[19]

The course of the war for Canada was followed with keen interest in Glasgow and Greenock, for it was realised in business circles that here was indeed a promising new field for enterprise that might well supplement the Virginia and West India trades in furthering the advance of Scottish commerce. John Rutherford, Scottish commentator on mercantile matters, expressed the view of many of his countrymen when he wrote in 1761: 'colonies will render us independent of the world, in point of trade'. In this new area there would be no chartered monopolies; the London shipping interests would have no preference. Hence the progress of the war in North America was watched closely.

With the fall of Quebec, a strong body of opinion developed in Glasgow and Greenock in favour of retaining Canada. A letter from 'Britannicus' to the editor of the *Glasgow Journal* in January 1760 stated:

of all our acquisitions the conquest of Quebec, and, consequently, of the country of Canada, is the most important and most beneficial to this Kingdom, for by the reduction of that place and country, the British Empire in America will be perfectly secured from all future attempts of our enemies; and also such a source of trade and commerce opened to us here, as will be fully sufficient, had we no other, to employ all our trading and commercial people; and find a vent or constant consumption for all our goods, products and manufactures. It is therefore above all things to be wished that the country of Canada may never be relinquished.[20]

This was only the first of a long series of letters which show the high hopes of the local business interests for a new and profitable outlet. The editor of the *Journal* echoed the views of his contributors, urging the completion of the conquest, regardless of expense, as 'the most thrifty disbursement ever made', expatiating on the benefits,

> An exclusive fishery! A boundless territory! The fur trade engrossed! and innumerable tribes of savages contributing to the consumption of our staple! — These are sources of exhaustless wealth! Ignorant and designing men have called this a quarrel for a few dirty lands or acres of snow, but the British public will soon have feeling [*sic*] proofs that Great Britain must sink or swim with her colonies.[21]

The direct commercial connection between Scotland and Canada began soon after the peace of 1763. Robert Finlay of Glasgow, agent for his brother James in Quebec, was advertising the first direct peacetime sailings for the province, the snow *Apthorp*, to leave Greenock in February 1764, and the schooner *Bonny Lass of Livingston* to sail for freights. He also sought skilled craftsmen for his brother and his brother's mercantile friends in Quebec, who had begun to acquire land and sought to build warehouses and stores. 'Masons skilled in building, gardeners, quarriers and millers, fabricators of dry stone dykes, and good and sober men skilled in the management of flour mills and saw mills' were asked to come forward for free passage and well-paid employment.[22] The two vessels owned by the Finlays were the first regular traders to operate between the Clyde and Quebec, and their services were supplemented temporarily later in 1764 by the full-rigged ships *Africa* and *Maria* (owners unknown) which were usually engaged in the West African slave trade.

From perusal of the shipping lists in the Scottish press, it is apparent that the Clyde shipping interest, centred on Greenock and acting on behalf of Glasgow owners' agency, had secured by 1776 a share of the shipping trade to Canada out of all proportion to Scotland's relative strength in shipping. The expectations of the Glasgow-Greenock mercantile interest were in fact fulfilled, and the founding of a consortium such as the North West Company of fur traders in Montreal in 1779 must be viewed as the natural outcome of 15 years of successful commercial operations in the conquered province by Scots, who were already well established as general traders and men of business. By 1770 at least eleven reputable firms in Glasgow, Greenock, and the surrounding area were engaged either fully or partly in the Quebec trade. Colin Dunlop and Son of Glasgow as agents, and James Wilson of Kilmarnock as owner were jointly advertising the fine ship *Diana*, not only for freight (she was a vessel of 400 tons – large for that time by Scottish standards) but also for passengers, with 'the highest class of cabin accommodation being available'. The Scottish debut in the Canadian shipping field was not made by the timber-ships of dubious quality which dominated the Miramichi and St John timber trade in the early 1800s, but by superior vessels, sailing to the new-won province of Quebec in the 1760s and 1770s.[23] Regular traders, Greenock vessels, were in fact plying between the Clyde and Canada from 1764, between the Clyde and Nova Scotia from 1768, and between the Clyde and New Brunswick from 1768 – long before Captain Alexander Allan of Saltcoats, founder of the Allan Line, sailed from Greenock for Quebec in June 1819. Yet Allan's voyage has often been described as the beginning of regular sailings between Scotland and British North America.

Ironically, it was not Scotland, but London, which benefited from the steady engrossment of the Montreal fur trade between 1763 and 1821. This was for two reasons. The first was the undisputed primacy of London as the British market for furs, with its long-established manufactures of hats and other fur products, its specialist buyers and handlers, and all the other appurtenances of the trade that had developed since the beginning of successful activities by the Hudson's Bay Company in the 1680s.[24] The other reason was the fact that the leading Scots firm in the British-Canadian fur trade, that of Phyn, Ellice and Co., composed of scions of the gentry of North East Scotland, was itself centred in London. The partners of their Canadian subsidiary, Forsyth, Richardson and Co. of Montreal, had a similar background. It was with this thriving firm that the North West Company and its predecessors dealt, and it was trade goods from London, rather than from Glasgow or Greenock that sustained the fur trade.

In London the friends and agents of the Company used their not inconsiderable political influence to maintain the co-partnery's position against the Hudson's Bay Company and its claim to have a monopoly in the north. David Macpherson, the Scottish commentator on trade, stressed the free enterprise character of the North West Company in his *Annals of Commerce* (1805, vol. 4, p. 129): 'without any exclusive privilege, or any advantages, but what they derive from their capital, credit and knowledge of the business, their prudent regulations, and judicious liberality to their clerks and servants of all kinds, they have carried their branch of commerce to a height never before attained'. As W. Stewart Wallace showed conclusively in his *Documents Relating to the North West Company* (Toronto, 1934), the Company was composed almost entirely of Scots, very largely drawn from Aberdeenshire, Banffshire and Inverness-shire, many of them with military, farming or small landholding backgrounds. Of the 255 persons listed in Wallace's 'Biographical Dictionary of the Nor' Westers' (Appendix A, pp. 425-505 of the *Documents*), 126 were Scots-born, 33 were of Scots descent, and others were possibly Scots. No fewer than eleven were established and operating in Quebec as early as 1763-5.

It was in the field of general trade, and after 1805, in the timber trade, that the province of Canada was to bring most advantage to Scotland. Montreal, Halifax, St John, and to a lesser degree St Andrews in New Brunswick were to become the principal centres of Scottish enterprise in North America after 1776. The 1760s and early 1770s were comparatively lean years for the connection, and the few Scottish merchants in Quebec appear to have had a thin time of it until the War of 1776 brought extended opportunities for trade and a further influx of enterprising fellow countrymen of the Loyalist persuasion from centres in the colonies which had declared their independence. By 1768 Scottish merchants were numerous enough in Halifax, Nova Scotia, for 16 of them to form a North British Society, which thrived and grew lustily from the time of its inception; but it was otherwise in Quebec and Montreal until the fur-trade magnates and the Loyalist merchants came in.

After 1776, with the influx of Scottish fur traders and general merchants, faith in Canada as an outlet for their energies was largely justified. War, as always in the period, gave further stimulus to the nation's commercial and industrial development. In the colony it also stimulated economic development by providing in the armed forces not only a market for colonial agricultural produce, but also an increased flow of currency in the form of soldiers' and sailors' pay in coin, officers' pay in Treasury bills, payment for supplies in Commissary and Artillery bills, and other useful media of finance. Scottish officers in the colonies, in this and in the Revolutionary and Napoleonic

Wars, had a particular proclivity for lending money to merchants among their countrymen, and occasionally even used them as fronts or agents in trading, privateering or prize buying activities.

The link between the Scots merchants in Quebec and Montreal and the Pitt and Liverpool governments through Dundas and his son, the second Viscount Melville, who succeeded to the political managership in Scotland, was a strong one. Henry Caldwell, naval officer in 1759 and merchant in Quebec thereafter, was influential in persuading Dundas, who headed the Admiralty, to develop Canadian timber resources for the Navy in 1804.

James Dunlop, Innovator and Entrepreneur in Canada, 1776-1815

The years 1774-80 saw the arrival of Scottish merchants in Montreal to augment the struggling Finlays and others of the first 'Conquest' wave. Simon McTavish, known to his familiars as 'The Marquis', uncrowned king of the Montreal fur trade, arrived in Montreal in 1775, after operating successfully out of Albany and Detroit.[25] James McGill appeared in 1774, after experience as a trader in several American colonies, and James Dunlop transferred his capital north from Virginia in 1776.[26] These three were to dominate the Scottish mercantile circle in the town, just as that circle dominated the trade of the town and province. It is unfortunate that the personal papers of McTavish and McGill have not survived. In the case of Dunlop, who is in many ways the most interesting of the three since he was not involved directly in the well-documented fur trade, such materials do exist in the series of letters which he wrote to his brother, sister, and brother-in-law in Glasgow in 1796-1815, preserved in the Scottish Record Office.[27]

Dunlop, as befitted a Glasgow-trained merchant, had strong free trade ideas. He was ebullient, even boastful, but he was undoubtedly successful. When the scale of his ship-owning, land-holding, property-owning, general trading and other diverse operations is considered there seems little reason to doubt the claim he made in 1814 that he was the wealthiest man in the province. He was convivial, enterprising, and bold; the impression he made in the community was strong enough for the Revd Robert Campbell to record with satisfaction 70 years after Dunlop's death, that this early parishioner of St Gabriel Street Presbyterian Church 'remitted to Britain, shortly before his death in 1815, the sum of £30,000, the largest bill of exchange ever sent from the colony up to this date'.[28] Between 1776 and 1796 Dunlop steadily built up a general trading business, dealing largely in imported textiles, liquors and groceries. The war with revolutionary France, as for so many other Scots merchants in this and other colonial centres, provided new opportunities, and Dunlop launched out in several new lines of activity, with boldness and verve, travelling frequently between Montreal and Quebec to promote his new ventures. Unlike the fur traders, he and his Quebec friend and agent, John Pagan, dealt largely with Scotland, through the agency of the important Greenock firm, Ker and Co. The increase in the scale of trading operations between the province and Scotland at the time is indicated by Table 3.2. Dunlop and his friends benefited greatly from the Act of Parliament of 1788, which permitted vessels carrying lumber, provisions and livestock from the province of Quebec to trade to the West Indies and to bring back thence sugars, rum, and other commodities, to the value of the outward cargo, free of duty. Even before the War of 1793 increased the demand for high-quality colonial timber, Dunlop was also exporting cargoes of choice Canadian oak to the important Leith timber firm of Allan, Stewart and Co., the first commercial concern on the East Coast of Scotland to show any interest in Canada.

Table 3.2: Scottish Trade with Canada, 1785-1801

Year	Scottish Imports from the Province of Canada (in pounds sterling)	Scottish Exports to the Province of Canada (in pounds sterling)
1785	344	3,670
1790	392	21,724
1795	2,564	21,055
1797	7,364	26,457
1798	9,920	63,136
1799	17,774	35,504
1801	49,800	63,157

Source: Abbreviated from the Glasgow Chamber of Commerce Abstracts.

By 1797 Dunlop was writing to his sister in Scotland that 'the variety and multiplicity' of his business made it necessary for him to recruit more clerks in Scotland. One of the new activities in which he was engaged was the wholesale purchase of grain in the country areas — an increasingly profitable business in view of the growing demand for flour in the colonies, the West Indies, and Britain, where scarcity was beginning to cause occasional disturbances, such as the Scottish 'meal mobs'. Fernand Ouellet, in his recent writings on the economy of the province, has stressed the importance of grain production at this time, and it is interesting to see from this Scottish merchant's angle just how much could be made from dealings in this commodity. In the autumn of 1797 Dunlop remitted to Glasgow bills to the value of over £17,000, derived largely from the sale of grain.[29] By this date he was importing consignments of rum – as many as 700 barrels at a time from Glasgow, but he considered that the export of Canadian grain and potash was his most promising line, though he had also developed a trade in Scottish gunpowder, which he re-exported from Canada to New York, and in Osnaburgh linens and Russian linen shirtings of which he held a very large speculative stock. Very large consignments of Madeira wines, Scottish woollens, teas, and olive oils were also being imported by him, and he showed considerable expertise in gauging the state of the market to avoid flooding.

The potash trade was particularly lucrative, a consignment of 951 barrels dispatched to the Clyde in 1798 sold in Glasgow for the high price of almost £63 per barrel, bringing in the handsome profit of £2,000. The scale of Dunlop's transactions in wheat and potash continued to increase as the War went on – no fewer than 20,000 bushels of wheat being exported to Halifax in 1798. From being essentially a large-scale importer Dunlop was changing to an exporting magnate, and it was only natural that he should develop shipping interests. The new Quebec-built ship of 250 tons, the *Caledonia*, of which he was a part owner with others of the Scottish mercantile clique, sailed for Port Glasgow early in 1799 with 12,000 bushels of Canadian wheat. Later in the year Dunlop purchased an extensive lot on the Saint Lawrence River with a good wharf, houses and stores, which he planned to be the largest mercantile establishment in the colony.[30] The bargaining and negotiating for grain with the growers and landowners was done by Dunlop himself, travelling with a pair of Scots clerks through the country areas while other Scots subordinates manned the Montreal establishment. As the finances at his command grew, the merchant found increasing opportunities for profit in the discounting of bills, a business in which he showed considerable acumen. In June 1800, to give only one example of how he worked, he purchased £21,000 of bills drawn on the Paymaster-General at a discount of 2 per cent, selling them in New York, at a premium of almost 2 per cent for specie. By July of the same year he stated that: 'For several years I have been a loser by my great importations', but admitted to his brother that he was

rapidly accumulating a large fortune in other ways.[31]

By 1800 whole cargoes of potash and grain were being dispatched by Dunlop for the Clyde and the Thames, and he was chartering sizeable ships and seeking to purchase other vessels. This trade particularly interested him, since he estimated that relations between Britain and the United States must inevitably deteriorate, and that this in turn would lead to a stoppage in supplies of the much needed potash to Britain from that quarter. If this came about, the Canadian product would be at a premium, and, gambling on the outcome, Dunlop began in 1801 to stockpile large quantities of potash and wheat. In 1801-2 his wheat and flour exports rose to a new peak, making a sizeable part (though the exact proportion is difficult to assess in view of the lack of his accounts) of the amazing total of wheat exports from the province in 1802, as calculated by Fernand Ouellet, of 1,151,530 minots. The short peace that followed the Treaty of Amiens upset his calculations and brought about a serious glut of British imports in Canada, but the setback was only temporary, and the resumption of hostilities enabled Dunlop to enter his most creative and profitable phase as entrepreneur and pioneer of new trades.

The export of grain to Britain, Nova Scotia and the West Indies, and of potash to the Clyde, with shipowning and bill discounting, were the four principal bases of Dunlop's later success, and the War of 1812 added other profitable sidelines. By 1810 he owned three vessels and was building two more for his fleet in Montreal, using a dozen ship carpenters brought in from New York and 50 local workmen. The new ships, named in honour of members of the Dunlop family, were sizeable craft of over 400 tons, and they plied regularly between the St Lawrence and the Clyde with wheat, potash, pine staves and pine boards, occasionally sailing for Jamaica with flour, pork, fish and lumber to load rum and molasses for the Clyde. Living now in a large mansion, with a retinue of servants, Dunlop was regarded as the town's most prominent shipowner, and his exports of wheat and timber were, on his own admission, bringing him great profits — sufficient for him to be able to weather the loss of £10,000 in 1811, when the London firm of Howard and Bell, which handled his potash in England, suddenly collapsed.[32] Domestic servants for the mansion, clerks and storemen for the business headquarters, and entire crews for the new ships were recruited in Scotland through Ker and Co. of Greenock, and from passing references in the Dunlop correspondence it is obvious that Dunlop's Scottish friends and associates in Montreal and Quebec followed the same policy of bringing in their countrymen wherever possible.

As war with the States appeared more imminent, Dunlop calculated, and correctly, that he stood to profit greatly by it. His two newest and largest ships would be suitable for service as privateers against American merchant shipping; there would be possibilities of a lucrative business in the discounting of Treasury, Army, and Navy bills; the rum trade from Jamaica and the wheat trade would benefit greatly from an increase in the armed forces in the North American colonies; the potash and flour trades to the Clyde would not suffer from the withdrawal of American competition; and the demand for oak and pine for British shipyards would increase even further. There is more than one suggestion in the correspondence that Dunlop and other members of the Montreal circle had formed a ring to hold down the prices of Canadian wheat, and to form a sort of corner in it. With three ships engaged in the Montreal-Jamaican trade by November 1811, returning on an average some £1,500 clear profit per voyage, Dunlop was in a good position to speculate in wheat, potash and timber, with a view to wartime profits.[33] By April 1814, Dunlop could declare: 'I have done more good business since the War began than ever I did in the same space of time, but I also have been more bold in my speculations than any other person or company in this province'. Even the import trade, marginally profitable since 1800, repaid Dunlop handsomely, and in May 1814 he stated that he had never gained more in any year than in 1813-14. Cases of import goods, mostly textiles, which he had wisely held during the glut period, rather than sell them at heavy losses in the public vendue, fetched remarkably high prices, and there were still large stocks on hand, valued at £40,000. Dunlop calculated in 1814 that his annual profit would be more than £20,000.[34]

Dunlop certainly stands out as one of the most colourful and imaginative of the early Scottish merchants in Canada. Here was a man who dealt not in consignments, but in full cargoes; who aimed at cornering the production of a whole province; who built and operated his own merchant fleet, and pioneered new trades. His importations in one cargo in November 1813 alone consisted of 800 tons of goods, valued at £50,000, including the duties. It is interesting to consider what he might have gone on to do had he not died suddenly in August 1815, for he had embarked on a massive speculation in importing Irish flour (thousands of tons of it), had purchased the fine East Indiaman *Earl St Vincent* of almost 900 tons for his fleet, and was on the lookout for similar vessels. At his death his inventory of imported goods in hand stood at £100,000. Having no partners and no heirs, the house of

Dunlop and Co. vanished at his decease.

Had he lived two years longer, Dunlop would almost certainly have played a leading part in the foundation of Canada's earliest bank, the Bank of Montreal, in which so many of his Scottish mercantile friends and associates participated in 1817. As Merrill Denison pointed out in the first volume of *Canada's First Bank* (Toronto-Montreal, 1966), half of the founding Board of Directors were Scotsmen, and the list of Presidents, Vice-Presidents and General Managers for the entire nineteenth century contains a preponderance of Scots. As in the new banks in the Maritimes, the first institutions in Upper and Lower Canada were deliberately set up on the Scotch principle, with branch banking and cash credits as prominent and successful features.

Canadian historians have tended to be so preoccupied with the stirring events, political and military, of the period 1794-1815 that they have been inclined to ignore the obvious fact that this, for the colonies, as for Scotland and the rising industrial areas in England, was a period of intense, unprecedented economic and social development. Never did the opportunities for trade, for selling, for exchanging, for dealing, loom so large for the inhabitants of the Canadas, of Nova Scotia, and New Brunswick. When the Peace of Ghent and the Vienna Treaty settled the clouds of war, a very different society emerged from the mists to that which had heard with some apprehension the declaration of hostilities against revolutionary France 20 years before. Under the new dispensation, the merchants in the trading centres had an even greater influence, politically and socially as well as economically. In Lower Canada, as the events of 1815-37 were to show, the almost total control of trade by British (largely Scottish) merchants had serious political consequences.

Scots Activities in Central Canada, 1820-1900

In the period between 1820 and 1900 the Caledonian influence remained strong, if less overwhelmingly pervasive than before, in the provinces which were to become known as Quebec and Ontario. In Montreal especially, Gerald Tulchinsky's *The River Barons: Montreal Businessmen and the Growth of Industry and Transportation, 1837-53* (Toronto and Buffalo, 1977) shows clearly in its analysis that Scottish firms such as Forsyth, Richardson and Co. (all successors of earlier fur-trading concerns) were involved in the export and import business of the entire St Lawrence empire, covering the River and the Lakes and providing credit, shipping, and service arrangements for this vast area. In broking, in the glass and china trade, and in the importation, wholesaling and retailing of dry goods (an ever growing and ever more profitable line of business as population increased), and in shipping, commission agencies and the infant industries of this time, including clothing manufacture (still a Montreal staple), and brass founding, the Scots, as Tulchinsky puts it, 'comprised the dominant group'. In shipping, the Allan family, based in Montreal and Scotland, had made themselves the principal operators of steamship routes between Britain and Canada by 1860; their Montreal Ocean Steamship Company started from extremely small beginnings with one tiny ship sailing out of Saltcoats in 1809.

Railway promotion, the importation of Scottish hardware and pig iron (the cheapest in the world in 1945-65) were the specialities of the Montreal-based concerns of all kinds, and of course, their home links with Lanarkshire producers gave them all the necessary edge in their transactions, a fact which their Canadian-born and American competitors often resented. Out on the frontier, in settlements such as York (Toronto) and Hamilton, Scottish firms were also to the fore, a fine example being the Glasgow-based concern which is the subject of Douglas McCalla's recent *The Upper Canadian Trade, 1834-1872: A Study of the Buchanans' Business* (Toronto, 1979). Typical of the heads of many energetically-run companies in the Canadian import-export trade, the Hamilton-based Isaac Buchanan built up a large and highly profitable business, but ran into difficulties in the 1850s and 1860s through diversification into the risky iron trade and the even more perilous route of railroad promotion and construction. Glasgow bankers helped stave off, but could not avert, eventual disaster. Yet, as in the earlier era, home mercantile and financial connections undoubtedly underpinned and sustained this and other Scottish ventures in Canada amid the vicissitudes of recession and bad judgement. On the whole firms which had a home partner, or which maintained a Scottish connection, fared better than those with neither. Isaac Buchanan, characteristic of his nation, attributed his handsome profits, averaging 30 per cent in the late 1830s, to picking Scottish settlers and storekeepers as his customers, and to 'distrusting Yankees as clients and accepting the Canadian born only after the most vigorous scrutiny of their means, their characters, and their possibility of prosperity'. He and his staff, recruited in Glasgow, acted as business consultants to their favoured fellow countrymen among the firm's merchant and farmer customers, and provide yet another instance of that Scottish web of connection which made Canadian business in its upper reaches seem to many colonials a preserve for the Caledonians, where they worked closely together for their mutual benefit.

The same process was at work in the growing manufactures of the country's central provinces of Ontario and Quebec later in the century. T.W. Acheson, in his studies of the social origins of the 'Canadian Industrial Elite' in the vital 1880s, shows that Scots, with Americans, Englishmen and Germans behind them in number and importance, 'were far more significant elements in the industrial life' of the Canadian heartland and of the Maritime Provinces than were 'Canadians from any other region, including the native born'. As Acheson further states:

It was the transfer of technology from the more sophisticated Scottish industrial economy to the more primitive Canadian, coupled with the traditional practice of providing some form of training for those sons who would not inherit that gave Scots their advantage . . . They came from an industrializing society in the mid nineteenth century and came prepared . . . to function in and to give leadership to the fledgling Canadian industries. Moreover, because of the Scottish-Canadians' tendency to perpetuate this system of 'providing a trade' for the sons, and because of the intense ethnic loyalties which characterized the outlook of most Scottish migrants, the group managed to preserve this technical superiority over members of most other ethnic groups even into the second generation.[35]

Acheson cites numerous examples in engineering, machine and tool making, iron founding and various service industries to point his argument and prove his case. Many Scottish artisans of lesser managerial or working-class origin (the Dunsmuir coal mining magnates of Vancouver Island were a classic example) were to find in the new land their pathway to wealth and industrial leadership in the 1850-1900 era, and to attain their realisation of the Scottish-Canadian dream. Emigrating from the Irvine Valley coalfield near Kilmarnock, the Dunsmuirs and their kin pioneered the industry in Western Canada and laid the foundation, still in place, of a vital part of the Canadian economy.

Scottish Enterprise in the Maritime Provinces

Many similarities with the Montreal circle are to be found in the Scottish mercantile groups in Halifax and St John, though they lacked the flamboyance of the fur trade magnates and the ebullient, calculating grandeur in concept that marked James Dunlop. As with Dunlop and the Newfoundland firms their closest links were with Greenock and Glasgow, for as a commentator noted in the *Scots Magazine* in 1805, Greenock had long been a centre, not only for the Newfoundland fisheries, but also for those of Nova Scotia.[36] As in so many other areas, wartime opportunities figured largely in attracting Scots merchants to Halifax, already an important naval base by 1756. The Seven Years' War saw the arrival of John Gillespie and John Taylor, Aberdeen men who had been traders in New York, and of Alexander Brymer, an enterprising and influential merchant, who had been in business in Glasgow and brought over a capital of £4,000 sterling. A handful of Scots merchants were already established in the town when these three arrived, notably Peter McNab of Inverness, merchant and organiser of salmon fishing ventures, and John Geddes of Glasgow, who came out in 1754 and 1755 respectively, but Brymer was to prove a key figure as 'Father of the Scottish Community of Merchants', for here too the Scots were to form a close-knit body, interdependent and often acting in concert in large-scale ventures. They formed the core of what Harold Innis called 'the little commercial group which dominated Nova Scotian behaviour'. According to the chronicler of the North British Society of Halifax, Brymer 'by his advice brought out several Edinburgh and Glasgow men, some of them with means, who, entering into trade, rapidly made their fortunes'.[37] By all accounts, he was prosperous, and lived in a handsome residence known as 'Brymer's Palace'. By 1768 the North British Society was formed and its *Annals* leave little doubt that this was essentially a mercantile club, though it had benevolent and charitable aims as well.

The wars brought a rapid increase in trade with Scotland (see Table 3.3). A distinctive feature of the Halifax group was the manner in which many of them combined general mercantile and shipping enterprises with a specialised trade or calling. James Thomson, for example, who arrived in 1768, was a cabinet maker and a skilled mason as well as a merchant. John Rider, in addition to being a trader and an organiser of fishing enterprises, kept an inn, reputedly the best in Halifax.

The merchants brought out by Brymer, like other members of the North British Society, speculated successfully in the purchases of

Table 3.3: Trade between Nova Scotia and Scotland, 1779-1800

Year	Scottish Imports from Nova Scotia (in pounds stering)	Scottish Exports to Nova Scotia (in pounds sterling)
1779	1,751	16,629
1785	1,443	19,653
1790	836	23,037
1795	2,015	29,938
1796	5,893	39,863
1800	7,863	37,857

Source: Based on the Glasgow Chamber of Commerce Abstracts.

prizes and cargoes condemned by the Admiralty Court — a Halifax speciality which was to prove increasingly lucrative.[38] The ships were sold to the highest bidder, and according to James MacDonald, 'after perhaps a slight inspection' so that full knowledge of cargo could obviously mean the securing of a bonanza profit. MacDonald further states, 'it was not unusual at this date to clear £5,000 on a single capture' (i.e. after paying for the ship and re-selling it and/or the cargo). It is difficult to avoid the conclusion that the close relations between the merchants and the naval officers and officials must have often proved most profitable to all concerned. Officers of the highest rank participated in this business and looked upon it with favour. At the St Andrew's Day Dinner of the North British Society in November 1813, Admiral Sir John Borlase Warren, guest of honour, spoke complimenting the Scottish merchants upon their sagacity and the rapid fortunes they were realising from the prizes brought into Halifax. He referred to one sale which had taken place on 19 March 1813, when 12 full-rigged ships, 8 brigs and 19 schooners were sold to the highest bidders.[39]

William Forsyth and His Trade Network

Not all of the Scots merchants regarded the traffic in prizes as entirely beneficial to their interests. William Forsyth, the key figure in early Nova Scotian commerce, whose vitally important letter book for the period from August 1796 to October 1798 is preserved in the Nova Scotian Archives, saw the dislocation which captures brought to business. Almost half of the hundreds of letters entered in the Forsyth letter book in 1796-8 deal with matters pertaining to prizes, for Forsyth built up a new branch of business in assisting American, German, and Dutch shipowners to save their vessels from condemnation by the Vice-Admiralty Courts.

By 1796 Forsyth was rising to a position of pre-eminence in the town, with his fleet growing steadily and his Nova Scotian, Quebec, West India, Newfoundland and mast-supplying branches of business developing rapidly. According to Innis, in his *Cod Fisheries*, there was a steep rise in prices offered for dried and salt cod, as much as 25 per cent in the period 1782-3, even before the French War of 1793 drove prices up further. Forsyth benefited greatly from this, and fish were the basic stock of all his trade.[40]

He had home partners in Greenock in the persons of Messrs Hunter, Robertson and Co., who ranked next to Ker and Co. in the scale of their business with the North American colonies. The web of communication which he maintained with agents and firms in all his areas of operation was entirely Scottish. His Newfoundland agents were the Greenock based firm of Andrew Thomson and Co., which maintained several branches in the island colony and supplied Forsyth with the fish he required as trading stock for his trade to Jamaica, Grenada, Barbados, and Martinique, especially the shipment of salted refuse fish as food for slaves on the plantations. In Grenada his agents were Cruden, Pollard and Stewart, a Scottish firm. In St Andrews, New Brunswick, there was Robert Pagan, in St John the Scottish family of Black. In Martinique he had Alexander Brymer, also a Scot. In Jamaica there were Bogle and Jopps, a Scottish house of good repute; in Charleston, Boston, and New York he dealt with Scottish firms, and through all these connections, Forsyth was able to develop some interesting, profitable, and novel lines of trade, such as sending his smaller vessels with codfish to Madeira for wine, which was then sold in Jamaica, the proceeds going into cargoes of rum and sugar for Halifax. Much of this West India produce was then reshipped into the firm's larger vessels which plied to Greenock.[41] Another speciality of the firm was the handling of entire cargoes of the prime Liverpool or Cheshire salt that was required in great quantities in the Arichat and Newfoundland fisheries. The vital importance of Halifax as an entrepôt for many trades at this time clearly emerges from Forsyth's records, and perusal of the *Greenock Advertiser* for the year 1805 shows that no fewer than 58 firms in Greenock, Glasgow, Port Glasgow, and Saltcoats were dispatching vessels to that port, or importing consignments from it.

According to R. G. Albion in his study of *Forests and Sea Power*

(Hamden, Connecticut, 1965, pp. 348-9), the firm of Hunter Robertson and Forsyth, of Greenock and Halifax, made a contract with the British Admiralty in 1788 for the supply of masts from New Brunswick for six years, and this was renewed in 1795 by a seven-year contract to supply no fewer than 30 full cargoes of masts to the naval bases in Halifax, Antigua, Jamaica and England. In the spring of 1798 Forsyth dispatched no fewer than five full cargoes of masts 'as fine sticks as were ever sent out of this country' to another London agent, the Scot Robert Livie.[42] There is no record of his actual profit on this mass of timber, but it was sufficient for him to decide to broaden these mast and yard-shipping operations, to supply the builders of merchant ships in Britain as well as the naval yards.

These successes attracted investment from the ranks of the local serving officers. Lieutenant General James Ogilvie, Commander of the forces in Nova Scotia, invested £20,000 as a silent partner in Forsyth's firm. Ogilvie's son joined the firm, and 'the young man retired after several years with £40,000'.[43] The Earl of Dalhousie, while in the colony, is also reputed to have engaged in large-scale speculations with Matthew Richardson, a prominent Scottish trader in Halifax. This was a tight group, and it grew as more Scots arrived. It would possibly be going too far to accept MacDonald's statement that 'the [North British] Society had by then [1789] enrolled all the leading citizens of the city, they being nearly all Scotsmen', but the new Scots arrivals of the period 1790-1812 did include some men of high ability in mercantile affairs, notably John Black, who came over from St John, New Brunswick, possibly attracted by the war-time activity in Halifax.[44]

The North British Society was not simply a commercial club and a social organisation. It was also giving aid to numerous impoverished Scots immigrants in 1785-6. When increasing numbers of their distressed countrymen in the northern states besought aid in the 1790s to enable them to return home to Scotland, the Society provided assistance. William Forsyth's ships on their voyages to the Clyde usually took back several of these poor Scots. Distressed emigrants were also assisted. As in Lower Canada and in Scotland, the War of 1793 was a great stimulus to trade and local production, and the emigrant flow from Scotland to the North American colonies, which had developed so strongly in the 1770s and 1780s, continued to increase, swollen by merchants who heard from their countrymen in Montreal, Quebec, Halifax, St John, and St Andrews of the good prospects in the new area, and by growing numbers of Highlanders feeling the pressures of the clearances, the falling in of tacksmen's leases, and the stagnation of agriculture in their home areas. By 1800 the emigration from the Highlands began to reach flood proportions, and Colin S. MacDonald has estimated that in the first six years of the nineteenth century no fewer than 10,000 people emigrated from the islands, the glens, and the Highland seacoast, mostly settling in the Maritime provinces.[45] Sir John Sinclair, author of the *First Statistical Account of Scotland*, estimated that 'between 1771 and 1790, no fewer than eight large transports sailed from the Island of Skye alone, with more than 2,400 emigrants to seek settlements, taking with them £24,000, ship freights included'.

Among the hundreds of mercantile Scots who took up residence in Halifax in the 1790s and early 1800s — traders, shipowners, master mariners and skilled craftsmen, and dissenting secessionist Presbyterian divines — the most outstanding in his contribution to the community's commercial development was John Black, who came on from St John, New Brunswick, in 1808. He had arrived in New Brunswick in 1786, as an agent of the Admiralty and as representative of the London (Scottish) firm of Blair and Glenie, entrusted with the shipment of masts and yards. He was quick to sense the importance of St John and the Passamaquoddy Bay as an entrepôt for trade between the West Indies and the United States, as well as for the timber trade, and invited several of his relations to join him in a trading venture in the colony. The Blacks, originally from Aberdeenshire, were prominent in the trade of St John, which they dominated, in conjunction with another of these Scottish mercantile circles remarkably similar to the one in Halifax. Black rapidly built up a fleet with which he traded to the West Indies and Scottish ports, especially Greenock and the old family home of Aberdeen. Black had thriving branches in Fredericton, St Andrews, Miramichi, and Montreal, and even a full-time representative in Aberdeen, Scotland, who handled his timber sales there.[46] In 1804 he was instrumental in the formation of the Halifax Committee of Trade to meet the threat to the town's commerce, due to the US Government's bounties on fish, which were attracting many fishermen south to American ports from the British colonial fishing centres. The flush wartime days of prosperity, privateering and dealing in prizes had been temporarily brought to a close by the Amiens Peace, and the merchants had been forced back on their West India trade in fish for survival. According to G. F. Butler, 'most of the fish caught in the province were being sold to the Americans [due to the bounties in the States] or exchanged for smuggled goods and then exported from Boston to the West Indies'.[47] In this crisis a committee of trade with an elected executive of five prominent merchants, four of them Scots, was formed and submissions were made to the British Government, asking for a monopoly of the West India fish trade for British subjects and pointing to the US bounties and the lower freight and insurance charges, which combined to give the Americans a competitive advantage. The submission was entirely successful, a remarkable early example of effective mercantile pressure in a British colonial society. Instructions were given to the governors of West Indian islands that articles from the United States should only be admitted in cases of great and urgent necessity. Bounties were declared for imports of fish to the islands in British vessels.

The Halifax circle was so numerous, influential, and prosperous, so daring in its new ventures, that another of its worthies should be mentioned as revealing a further aspect of Scottish enterprise. This was John Young, later known by his *nom de plume* of 'Agricola', who left off trading in Glasgow in 1814, hearing of the boom that Halifax had enjoyed since the outbreak of the American war in 1812. Young was a graduate of Glasgow College. In his own words he had 'laboured in vain' in Scottish commerce for ten years. On his arrival in 1814 with a large stock of dry goods, he set up at once as John Young and Co., operating in the captured port of Castine. There he conducted both legal and illegal operations, the latter being undoubtedly the most lucrative. This was the practice of trading on the line that was bringing so much wealth to Nova Scotia and New Brunswick in the War of 1812, and Young's graphic letters give a fascinating account of the ruses that were involved in an illicit trade with the enemy.[48]

The third and final centre where Scottish merchants established a rapid dominance in the period of their home country's dramatic surge forward in commerce was St John, New Brunswick, with the neighbouring settlement of St Andrews. The Loyalist influx of 1784 brought many Scots, but even before this Scots were active in the fields of fisheries and timber-getting. There is evidence that development of New Brunswick fisheries was an extension of Scottish interest in the Newfoundland fisheries. William Davidson and his partner John Cort, who hailed from Inverness and Aberdeen, secured a large grant of 100,000 acres on the Miramichi River in the 1770s and appear to have been chiefly interested in the export of barrelled salmon to the West Indies and the Mediterranean, but they rapidly developed an interest in the timber trade as well.[49] Davidson and Cort, according to Rattray, were established on the Miramichi as early as 1765, in an area abandoned by the French, from which they were able to export from 1,400 to 1,800 tierces of salmon [about 1,000-1,200 barrels] annually in the mid

1760s. It is probable that they both had experience of large-scale salmon fishing operations on the Don or the Dee in their home country and of the salting and pickling methods followed there. Yet another Scot, Alexander Walker, who settled at Alston on the north side of Bathurst Harbour in the 1760s, traded extensively in fish, furs, walrus tusks and hides, oil, and other local products. Tragically little is known about these early entrepreneurs, who were the true pioneers of commerce in that area, or of Edward Mortimer from Keith, Banffshire, the 'King of Pictou', who made Pictou the business centre of the Gulf of St Lawrence in the 1780s. Mortimer's partner, George Smith, another Scot, who was Pictou's leading businessman in the early 1800s, is also an obscure figure. The Patterson brothers, from Greenock, who traded on a large scale from Pictou to Jamaica and built hundreds of fishing vessels and small merchant ships, are also lost in the mists, for none of their records have survived. Yet these were key people in the economic development of the Maritime Provinces.

During the 1790s the difficulties of carrying on the Russian trade increased. The shocks of the 1798 Ukase and the seizures and confiscations inclined many timber merchants and shipbuilders in Scotland to turn their attention to the North American timber trade long before the first large contracts for colonial timber were awarded in 1804-5. These firms were centred chiefly in the Glasgow, Greenock, and Port Glasgow area, but several Grangemouth and Leith firms on the east coast also began to seek North American contacts in the 1780s, for the gradual completion of the Forth and Clyde Canal enabled timber cargoes to be shipped to them after being landed in the Clyde. As early as 1785, the press of St John recorded two departures of vessels with loads of timber for Glasgow. By the following year Scots were obviously the most numerous element among the town's mercantile men, their centre of operations being Scotch Row and their principal rendezvous McPhail's Tavern.[50]

Again, in this New Brunswick port, as in Halifax, the list of thriving commercial houses in the later 1780s reads like a Scottish census list: James Stewart and Co., importers on a grand scale of rice and molasses from the United States; Campbell, Stewart and Co., importers of books, rum and foodstuffs from the Clyde; McGeorge, Elliot and Co., importing textiles of all types; McCall and Co., importing British textiles and India goods; and John Colville and Co., David Blair's Co., Hector Scott and the brothers William and Thomas Pagan, formerly of Greenock, all exporting timber and bringing in rum, bibles, and gunpowder, often in Scottish vessels, mostly from the Clyde. There were a few non-Scottish merchants, but they were sorely outnumbered.[51]

The dependence on a web of Scots connections and contacts, not only in the homeland but in foreign ports, is strikingly obvious. St John traders dealt with Scots firms in American, West Indian, English, and even Spanish and French colonial ports. Many vessels from the Clyde unloaded part of their cargoes in Halifax, passing through the hands of Blacks, Bremners, Brymer, Forsyth and other Scots houses there as agents, before proceeding to St John for their timber cargoes. Lesser centres like Shelburne and St Andrews also had Scottish houses which acted for St John, Halifax, and on occasion, for Montreal merchants of the Scots connection. In the first decade of the town's existence the number of Scots merchants increased, swollen by new arrivals, mainly from Glasgow and Greenock, lured by the timber trade. By 1797 the houses of Pagan and Co., Hugh Johnston and Co., John Black and Co., and Andrew Crookshank and Co., stood out as pre-eminent among the 25 Scottish firms which essentially controlled the trade of the new province's major port.

As the need for shipbuilding materials grew desperate on the Clyde, due to Russian difficulties and the exhaustion of home resources, and as the premium on ships of any quality rose due to war losses to privateers, it was natural that Scottish builders should hear of the possibilities of establishing yards in the new timber-rich area of New Brunswick. Through his agents in Greenock, Alan Ker and Co., Andrew Crookshank encouraged the already famous firm of Scott and Co., shipbuilders at Greenock, to build new vessels on the St John River. Remarkably, while the entire early-eighteenth-century records of Scotts Ltd were destroyed in the Greenock Blitz of 1941, the letter book covering the years 1798-1800 has survived, and it contains a full account of the transfer of Scottish shipbuilding techniques, men, and material to the distant shores of New Brunswick. It is interesting to note, as an example of the close-meshed web of Scottish commercial connections at the time, that the Scott firm shared with Forsyth the same Liverpool, London, and Jamaican agents.[52]

The Scotts' scheme was one of the earliest examples of the exportation of an industrial installation, involving the shipment of craftsmen and such materials as nails, iron spikes, jobbing iron, anchors, and copper spikes (all manufactured in the Muirkirk Ironworks) and the nucleus of the crews for the first vessels. Heading the expedition was Christopher Scott, younger brother of James and William Scott, the firm's principals. He was an experienced supervisor of ship construction and a master mariner in his own right, who sailed in March 1799.

By mid-April he had two vessels under construction and further ship-loads of materials, including Archangel tar, Russian cordage and Scottish sailcloth, were being shipped to him. Furthermore, with the continued shortage of shipping in British ports Christopher Scott was instructed to purchase any colonial-built vessels of quality that might be available, even if they were only half or quarter built, and even although he was required to pay in advance.[53] Skilled shipwrights, carpenters, blacksmiths, and caulkers were sent out continuously by the Scotts to their new yards during this period, often in small groups in vessels sailing from the Clyde, but occasionally in larger numbers in the Scotts' own vessels. It is interesting to speculate on the impact of these men and the techniques they brought from Scotland on shipbuilding generally in the Maritimes. Entire crews for new vessels, from commanders to cabin boys, were also shipped out.

By April 1800 the Scotts had built, commissioned, purchased, or otherwise acquired the surprising total of 27 vessels constructed on or around the St John River, a remarkable total, which does not include eleven other vessels in various stages of construction also owned by them. The achievement was possible only because of Christopher Scott's contacts in the dominant Scots mercantile community and the co-operation of local builders, timber suppliers and workmen, as well as the backing of the powerful home firm on the Clyde. It was an outstanding example of the projection of early industrial Scotland into the colonial scene, an amazingly large-scale operation for the time, involving the transfer of hundreds of artisans, hundreds of sailors for crews, and thousands of tons of cordage, copper, iron-work, sheathing paper, and chandlery across the Atlantic from the Clyde to service the new vessels.

The years after 1804 saw the beginning of the golden age of the New Brunswick timber trade, and the apogee of Scottish mercantile influence in the colony. The key figure in conceiving the giant among contemporary timber companies was Allan Gilmour. Temperamental and adventurous, he began his business career as a small importer of lumber from the Baltic area. As one of the first Scottish timber merchants to recognise the advantage of importing North American wood, Gilmour moved his headquarters from Grangemouth at the mouth of the Great Canal to Port Glasgow on the Clyde. In 1804 he established a branch in Quebec City and in 1812 another at Miramichi; from that time on the firm grew rapidly. In the late 1820s they were operating eleven shipyards in the North American colonies, and between 1822 and 1832 their fleet increased from 54 to over 100 vessels, the largest fleet under one house flag in the British Empire. In the 1830s, apart from the 5,000 men employed in the ships and shipyards, over 15,000 were working in the forests of New Brunswick to obtain the timber, although in Canada they bought directly from the lumbermen as they rafted their logs down the St Lawrence and Ottawa Rivers. In 1834 the firm exported 300 shiploads from Miramichi, St John, Quebec, Montreal and Bathurst, probably amounting to some 150,000 tons, if the average ship's capacity was 500 tons, although some were much larger. Pollok and Gilmour also acted as agents for shipbuilders in the Maritime colonies, selling large numbers of their vessels on the London market. We may gain some idea of the way in which the wealth of the partners increased during this period by the fact that Gilmour between 1815 and 1836 bought a number of country estates and finally in 1838 sold out his share to the Polloks for £150,000, not a bad capital gain on his original £1,000 investment.[54]

Of the 20 original board members of the Bank of New Brunswick, established in 1820 at St John, no fewer than ten were Scots, or of Scots descent, including Christopher Scott, the shipbuilding entrepreneur. In the Charlotte County Bank, set up in St Andrews in 1825, there were 14 Scots in a total directorate of 25. These are typical, and not outstanding examples of Scottish participation in the formation of the early Canadian banks. In the circumstances it was natural that these banks should follow the design of the new Scotch institutions which had revolutionised the whole concept of banking in Britain, if not in Europe.

As the nineteenth century wore on other Scottish names appeared. George Stephen, Lord Mount Stephen, and his cousin, Donald Smith, Baron Strathcona and Mount Royal, both played important parts in the financial world of Montreal and were the two men responsible, along with the engineer Sandford Fleming, another Scot, for the successful completion of the Canadian Pacific Railway. Many of these Scots were the leading philanthropists of the city, being responsible for the founding of institutions such as McGill University, the Royal Victoria and the Montreal General Hospitals, the building of churches and the establishment of commercial organisations such as the Board of Trade and even the Mercantile Library Association, a kind of merchants' mechanics' institute. To the west of Montreal from Toronto and Hamilton as far as Fort William and Port Arthur at the Lakehead, the same phenomenon was observable. Whether it was Sir Alan MacNab, who with J.B. Ewart and Peter Buchanan pushed through the construction of the Great Western Railway, or Robert Simpson, the originator of the chain of retail departmental stores, Scots seem to have dominated the business world.

In Victoria — founded by a Scot, James Douglas — on the west coast we find that the eastern pattern tends to repeat itself. Although many different ethnic groups were represented in the thousands of people who came in with the gold rush in the Fraser River Valley, Scots soon made their appearance and gradually became some of the most important and influential businessmen in the area. Thomas and James Lowe were two of the first to come, arriving in 1861-2, and eventually became leaders of the business community. Other Scots who came about the same time were J. Robertson Stewart and Gilbert M. Sproat, president of the local St Andrew's Society in 1863. Sproat represented Anderson and Co., which was interested in shipbuilding and the lumber trade. In 1859 the first private bank was established by Alexander Macdonald. Gradually more Scots moved in. One of the most important was Robert Dunsmuir who had been selling coal from Nanaimo since 1855. In 1869 he discovered the Wellington mine which enabled him to form a large coal mining company. In the 1860s men such as William Irving and Alexander Murray operated the first steamships in the area. A little later another Scot who was to wield a great influence settled inVictoria: Robert Paterson Rithet, who in 1868 was working for Sproat and Co. but later joined J. Robertson Stewart.

Pierre Berton in *The National Dream* (Toronto, 1971) states the Scots' accomplishments most clearly. He quotes from Lord Mount Stephen's address when the latter received the freedom of the City of Aberdeen:

Any success I may have had in life is due in great measure to the somewhat Spartan training I received during my Aberdeen apprenticeship, in which I entered as a boy of 15. To that training, coupled with the fact that I seemed to have been born utterly without the faculty of doing more than one thing at a time is due that I am here before you today. I had but few wants and no distractions to draw me away from the work I had in hand. It was impressed upon me from my earliest years by one of the best mothers that ever lived that I must aim at being a thorough master of the work by which I had to get my living; and to be that I must concentrate my whole energies on my work, whatever that might be, to the exclusion of every other thing. I soon discovered that if I ever accomplished anything in life it would be by pursuing my object with a persistent determination to attain it. I had neither the training nor the talents to accomplish anything without hard work, and fortunately I knew it.[55]

The words, so Victorian in style, seem in the late twentieth century rather trite and sententious, but they represent the feelings of one who successfully, and characteristically for many of his fellow countrymen, fulfilled the Scottish-Canadian dream.

The sheer preponderance of the Scots in business, their wholesale pervasion of commerce in the area would, perhaps, have received more attention had it not been for two decisive developments. The first was their rapid assimilation. Even James Keith, who had commanded on the Columbia River in 1814 for the North West Company, living in retirement in Aberdeen, Scotland, in the early 1850s, often wrote nostalgically to his friends in Lachine and described himself as 'in some sort . . . a Canadian'. Those who did not go back must have assimilated even more easily than this particularly patriotic and stiff-necked man from the heart of Scotland's North East. The other reason was the fate of Scotland itself in the later nineteenth century, when the country became materially absorbed in the affairs of Great Britain, when 'Hungry London', as Lord Cockburn put it, attracted the best of Scottish talent, as well as the most profitable of Scottish companies.

It has been argued that Scotland exhausted itself in its rapid social and economic transformation, and there are grounds for holding the argument a valid one; but if it is valid the main beneficiary, in people, initiatives, and economic strength gained by investment, trade and enterprise, was undoubtedly the group of colonies which were eventually to confederate as Canada.

If the theory of the metropolitan focus of Canadian history is a valid one, as suggested by some historians — the foci comprising London as well as the cities of the St Lawrence System — then Glasgow and its Clyde port of Greenock should surely be included in the list of urban centres from which Canadian economic development was planned, organised, and effected.

Notes

I am indebted to the Social Sciences and Humanities Research Council of Canada, and to the Research Committee of Trent University for grants which have enabled me to carry on the work upon which this chapter is based. D.S.M.
    1. Bruce Lenman's *Integration, Enlightenment, and Industrialization: Scotland, 1746-1832* (Toronto, 1981), pp. 80-4. The degree of Scottish participation in

Canadian business management today can be ascertained by reference to the Business Section of the *Toronto Globe and Mail*, and to the lists of directors of Canada's 255 leading corporations where Scottish immigrants, and first, second, third and later generation Scots is highly impressive.

2. The Alexander and Ochiltree projects were ably treated by George Pratt Insh in his definitive studies of early ventures, especially *Scottish Colonial Schemes* (Glasgow, 1922). For the other colonisation projects, see J.M. Bumsted 'Lord Selkirk of Prince Edward Island' in the *Island Magazine*, No. 5, 1978, pp. 3-8, and articles (forthcoming) in the *Dictionary of Canadian Biography*, on Archibald MacMillan, founder of the Ottawa River Settlements, and on James Douglas, Montgomery's agent in Prince Edward Island, by David S. Macmillan.

3. See David, S. Macmillan, *Scotland and Australia, 1788-1850: Emigration, Commerce and Investment* (Oxford, 1967), Chapters I-VI.

4. The development of an efficient, indenture system of emigration is considered in Charles Cargill Graham, *Colonists from Scotland: Emigration to North America, 1707-1783* (Ithaca, 1956), and A.E. Smith, *Colonists in Bondage: White Servitude and Convict Labour in America, 1607-1776* (Chapel Hill, North Carolina, 1947), as well as in the more recent *Scotus Americanus*, by William R. Brock (Edinburgh, 1982). Jacqueline A. Rinn has also contributed a useful and informative article on the subject in *History Today*, vol. 30, (July 1980). A general assessment of the emigration and market-seeking activities of the Scottish merchants in 1650-1850 is contained in David S. Macmillan 'The Neglected Aspect of the Scottish Diaspora, 1650-1850: The Role of the Entrepreneur in Promoting and Effecting Emigration' in *Institute of Commonwealth Studies Collected Seminar Papers, No. 31, The Diaspora of the British* (London, 1982).

5. Figures based on Customs Records in the Scottish Record Office, Edinburgh, Collections of Business and Family Papers there, and on similar collections held in the National Library of Scotland, Edinburgh, and on the files of Edinburgh and Glasgow newspapers there. The Mitchell Library, Glasgow, and the Business Archives Collections in the University of Glasgow and the Library of King's College, the University of Aberdeen, also contain useful references.

6. Lenman, *Integration*, pp. 2, 9.

7. For examples of Scots activity in the various fields, and of the ways in which localism prevailed among them, see the Revd Robert Campbell, D.D., *History of the Saint Gabriel Street Church, Montreal* (Montreal, 1887), pp. 84-149; James S. MacDonald, *Annals of the North British Society, 1768-1903* (Halifax, 1905), pp. 39, 63, 107, 122; Navy Board Records – Disposal of Prizes 3/143-8, 1813, Public Record Office, London.

8. For 'trading on the Line' see D.C. Harvey, 'Pre-Agricola John Young' in *Collections of the Nova Scotia Historical Society*, vol. 32, 1959; Esther Clark Wright, *The Saint John River and Its Tributaries* (Toronto, 1949); and Guy Murchie, *Saint Croix: The Sentinel River* (New York, 1957). For the traffic in gypsum, see W.S. McNutt, *New Brunswick: A History, 1784-1867* (Toronto, 1963).

9. See Daniel Weir, *History of the Town of Greenock* (Glasgow, 1829).

10. R.G. Lounsbury, *The British Fishery at Newfoundland* (Archon Reprints, 1969), p. 44.

11. Ibid., pp. 198-9.

12. Ibid., p. 201.

13. Ibid., pp. 203-6.

14. A.C. Wardle, *The Trade Winds: A Study of British Overseas Trade During the French Wars, 1793-1815* (London, 1958), pp. 243-44.

15. The Lang Papers are housed in the Business Archives Collection in the Department of Economic History, the University of Glasgow.

16. Abstract of the General Customs of Scotland, 1755-1801, Archives of the Glasgow Chamber of Commerce, probably compiled by George Chalmers; Customs account book, *Newfoundland, 1771-85*, R.H. 20/22 in the Scottish Record Office, Edinburgh.

17. H.A. Innis, *The Cod Fisheries: The History of an International Economy*, revised edn (Toronto, 1954), p. 289.

18. Ibid., pp. 212, 245, 297.

19. W. Stewart Wallace, *The Pedlars from Quebec and Other Papers on the Nor'Westers* (Toronto), p. 21.

20. *Glasgow Journal*, 14 January 1760.

21. Ibid., 28 January 1760.

22. Ibid., 2 February 1764.

23. Ibid., 8 March 1770. See also shipping lists, 1765-1770, *Glasgow Journal*.

24. For the development of this trade see E.R. Rich, *The History of the Hudson's Bay Company, 1670-1870* (London, 1958-9).

25. W. Stewart Wallace, *Pedlars from Quebec*, pp. 485-6.

26. *Glasgow Burgh Court Records*, October 1777; *The Macmillan Dictionary of Canadian Biography* (Toronto, 1963).

27. Letters of James Dunlop, G.D. 1/151, Scottish Record Office, HM General Register House, Edinburgh.

28. The Reverend Robert Campbell, *A History of the Scotch Presbyterian Church, St Gabriel Street, Montreal* (Montreal, 1887), pp. 96-8.

29. Dunlop Letters, Dunlop to Alexander Dunlop, 15 April 1798.

30. Ibid., same to same, 29 December 1799.

31. Ibid., same to same, and to Mrs Janet McNair, 1, 7, and 24 July 1800.

32. Ibid., Dunlop to Mrs Janet McNair, Glasgow.

33. Ibid., same to same, 9 and 30 November 1811.

34. Ibid., same to same, 17 May 1814.

35. T.W. Acheson, 'Analysis of the Industrial Elite' in *Canadian Business History, Selected Studies, 1497-1971*, D.S. Macmillan (ed.) (Toronto, 1972), p. 154.

36. 'View of the Situation and Trade of Greenock' in the *Scots Magazine*, vol. LXVII, 1805, p. 10.

37. MacDonald, *North British Society* (Halifax, 1905), p. 27.

38. Ibid., passim.

39. Ibid., p. 122.

40. Forsyth to Crawford, 16 September, 1796, Letter Book of William Forsyth and Co., 1796-8, Archives of Nova Scotia. Harold Innis, *The Cod Fisheries* (Toronto, 1954), pp. 288-9.

41. Forsyth Letter Book, passim.

42. Ibid., Forsyth to Livie, 21 June 1798.

43. MacDonald, *North British Society*, entries of 1784.

44. Ibid., p. 62.

45. Colin S. MacDonald, 'Early Highland Emigration to Nova Scotia and Prince Edward Island from 1770-1853' in *Collections of the Nova Scotia Historical Society*, vol. 23, 1936, p. 48.

46. James S. MacDonald, *North British Society*, p. 114; *The Judges of New Brunswick and Their Times* (St John, 1912), pp. 223-4.

47. G.F. Butler, 'The Early Organisation and Influence of the Halifax Merchants' in *Collections of the Nova Scotia Historical Society*, vol. 25, 1942.

48. See D.C. Harvey, 'Pre-Agricola John Young', in *Collections of the Nova Scotia Historical Society*, vol. 32, 1959, pp. 125-39.

49. George MacBeath and Dorothy Chamberlin, *New Brunswick* (Toronto, 1965).

50. *Royal Gazette and New Brunswick Advertiser*, 11 October 1785.

51. Ibid., Advertisements, 1785-6.
52. Letter book of Scotts Ltd, Greenock, September 1798 – August 1800, Archives of the Scotts, Cartsburn Dockyard, Greenock.
53. Ibid., John Scott to Christopher Scott, 25 May 1799.
54. John Rankin, *A History of Our Firm* (Liverpool, 1921).
55. Quoted in Pierre Berton, *The National Dream* (Toronto, 1971), p. 319.

4 THE SCOTS IN THE UNITED STATES

Bernard Aspinwall

'The Scottish Whigs', wrote the emigrant novelist William Brownlee, 'achieved in their nation what the patriots of every nation will achieve in the day they rise to vindicate their rights. Theirs is the proud honour of having struck the first blow, as the van of patriotic hosts who will overthrow tyranny; and give liberty to the world.'[1] With this sense of manifest destiny in bringing reinforcement to civil and religious liberty in the growing American nation, Scots were especially welcome. As Neal Dow, the Maine entrepreneur and prohibitionist wrote of one Scottish visitor: he was

> a downright hearty Scotsman; a capital specimen of their race and blood, so heroic in many a field, so true and tenacious in church and council. May the race never be fewer; the blood cannot be purer. Of all immigrants to our country the Scotch are always the most welcome. They bring us muscle and brain and tried skill and trustworthiness in many of our great industries of which they are managers of the most successful ones.[2]

So pervasive was this view that almost 30 years later, a one-time Lord Provost of Glasgow, Sir Samuel Chisholm was able to tell a New York audience 'Does not the persistence of Protestantism and Calvinism and Puritanism and Presbyterianism and the general democratic spirit suggest that the ever coming Scot has assimilated and is assimilating the American people.'[3] Scots seemed to be everywhere. As David Macrae observed, 'I begin to think that either the world was very small or Scotland very large.'[4] America, as Andrew Carnegie saw, 'would have been a poor show had it not been for the Scotch'.[5]

Scottish ethnic self-assertion confirmed — and contributed to — American social, political and religious attitudes to produce a confident belief in progress. In celebrating their ethnic success Scots were celebrating America. They were constructing and identifying with American nationality. The typical Scottish immigrant to America went with a stable, consistent character. Though Scottish emigrants retained a strong affection for their homeland, they did not develop that intense nationalism like Polish, German, Italian, or above all, Irish immigrants. Unlike these groups, Scots could not easily identify an alien oppressor: they saw only aristocratic, industrial or Anglicised privileged groups of their own kind at home. For that and other reasons, Scots tended to develop a portable, almost messianic vision which was appropriate to their role in the expanding English speaking world of the last century.[6] In a developing, expanding economy their education and technical skills gave them considerable advantages. In a fluid American society their opportunities for self-improvement and self-fulfilment were vast and rewarding. America represented the realisation of those potentialities denied them at home by privilege in its various guises. The United States was Scotland realised beyond the seas. Accustomed to hard relentless toil on unrewarding land and heavy industrial work at home, Scots came highly motivated with a sense of religious crusade, duty and the work ethic: they like Robert Burns were universal men. Disciplined through education, religion, and hardship, they arrived with a well-regulated internal moral mechanism. Sometimes they had been able to save the fare through adherence to temperance principles. With these qualities they were well equipped as the shock troops of modernisation.[7] In effect they confirmed Weber's thesis regarding capitalism and protestantism. Scots in general accepted that the benign operation of natural law in economics depended upon the possession of certain qualities, thrift, the postponement of immediate gratification, industriousness and 'being frank and honest with oneself about affairs'.[8]

Scottish emigrants to America were committed to the realisation of an efficient moral social order. In general they held an alternative vision, one which they could invoke consistently throughout the period to 1920, as we shall see, to criticise the failings of the existing order to evolve more purposefully towards a providential order in America. Their cultural 'package' gave them this insight. That Scottish outlook enabled them to champion capitalist enterprise and to sustain labour union critics. In both cases their Protestant ethic railed against privilege and monopoly. Andrew Carnegie, the millionaire son of a Scottish Chartist is a case in point. His famous letter of December, 1868, shows that heritage emerging: 'To continue much longer overwhelmed by business cares and with most of my thoughts wholly upon the way to make money in the shortest time, must wholly degrade me beyond the hope of permanent recovery'.[9] That paradoxical approach worked until technology undermined the old work ethic and mass immigration eroded the cultural base and status of the Scots as a group. The Great

Depression, the post-war expansion of higher education and the emergence of a more pluralist American society completed the transformation.

The reordering coincided with the changing Scottish perception of America.[10] In the early days of the United States, Scots saw America as the work of an enlightenment and Christian providence. In removing religious, class and educational barriers to individual self-improvement, America seemed to be an ideal, peaceful, democratic state. A reformed Scotland might achieve similar goals. Her failure to do so allowed America to become a useful myth, an escape valve and the hope of the future, whatever the disappointments at home. Though Scottish conservatives might carp at American democracy, they must have realised that emigration to America provided a guarantee of domestic stability. By the 1880s the consolidation of big business, the conflicts with labour and the erosion of Scottish skill and status was dimming the attractions of America. By the close of the First World War, the decline of Scottish industry and the emergence of Soviet Russia made other models somewhat more attractive. The persistent 'Red Scare' and the Depression reinforced that view of dry America. In so far as America provided a dream world, Hollywood was that.[11] Though Scots might recognise the American contribution in the Second World War and after, the old strong identification was much weakened.

Scots were neither radical nor reactionary but consistent. In a sense Albert Brisbane, the Fourierist American, was not far wrong in believing a brand new idea was not easily hammered into a Scottish head.[12] Scots reasoned from common-sense tradition, from experience and from an organic evolutionary view. They did not radically alter their position, though massive social changes took place around them. Sufficiently 'modernised', they had an internal, resilient moral sense which could cope with varied challenges. Theirs was a republic of the mind which gave no hostages to fortune. They did not identify with fixed positions, fixed hierarchies or static social orders. Their essential convictions, their belief in Providence, Protestantism and Progress remained secure and readily evolved satisfactory responses to the changing circumstances.[13] In a very important sense Scots were the engineers of American social and political progress.

The Scots undoubtedly contributed talent and skill to the developing country. But they were also pugnacious and aggressive. They placed great store on the church and the schoolhouse, 'these fortresses against ignorance and the devil paralleled a chain of blockhouses and forts against the French and Indian. The Scots were as eager to fight one as another.'[14] Even in the earliest days of the American revolution, Ezra Stiles, the president of Yale College, found Scots too ready to place a liberal gloss on their pugnacity.

From the earliest days of British colonisation there had been Scottish interest in the new settlements. Captain John Mason, the founder of New Hampshire, had published a pamphlet in Edinburgh in 1620 encouraging settlement in North America. Four years later, Sir William Alexander, a promoter of the Newfoundland colonies and associated with New England interest, published his *Encouragement to Colonies*, while the following year Sir Robert Gordon of Lochinvar published his tract dedicated to the 'undertakers in the plantations of New Scotland in America'.[15] As early as 1638, John Burnett of Aberdeen was trading with Virginia.[16] With the growth of the American trade, particularly tobacco, the pressure on land at home and the prospect of better land in America, interest greatly increased.[17] In the late eighteenth century the consolidation of landowning into a few hands, the increasingly unrepresentative and unresponsive parliamentary body from Scotland, and the lack of self-esteem of prospects in Scotland made the prospect of America increasingly attractive.

The merchants and talented men of business were leaving in great numbers to go to America. The middle and lower classes were being neglected to the detriment of the long-term good of Scotland. Naturally with a literate public, ample publicity, and available ships to America, considerable numbers were forming themselves into companies to emigrate.[18] Earlier emigrants were sending letters back home encouraging migration: 'North America is the best poor man's country in the world for the price of grain there is very low and the price of labour very high.'[19] The landless, forced into town, and mechanics, faced with high costs through the monopoly of landownership, readily took themselves to America.[20] In a freer American atmosphere higher aspirations might be fulfilled.[21] Many factory workers left to better their lot, but rural emigrants were also numerous. The pace at which they left is debatable but the flow was continuous over the period.

The emigration traffic was but a logical extension of the considerable seaborne trade through the 'Amero-mania' which seized so many Scots in the early nineteenth century.[22] Following the initial rush of immigrants in the years after 1815, a number of passenger companies emerged. In 1840 the Cunard Company was established with the considerable backing of George Burns of Glasgow and the Glasgow-born David MacIver for its service between Liverpool, Halifax and Boston.[23] Other direct connections between Glasgow and America followed later;

the short lived New York and Glasgow Steamship Company (1851-9); the Anchor, Allan and Donaldson Lines.[24] From 1856 the Anchor Line operated between Glasgow and New York. In 1869 it began feeder services from Scandinavia and Naples. In the following year 23,000 of its 25,000 passengers went to America in the steerage, an indication of the extent of their immigrant traffic. In 1872 the company shipped the first live cattle to Scotland from America and three years later made the first ever shipment of refrigerated meat. Anchor claimed to offer a ship to America every other day of the year. The Allan Line offered services to New York from 1856, Baltimore from 1871, Philadelphia from 1884, and briefly to New Orleans in 1872. The Donaldson Line offered services to Portland, Maine from 1879 and to Baltimore from 1881. In time the Allan Line was absorbed by the Canadian Pacific, and the others, affected by severe competition, war losses and changing habits of travel, were wound up. In their time, however, they had provided an important tangible link with America. If Scottish lines did not convey emigrants to America, an astonishing number did go in Clyde-built ships.

The many later travel books on America written by Scots show writers moving within a world of Scots, better fed, clothed, housed and greatly improved on their native land. It seems to be a world of numerous friends and acquaintances who have moved *en masse* to America from Glasgow, Paisley, Ayrshire or wherever. The same Presbyterian church services with local Scottish born ministers served their flock, who were working in similar industries as at home. More might be in white collar jobs over more recent immigrants from other lands, as in textiles or mining. Such travel books spread reassurance, encouragement and confidence among those contemplating emigrating. They also suggested areas where their skills might be most welcome among ethnic kin. Reinforced in that knowledge by numerous American visitors to Scotland, politicians, writers or more popular preachers, the break would not seem so dramatic compared to other lands. The Atlantic was progressively shrinking through the century so that seasonal migration or hard times in either might encourage transatlantic traffic. America was not so much a foreign land as an upmarket, or idealised, Scotland. The American wore a well-cut and well-kent kilt — or so it seemed.

How did Scottish visitors fare in America? They like their American counterparts frequently found much to reinforce their prejudices. The vast majority found their countrymen flourishing in comfort and affluence as a result of their own endeavours. Everywhere in Vermont, Maine, New York or California the emigrants had prospered.[25] In travelling through the country Scottish visitors invariably met large numbers of their countrymen, old friends, relatives or members of their old congregations in Scotland.[26] America was hardly a foreign land in any real sense.

The sons of radicals, Andrew Carnegie and Allan Pinkerton, both emigrated and enjoyed astonishing success, respectively as an industrial entrepreneur and as the founder of a detective agency which specialised in breaking industrial unions.[27] They like many of their compatriots were able to succeed with their native Scottish qualities in a land which they found highly valued those virtues. Scotland and America seemed one and the same:

> Sobriety, love of work and perseverance in both; the same attachment to religion, mingled with more caution in Sanders and more enterprise in Jonathan. Both are inhabitants of a poor country and both have become by habits of steady industry and frugality. Both send forth a large portion of their population to participate in the wealth of more favoured regions. The Scot, however, never loses his attachment to his native land. It has probably been to him a rugged nurse yet wander where he will, its heathy mountains are ever present to his imagination and he thinks of the bleak moorland cottage in which he grew from infancy to manhood, as a spot encircled by a halo of light and beauty. Whenever fortune smiles on him he returns to his native village and the drama of his life closes where it commenced.[28]

These highly prized virtues stemmed from his home experience which demanded 'sober habits and well directed industry' and gave him advantages in America.[29] His strong religious sense also contributed to his purposeful drive to economic success here and salvation in the hereafter. Whether explained by terror, a sense of duty or ambition that quality made him well equipped for self-improvement in America.

The Scottish tradition of education had won a great reputation during the eighteenth century. The Scottish intellectual contribution to developing American self-consciousness is well documented. Scotland provided the sociological tools for American Independence. By establishing a science of society, the Scottish academics of the Enlightenment provided the colonies with the means of critically assessing their governors.[30] The numbers of colonials studying medicine and other subjects in Scottish universities and the migration of talented leaders of education to America further consolidated the hold of Scottish letters. The work of Francis Makemie and Francis Alison (both Ulster born and Glasgow trained) in consolidating education and the Presbyterian Church, William Smith of Aberdeen at the University of Pennsylvania, the former Montrose minister Charles Nesbit at Dickinson College, and above all, John Witherspoon, president of Princeton and the only clerical signatory of the Declaration of Independence were substantial and are well known.[31] Scotland provided the personnel, leadership, and intellect for the new independent nation. For example, Princeton under Witherspoon's presidency produced 13 college presidents who combined energetic democratic sentiments and evangelical piety; one president of the United States; one vice-president; 9 cabinet officers; 21 senators; 39 congressmen; 3 Supreme Court justices; 12 governors; 33 judges; and six members of the Continental Congress. At the same time the numbers entering the ministry declined to about one quarter of all graduates as more entered the public service and professions.[32] That tradition was to continue under the presidencies of John Maclean, son of a Glasgow graduate who held the first ever chair of chemistry in America, and the former Glasgow and Edinburgh student, James McCosh, until 1894.[33] The contribution was not merely at the level of college presidencies, but throughout all levels of education. At Princeton John Maclean, a Glasgow graduate, taught the 'father of American chemistry', Benjamin Silliman, a fact Silliman gratefully recognised. Silliman subsequently went to Scotland and examined facilities in Edinburgh and Glasgow while he was securing chemistry equipment in 1805-6.[34]

Granville Sharp Pattison, Professor of Anatomy and Surgery at the Andersonian Institution, Glasgow, emigrated to America in the wake of a divorce scandal. Failing to secure a chair in the University of Pennsylvania, he then became Professor of Anatomy at the University of Maryland, Baltimore. After an unhappy spell in the University of London he returned to America to be Professor of Anatomy at the Jefferson Medical College, Philadelphia from 1832 to 1841, then at New York University until his death in 1852. His reputation as a teacher was allegedly unsurpassed on either side of the Atlantic.[35] That contribution to medical education was further extended by Abraham Flexner, who returned from a European tour deeply impressed by the methods and techniques of Glasgow University.[36] He sought to copy them in his homeland.

In the late nineteenth century the recently established Johns Hopkins University sought aid from Scottish universities, as much as from the much publicised German universities, in developing more scientific courses of instruction. President Gilman visited Glasgow and consulted with Principal Caird. Professor Thomson, later Lord Kelvin, gave considerable advice, spent a period teaching in the new university, and encouraged research work there.[37]

That innovative cast of mind took several leading Scottish academics to American state universities in the late nineteenth century. W.M. Wenley, the pioneer of extra-mural education in the west of Scotland and one of Edward Caird's pupils, emigrated to Michigan in 1896, where he remained until 1929; James Mavor, after associating with Hyndman and William Morris and more modest social democratic reformers, followed W.J. Ashley as professor of political economy at Toronto. From there he was able to beam his influence into the United States in support of municipal reform.[38]

The traffic was not entirely one way. Glasgow University must have had one of the first American born professors in any British university. Professor Henry D. Rogers of natural philosophy, after holding chairs at the University of Pennsylvania and Dickinson College, came to Glasgow in 1852 until his death in 1866.[39]

The foundation of the American common school system owed far more to Scottish influences than American historians of education have been prepared to admit.[40] In the early nineteenth century, Scotland faced a similar problem with the growth of cities, the physical separation of classes and the accompanying decline of influence for desirable ends. As W.E. Channing observed:

> It is the unhappiness of most large cities that instead of union sympathy, they consist of different interests so widely separated as indeed to form different communities ... The happy community 'is where' human nature is held in honour, where to rescue it from ignorance and crime, to give it an impulse toward knowledge, virtue and happiness is thought the chief end of social union.[41]

The respectable, influential, and property owning groups were naturally concerned at the prospect of growing democracy. The spectre of the French Revolution and more local popular disturbances gave cause for alarm. The decline of church influence and its inability to inculcate virtuous conduct was further cause for alarm. To some that was attributable to the fewer university men entering the underpaid, onerous, profession.[42] The need for a new professional teacher, well instructed and trained in the psychology and techniques of teaching was apparent.[43] To secure intelligent, dedicated career people, the state must establish training institutions, improve the salaries and conditions as well as the public image of teachers.[44] The teacher was to be 'the very life and soul of the system'.[45] In short the teacher was to be a new priesthood, an instructor in morality and knowledge. Such training was put into effect in David Stow's school in Glasgow.[46] The child was made the centre of his scheme of training, being drawn out through the appreciation of objects, by playground activities and by the regulating social moral code of his peers. Similar methods were employed at New Lanark by Robert Owen. With their emphasis upon practical rather than classical education, the schools appealed to American visitors.

The new pedagogy was transmitted to America in several ways. The ideas of Pestalozzi, centred on the child, were published in the *American Annals of Education* by its editor, William Russell, a Glasgow graduate and former student of Professor Jardine.[47] He was the first to publish any translation of Pestalozzi in America. But Pestalozzi had already been carried to America by Scottish writers. Elizabeth Hamilton, the novelist, had written two books on Pestalozzi's methods, *Popular Essays on the Elementary Principles of the Human Mind* and three years later, *Hints Addressed to the Patrons and Directors of Public Schools*. The writings of Robert Owen and the visits of numerous Americans to his school at New Lanark, the growing reputation of Stow's school, and others reinforced that influence.[48] The foundation of school at New Harmony under the influence of William Maclure, the Ayrshire merchant who had made a fortune in America further widely disseminated the new ideas.[49] The school included teachers direct from Pestalozzian influence in Europe.

Maclure represented the radical extreme. With Frances Wright, the Dundee epicurean, he wanted to reorder society through educational innovation. By eliminating all superstition in childhood, the basis for a new society based upon reason, merit and ability would be firmly established.[50] On the other side, the former Glasgow Virginia merchant, J.C. Colquhoun, sought to use education in a counter-revolutionary way. By inculcating correct attitudes he hoped to secure more honest, obedient, and productive servants.[51]

The main stream contribution was to combine moderated evangelical and enlightened zeal into one synthesis. The means seemed to have been George Combe and phrenology. The impact of phrenology upon America was far reaching in the 1830s, the period of Jacksonian democracy. Gall and Spurzheim had brought the idea to Edinburgh in the aftermath of the Napoleonic Wars. Spurzheim had then gone to spread the message in North America but died in Boston in 1832.[52] In cutting through Calvinist tradition, the barriers of class and social standing, phrenology was essentially democratic. Its psychology, by emphasising the need for fresh air, healthy exercise, proper diet and self expression rather than enforced intellectual learning by rote, allowed the child to learn himself. George Combe through the *Phrenological Journal*, established in Edinburgh in 1824 and his best seller, *The Constitution of Man* (Edinburgh, 1828), exercised a decisive influence. He was in correspondence with W.E. Channing and many leading American thinkers.[53] By emphasising environment, the debate in education shifted ground to the provision of a pleasant atmosphere in which learning became a joyful enterprise. To stimulate and to win the assent of the individual to certain truths in science or moral sense was its aim. It fitted the needs of the day.

Robert Cunningham, one of Dr Pillans' students, had left Edinburgh University to establish a new thriving school in the city. Winning the plaudits of local professionals he soon attracted American attention. In 1836 he decided to go to Easton College, Pennsylvania. A close friend of Combe, he had hoped to inaugurate new teacher training colleges attached to the university. His enthusiasm took him to lecture in several neighbouring states. It is possible he may have met Alexander Kinmont, an Aberdeen emigrant, who had settled in Cincinnati to play a brief but influential role in developing western education.[54] Disappointed in his expectations, Cunningham returned to head the first purpose-built teacher training college in Glasgow. He was to continue in that role until the Disruption in 1843. He then founded a successful school at Polmont before gradually withdrawing into retirement in Stranraer.[55]

Combe, however, went to the United States for almost two years.[56] Travelling and lecturing throughout the country he soon won considerable attention. His message of benevolence, amelioration, and self-fulfilment had obvious appeal. He won the attention of Samuel Gridley Howe, Orestes A. Brownson, the Boston intellectuals and reformers and many more. He was pressing home the message which had attracted educational reformers like Alexander Dalrymple Bache to Glasgow High School. There Alexander D'Orsey had espoused Combe's ideas and was giving them immense practical effect in his teaching.[57] In time that interest extended to various health concerns and so encouraged a more efficient society.[58]

In addition to the naturalist Douglass, several Scots prospered from a very early stage in California. Among the most fascinating were Hugo Reid and the Donahoe brothers. Born in 1810, the son of a Cardross shopkeeper, Reid spent two years at Cambridge University before settling in southern California.[59] There he seems to have joined up with an earlier emigrant from Cardross, James McKinley, in a thriving hide and household goods business. After marrying a Catholic Indian lady, Reid built up considerable landholdings, began a school and showed considerable respect for the native Indian population. When California became part of the United States, Reid attended the first constitutional convention, where he championed the foundation of a state school system, the protection of Indians, and the abolition of slavery. His stance on the Indian question was so marked that he later became a model for Helen Holman Jackson's *Ramona*, a novel in which the injustice perpetrated against the Indian was attacked.[60] Unfortunately he was to contract tuberculosis and die in 1852. Reid was one of a handful of Scots who settled in California before 1840.[61] Three doctors, a shipowner, a packer and a blacksmith were but a prelude to the flood of immigrants drawn by the discovery of gold in 1849. Among this flow were the three Donahoe brothers.

The case of the three Donahues (sometimes Donahoes), Peter (1822-85), Michael (1817-84), and James (died 1863) is worth discussing at length. Neglected in recent studies of San Francisco, they deserve attention since they challenge several stereotypes about the nature of the Scottish immigration and its Catholic component.[62] Born in Glasgow of Irish parents, Michael emigrated with an uncle to New York in 1831. Peter worked for two years in a Glasgow mill before he went out in 1833 with his mother. Two years later his father emigrated. All three boys served apprenticeships in Thomas Rogers, locomotive builders, Paterson, New Jersey, in moulding, machining and foundry work. Following the death of the mother, the boys scattered. James, a sickly fellow, went to Alabama, sailed to the West Indies, then lost his newly acquired ship. Michael went from the Union Iron Works to sea and then moved to Cincinnati in 1844. After serving in the First Ohio Volunteers during the Mexican-American War he established a foundry to repair US Navy vessels on the Rio Grande. With the discovery of gold he made a remarkable journey across country to the California rush. There he met up again with Peter, who had helped build a gunboat for the Peruvian navy and sailed round the Horn in the first steam vessel ever to round the Horn. On arrival in San Francisco he had some $6,000. Peter and Michael then opened a foundry after six unsuccessful months prospecting; manufacturing stoves and shovels was lucrative work. James joined them in 1851-2 in the Union Iron Foundry, named after the works in the East. In 1852 Peter secured the franchise for gas in

San Francisco; later it was alleged to pay between 60 and 90 cents on every dollar. Shortly afterwards James retired from the business and Michael went East.

Peter Donahoe now went from strength to strength. He ran a steamship company between San Francisco and Sacramento, built the first steam engine for a US naval vessel on the west coast; the first quartz mill in California; the first printing press there; assembled the first prefabricated ironclad on the west coast; built the first locomotive in California and introduced the first street railway to San Francisco. The president of the Omnibus Railroad Company for 20 years, he became a director of the Hibernia Savings and Loan Society and the First National Gold Bank. Meanwhile he built the San Francisco and San Jose Railway, owned one third of its stock and eventually sold out to the Southern Pacific in 1870 for around $3.5 million. The railroad even had a town named after him in Sonoma county, where he built a carriage works. A generous benefactor, he redecorated St Mary's Church, Glasgow on a trip back to Europe, as well as giving to various charitable institutions in California. At his death his will required all bequests to be paid in gold coin.

Michael Donahoe, a millionaire also, bought a foundry in Davenport, Iowa and quickly made it the largest in the state. Building steam engines and agricultural machinery, he played a major role in the organisation of the Davenport and St Paul Railroad. After serving as mayor for two terms he refused a third and went on a year's tour of Europe. He returned to undertake the construction of a vast modern waterworks for the city, allegedly the best in America. A charitable and respected man, at his death he was described as 'a citizen who did as much if not more to advance her [Davenport] in growth and prosperity than any other resident that ever lived here'. By his death bed his niece, Baroness von Schraeder stood. From the slums of Glasgow to millionaire and aristocratic family was a remarkable step.

The Donahoes never employed Chinese labour, whether for reasons of social justice or racial antipathy is unclear: Peter Donahoe was the only major local employer not to be attacked by the 'Sand Lot' orators in the late nineteenth century.[63] The policy must have helped Robert Forsyth, a Lanarkshire immigrant who after an apprenticeship with Randolph Elder of Glasgow and various periods with steamship companies, rose to be president of the Union Iron Works Company. A foreman from Forfar, William Rutherford, a strong supporter of the temperance movement, emigrated to Oakland and ran the only cotton mill on the Pacific slope.[64] The most colourful character was perhaps

Andrew Smith Hallidie, the London born son of Dumfriesshire parents who developed the cable railways of San Francisco, and with Scottish educational zeal built up the Mechanics Institution and the public library.[65]

The romantic image of the west also had a Scottish contribution. The trips Sir William Drummond Stewart made to the trappers annual rendezvous in the far west were significant in this respect. A former officer in the Napoleonic Wars, Sir William, the younger son of a substantial aristocratic Perthshire family, left the army and later went to America.[66] He travelled extensively in the largely virgin west, met most of the leading figures of legend like Jim Bridger, associated with the St Louis entrepreneurs and thoroughly enjoyed himself. After returning to Scotland to take up his inheritance, he made one last trip west in 1843. It was a splendid affair. His party included some 93 people, more than half paid for by himself. Among them was Alexander Gordon, the Scottish naturalist, two American newspapermen and two American army officers; James J. Audubon, unfortunately, was unable to join the expedition. Those who did go were royally treated. Stewart had secured a special licence to take 'as much spiritous liquors as he may deem necessary for himself and his party'. By all accounts an abundant supply of the finest wines, cognac, gin and cigars were taken; some ten wagons were needed for transport. In addition, Stewart took two india rubber boats. These relatively new inventions, though claimed by some as American inventions, were probably Glasgow products.

Stewart frequently visited Glasgow on business where Charles Macintosh of raincoat fame had perfected inflatable rubber boats in 1839. At the Green River gathering there was the usual feasting, drinking, gambling and racing. His supplies of champagne and playing cards proved useful. Various Indian tribes performed ceremonial dances and processions in his honour. After two weeks fishing, Stewart and his party returned to St Louis at a leisurely pace. It was the last he was to see of his idyllic wilderness.

Scottish emigrants were to be found scattered throughout the United States. Illinois attracted many settlers. Some of the early emigrants to Birkbeck's model development at Albion, Illinois included some 20 kith and kin from Perthshire.[67] A few years later another visitor, William Oliver, dedicated his *Eight Months in Illinois* 'to the labouring men of Roxburghshire with sincere wishes for their welfare' amid the fertile lands, happy diverse religious groups and politically enfranchised people.[68] Later Scottish emigrants like the temperance advocate Robert Reid would settle in the state after the Civil War with their friends and relatives.[69] In addition considerable numbers of Scottish miners would find employment either for a brief period or permanently before returning home in Braidwood and similar communities.[70] There were many settlements of Scots in Minnesota, Wisconsin and the Dakotas in the late nineteenth century but the biggest concentration was in the Pacific north-west around Seattle.[71]

Alexander McDonald, the Scottish miners' leader reported that California was 'bound to become the garden of the universe to some extent', unequalled for health and productive capacity.[72] Its beauty brought Scottish naturalists. James Wilson of Paisley had already built up a considerable reputation in Pennsylvania when James Douglas, one of Professor Hooker's Glasgow students came out to gather specimens for the British scientists. A second visit soon followed over several years until he died in an accident in Hawaii.[73] The most influential, however, was perhaps John Muir, the legendary Scot who played a major role in the establishment of the US National Parks and the preservation of the wilderness. In particular he was to safeguard the Californian mountains through his presidency of the Sierra Club from 1892 to his death in 1914.

Some others went to America as part of colonisation companies. In the late eighteenth century John Witherspoon had been anxious to promote immigration to his lands in North America. As one critic suggested 'the doctor seems to be taking care of this world as well as that which is to come'.[74] Many who had been radical addicts in the west of Scotland went to America and simply made money.[75] Others 'not being able at home to make England like America, they come here and then first work to make America like England'.[76] Other companies were formed in the period after 1815, as Scottish textiles found themselves in difficulties in the American market and as handloom weavers were displaced.

Ohio reportedly had great prospects. According to one Scottish writer,

> no country in the world was more favoured in respect to natural advantages than the state of Ohio in North America; the soil is of inexhaustible fertility: the climate temperate: the rivers navigable for many hundreds of miles: the forests with the finest timber and even the bowels of the earth pay, in various kinds mineral, abundant contribution to the general wealth.[77]

With such attributes, not surprisingly, a company was formed to exploit its resources in 1786. In the first decade of the nineteenth century, many Scottish families emigrated to Ohio to found townships at Inverness, Washington and Wayne.[78] An Ohio landowner, Nahum Ward went to Scotland to publicise his landholdings in 1822. Emigrants were attracted to his lands in Marietta but again the scheme did not flourish as anticipated.

If Witherspoon was accused of trying to harbour treasure in this world and the hereafter, the Mormons might be considered a more effective and successful co-operative venture in that regard. Some of the earliest Mormon missionaries were Scottish-born converts. Alexander Wright of Banffshire had emigrated to Canada in 1838, became a Mormon and returned to proselytise among his fellow Scots.[79] Travelling through Scotland from Aberdeen to Edinburgh he recruited some 17 relatives among his converts and arranged for their passage to America from Liverpool in 1842. Another missionary, Samuel Mulliner of Haddingon, East Lothian began his campaign in Bishopton and soon encountered challenges from clergymen in the district. Such opposition and even mobbing were not infrequent. Success continued and the first emigrants left in September, 1840. In 1843 James Macaulay, one of the earliest Glasgow converts left from Liverpool with over 200 others. Others, including several fascinating characters, followed in the 1850s. Peter McIntyre of Succouth, Ayrshire, who had fought in the Napoleonic Wars and in the War of 1812, became president of the Greenock branch of the church and eventually reached Utah in 1853. John McNeill, a graduate of Edinburgh University, became president of the Lochgelly branch and eventually reached Utah in 1850 where he fathered 29 children.[80] David Budge, a former editor of an Owenite newspaper in Lanark, converted to Mormonism and became a missionary before settling in Utah.[81] A Lanarkshire miner, William Richardson (1829-94) converted in the 1850s, saved to emigrate, then worked in Pennsylvania before settling in Utah working in the silver mines. Some Scottish Methodists were among those who went over to Mormonism like Robert Scott. Dundee and Aberdeen also provided some members. There were 5 converts through a Gaelic speaking missionary, William Mackay in 1847. Tracts in Gaelic were published though they met with little success. In 1841 baptism had taken place in the Clyde estuary at Irvine. Missionaries seemed to have paid their way in the early days by casual work at their calling in the localities they visited; in pits, woodworks, or gardening. In Hunterfield near Edinburgh 70 of the 90 population were enrolled in the Mormon ranks in 1848. Mob violence, general curiosity and astonished relatives were all part of the response in Scotland. The *United Presbyterian Magazine* was deeply concerned at the apparent success of the Mormons.[82] Between 1840 and 1900 some 9,200 had joined the Mormon Church in Scotland and about one-third had emigrated to Utah. Successful businesses followed.

The Mormons were the most outstanding effort at community migration. There were others. The experiments of Robert Owen at New Harmony is perhaps the best known.[83] Others like the Mauchline Chartist, John Alexander, unsuccessfully tried to establish a colony in Texas. He had to return to Britain. The Scottish miners' leader, Alexander McDonald, considered a co-operative mining scheme in Eastern Kentucky in 1874. Though co-operation was fashionable at the time, it came to nothing. Yearly, Revd Robert Kerr, the congregationalist minister in Forres, tried, with the aid of the state government and the railway, to establish a temperance colony in Minnesota. Unfortunately he was able to attract only a handful of supporters. Severe winters and intense hot summers destroyed the idea that Minnesota was the sanitorium of the West.[84] The community of proper values would have to be built in some other way.

The Scottish textile industry spearheaded the industrial revolution at home as the new factory machinery spawned new technology, in iron, chemicals, engineering, and entrepreneurial skills. If factories proliferated in the squalid industrial cities of England, in Scotland there were many instances of model villages where factories were established under the benevolent despotism of their owners. Robert Owen's New Lanark, Smith's at Deanston and several others were markedly different from their English counterparts. Ideally they were provided with model housing, schools, churches, libraries and other institutions of self-improvement in either a drink free or carefully controlled licensed environment. Well-kept houses, strict discipline and sobriety were their essential characteristics. In short Scottish textile industry was a model to the world.

The structure, technology and skilled manpower of this industry were attractive to Americans. Anxious to develop their own textile industry free from the frequent fluctuations and interruptions caused by the various European wars from 1789 to 1815, the Americans were eager to acquire Scottish expertise. Unfortunately British law forbade the export of machinery and the emigration of skilled artisans. American entrepreneurs sought to evade these restrictions by bringing over experienced Scottish craftsmen, employing industrial spies or by going on tours of British factories themselves. Even before the stimulus provided by Eli Whitney's cotton gin in 1793, and the arrival of Samuel

Slater in America with some of the British textile industry's technical secrets in 1790, Americans were attempting to recruit Scottish technicians. The Pennsylvania Society for the Encouragement of Manufactures, established in 1787 unsuccessfully tried to secure cotton manufacturing information from a Scot, John Barber. Significantly almost 20 per cent of textile workers who had emigrated to America in 1773-6 were located in the Philadelphia area. A few years later, in 1792, John Douglas, a Scots machinist, was offering plans of a gig mill and a slubbing billy to a group of merchants, but was persuaded to return to Britain by the British consul before he could establish himself in Pennsylvania. In 1816 misgivings about the large investment which might be required prevented a Scot, Gilmore, from introducing a model loom into American factory production. The following year, however, Scottish looms were introduced into Rhode Island and began to spread throughout most of New England. They gradually superseded the Waltham loom which had been introduced earlier, in the model American textile town of that name. The town had been intended to be an ideal moral centre of industry. That and still more the model town of Lowell seem to have been influenced by model Scottish textile towns more than American historians have been prepared to credit. Nathan Appleton, the textile entrepreneur, had spent much time in Britain and in 1810-11 went on a tour of model Scottish mill towns including New Lanark, probably Deanston and others around Edinburgh and Paisley.[85] Suitably impressed, they returned to begin the construction of the textile town of Lowell. Scots and other British weavers were already established in early American mills: many Scottish mechanics became industrial manufacturers. According to Caroline F. Ware, 'nearly every company reveals the important role of the skilled foreigners'.[86] New Ipswich, New Hampshire, was a Scottish weaving settlement, though by 1877 Scottish weavers were an exception in that locality. Other areas utilised Scottish workers to teach their skills to their workers. By 1860 Scots seemed to be dominant in the managerial and clerical sections of many factories.[87] The lack of a skilled experienced workforce, high rates of pay and the availability of other well-paid jobs contributed to a high turnover rate in the American mill workforce.[88] Aware of their value, ready to strike to enforce demands for even higher wages and better conditions, Scots gradually became less attractive to employers. In an effort to stabilise their workforce employers had actively recruited in Scotland. In 1853, an agent for the Hadley Falls mills secured some 82 women weavers while in 1853-7 an agent for the Lyman mills was recruiting in Glasgow.[89] Another agent for the Holyoke mills secured 67 women for his sponsors. Their success in paying off their transatlantic fare, buying new clothes and shoes within a few months confirmed the roseate views in emigrant letters home to other workers.[90] The later emigrants sometimes proved less reliable in the fulfilment of obligations. Some women deserted in New York *en route* to the New England mills. Employers responded with heavier deductions from wages. That and the deportations of some women as public charges may have contributed to later difficulties in recruitment. In 1865 Holyoke mills could only secure 200 women from Scotland although they needed 1,000.[91] Though further efforts at recruitment were to continue, employers began to look to Belgium and to new machinery to replace their skilled Scottish workers. By 1881 Scotland was no longer supplying mill workers.[92]

New technology, the increasing availability of cheap unskilled immigrant workers, and the maturing of the American industry meant less dependence upon Scottish labour. By the late nineteenth century Scottish workers came in with their employers as Scottish manufacturers became apprehensive about American tariffs and became internationalised. As early as 1850, Coats of Paisley had established plants in Pawtucket while the Glasgow Linen Company had an almost entirely Scottish workforce at Grafton, Massachusetts. Following the 1890 tariff, Kerrs of Paisley moved their mill to Fall River with their workforce. With workers receiving about double the Scottish wage they were satisfied. At the same time the Cumnock brothers rose to prominence as major figures in the textile field: two of the three had been born and bred in Glasgow.[93] Their role was perhaps indicative of the upward social mobility of the Scots not merely within the textile industry but in the larger American world. Some expressed considerable reservations about the prospects in America. The departure of industrious, sober artisans from Scotland left a gap at home into which unintelligent, disorderly, ill disciplined, uncivilised Irish poured. As early as 1829, an Edinburgh authority was suggesting that the golden opportunities had passed: 'To earn simple plenty by a life of labour is all that America now offers.'[94] Though openings remained for clergymen, the professions were overcrowded.

The bulk of the emigrant population, then must long consist of wealthy peasants dressed in home spun clothes, cultivating their own ground with their own hands and living in simple plenty. For the higher ranks this continent affords no refuge; and scarcely for any in the middling classes who do not stand at the bottom of the scale.

> The exclusion from social intercourse, the distance from church, the want of any opportunity of attaining the higher branches of education, must operate strongly with those accustomed to the accumulations and elegances of European life.[95]

To some extent that must explain the success of the Scots in America. The migration of the less fortunate if highly motivated people was in marked contrast to the pretentious English who bewailed their lot and the shortcomings of their hosts with boring frequency. The fortunes of Scottish immigrants have a bearing on the current discussion of American social mobility and 'success'.[96] Carnegie obviously fulfils the wildest dreams of avarice in his surge from rags to riches but for most emigrant Scots the improvement was less spectacular but in many instances considerable.

Urbanisation, increased purchasing power among the populace and new forms of enterprise, consolidating producer, distributor, wholesaler and retailer into one company became the norm. Scots with their penchant for dry goods were well placed. Scotland and America contributed to the somewhat neglected retailing revolution. By the later nineteenth century, popular shopkeeping began to develop. Thomas Lipton, the Glasgow provision merchant, soon built up a chain of 245 shops providing cheap food and one tenth of the tea trade.[97] He would become famous in the transatlantic world for his yachts and competitions. But he was symptomatic of deeper social and organisational changes which were taking place. For some time ideas of the modern department store had been taking shape in Britain, as in Andersons of Glasgow and elsewhere, but Bon Marche of Paris was to revolutionise the retail trade. By gathering all merchandise under one roof in various departments, that store inspired many others like Wanamaker of Philadelphia and Macy's of New York.[98] Enterprising individuals who were astute enough to realise the new democratic nature of merchandising, the subtle status shifts and potential of free access to a wide range of departments without sales pressure flourished. Needless to say several Glasgow-trained dry goods merchants were to the fore in America.

The department store seems to have been a favourite route to wealth. St Louis provided the opportunity for two Scottish entrepreneurs to rise to considerable wealth. David Nicholson, 1814-80, was born in poverty in Fowlis Wester, Perthshire. After working in Glasgow and Oban merchant houses, he emigrated to Canada, where working as a carpenter he moved on to Pennsylvania, Chicago and then to St Louis in 1835. Eight years later he began his own business, importing high quality goods, new commodities and 'more than any other man in St Louis trade' educated his customers to superior quality.[99] By 1870 he had a five storey store which employed 50 assistants. At the same time he ventured into real estate with considerable success, erecting the Temple Buildings at 5th and Walnut Street and also Nicholson Place. A staunch Presbyterian, he frequently returned to Scotland. Dugald Crawford established his store in 1866, which developed into one of the largest dry goods stores in America. From a start with $2,000 capital he had by 1880 a capital of $10,000,000 and a turnover of $35,000,000. Crawford was born in Argyllshire, 1830, served an apprenticeship in a Glasgow dry goods shop, went to Dublin and then returned to the Glasgow firm of Arthur and Company, the largest wholesale and retail dry goods firm in Britain. In 1856 he went to Canada before moving to St Louis in 1864. Crawford was also president of the Congregational Missionary Society, of the Caledonian Society of St Louis, trustee of Drury College and a leading figure in various mercantile organisations.[100]

In Buffalo, Robert B. Adam Borthwick established a similar thriving concern. Born in Peebles (1833-1904), Borthwick was apprenticed to an Edinburgh fabric exporter and emigrated to America in 1857. After ten years he established his firm in Buffalo, which soon became the largest store with interests in New York, Pennsylvania and Ohio. He was also very active in community life as the head of the YMCA, trustee of the Buffalo Hospital and of Cornell University as well as chairman of the New York State Grading Crossing Commission. In 1881 his brother J.N. Adam came over from Scotland and began a store immediately opposite that of his brother. His business also grew and he served as mayor of Buffalo from 1906-9. Robert Adam pioneered the modern buying office by combining the purchasing power of a large number of department stores across the country. The first organisation was the Scotch Syndicate with buying offices in Europe and Britain. His son continued the business and established a glove factory in France and built a reputation as a Samuel Johnson specialist, which gained him an honorary degree from Yale. He died in 1940. The firm still continues.

In Syracuse the Deys, also Scots, built a thriving business. Robert Dey, 1849-1943, was born in Abernethy, educated at Kirkmichael and served an apprenticeship to an Aberdeen dry goods merchant, Pratt and Keith, before emigrating to America in 1871. He began work in the largest dry goods store in Rochester, Sibley, Lindsey and Kerr. After five years, by which time his brothers Donald, Charles and James had all followed him across the Atlantic into the same firm, Robert established his own firm in Elmira, New York, in 1877. Another brother, John, also came to join the company. He was to invent the time register. Robert and Donald remained with the firm and moved it to Syracuse, where they soon built a six storey building for their business. A member of the board of St Paul's Episcopal church, director of the Syracuse Trust Company and associated with the local hospital, he was also a member of several social and business associations. His brother Donald, 1853-1946, was a philanthropic character who vigorously promoted the American flag: a Republican and the president of the chamber of commerce, he was credited with introducing golf into the city. Other Scottish department store innovators included John Forbes, Kansas City; Samuel Williamson, Salt Lake City; J. C. Livesey, Omaha.

More substantial Scottish interest in the west came later with the development of the cattle industry. The completion of the transcontinental railroads, the invention of refrigeration, and large scale companies catering to mass European markets encouraged considerable Scottish investment in American cattle companies. These funds and their headquarters were centred mainly in Dundee and Edinburgh, although Glasgow and Aberdeen had a very small interest. Between 1879 and 1888 at least 33 British registered companies were investing in cattle ranching. By 1896 the Scottish investment in the American west was of the order of $60 million.

Scottish interest in American lands was well established. In 1864 the Earl of Airlie had travelled extensively in the west and returned to play a leading role in some investment companies. Various land companies were established to promote development and Scottish emigration to various parts of America but the majority seem to have quickly faded. Railway investment was considerable, though that too could be a costly affair.[101] Whatever the results, Scottish interest helped to oil the general movement forward.

Engineering was another transatlantic industry. The 'hot blast' technique had been imported from Scotland at an early stage and introduced into iron production. The Glasgow and Port Washington Iron and Coal Company established two blast furnaces in the Hanging Rock district of Ohio after the Civil War: all the officers of the firm were brought over from Scotland.[102] Scots seem to have been the foremen and managers in many plants according to visitors. Andrew Carnegie, of course, was the exceptional success in this industry, but many other Scots enjoyed major, if modest, success.

The coal mining industry attracted many Scots across the sea. Some migrated for a term or merely for a season, others permanently. The main areas of settlement were Pennsylvania, Ohio, and Illinois. In Illinois, at Braidwood, there was a major settlement of Scottish miners mainly from Lanarkshire, as Alexander McDonald found. He himself had acted as a recruiting agent for an American coal mining company in 1864. Parties of miners had gone out in the following year and continued to do so until 1870. By then new mines and better wages at home dissuaded many from going. Others clearly continued to emigrate, as Keir Hardie indicated in his reports in 1912, though increasingly masses of other European ethnic groups were entering the mines.

Around the close of the nineteenth century, the new American automobile industry was beginning to seek a mass market. Among the early pioneers was Alexander Winton, a Clyde-trained marine engineer. In 1884 he had established himself in Cleveland, Ohio, as a cycle manufacturer. Soon he was building motor cars, promoting them with publicity stunts like record breaking drives to New York or the first trans-America car run. Though somewhat less successful in European competition and with Ford, he continued in business until the firm was absorbed by General Motors in 1930. Winton's industry was to destroy irrevocably the old order. By democratising mobility, generating new industries of leisure and life style, it finally ended the old Scottish idea of a cohesive community. It changed habits in religion, social customs and interest. People defined themselves by what they did in their leisure time rather than by what they worked at. The shift was momentous and decisive.

Business, trade, enterprise and thrift could only flourish in a peaceful society. Not surprisingly Scots were active in promoting Anglo-American peace movements thoughout the nineteenth century. In 1815 William Ladd had helped to inaugurate the New England peace movement with his essay. Thomas Chalmers had echoed his hope in his sermon on peace, while W. E. Channing had committed himself to that enterprise.[103] With Arthur O'Neill, the Baptist minister of Birmingham and former Glasgow student, Burritt constantly tried to win public opinion to his side.[104] Henry C. Wright, the abolitionist, spent some time in Scotland promoting peace sentiment, while in the Shaker colony of Mount Lebabon, Daniel Fraser, a former Paisley weaver and confidant of Michael Thomas Sadler, MP, the factory reformer, firmly endorsed peace addresses. The activities of Glasgow and the west of Scotland peace groups in supporting peaceful solutions to potentially dangerous diplomatic wrangles with America contributed to the formation of much greater Anglo-American understanding.

The demands for popular moral control in an immoral world found further expression in the movement for municipal reform. American cities were rapidly expanding in an almost uncontrolled way. Their sheer size, together with the flood of new urban dwellers from southern and eastern Europe as well as from rural America produced immense social problems. Almost nine out of ten were newcomers to the cities. The demand for various public services gave rise to innumerable opportunities for graft and corruption. To shocked observers the 'robber barons' of monopoly capital and the corrupt ethnic politicians were undermining the quality of American democracy and the promise of American life.[105] Men of good will and moral stature, William Allen White's middling people, would have to get involved to save the city for themselves, their kind and their culture.

Most British cities, above all Glasgow, seemed to have developed an excellent system of local government regulation and control. In Glasgow gas, electricity, markets, even telephones, and above all the tramways were run by professional public servants under local democratic control to produce handsome profits. Councillors drawn from the 'best people' served with disinterested pride. Cleanliness, efficiency and cheapness impressed American observers. Even more impressive was the pride of the citizens in *their* city, their identification with its history, fortunes and future. To Americans suffering from corrupt local government, apparently excessive tax burdens, indifferent or non-existent public services and extortionate private services, Glasgow seemed a working model of the reform ideal.

Academics, journalists, and politicians dutifully poured in to study the Glasgow success story. They came, admired, and returned home to spread the wonderful gospel of municipal ownership. Many were of Scottish ancestry and so might be seen as bolstering their sagging ethnic pride and status in America by bolstering the Glasgow image. The reforming mayor of Toledo, Brand Whitlock, the historian J.R. Commons and the economist R.T. Ely among others could claim Scottish ancestry. Albert Shaw, significantly a Johns Hopkins graduate who had attended James Bryce's seminars on government there, was foremost in publicising the Glasgow achievement in lectures, journals and books. His lead was followed by many others, notably, F.C. Howe, in his *The British City and the Beginnings of Democracy*, London, 1907, which was largely a eulogy of Glasgow and the famed prohibitionist, Lord Provost, Sir Samuel Chisholm: 'the glory of Glasgow's government is not an American myth. It is a concrete reality.'

Such propaganda encouraged practising politicians like mayors

Phelan of San Francisco, Sam Jones of Toledo, aspiring mayors like Edward F. Dunne of Chicago, and former mayors like Tom Johnson to visit the city. The unsuccessful Democratic presidential nominee William Jennings Bryan basked in wonders of municipal achievement compared to his own land.

A full-scale debate commenced in America on the issue. Edward Dunne won election as mayor of Chicago on a promise to make the city 'a second Glasgow'. An invitation to James Dalrymple, the Glasgow tramway manager, to visit and advise on municipalisation badly misfired on Chicago and Cleveland. Unfortunately, statements, misrepresentation, and inept behaviour on both sides undermined reformist hopes. The visit and inconclusive report of a commission from the National Civic Federation to Glasgow in 1907 further eroded confidence. When the Glasgow tramway workers went on strike with considerable violence in 1911, the vested interests widely circulated these 'truths' about municipal ownership and social harmony. Thereafter municipal ownership fell back on the defensive in the face of renewed business self-confidence, increased private affluence and suburbanisation and the emergence of a self-indulgent approach to life.

The shift in emphasis reflected the failure of the older ethnic groups in American society to capture permanently the commanding height of its culture. The disenchantment and affluence in the wake of the First World War made the 1920s a battle between the old puritanism and the new gods of leisure and pleasure. The new technologies, industries and life styles increasingly weakened the old moral certainties of the work ethic, so strongly maintained, particularly by the declining numbers of Scots in America. The demise of the two seemed to go together. In a sense even the Scottish ethic was divided in public now. The moral utopia envisioned by temperance advocates seemed to be a materialistic employers' utopia in which the unions were in decline. At home in Scotland the more militant left was in the public eye, emphasising the class conflict as the key to social salvation. To most influential Americans that had very little appeal.

The labour movement had been building up its forces during the previous decades. Hitherto America had been seen as a haven, a place to realise the democratic dream and to secure jobs in difficult times. Trade unions had even aided their members to go out to America. Coal miners' leaders like Alexander McDonald and Robert Brown of Mid and East Lothian miners had spent some time in America. The idyllic dream of Robert Owen and New Harmony was giving way to a much more class-conscious view under the influence of American consolidation and monopoly. The series of bloody confrontations on the railways, Homestead and Pullman as well as the Haymarket trials confirmed that impression from the 1870s through to the 1890s. The emergence of American labour movements, both political and trade union, with close associations with Scotland reinforced the negative view. The visits of Lawrence Gronlund, secretary of the American Socialist Labour Party, Charlotte Perkins Gilman, the American Fabian, Gaylord Wilshire, the millionaire socialist and 'Big Bill' Haywood, the International Workers of the World leader, gave added confirmation. The sense of international solidarity was carried further by the several visits of Keir Hardie to America between 1896 and 1912. On the latter occasion he travelled some 7,000 miles, attending 42 meetings. Wherever he went he found old friends from Larkhall and Cadzow in Colorado; from Ayrshire in Terre Haute, Indiana; from Lanarkshire in Gillespie, Illinois. The President of the Pennsylvania Central miners, Patrick Gilday, hailed from Luger. At the American Labour Congress in 1912, Bob Smillie, president of the British Miners Federation attacked the claim that American workers were sharing in the wealth. That socialist alliance strengthened during the First World War and afterwards as Bill Haywood sent full reports on the suppression of the IWW in America. Crystal Eastman, the socialist writer, came to Scotland in 1919. Her reports to American socialist papers emphasised the strength and forcefulness of the various Clydeside leaders she met; John McLean; John Kirkwood; William Gallagher and the rest.[106]

The common interests were well developed. Though a socialist solution might appeal to Scots, the American public were less than enthusiastic in the wake of the Russian Bolshevik Revolution and the recent bomb outrages at home in America. The general common outlook was fragmenting into disparate elements. By 1900 the old Scottish importance was being eroded. The decline of Scottish immigration to the United States, the levelling off of the birth rate and the attractions of other lands like Canada and Australia, the introduction of new technology which allowed the use of the new mass unskilled immigration in industry, guided by new management techniques meant the Scot became somewhat 'invisible'.[107]

It is significant that Glasgow became a model for municipal reformers in America at the very point the broadly 'Scottish' ethos was under attack. Many reformers themselves of Scottish or Scots-Irish background were seeking to save their moral traditions by capturing the city for themselves and their kind through temperance, referenda and other reforms. At the same time in those campaigns, by appealing to the

anti-party sentiment, the men of good will and disinterested professionalism were reiterating old notions which had been used earlier by
their ancestors. Equally Scotland as a nation was in industrial decline,
had developed a 'red image', and was less attractive to a business civilisation. In a more leisured society of the 1920s, the old Scottish
inspired work ethic, temperance and sabbatarianism would seem too
restrictive. By the crash of 1929 the sturdy self-improvement, self-help
philosophy was in eclipse. The Second World War contributed to the
consolidation of big government and big business. In the aftermath the
old individualistic Scottish entrepreneurial skills would be lost within
larger concerns. With the greater job, educational, and leisure opportunities after 1945, a far more pluralist society took shape. The old
monolithic 'official' culture rapidly disintegrated, as previously submerged ethnic groups emerged. To this more affluent generation of
Americans, Scotland would appear more as a tourist centre for gold and
scenic recreations. To American government it would appear as a useful
base for the submarine nuclear defence of Europe. It would not be so
prominent as a place of ethnic resort. At best it might become a branch
factory for large American concerns or a recruiting ground for talented
graduates in the new sciences. The whole relationship had been transformed. Whether for better or worse was irrelevant. It was different.

Notes

1. W. Brownlee, *The Whigs of Scotland: or the Last of the Stewarts* (2 vols.,
New York, 1833), vol. 1, p. ii.
2. Letter describing J. Jamieson of Ayr to R. Mackay, editor of the *Social
Reformer*, published in the July, 1880 issue.
3. Remarks to the New York Council Presbyterian meeting Pan Presbyterian
Congress reported in *Temperance Leader*, 7 August 1909.
4. D. Macrae, *American Presidents and Men I have Met* (Glasgow, 1908).
5. Ibid., p. 123.
6. See Bernard Aspinwall, 'The Scottish Religious Identity in the Atlantic
World, 1880-1914' in S. Mews (ed.), *Religion and National Identity: Studies in
Church History* (Oxford, 1982), vol. 18, pp. 505-18.
7. See Richard D. Brown, *Modernisation: The Transformation of American
Life, 1600-1865* (New York, 1976).
8. J.D. Rockefeller quoted in Edward C. Kirkland, *Dream and Thought in the
Business Community, 1860-1900* (Ithaca, 1956), pp. 20-1.
9. Quoted in R.G. McCloskey, *American Conservatism in the Age of Enterprise, 1865-1910* (Cambridge, Mass., 1951), p. 144.
10. James D. Young, 'Changing Images of American Democracy and the
Labour Movement', *International Review of Social Studies*, vol. 13 (1973),
pp. 69-89.
11. See J. Cunnison and J. Gilfillan, *Third Statistical Account: Glasgow*

(Collins, Glasgow, 1958), p. 619.

12. Redelia Brisbane, *Albert Brisbane* (New York, 1969 edn), p. 159.

13. See Bernard Aspinwall, 'The Scottish Religious Identity', pp. 505-18.

14. Louis B. Wright, *Culture on the Moving Frontier* (Bloomington, 1955), p. 40.

15. Quoted Richard Eburne, *A Plain Pathway to Plantations* (Louis B. Wright, Ithaca, 1962), p. xxv.

16. E. Keble Chatterton, *English Seamen and the Colonisation of America* (London, 1930), p. 288.

17. Tom Devine, *The Tobacco Lords* (John Donald, Edinburgh, 1975).

18. William Thom, *A Candid Enquiry into the Causes of the Late and the Intended Migrations from Scotland in a Letter of J.R. Esq of Lanarkshire* (Glasgow, 1771), pp. 28-9, 40-1, 50-3.

19. Ibid., p. 39.

20. Ibid., p. 37.

21. W. Thom, *The Defects of a University Education and Its Unsuitableness to a Commercial People With the Expedience and Necessity of Erecting at Glasgow an Academy for the Instruction of Youth* (London, 1762).

22. John M. Duncan, *Travels*, vol. II, p. 338.

23. Edwin Hodder, *Sir George Burns Bart., His Times and Friends* (London, 1890), pp. 189-203; F.E. Hyde, *Cunard and the North Atlantic, 1840-1873* (London, 1975), pp. 2-19.

24. See P. Bonsor, *North Atlantic Seaway* (Prescot, 1955), pp. 54, 72, 83, 136, 341.

25. P. Neilson, *Six Years in America* (Glasgow, 1830). Letter of Neal Dow on Maine in *Scottish Reformer*, July, 1880.

26. See Fergus Ferguson, *From Glasgow to Missouri* (Glasgow, 1878) which is a catalogue of such meetings.

27. See Bernard Wall, *Andrew Carnegie* (New York, 1970), and Sigmund A. Lavine, *Allan Pinkerton* (London, 1965), pp. 1-7.

28. Thomas Hamilton, *Men and Manners in America* (Edinburgh, 1833).

29. See Allen, *The Practical Tourist*, vol. II, pp. 349-50.

30. See for example Douglas Sloan, *The Scottish Enlightenment and the American College Ideal* (New York, 1971); W.C. Lehmann, *Adam Ferguson and the Beginnings of Modern Sociology* (New York, 1930); and his *Henry Home, Lord Kames and the Scottish Enlightenment* (The Hague, 1971).

31. See Sloan, *The Scottish Enlightenment*, pp. 26, 41, 76.

32. Nelson R. Barr, *Education in New Jersey, 1630-1871* (Princeton, 1942), pp. 135-7.

33. See John Maclean, *History of the College of New Jersey from its Origins in 1746 to the Commencement of 1854*, 2 vols. (Philadelphia, 1877); and J. David Hoeveler, *James McCosh and the Scottish Intellectual Tradition: From Glasgow to Princeton* (Princeton, 1981).

34. Benjamin Silliman, *A Journal of Travels in England, Holland and Scotland and of Two Passages of the Atlantic in the Years 1805 and 1806*, 2 vols. (New York, 1810), vol. 2, pp. 360-1; also G.P. Fisher, *Life of Benjamin Silliman*, 2 vols. (New York, 1860), vol. 1, pp. 109-10.

35. See the details given in Thomas Kelly, *George Birkbeck: Pioneer of Adult Education* (Liverpool, 1957), pp. 282-3.

36. A. Flexner, *Medical Education in Europe* (New York, 1912).

37. See his correspondence with President J.C. Gilman, Gilman Papers, Johns Hopkins University, Baltimore, and Hugh Hawkins, *Pioneer: A History of Johns Hopkins University* (Ithaca, 1956).

38. R.M. Wenley, *The University Extension Movement in Scotland* (Glasgow,

1895); Wenley Papers, University of Michigan, Ann Arbor, Michigan has much relevant material.

39. *Roll of Glasgow University Graduates to 1897* (Glasgow, 1897), appendix.

40. For example see virtually any treatment from Edwin Grant Dexter, *A History of Education in the United States* (New York, 1904), to Carl F. Kaestle, *The Evolution of an Urban School System: New York City, 1750-1850* (Cambridge, Mass., 1973). Paul H. Mattingly, *The Classless Profession: American Schoolmen in the Nineteenth Century* (New York, 1975) has begun to redress the balance by recognising the importance of William Russell.

41. W.E. Channing, *The Obligation of the City to Watch Over the Moral Health of Its Members* (Glasgow, 1841), quoted in Thomas Bender, *Toward an Urban Vision: Ideas and Institutions in Nineteenth Century America* (Lexington, 1975), pp. 80-1.

42. See the American educator J.G. Cogswell in *Blackwoods*, vol. 4, 1818-19, pp. 546-53 and pp. 641-9.

43. See John Pillans, *Principles of Elementary Education* (Edinburgh, 1828), pp. 7, 66, 70; and his collected essays, *Contributions to the Cause of Education* (London, 1856), pp. 37, 184-5.

44. Such as John Gordon, *Report on the Deficiencies of Elementary Education in Scotland* (Edinburgh, 1845), pp. 372-3.

45. John Wood, *Account of the Edinburgh Sessional School* (Edinburgh, 1828), p. 81.

46. William Fraser, *Memoir of the Life of David Stow* (London, 1868), p. 81 *et seq.*

47. *American Annals of Education*, 1826-30; George Jardine, *Outlines of Philosophical Education* (Glasgow, 1825); George Davie, *The Democratic Intellect: Scotland and Her Universities in the Nineteenth Century* (Edinburgh, 1961), pp. 3-25.

48. E.G. John Griscom, *A Year in Europe*, 2 vols. (New York, 1823), vol. 2, pp. 373-93; and Alexander Dalrymple Bache, Diary, 1837, Bache Papers, Library of Congress.

49. William Maclure, *Opinions on Various Subjects dedicated to the Industrious Producers*, 2 vols. (New Harmony, 1831); J. Percy Moore, 'William Maclure: Scientist and Humanitarian', *Proceedings of the American Philosophical Society*, vol. 91, 1947, pp. 234-49.

50. Frances Wright, *Views of Society and Manners in America* (Cambridge, Mass., 1963), p. 217.

51. See *A Treatise in Indigence* (London, 1806).

52. John D. Davis, *Phrenology, Fad and Science: A Nineteenth Century American Crusade* (New York, 1971).

53. See the Combe Papers, National Library of Scotland, Edinburgh for an indication of the immense breadth of his contacts.

54. See Alexander Kinmont, *The Natural History of Man and the Rise and Progress of Philosophy* (Philadelphia, 1891).

55. Obituary, *Free Church Monthly*, 1 Dec. 1883.

56. G. Combe, *Notes on the United States of America*, 3 vols. (Edinburgh, 1841).

57. Bache Papers, Diary, 1837 and *Phrenological Journal*, 1839, p. 105; 1840, pp. 186-7; 1841, pp. 51-2.

58. Madeleine B. Stern, *Heads and Headliners: The Phrenological Fowlers* (Norman, 1971).

59. See Susan Bryant Dakin, *A Scotch Paisano in Old Los Angeles: Hugo Reid's Life in California, 1832-1852, derived from his Correspondence* (Berkeley, 1978).

60. Ibid., p. vii and H.H. Jackson, *Ramona* (Boston, 1907).

61. Dakin, *A Scotch Paisano*, p. 203 lists eleven Scots who are known to have resided in California between 1824 and 1831.

62. Roger W. Lotchin, *San Francisco, 1846-1856: From Hamlet to City* (New York, 1974) and R.A. Burchell, *The San Francisco Irish, 1848-80* (Manchester, 1979), pp. 9-10, 22, 27.

63. The background will be found in Robert Seager, 'Some Denominational Reactions to Chinese Immigration to California, 1856-1892', *Pacific Historical Review*, vol. 28, 1959, pp. 49-66.

64. A.R. Kimball, *The Blue Ribbon* (New York, 1894), pp. 22-222; John Leng, *America in 1876* (Dundee, 1877), p. 85.

65. Edgar Myron Kahn, 'Andrew Smith Hallidie', *California Historical Quarterly*, vol. 19, 1940, pp. 144-56; and Fulmer Mood, 'Andrew S. Hallidie and Librarianship in San Francisco, 1868-79', *California Historical Quarterly*, vol. 25-6, 1941, pp. 202-9.

66. See Mae Reed Porter and Odessa Davenport, *Scotsmen in Buckskin: Sir William Drummond Stewart and the Rocky Mountain Fur Trade* (New York, 1963).

67. Anon, *An English Gentleman, An Excursion Through the United States of America and Canada during the years 1822-23* (London, 1824), p. 153.

68. *Newcastle-on-Tyne 1843*, 1966 n.p. reprint edn, frontis, pp. 29, 47, 54-5.

69. 'R. Reid Obituary', *Scottish Temperance Leader*, 8 Feb. 1908.

70. See Gordon M.Wilson, *Alexander McDonald: Leader of the Miners* (Aberdeen, 1982); unpublished paper by Professor John M. Laslett to the Scottish Labour History Society, November 1982.

71. O.O. Winther, 'English Migration to the American West', *Huntington Library Quarterly*, vol. 27, 1963-4, pp. 159-73.

72. Quoted in M. Wilson, *Alexander McDonald*, p. 179.

73. D.N.B. and *Journal Kept by David Douglas during His Travels in North America, 1823-27*, W. Wilks (ed.) (London, 1914), pp. 295-9.

74. Dr. Stiles quoted Collins, *Witherspoon*, p. 151.

75. John Galt, *Lawrie Todd*, 3 vols. (London, 1830), vol. 2, p. 249.

76. Ibid., p. 239.

77. Charles Augustus Murray, *The Prairie Bird* (London, 1845), p. 1.

78. I am grateful to Andrew Gibb's unpublished paper 'A Scottish Venture in the United States: The Glasgow Ohio Company' for this information. Alexander Mackay, *The Western World and Travels in the United States, 1846 and 1847*, 3 vols. (London, 1849), vol. 3, p. 79.

79. MS. Missionaries of the Church of the Latter Day Saints, Church Archives.

80. Autobiographical Collections, Church archives. A summary of numerous lives is given by Davis Britton, *A Guide to Mormon Diaries and Autobiographies* (Provo, 1977).

81. See Frederick Stewart Buchana, 'The Emigration of Scottish Mormonists to Utah, 1849-1900', unpublished MSc dissertation, University of Utah, 1961, pp. 53-4.

82. October, 1852.

83. See Harrison, *Robert Owen and the Owenites in Britain and America* (London, 1969).

84. *Forres Gazette*, 23 Oct. 1872; *Scottish Temperance League Journal*, 3 May 1873; Letter of Mrs Margaret Kerr, 31 Jan. 1892, Minnesota Historical Society, St Paul, Minnesota.

85. David J. Jeremy, 'British Textile Technology Transmission to the United States: The Philadelphia Region Experience, 1770-1820', *Business History Review*, vol. 47, 1973, pp. 24-52, especially pp. 30 and 51. Also see Cynthia

Shelton, 'Labour and Capital in the Early Period of Manufacturing: The Failure of John Nicholson's Manufacturing Company, 1793-97', *Pennsylvania Magazine of History and Biography*, vol. 106, 1982, pp. 341-63. Frances W. Gregory, *Nathan Appleton, Merchant and Entrepreneur, 1779-1861* (Charlottesville, 1975), vol. 1, pp. 143-5.

86. Caroline F. Ware, *The Early New England Cotton Manufacture: A Study in Industrial Beginnings* (Boston, 1931), p. 203.

87. See Daniel J. Walkowitz, *Worker City, Company Town: Iron and Cotton Workers Protests in Troy and Cohoes, New York, 1855-84* (Urbana, 1978), p. 61. Tamara K. Hareven, *Family Time and Industrial Time: The Relationship Between the Family and Work in a New England Industrial Community* (Cambridge, Mass., 1982), pp. 16, 20, 43, 123.

88. See Ray Ginger, 'Labour in a Massachusetts Cotton Mill, 1853-1860', *Business History Review*, vol. 28, 1954, pp. 67-91.

89. Ibid., p. 78.

90. Ibid., p. 80.

91. Constance McLaughlin Green, *Holyoke, Massachusetts: A Case History of the Industrial Revolution in America* (New Haven, 1939), pp. 48-9, 76.

92. Charlotte Erickson, *American Industry and the European Immigrant, 1860-1888* (Cambridge, Mass., 1957), pp. 36-8.

93. Rowland T. Berthoff, *British Immigrants in Industrial America, 1790-1850* (Cambridge, Mass., 1953), p. 44; Frances W. Gregory, 'The American Industrial Elite in the 1870s: Their Social Origins' in William Miller (ed.), *Men in Business: Essays on the Historical Role of the Entrepreneur* (New York, 1962), p. 197.

94. Hugh Murray, *Historical Account of Discoveries and Travels in North America with observations on emigration*, 2 vols. (London, 1829), vol. 2, p. 528.

95. Ibid., p. 531.

96. See S. Thernstrom, *The Other Bostonians* (Cambridge, Mass., 1973).

97. Maurice Corina, *Fine Silks and Oak Counters: Debenhams, 1778-1978* (London, 1978), p.42.

98. See H.A. Gibbons, *John Wanamaker*, 2 vols. (New York, 1926); Alfred D. Chandler Jr, *The Visible Hand: The Managerial Revolution in American Business* (Cambridge, Mass., 1977), pp. 209-26.

99. John Thomas Scharf, *History of St Louis City and County*, 2 vols. (Philadelphia, 1883), vol. 2, pp. 12, 41-2.

100. James Cox, *Old and New St Louis* (St Louis, 1894), pp. 216-18; *St Louis Hornet*, 8 April 1882; J. Thomas Scharf, *History of St Louis*, vol. 2, p. 130.

101. R.E. Tyson, 'Scottish Investment in American Railways: The Case of the City of Glasgow Bank, 1856-81' in P.L. Payne (ed.), *Studies in Scottish Business History* (London, 1967), pp. 357-416.

102. Dorothy R. Adler, *British Investment in American Railways* (Charlottesville, 1970), p. 125; Peter Temin, *The Iron and Steel Industry in Nineteenth Century America* (Princeton, 1964), p. 59.

103. On the whole background see Merle Curti, *The American Peace Crusade, 1815-1860* (Durham, 1929).

104. 'A. O'Neill obituary' in *Herald of Peace*, 1 Jan. 1896.

105. Blake McKelvey, *The Urbanisation of America, 1860-1915* (New Brunswick, 1963), and his *The Emergence of Metropolitan America, 1915-1966* (New Brunswick, 1968), Chapter 1.

106. See Blanche Wiesen Cook (ed.), *Crystal Eastman: Woman and Revolution* (New York, 1978), pp. 336-49.

107. See Daniel Nelson, *Managers and Workers: Origins of the New Factory*

System in the United States, 1880-1920 (Madison, 1975), and Gerald Rosenblum, *Immigrant Workers: Their Impact on American Labour Radicalism* (New York, 1973).

AUSTRALIA AND THE SCOTTISH CONNECTION
1788-1914[1]

Eric Richards

When European civilisation came to be imprinted on the Australian
continent, the two most influential Scots were, almost certainly, John
Knox and Adam Smith. Their philosophies pervaded most aspects of
the business of colonisation, and the creation of the Australian
societies. Presbyterianism and classical political economy, together a
powerful concoction, shaped the culture, determined the role of the
state, allocated resources, and inspired the energies of the first eight
generations of colonists in Australia to such a degree that it is difficult
to imagine colonial Australia *sans* Knox and Smith. Indeed, the most
outspoken modern historian of Australia has chosen to interpret the
colonial experience largely in terms of a vast antipodean struggle
between the forces of the Enlightenment, Protestant Christianity and
Catholic Christendom.[2] The Scots were ubiquitous; they were the
nineteenth-century colonists *par excellence*. Their impact on Australia
has never been in doubt.

The Scottish influence was carried to Australia by legions of immigrants: convicts, governors, merchants, administrators, labourers,
capitalists, domestic servants, pastoral pioneers, artists, writers, doctors,
educators, miners, men of religion, drovers' wives, and many more.
Some had capital, some education, some both and some neither. Their
collective record leaves a clear impression of a people highly mobile,
and strongly motivated in the business of grasping opportunities created
in the virgin territories of colonial expansion.

Yet there is something artificial in abstracting the Scottish influence
from the manifold agencies which created Australian society in the
nineteenth century. For one thing, it is the sort of exercise which leads
to cultural stereotypes much loved by the Victorians themselves — con-
ventionally expressed in terms of the canny, pertinacious, calculating,
dour, upwardly mobile Scot. For another, it requires some demonstration of the proposition that the Scottish influence was disproportionate, perhaps because of the *per capita* supply of energy, capital, and
culture. Such claims would require a systematic comparison of the
Scots with the rest of the population, or with another regional group

(for example, the Welsh, or Yorkshiremen). In general, the numbers and proportions are simply not known, and the relative qualities inherent in Scottishness are not analysable. Consequently, the purpose of this chapter is not so much a celebration of the Scottish influence on Australia, as a commentary on the Scots as representative elements in the process of colonisation and the making of Australia.

Most Scots merged anonymously into the life of colonial Australia. Many had arrived in Australia not so much as contributors to, but dependents upon, colonial society. Those who remained distinguishable in the historical record did so by virtue of their wealth or their literacy or their distinctive contribution.

I

The impact of Scotland on Australia depended largely on historical timing: on the timetable of modernisation in Scotland and its relationship to the phases of colonisation in Australia. The extraordinary mobility of the Scots (within and beyond the British Isles) derived mainly from the early and rapid industrialisation of parts of the central lowlands in the late eighteenth century. At much the same time Scottish agriculture was modernised, a process which dislocated much of the population, improved productivity rapidly, and permitted the swift urbanisation of the increment of population growth that accompanied economic development. In the Highlands and Islands the story was quite different. There a peasant society was in retreat, traditionalism persisted, and the population outgrew the region's economic needs until emigration (southwards or abroad) relieved the pressure. Consequently Scotland became a dual economy in which social and economic changes released the people from old ways, while demographic revolution yielded large numbers who could be accommodated in neither the peasant Highlands nor the new agriculture. Meanwhile the success of the commercial and industrial base, by the turn of the nineteenth century, generated savings at an unprecedented rate, even to the point at which local needs were overfed. Surpluses of capital began to seek overseas investment opportunities just as manufacturers and traders sought wider markets for output.

The economic circumstances of nineteenth-century Scotland generated outward pressures which were expressed in the emigration of labour, capital and enterprise. It was inevitable that the Scots would reach the furthermost colony of New South Wales. The first links came,

Map 5.1: Centres of Scottish Settlement in Australia

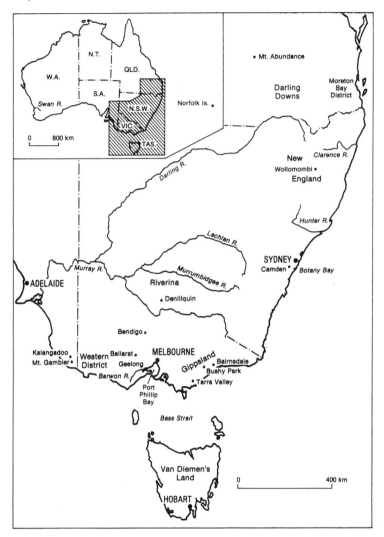

in most instances, from the initiatives of merchants and colonial administrators who often had prior connections with India. A more broadly based incursion of Scots developed in the second quarter of the new century. The establishment of settlement in South Australia, Victoria, Queensland and Western Australia, and the great push into the continental interior, coincided with the decades in which Scottish trade and industry advanced most vigorously. Capital and enterprise from Scotland came to Australia in concentrated flows which favoured specific sectors, most notably pastoralism and commerce. In all, it illustrated the changing relationship between the two economies in the *laissez-faire* world of the *Pax Britannica*.

II

Scotland provided Australia with bone and sinew. Scots first came in 1788 either as criminals or as members of the militia. A trickle of wealthy agriculturalists followed, seeking new fields for their capital or to rebuild a social status lost in Scotland; then came the poorest Scots, beneficiaries of charity or colonial bounties in the 1830s. These were the precursors of the great movement of colonial-financed immigration programmes which operated for most of the following century. Parallel, however, was the much smaller influx of wealthier Scots, self-financed immigrants, who took advantage of disproportionate opportunities which existed in the early stages of settlement and mercantile development.

The colony established in 1788 at Botany Bay was a convict scheme (which had been opposed in Scotland by Lord Gardenstone as a ridiculously expensive method of dealing with the problem of crime) and a staging post in the trading network of British influence in the East. It brought Scots to Australia in three capacities: as convicts, administrators and settlers. In many cases the colonial administrators came from a previous career in the armed forces or in the East India trade. There was a sprinkling of Scots who, nevertheless, were able by example to demonstrate the feasibility of voluntary emigration to fellow countrymen who possessed moderate capital. It was several decades before Australia emerged in the consciousness of footloose Scots as a place of settlement.

The best known of the convict immigrants were 'the Scottish Martyrs' of 1793-4 who are clearly to be numbered among the political prisoners leavening the convict mass. Convicted of sedition, they were in a special category and received privileged treatment. It is unlikely that they made any permanent mark on Australia though they may have strengthened, however briefly, the egalitarian outlook which developed from the earliest days of the colony.[3] The total number of Scots convicts who came to Australia was small: they were less than 3 per cent of the criminal population, and in the first dozen years of settlement only 70 Scots were transported. By 1823 the number amounted to 855. As A.G.L. Shaw has demonstrated, the Scots were greatly under-represented. (In *per capita* terms in the years 1810-21 the English sent four times as many convicts.)[4] But although the Scots lacked numbers they compensated in the severity of their criminality. The Revd John West, referring to the convict population, said 'the most base and clever are the Scotch'. In general they arrived at Botany Bay after experience in the hulks at Portsmouth or Woolwich, and their crimes were more serious than the average. Hence the Scots developed the reputation as the most hardened and dangerous of the criminal fathers of the new continent — it was said that 'A man is banished from Scotland for a great crime, from England for a small one, and from Ireland, morally speaking, for no crime at all.'[5] This opinion was based on a deduction from the comparative crime statistics — fewer persons were convicted in Scotland than in the rest of the country, and of these a smaller proportion were transported.

Colonial opinion tended to confirm the deduction. In 1847 Majoribanks commented

Both in New South Wales and Van Diemen's Land, Scotch convicts are considered the worst, and English the best. This seems to arise not so much from the laws of the two countries being so essentially different, as their being differentially administered; the punishment for minor crimes in particular, being infinitely more severe in England than in Scotland. Hence, hundreds are transported annually from England for offences which, in Scotland, would be punished by sixty days confinement in jail at Bridewell . . . In Scotland . . . they are mostly old offenders before they are transported.[6]

It was a view reaffirmed in 1850 by Archibald Alison, who stated baldly that, of those transported in Australia, 'the Scotch beyond all question, [are] the worst who arrived'. He explained thus:

The Scotch law, administered almost entirely by professional men, and on fixed principles, has long been based on the principle of transporting persons only who are deemed irreclaimable in this country. Very few have been sent abroad for half a century, from Scotland, who had not either committed some grave offence, or been four or five times, often eight or ten times, previously convicted or imprisoned.[7]

It was not surprising that in the dawn of civil society colonial Australia regarded the highly selective Scottish system with considerable distaste. Indeed by mid-century there was alarm in the colonies that the Irish, English and Welsh magistrates were moving towards the Scottish principles of sentencing, there being a fear of 'a class of repeatedly convicted and hardened offenders'.[8]

In reality most of the Scottish convicts were burglars or housebreakers, who came by way of trial in Edinburgh or Glasgow after previous convictions. Lloyd Robson's statistical studies confirm that they were 'the worst of a bad lot', a remark which applied to the female convicts also, who included the longest serving prostitutes.[9] Yet, while opinion of the Scottish convicts was unanimous, there is little evidence that a race of hardened criminal Scots darkened the continent in any permanent sense.[10] Certainly the virtues of the free immigrant Scot rapidly erased the old reputation.

The convict reputation could also be set beside the labours of the class of administrators from Scotland who were prominent in the convict colony – notably John Hunter who came with the First Fleet, and was the second Governor, and most illustriously, Lachlan Macquarie, Governor of New South Wales in the wake of the controversial Bligh, and the man who may be credited with a new vision of civilisation in the antipodes. More specific compensation for the dumping of hardened Scots criminals in Australia was contributed by Captain Alexander Maconochie (1787-1860). Orphaned son of a Scottish land agent, he pursued a naval career until he became the first Professor of Geography at University College, London, in 1833. Four years later he visited Port Phillip and made a report on the penal system in Australia for the Society for the Improvement of Prison Discipline. He advocated a work system for prisoners with the aim of early release by rehabilitation, and in 1839 he was appointed to the command of the penal colony at Norfolk Island. Putting into practise his controversial ideas, Maconochie humanised the hell-hole of Norfolk Island within a few years, and although his penal career was dogged by opposition his permanent influence on penological ideas (notably in the form of the so-called 'indeterminate sentence') has been widely recognised. It was fitting that, in Maconochie, Scotland should give Australia a progressive penological theorist, as well as its most hardened criminals.[11]

During the infant days of colonial Australia the tasks of administering and developing the convict settlement created opportunities in which could be demonstrated the exportability of Scottish talents. The Scots' career paths usually involved army service, time in India, and then a natural progression into the officer corps in New South Wales, followed by land grants in the colony and family settlement.[12] Moreover much of the security of Australia in the first decades was placed in the hands of battle-hardened Scots units, notably the 73rd Highlanders, the Perthshire, and the 2nd Battalion of the Black Watch. Unthreatened by external forces, they contributed to the development of the colonial infrastructure, especially in great road construction programmes.[13]

In the long run, however, the greatest challenge in Australia was the transformation of the penal settlement into a self-sufficient civil society capable of cumulative development without the subsidies necessary within the convict system. The task required capital, enterprise and free immigration; it needed also an exploration of the economic potential of the new continent. In essence Australia wanted mercantile initiative and to Robert Campbell (1769-1846) is due the credit for the first steps in this vital process. His biographer described him as Australia's first merchant, 'the first man to come to the colony with a command of capital and the means of mobilising colonial resources'. His pioneering initiative in New South Wales was a natural extension of a family enterprise which already linked Scottish trade between Glasgow and Calcutta. His commercial activity in Sydney was an offshoot of the East India trade.[14] It was Campbell's achievement, first, to introduce Australia into the network of Asian trade and, second, to challenge the trading monopoly of the East India Company and its officers. He arrived in New South Wales in 1798 to explore its trading possibilities, and to establish a branch of Campbell, Clark and Co., merchants of Calcutta. Once in Australia Campbell swiftly discovered wide scope for his talents; his career embraced the collection of taxes, banking and politics, as well as trading. Eventually he settled as a wealthy pastoralist and exhibited his success in substantial philanthropy. From the beginning he made a conscious effort to liberate colonial trade from the clutches of the ruling officer corps. Rebuffed in the early stages he nevertheless identified the commercial possibilities for the export of whale oil and sealskins, the first staples of Australian commerce. By 1805 he was exporting skins directly to London in contravention of the rights of the East India Company. (He was saved from their litigation by the intervention of Sir Joseph Banks.) In the following decade he campaigned for free trade to Australia, the success of which came in 1815 when Sydney was at last declared a free port. During the intervening years Campbell had accepted government contracts to import livestock from India. In 1819 he helped organise the first savings bank in Australia. These activities helped build the new colonial economy, without which Macquarie's vision of civil society would have come to nought.[15]

III

Until the 1820s Australia remained low in the Scottish consciousness; it did not emerge as a potential destination for capital and emigrants in any significant fashion until the following decade. Before 1815 Australia remained remote and entirely clouded by its penal function. At this time Scottish emigration, even from the Highlands, remained relatively slight and was primarily directed south or across the Atlantic. David S. Macmillan, historian of the Scottish-Australian link, detected a change in the relationship in the post-Waterloo years. Scots then sought new markets, more scope for entrepreneurial expansion, and new outlets for emigration to act as a solution to structural unemployment in agriculture, as well as cyclical difficulties in industry. He regards Scotland at this time as a backward country, 'only beginning to look beyond its borders to the new opportunities opening in the antipodean empire.'[16]

Yet this was a period of awakening rather than of achievement. There was certainly much Scottish discussion of the potential of British North America, the Cape of Good Hope, and Australia (even as early as 1817), but little came of the Pacific idea until the 1830s. The Royal Commission on Emigration from Scotland in 1827 made no reference to Australia, although at that time it was emerging as a free enterprise economy with promise of a capacity to yield staple export output, primarily for Britain. There were pre-conditions at both ends of the chain before immigration could develop on a significant basis.

Free settlement in Australia before the 1830s was highly selective, partly because of the great expense of emigration, and also because colonial land policy was deliberately exclusive. In Australia, until the inauguration of the Ripon Regulations in 1831, land was allocated freely in large grants, but only to men whose capital was sufficient to warrant the grant. Hence, for the first 40 years of colonisation, the

Scots free settlers were primarily ex-officials and army officers; this stream was augmented by a growing trickle of men who came out directly from Scotland, mostly merchants and former farmers. There were singularly few Scots emancipists among the land grantees; nevertheless the Scots began to blossom, especially in Van Diemen's Land where, in the 1820s, they constituted one sixth of free settlers, a proportion which rose to a third within ten years.[17] They tended to be relatively well-heeled, middle-order men, with greater than usual mobility, searching for land. As Macmillan says, 'Throughout the 1820s it is the rank, the standing, and the wealth of the Scottish Agricultural settlers that is impressive.' Men of substance, often at the end of their Scottish leases or else squeezed by falling agricultural prices, and ready to make an adventurous start in the antipodean landscape, they were not unlike the relatively wealthy tacksmen who had led emigration from the Highlands to North America in the 1770s.[18] Aspiration rather than desperation was the propelling force, says Macmillan, and the property qualification for land grants excluded the poorer elements.

Some, indeed, were Highlanders, probably inspired by the success of Macquarie and the network of news from the regiment which had served in Australia. The best known example was Major Donald Macleod, a tacksman of Talisker in Skye, who sold his lease in 1820 (after years of service with the 56th Regiment) and sailed to Van Diemen's Land with his family of nine. He was given a grant of 2,000 acres (called 'Talisker') which he farmed until 1837, when he went to Sydney. His third son followed the pioneering effort by a squatting venture in the newly opened pastures of Port Phillip in the 1830s when he took over 25,000 acres after a succession of blood-curdling clashes with aborigines.[19] The Macleods eventually emerged from their emigration as wealthy squatters typifying the energy released from the Highlands. There were other footloose elements in the Scottish economy which sought opportunities in Australia — merchants who found business conditions too much in the post-war depressions, or military men whose careers were cut short by peace. The papers of James Wilson track the life of a small merchant from Banff who emigrated to Hobart in 1829 where he set up in various fields until he became a brewer, and then manager of the Cascades Brewery. Nostalgia for Banff did not prevent his eventual rise to political office and a knighthood.[20] Less affluent Scots, brought out under contract, were also trickling into the colony. In May 1823 an employer exulted in the fact that 'now there are so many Scotsmen arriving daily that I can get them for almost nothing.'[21] Over the next decade money could be made on pastoral land with relative ease by those prepared to go into the out-back. David Waugh told his brother in Edinburgh in 1834 that 'All the settlers are making money if they use common prudence. One Scotsman has been here 8 years, and come without a shilling, cleared £1,300 from his wool this last year and so on with all the rest.'[22]

From these various groups were drawn the first permanent threads which held Scotland to Australia. Between them they built a network of links and information, and, most of all, established the plausibility of Australia in the public mind of Scotland. Such, indeed, were the prerequisites for large-scale emigration to, and investment in, Australia. Experimental corporate beginnings for both were attempted in the second quarter of the century, though sustained interest was not captured before 1840.

The Australian Company of Edinburgh and Leith, formed in 1822, was a prototype development for Scottish investment. According to D.S. Macmillan it was itself the product of a sense of emulation in east Scotland, an expression of the fear that Edinburgh was losing mercantile opportunities to the more dynamic men of the west of Scotland, waxing rich on their manufacturing success of the lowlands. It was therefore a conscious effort by the merchants of Leith, a port hitherto bound to coastal trade, to break into overseas markets in the manner of their rivals in the Clyde ports and Dundee.[23] It was regarded as a way of making up lost ground, and the relatively new and neglected Australian market was to be the forcing ground of the new initiative. The new company, making a virtue of diversity, hoped to take commercial pickings that might arise in such a remote place. In form it was a shipping concern but it looked also for new trade and credit operations in the Australian market. Beginning with a proposed stock of £1 million, it anticipated, vainly in the event, a consistent growth of the emigrant trade from Scotland. 'The motives which prompted the partners ranged from the investor's drive for good returns on capital to the shipowner's wish to open up a new trade route and the manufacturer's interest in a new market.'[24]

The company succeeded in establishing its facilities in Hobart and Sydney and thereby reinforced the predominance of Scots in the mercantile community of Van Diemen's Land where, in 1823-4, the majority of the merchants were said to be Scots. Given a warm welcome in the Hobart press, as a new source of credit, the company sought to elbow its way into the emigration trade and searched for colonial staples which would yield profit on the return freights. Both tasks were fundamental to the development role of merchants in the nascent economy. In practice the company was able to organise regular voyages, two per year, between 1823 and 1826. It experienced the greatest difficulties in generating sufficient return cargoes, but it made notable progress in its experiments with new routes in the Far East, in forging links with the India and China trades, and in the articulation of intercolonial and New Zealand commerce. It ran into difficulties of credit in Scotland in the crisis of 1825-6 and, much buffetted by competition in far eastern trade, began selling off its ships in 1829. Though the company was short-lived its significance should not be underrated. Macmillan judges that it was 20 years ahead of its time – during those years Australia developed mechanisms of sustained institutional growth and much higher productivity in its staple exports. Ultimately, from the 1840s onwards, companies similar to the Leith and Edinburgh enterprise were to enable absentee creditors to invest with confidence in so remote a place as Australia. The achievement of such companies was best displayed in the golden age of Scottish investment in the 1870s and 1880s, when they appeared to dominate the Australian capital market. The evolution of these mechanisms was essential in the process which diminished the risks inherent in long-distance speculation.

IV

In the 1830s Australia emerged as a series of rapidly developing colonial economies, no longer dominated by Hobart and Sydney. New settlements at Swan River in the west, at Adelaide in South Australia and at Port Phillip demonstrated the impact of discovery and revealed the scale of continental possibilities. The immensely successful development of wool production, followed in the next decade by mining in copper and then gold, changed the complexion of Australian colonisation. Already, by 1831-2, pressures were rising for institutional changes in both immigration and land policies. Within a decade mass immigration began to link the labour surpluses of Scotland with the demands of Australia.

In simplified terms the old Australian land grant policy was replaced by a system (much influenced by the ideas of Edward Gibbon Wakefield) of land sales at a minimum price. The revenues yielded by land sales could be harnessed for many purposes, but there was a strong feeling that the subsidisation of immigration was the best use of funds. Consequently, in the 1830s schemes were evolved which improvised various formulae to employ bounties to finance immigration programmes. Eventually systematic arrangements were designed which efficiently channelled labour from Britain to Australia, so diverting immigrants away from North America to the antipodes. The current political problems of Canada assisted in this process, and Australia found itself in a propaganda war with Canada in the competition for people.

In the first phase of the new era the Scots were not well placed. In the years 1832-7 they accounted for a mere tenth of Australian immigration probably because of the dominance of London in the bounty system. It was not until shipping interests in Leith applied some persuasion that the system was extended to Scotland. By 1836 there were three government emigration agents appointed to Scotland. In the following five years they were instrumental in bringing the interests of the two countries together. Recurrence of famine in the West Highlands reached national attention at a time when the labour needs of Australia became critical, as evidenced in the rapid inflation of wage rates in Sydney, Hobart and in the new colonies centred upon Adelaide and Port Phillip. David Waugh in New South Wales in September 1837 observed the possibilities: 'I see by the papers the lamentable state of the Highlands and Islands of Scotland. If we had some twenty or thirty thousand of them here we would get on as fast again.'[25] Urged on by the propaganda of J.D. Lang and the influential encouragement of James Macarthur, Scotland, and especially the Highlands, became a prime recruitment zone for Australian emigration in the years 1837-40. The campaign brought the first great inflow of Scottish artisans and peasants to Australia, in company with even more from Ireland.

The bounty emigration of the late 1830s was the first concerted effort by colonial authorities to seek out large numbers of emigrants suitable to Australian conditions, particularly for pastoral work in the outback. The effect of the government agents in the West Highlands was to generate great local interest in Australia, which was further reinforced by the concurrent private bounty scheme also in operation in the north. Perhaps 10,000 Scots went to Australia between 1837-42, many shipped directly from West Highland ports. While the emigration broke down some of the prevailing prejudice against Australia, there was complaint in Scotland that the emigration schemes were creaming off the best of the population. It was a complaint sometimes ironically reversed within Australia where some of the Scots immigrants were described as the dregs of the Scottish world.[26] Many of the Highlanders arrived in a condition of severe poverty and their traces in Australia were not easily followed. It was said that Caroline Chisholm, the humanitarian reformer, came across some needy Highland immigrants in 1838 who could speak no English, and 'gave them tools and wheelbarrows wherewith to cut and sell firewood'.[27] These people were precursors of many more immigrants, notably in the 1850s, who arrived in Australia in a pitiful condition and were dependent on private charity or the state for some time before they were able to contribute to the colonies.

The bounty schemes came to an abrupt halt during the economic crisis in the colonies in 1841-2 when labour became a drug on the market, just as a resurgence of Scottish interest in North America helped to divert attention away from Australian possibilities. Still the thin stream of unassisted newcomers continued to flow throughout the 1830s and 1840s. Bourgeois Scottish immigrants, prominent among settlers and investors in South Australia (founded in 1836), made their biggest impact in the Port Phillip district (later to become Victoria) where they dominated the earliest phases of economic development, and created a remarkable plutocratic circle of merchants and settlers in pre-gold-rush Melbourne. In opening new opportunities in the infant colonies the second generation Scots Australians made the running but were strongly sustained by new blood from home. In the rough work of colonisation it was the squatter fastest off the mark who was most likely to become the richest and most respectable pastoralist of the mid-century.

The Scottish influence in early Melbourne and its hinterland, was proverbial. William Kelly in 1859 remarked that Melbourne 'strongly reminded [him] of Scotland in everything around [him] . . . except the pure air'. In the early pastoral days 'Scotchmen vastly predominated over all the others', a view supported by William Howitt who claimed that 'Before the gold discovery, the colony was almost entirely Scotch.'[28] Eventually, during the gold rushes, the Scots were partly displaced by the Irish. But when the great pastoralist from Argyll, Neil Black, arrived in the Western District in 1839 he remarked that 'Melbourne is almost altogether a Scotch settlement, and the people are so far as I can judge altogether Scotch in their habits and manners.'[29]

The vast lands of southern Australia provided the amplest scope for Scottish initiative and capital. The way was prepared by Vandemonian men who began a great squatting push north and west from Port Phillip during the early 1830s. Some were Scots and they were followed by fellow countrymen with connections or capital, or both. It was a great time to establish the foundations of a colonial fortune, but it required a risk-taking temperament. The extraordinary story of the establishment of British settlement at Port Phillip in 1835 — after John Batman and his friends had bartered blankets, knives, tomahawks, looking glasses, beads, scissors and flour, and the promise of a yearly tribute, for 600,000 acres of land to some Aboriginal leaders – was strongly influenced by Scotsmen. The man chosen by the Port Phillip Association to perform the daunting task of persuading the British government that its 'treaty' with the aborigines was equitable, reasonable and legal, was George Mercer of Edinburgh. Having retired from a lucrative career with the East India Company, he had settled in Van Diemen's Land, and he found himself at the centre of negotiations between London and Hobart in the years 1835-7. He attempted to persuade Lord Glenelg at the Colonial office that the intentions of the Association were entirely honourable and that its treaty should be confirmed forthwith 'as an act of common justice'. The Association intended to create 'a free colony without pecuniary sacrifice to the Mother Country'; the new colony would however require British local authority to give protection to all, most especially to the 'Aborigines whose welfare and general improvement the association takes a pride in declaring to be one of the great objects as evinced by the tribute paid to and arrangements made with the Natives'. While Mercer made great play of the amiability of their relations with the Port Phillip aborigines, he added more plausible arguments when he anticipated that Port Phillip would become 'a new field for emigration and British industry'. It would be

a nucleus for a free and useful Colony founded upon principles of Conciliation and Civilisation, of Philanthropy and Temperance, without danger of it becoming onerous to the Mother Country, and calculated to insure the well being and comfort of the Natives, the proposed system instructing and protecting, not exterminating.[30]

Mercer's colonising pieties towards the native people were typical of his age; the reality diverged monstrously from the promises of the Port Phillip Association. It was an ugly story of aboriginal destruction, repeated many times across the Australian continent, in which Scots figure as strongly as any of the other white immigrants.

Mercer cited his own career as proof of the sterling credentials of the Association and his story demonstrated the advantages of a large capital in the business of colonising. As a settler in Van Diemen's Land he had brought out from Britain many overseers and ploughmen, and their families, and in the process, had 'vested already in these colonies in agricultural and pastoral pursuits a sum exceeding twenty thousand pounds, five thousand of this forwarded in gold at a great sacrifice to myself but of much benefit to the Colony'. It was a classic instance of Scotch enterprise and East Indian profits finding a new channel in Australia. Mercer said he was now prepared to replicate his investment for the sake of Port Phillip. Both Mercer and the association which he represented anticipated the highly predictable resistance of the Colonial Office to their opportunistic entrepreneurial colonisation of the southern mainland. It was a typical case of the colonist *in situ* dragging Britain into further expansion of settlement. Mercer, in December 1836, was prepared to say that:

> The fact I believe to be that the Colonial officials know little and care less about Australia destined in my humble opinion to become for a period the brightest jewel in the British Crown and in the common course of mundane matters to quit . . . the protecting Parents wing and assume independence.[31]

And although Mercer failed to convince Whitehall of either the justice or legality of their outrageous initiative, his vision was brought to fruition within an astonishingly short period of time. He himself sent out his sons to manage his property; by their landgrabbing they quickly gained a foothold in the Port Phillip district during the late 1830s.

V

Squatting in the mid-century required both adaptability and capital. Pastoralism was a selective process because the costs of entry were high: huge tracts of land were required and the accumulation of the minimum economic size of flocks excluded the small men. Reliable supervision was also vital. Scots appear to have been disproportionately successful in meeting these requirements. Defining the 'average' squatter of this time Stephen Roberts said 'the mixture is Scotch, somewhat military, and intolerant alike of obstacles and authorities'.[32] Some were perhaps tenant farmers direct from the Scottish lowlands, looking for better promise than the depressed profits which clouded British agriculture during the 1830s. But it was more likely that they were guided into pastoralism by a series of stepping stones in the colony — perhaps through a family connection or by employment from fellow Scots. For example George Russell was born in 1812, tenth of 13 children of a tenant farmer who had seen his finances deteriorate at Banchory and in Fife. Unable to offer him a future at home, in 1830 his father had encouraged George to follow his older brother, who had emigrated to Van Diemen's Land in 1821. There George helped manage a property; in 1836 he crossed the Bass Strait to explore Port Phillip where he represented the Clyde Company, a Scottish-Vandemonian enterprise of rich pastoral capitalists, which operated in the western district of Victoria. It was a typical pastoral company, backed by a group of merchants and landowners in Glasgow, Edinburgh and Fife, connected by several ties of family and able to exert considerable parliamentary influence when the need arose.[34] Pioneering in the wilderness, by 1839 Russell was managing 8,000 sheep for the company which paid him a salary of £100 a year, and a share of the profits. He eventually set up on his own account and when he died in 1887 was worth £318,110.[34]

It would be easy to underestimate the sheer adventurousness and gumption of many immigrants, and perhaps especially the Scots, who came to Australia before the gold rushes. John Peter came from a prosperous family of farmers near Milngavie, the first son, and born to inherit a steady living in Scotland. It was said that 'he relinquished a respectable position there, with the view of acquiring a more ample independence than even the fair expectations he had at home presented'. Not in any way pushed out of an ailing homeland, he was attracted by sheer *jeu d'esprit* to New South Wales in 1832. His father paid his passage and presented him with £50. Peter, through Scottish connections, quickly picked up employment in that great field for immigrants with talent but little capital — managing, superintending and overseeing. Soon he had charge of a large run on the Lachlan River, with 2,000 sheep and a dozen assigned convict shepherds. He said, 'I now found myself, without any colonial experience, placed in a position of great responsibility, alone, and without anyone to assist me.' His biographer says that the Scottish connection was critical, and the 'Scottish values of prudence, application, doggedness and endurance, self-discipline and the capacity for preferring work to the call of pleasure' counted for still more. An English contemporary remarked 'You must recollect that he is a Scotchman which is in itself a sort of passport to fortune.' Peter had another advantage: he married a rich propertied widow and set up for himself as a pastoralist on the Murrumbidgee where he eventually generated an income of £40,000 a year. The ultimate badge of his success was the acquisition of a superior house in London and a lease of a shooting estate in the Highlands which placed him on a par with contemporary American plutocrats in the north.[35]

More modest and perhaps more typical was the case of the Highlander who arrived in New South Wales in 1836, from Strathconan, Ross-shire, where he had been in the employment of Sir George Mackenzie. In his first year he earned £20 with rations, in the second and third years £30, and then £45 per annum. By 1845 two of his family were old enough to work and he possessed a farm on which he also employed labourers, running 200 sheep and 50 head of cattle. 'I would like my relations out', he wrote at the time. His was one of the cases collected by Caroline Chisholm to use as propaganda in favour of further emigration at the time of the famine of 1847.[36]

A relatively new model of direct land investment emerged in the middle decades of the century. On occasion respected Scottish institutions gave their colonial representatives considerable discretionary authority, and thereby led the way in speculative pioneering. Benjamin Boyd of the Royal Bank of Scotland was an early starter into the Deniliquin country in the early 1840s. On behalf of the Bank he acquired great tracts of new country, animated by 'an insatiable attack. . . of earth hunger, and was not satisfied with less than what would comprise several English counties'. He bought up large Murray River frontages, contracted a manager to run the property, and named it the Royal Bank Station. This was corporate wealth reined to managerial initiative and energy.[37] The same process was pursued by personal connections. Joseph Anderson, a man of Sutherland, born in 1790, served in the French Wars and continued his military service which eventually brought him to Norfolk Island. In about 1838 his brother suggested that they take up a sheep station in Port Phillip, employing a manager to acquire and maintain the stock. This was typical vicarious pioneering, that is until the persistent drunkenness of the manager caused the brother to intervene personally in the management of the property. Eventually John Anderson retired on a pension of £6,000, and chose to live in the land of his adoption, combining the fruits of an army career and his lucrative pastoral speculation to become a considerable patrician figure in mid-Victorian Melbourne society.[38]

The urgent need for managerial experience in the pioneer economy generated considerable opportunities for well-educated Scots, especially where they were able to connect themselves with Scottish partnerships or individual pastoralists. A man of ability could rise rapidly in responsibility if he showed the capacity to take on the running of a great pastoral run. J.G. Johnston, writing in 1839, recorded an example from the 1820s, whose motif recurred through the middle decades of the century:

I know an individual who went out as a farm servant to Van Diemen's Land fifteen years ago, without taking as much as £5 with him; but when leaving last for this country, the proceeds of his farm establishment amounted to upwards of £15,000, which he laid out on good security, at interest varying from £10 to £12 per cent. This individual is now in the East of Fife, with his numerous and healthful family, giving them an education suitable to their rank and prospects.[39]

Social advance, naturally, was a great propellant for emigration, and though it is not known how many sent their children back home for their education, or retired there, the rapid growth of superior Scots schools in the colonies suggested that most made a long-term accommodation with colonial society. The ladder of social advancement in Australia — pioneering management, then ownership and independence, and perhaps fortune — suited perfectly the aspiring immigrant Scot's mentality.

Corporate enterprise from Scotland in pastoral pioneering was a phenomenon of the middle years of the century. The Hunter brothers of Kalangadoo, but originally of Forfarshire, came to the Western District of Victoria with capital raised in a partnership in Scotland. One of the partners was the Marquis of Ailsa whose grandson, Lord Gilbert Kennedy, emigrated as manager. An early start, with strong financial support, were great advantages and although the original partnership crashed in the crisis of 1842 the Hunters developed other Scottish connections and became large pastoralists in the classic Scottish mode.[40] More illustrious still was the case of Neil Black (1804-80) who arrived at Port Phillip from Argyll at the age of 35 to be managing partner in the firm of Neil Black and Company. This was a Scottish/ Australian subsidiary of the Liverpool firm of Gladstone, Sergeantson and Company. Black himself had little capital but provided the managerial framework for the utilisation of Scottish capital for pioneer squatting in the newly opened tracts of the rich, western district of Victoria. In Margaret Kiddle's illuminating phrase, Black was 'the very type of a Scots pioneer — righteous, frugal, hardworking, no one's fool, with an instinctive knowledge of how the commercial cat might jump that amounted almost to clairvoyance. Every risk he took was a well calculated one.'[41] His single-minded devotion to his partners', and then his own interest, rewarded him with a fortune, a princely mansion and a long membership of the Victorian Legislative Council. He had taken the track, well worn by Scots, from management to ownership, and entry into the colonial plutocracy. Managerial skills in the early colonial phase were in short supply, as the case of Black's contemporary, Neil Campbell of Sunniepol in Mull, further demonstrates. After two years, in 1840, he was able to command a salary of £1,000, better than a top level aristocratic estate agent in England at that time. Black and Campbell, in common with other successful squatters, expressed a preference for Scottish labour and made specific arrangements for their immigration throughout the 1840s and 1850s. Though he expostulated against the laziness and unreliability of many of his men, Black remarked in 1841 'to have them bound for Three Years is an advantage and a good Scotch Shepherd is at anytime worth £30 to £32 a year whatever the wages are'.[42]

The most exotic of the relatively wealthy Scots to attempt a new start in colonial Australia was the Highland chief, Macdonnell of Glengarry, who emigrated with a full entourage in the year 1842. He had sold off his debt-ridden ancestral estate, hoping to achieve financial recovery in Australia, and emigrated to Gippsland, with a depasturing licence for a head station on the banks of the Tarra, a great stretch of country for which he bought 500 dairy cows at £10 each. The entire enterprise was ill-fated: the Highlanders had no experience of management, they learned their farming lessons at awful cost, they fell into appalling conflict with aborigines, and the dairying venture collapsed. Glengarry, failing utterly, sold off his stock at a great loss and returned home to an early grave. Stephen Roberts judged that 'He was too feudal to succeed as a pastoralist in that business age.'[43]

More successful, more ruthless, and with a better head for business, Angus Macmillan of Bushy Park had been born in Glenbrittle in Skye in 1810, the fourth of 15 sons. A man of substance, he had paid £55 for a cabin in which he emigrated to Sydney in 1838 with a letter of introduction to another Skyeman, Captain Lachlan Macalister, and quickly gained employment as a station overseer at Camden in New South Wales. Very soon he looked south to new lands for settlement on his own account. Financed in part by Macalister, and animated by a self-confessed godly mission, Macmillan undertook much arduous and exacting exploration in the southern limit of the colony. With the aid of aboriginal guides (he possessed 'a peculiar capacity for winning the fidelity of the natives') this hardened frontiersman opened up large tracts of country and earned the title of 'the Gippsland pioneer'. Eventually he carved out a territory for himself at Bairnsdale. It was land for cattle and sheep, hard won from the aborigines. When, during 1843, he came across the mutilated body of Ronald Macalister (the fifth white in the locality so treated) the Skyeman assembled a posse of 20 settlers (mainly Scots — called 'Macmillan's Highland Brigade') and surprised a body of blacks at Warrigal Creek. It was thought that 150 aborigines died in the slaughter. Macmillan himself thought that the country there-abouts was a suitable refuge for his fellow Highlanders: it was 'Country capable of supporting all my starving countrymen'. Indeed the district attracted a cluster of *emigré* Highlanders, usually men of means, but their record, here at least, was not one of financial success. Hal Porter's opinion was that

> seemingly intoxicated by space and affronted by freedom, their wits dislocated, they plunged too many irons in the fire, found them-selves momentary lords of tracts of land too far-spreading properly to look after, and victims of their own tangled visions.

Perhaps the leap from land-hunger in Scotland to Victoria was too much for the mind.[44]

But most of the pre-gold-rush Scottish pastoral story is one of triumph matched by a remarkable social dominance. The Scots were inordinately influential in establishing the social style of the first colonial community in the Port Phillip district. Margaret Kiddle esti-mated that two thirds of the pioneer settlers of the Western District of Victoria were Scots, and almost all had been lowland farmers.[45] A recent study has suggested that there existed a distinctive pre-democratic society in the early days of each colony, a time in which 'gentlemen and their families . . . attempted to reproduce as far as possible the life they had left at home'. After responsible government they lost their dominance and 'the enclaves became islands of gentility in a demo-cratic sea'. In Melbourne the Scots predominated — often with good lineage in the homeland and linked together in the colony by marriage, and much governed by 'a Celtic passion for genealogies'. Their tendency towards self-congratulation and exclusivity created social tensions, but most of all their success as pastoralists made them the source of envy in Port Phillip society. It was a patrician growth in a colonial setting, building monuments to its own thrift, frugality, industry and rapid upward mobility:

> The Scottish squatters of the Western District took over the public leadership of society and purposefully established themselves in their bluestone houses on the volcanic plains as a 'colonial landed gentry', while in Melbourne they and the new rich of the city build heavy

palaces in the Italian manner.

Among their ranks were lesser lights of the Scottish aristocracy, many managers who became masters, fully kilted Highland lairds, opportunist Scots squatters from Van Diemen's Land, and the extraordinary Anne Drysdale, who hailed from Pittenchar in Fife, an emigrant who set herself up as a squatter and prospered independently in the outback.[46]

The patterns of Australian settlement at mid-century revealed several concentrations of Scots. For despite their ubiquity there were notable clusters, not only in western Victoria but also in New England, Moreton Bay and the Clarence River. Pioneers of frontier pastoral development in Queensland included a group of dominant Scots. Notable among them was Allan MacPherson who, in 1847-8, tried to take up 400,000 acres of country at Mount Abundance. Young, wealthy, courageous and a gambler, he moved 8,000 sheep and several hundred cattle through 350 miles of trackless country, with the object of establishing a great pastoral enterprise. Aided by a stockman and 20 workmen, whose fears of the aborigines he scorned, MacPherson, pressed into the outback well ahead of police supervision. In the outcome he met massive resistance from the aborigines, five of his men lost their lives, and eventually he was forced to sell up and leave. MacPherson's experience was a demonstration of the stark confrontation between Scottish colonial energy and the unusually well co-ordinated resistance of the aborigines.[47]

VI

In the late 1830s there was a resurgence of Scottish mercantile interest in Australia which extended beyond the pastoral focus of many of the co-partnerships of the time. It ran parallel with the emergence of larger inflows of immigrants to the new colonies in which mercantile requirements were quickly identified. Each of the colonies had established a complement of Scots among its nascent mercantile community. Elder and Company sprang up in Adelaide in 1839. Names such as Gilchrist and Alexander, Craig and Bradfoot, and Alexander Dick, rose to early prominence in New South Wales and Victoria. Another was Alexander Brodie Spark (1792-1856), who had left Elgin in 1811 for lack of local opportunities. With a good education and some inherited money he first tried to advance in London but, at the end of a decade, applied for a land grant in Van Diemen's Land. He arrived in Sydney in 1823 and decided to stay. Within three years he was a leading member of the business coterie, prominent in banking, and by 1840 owned £40,000 of land. His contribution was to reconnoitre possibilities of trading enterprise and he became the agent for a variety of bodies in Scotland: in Sydney his business became the centre of a commercial web linking various colonies to Britain. Among the business undertakings represented were the Australian Gas Company, several shipping ventures, and the Bank of Australasia. He over-reached himself, like many others, and in the 1841-2 colonial crisis lost most of his wealth; he lived out his days in relative quietude.[48]

Merchants such as Spark created an informal Scottish network in Australia, a string of agencies linked by personal knowledge of economic conditions, and a vital source of information for further enterprise from Scotland. They gave confidence for a renewed bout of enterprise by Scottish capitalists in Australia at the end of the 1830s. The initiative came from two Aberdeen-based companies which, in seeking investment outlets in a new territory, connected legal and banking interests in the city with Aberdonians already settled in Australia. As Dr Michie suggests 'It was formalising an already widespread practice – whereby private individuals in Scotland sent funds to connections overseas in order to obtain higher capital gains.'[49] Still more, however, these companies were the first of the international investment trusts endeavouring to connect small Scottish savings with the very high interest rates associated with the Australian pastoral boom of the 1830s. Advances on mortgage were the first mode, but the investors shifted into direct property acquisition, and thereby introduced a new element into the economics of colonisation. The times seemed propitious – by the late 1830s there were confident promises of profitable investment in Australia, and of returns on capital of 20 per cent and more. According to the propaganda it was 'obvious that on the security of lands, ships, houses, sheep and capital, a very large amount of capital would find lucrative employment'.[50] Capital in Australia, said another, would yield between 30 per cent and 60 per cent compared with profits of four to eight per cent in Britain. The Aberdonian enterprise which responded to these challenges was modelled on similar corporate enterprise in America; it demonstrated that Scottish capital was switchable from the North Atlantic to the Pacific.

The first to emerge was the North British Australasian Company which started with a capital of £50,000. It hoped to attract a wide range of small investors and spoke of likely profits of 40 per cent per annum. It began operations in Sydney in 1839: it bought an estate on the Hunter at 'Lochinvar' at an inflated price as a start in the company's pastoral and agricultural activities, and planned to send out labourers under the free passage scheme. Reports continued to be optimistic into the autumn of 1840. It was, however, rapidly overtaken by the deterioration in colonial finances in 1841-2 and became involved in a controversy about the treatment of its debtors. Its principals in Aberdeen, failing to comprehend the gravity of events in New South Wales, were decidedly unsympathetic to the proposal of a voluntary moratorium for their debtors, or even a mitigation of interest rates.[51]

The second Aberdeen-based venture – the Scottish Australian Investment Company – was also the child of the latter stages of the boom. Established in 1840 with a capital of £100,000 it advertised 'the great returns obtained for the employment of capital in Australia', and 'the wonderful aptitude of this colony to absorb capital without bringing down or altering the rate of interest'. Although strongly directed to mortgage business the Company emphasised the range of its coming activities which would also include banking, insurance and investment across the board. It sought the contributions of small investors across Scotland, and employed agents in Edinburgh, Glasgow, Dundee, Montrose, Stonehaven, Banff, Elgin and Inverness. This was a distinct precedent for Scottish enterprise in Australia and it too became a dominant model in the coming half-century. But its first prospectus was vague – there was reference to the construction of brick houses in Melbourne and Sydney, importing Baltic timber, land purchases at Port Phillip, and whaling in South Australia. By far the most sensible move made by the Company was the despatch to Sydney of an intelligent and cautious manager, R.A. Morehead, who navigated the enterprise through the coming years of depression and recovery. Whereas the North British had paralysed itself with badly-timed land investments, Morehead selected its rival's ventures with great caution, rode out the depression, and found his company well placed for positive investment in the revival, especially in the copper boom. It laid out its funds primarily in mortgages and shares in colonial companies. It became a channel of capital to the Australian market and reaped good interest rates. As David Macmillan says, 'by 1846, for the first time, a business venture based in Scotland (as distinct from the pastoral partnerships like the Clyde Company) had established itself in the front rank of Australian commerce'.[52]

There was a swift annihilation of capital in the crisis of 1841-3, and a seething controversy about usury in the colonies. Colonial opinion swung between enthusiasm for the fructifying effects of imported credit and hostility to the profits achieved sometimes with apparent ease. The extraction of interest and the recovery of debts in a time of bankruptcy made investment companies exceedingly unpopular. When R.A. Morehead came to defend the race of absentee creditors to Australia, he invoked the vision of a multitude of small people making daily sacrifices to render Australian development possible:

> Many have earned the money by which they have acquired their shares, by the exercise of persevering industry. Some of them are females, some men in the vale of years, who, perhaps, require every shilling of their incomes.[53]

The controversies, and the depression, caused a dissolution of confidence in Australia: the Company raised no capital in Scotland between 1843 and 1847. The Aberdeen Company did not seek expansion until 1845 when it opened up a good connection with Elder in South Australia. The depression persuaded it to seek wider prospects and it became involved in the South Australian copper boom which obsessed the mind of the Scottish investor. The greatest contribution of the Company and its successors was to mobilise savings in Scotland, both large and small, and to mitigate the risks involved in investment in a remote new field. It demonstrated the possibilities for Scottish capital and led the way for a succession of pastoral and investment companies in Australia in the following half century.

By mid-century Scots were entrenched in several leading sectors of the Australian economy, most prominently in trading, shipping and banking in New South Wales. They completely dominated the grazier community in the western district of Victoria. They had introduced new modes of investment and provided the trained labour for much of the pastoral industry. Though Scottish immigration was not particularly high the role of the managers was, almost certainly, disproportionate. The career of R.A. Morehead illustrated well the critical importance of managerial skills in the development of the mid-century Australian economy. Company management and colonial administration were sectors in which well-educated and experienced Scots were able to contribute with special success. Another key exemplar was Edward Dea Thomson, an immigrant from Edinburgh who helped shape the development of political institutions in New South Wales in the middle decades of the century.[54] It is likely that the educational background of many Scots was important in their colonial success, and it was not surprising, therefore, that Scots figured strongly among the medical practitioners of colonial Australia, or that a training in Edinburgh opened a career in the outback.[55]

VII

It is not easy to disentangle the Scottish element from general Australian immigration, but it seems unlikely that the Scots were much better represented than their fellow Britons. In the years 1853 to 1880 they comprised about 10 per cent of all British emigrants to all destinations, and 13 per cent of those destined for Australasia; far more went to North America. Official records indicate that 138,036 Scots migrated to Australasia in the same period, though the flow varied greatly from year to year. In the middle decades of the century the Scots immigrants were predominantly domestic servants and general labourers; they got to Australia mainly with the assistance of colonial governments. The Scots offered a general range of proletarian skills for the benefit of Australian development. Colonial policy made a conscious effort to replicate in the colonies the proportions that prevailed in the United Kingdom, and there was some attempt to compensate for the relatively large numbers of Irish and Catholic already resident in the colonies. For this reason, and others, most Scots were regarded as eminently suitable immigrants. Each colony organised assisted immigration schemes from time to time, according to its labour needs, and, as well, there were specialised societies facilitating the flows. Within the United Kingdom the Colonial Land and Emigration Commissioners also responded to special circumstances in which groups requested assistance. In 1852 for instance the Commissioners despatched several groups requesting relief by emigration, including shepherds (almost certainly Highlanders) and broadloom weavers (from the Scottish lowlands). In each case the emigration clearly identified declining elements in the Scottish economy, highly suitable to fill labour shortages in Australia resulting from the gold rushes. Another flow was promoted by the Scottish Australian Emigration Society, formed in Glasgow in July 1853, which also sought to alleviate the problems of the redundant handloom weavers. In the same period a Victorian agent, Bonney, was sent to Scotland with £3,500 to mobilise 5,000 Scottish immigrants. An even more ambitious scheme, the brainchild of Charles Trevelyan, was the Highland and Island Emigration Society, which sought to match the population crisis in the Highlands with the needs of the colonies. The Society transmitted 5,000 in the mid 1850s, many of whom arrived in the poorest physical and mental condition, often to meet a mixed if not hostile reception. Some of these Highland immigrants were described as 'poverty-stricken Gaels', likely to be 'too indolent' to suit the needs of employers. More to the point, many arrived after the end of the gold boom, to face conditions of severe oversupply on the labour markets.

There were many tragedies amid the general success story of Scottish immigration. In contrast one of the successful Highland immigrants of the 1850s wrote home

> Now Sandy, it is no profit to me to tell you lies. That I will not . . . this is the richest town of its size in the world . . . How long I would be in Skye before I would gather as much . . . we did not feel any hunger since we left home.[56]

Those who survived the voyage and the adjustment to Australia usually joined the rural proletariat. Nevertheless there were some specific concentrations of Highland settlement. In 1854 there were 1,500 Highlanders in Geelong alone, and when they rose to the ranks of squatters or selectors they tended to congregate in particular areas such as New England or the Mount Gambier district.

Anthony Trollope, touring Australia in 1873, remarked that 'In the colonies those who make money are generally Scotchmen, and those who do not are mostly Irishmen'[57] William Kelly made an effort to capture the national character of the Scots immigrants of the 1850s, and it led him (like so many others) into inevitable caricature. In contrast to the English in the colonies – who prospered and then increased their standard of living and bought, for example, a horse and gig – the successful Scot tended far less towards consumption. Thus, 'instead of squandering his savings in fleeting amusements, he erects them into a balance at the bankers, the contemplation of which never fails to suffuse him with rapturous delight'.[58] On the goldfields Kelly reported that the Scots diggers (in company with the Americans) were high in the ranks of the agitators who made radical demands for their rights.[59] There is, indeed, evidence of a democratic spirit among the Gaelic Scots on the goldfields.[60] George Dunderdale, remarking on the prominence of Highlanders in Victoria, said that 'the news of the discovery of Gippsland must often have been imparted in Gaelic, for many of the children of the mist could speak no English when they landed'.[61] William Craig reported from Bendigo that 'The German camps were strong in music, but they lapse into silence when stirring martial strains are commenced on the bagpipes by enthusiastic Scottish Highlanders, who are numerous in Bendigo, every gully, indeed, having its pipes and pipers.'[62] Some of the diggers rejoiced in their escape from 'the tyranny and oppression of Lairds and Factors'.

Contemporary observations, which revealed little beyond the diversity of colonial behaviour, were reinforced by William Howitt who also observed the goldfields in 1854. He gave voice to the growing irritation of the English with the Highlanders.

Ten times Scotch . . . are all the Highlanders we have hitherto come across. Poor as rats at home, they are as rapacious as rats abroad. There is scarcely a year at home that there is not a piteous outcry about the poor famishing Highlanders; but catch a Highlander out here that has any feeling for an Englishman except that of fleecing him.[63]

Both the merits and the personality defects of the colonial Scots were reported almost always with journalistic exaggeration. The search for the typical Scot was illusive then and since.

The response of ordinary Scots is not easy to capture from the fragments of letters that survive. One Kenneth McCrea, who arrived in Melbourne in 1852, was initially shocked by the violence of colonial society, but thought it 'a first rate country for poor hard working men if they can keep sober'. He testified that 'good servants always get ready employment, especially Scotch'. Neil McCullum, from Argyll and then Glasgow, arrived at Geelong in 1854 and wrote feelingly, 'I will be wealthier at the end of one year here than I was at the end of seventeen years of slavery.' Catherine Dickson, a domestic servant, had left Scotland in about 1846; 14 years later she recommended Victoria to her girlhood friends — 'Tell them they will all get married if they come out here. Cripple ones, deaf and dumb females, all get married over here.' An Aberdonian blacksmith of Mt Prospect in Victoria also spoke praise — 'This is a very fine healthy country and very civil country. Everyone is thought as good as another and no pride among them like the poor creatures of farmers in Scotland.'[64]

There was a district in New England (perhaps wrongly so named) which, in its local history, summarised the mechanisms of immigration, capital investment, and settlement which linked Scotland and Australia in the middle decades of the century. Wollomombi was first occupied by squatters in the 1830s and 1840s, large dominant landowners in good grazing country. They employed shepherds many of whom were Scots, brought out as free immigrants with skills and muscle. When much of the land was thrown open for selection by the Robertson Land Acts in the 1870s these people were able to gain their own foothold.[65] Among them there was an unusual concentration of people at Wollomombi who had originally hailed from the Lochiel and Fort William districts; it was said that 'at least four-fifths of the early settlers in this region were Highlanders of the best type, courteous, kindly, hospitable and absolutely trustworthy'. To begin with they lived in primitive pioneering conditions, bringing a native self-sufficiency to their household economies, their energies much consumed by the labour intensive pastoralism of the day. They engaged in appalling conflict with the aborigines, raised large families and lived within a strict Presbyterian regime. Some spoke only Gaelic; most began as shepherds and had graduated through overseeing prior to taking up a selection of their own account. Some became very rich.[66]

On the Darling Downs, the story was similar in most essentials. The first squatter was a Scot, John Campbell of Beebo, and it was Aberdonian capital which helped finance the Leslies, Gammies and Dalrymples when they too settled in the region. Stations and pastoral companies were financed through the North British Australasian Company and the Scottish Australian Investment Company, both of which invested heavily during the 1870s. The ladder of upward mobility was clear: 'Scots squatters were shrewd, hardworking and successful pastoralists, most of whom had risen from the ranks of the pastoral employees.' Often of humble origins such Scots arrived as general utility labourers, became overseers, rose to be managers, and meanwhile saved enough to become owners of freehold property. Steele Rudd defined the progressive lowland Scots agricultural capitalists — 'they believed in land — these Scottish pioneers, and in sheep, and in wheat, and in horses, and cows — in all things in fact pertaining to the soil — and the soul.' They imported from the Scotland of the age of improvement the vital concept of agriculture as a business. Many had left Scotland to escape the monopoly landlords; they were able to make rapid fortunes if they got in at the right time. Until the 1870s it was possible to advance in this manner in many theatres of colonisation, but thereafter the costs of entry rose steeply against the small man. When the Downs were opened for selection, after 1865, the smaller man, with little cash and few connections, stood little chance.[67]

When Anthony Trollope toured Australia he was much impressed by the reproduction in the colonies of the caste of the countrymen who could be seen 'occasionally at the clubs and dinner tables in Melbourne, exactly as he finds those of England up in London during the winter frosts or in the month of May'. He thought most had come from Scotland, and then had made their fortunes in Australia: 'Some were butchers, drovers or shepherds themselves but a few years since. But they now form an established aristocracy, with very conservative feelings, and are quickly becoming as firm a country party as that which is formed by our squirearchy at home.' Trollope had identified a Scottish contribution to political life in rural Australia which, indeed, remained powerful into the latter part of the twentieth century.[68]

The success of the Scots in Australia has yet to be demonstrated in any relative, quantified sense.[69] But there were sectors where their role was palpably disproportionate, and the reasons may connect with those which have been attributed to Scottish success in Britain itself. Grappling with the most slippery of historical problems, T.C. Smout has couched part of the explanation in terms of national character, and the effects of 'a remarkably strong native culture below the elite level of the landowners'. The high level of literacy among both peasants and artisans made them 'welcome emigrants and quick learners, disseminators, and adaptors of new technologies when they became available'. He also allows that Calvinism gave them 'a seriousness of purpose that assisted capital accumulation and the processes of economic growth' — and a 'pervasive commitment to the ideology of improvement'. In all it gave Scots people a propensity to emigrate and an aspiration towards higher achievement.[70] In Australia there is plenty of impressionistic evidence of 'the achieving Scot', but the historian Duncan Waterson has questioned part of the conventional thesis. He concedes that the Scots Presbyterians in Australia equated material success with individual virtue, and that their Calvinism was well adapted to successful pioneering; but he doubts that the full Weber thesis can apply to colonial society:

> That the Scots considered that thrift, frugality and hard work led to inevitable rural success can be accepted. But these beliefs were also held by many successful Irish Roman Catholic boss-cockies. What is undisputable is the triumph of urban capitalistic techniques and controls in New World agriculture. Religious beliefs as such, however, played only a small part in this economic development.[71]

The Scots abroad provide some useful tests of several hypotheses relating to the Scots need for achievement and their economic success.

It may well be that the Scottish influence in Australia was most fully exercised in the broadest and least definable cultural forms. Some would say that the austere requirements of Presbyterian doctrine have exerted a profound (and not always welcome) influence on Australian life and culture ever since white settlement. It is literally impossible to know the influence, for good or bad, of John Dunmore Lang, 'the old disturber', who sought to found a Scottish colony in eastern Australia, to which he assumed an inevitable independence would eventually be accorded. The cultural impact of his fellow churchmen, religious imperialists all, was probably greater and much reinforced through the medium of education. Sometimes they introduced a form of education potently combined with Benthamism and Presbyterianism. As Geoffrey Serle says, Lang's migrants 'were conscious cultural missionaries, who brought with them the superior achievements of Scottish education', and invaded Australian schools with the weapons of arithmetic, geometry and Adam Smith.[72] They transferred endless theological controversy and schism to Australia.[73] At all levels, including the universities, Australian education bore the marks of Scottish parentage.

The cultural influence was indefinable and was probably carried as much by the Scots philosophy and morality contained in English baggage, as in that of the Scots themselves. One Scot is worth individual notice: Nicol Drysdale Stenhouse (1806-73) was Australia's first and probably only important literary patron in the nineteenth-century. A 'Maecenas of Australian literature', he gave encouragement to writers in the Sydney of the 1850s and 1860s, and shaped the intellectual development of Australia. A quiet lawyer, born in Melrose, educated at Edinburgh University, he left Scotland partly because of poor prospects of employment at home, and partly because of the encouragement of family friends in the colony. He brought to Australia the vision of the Scottish humanists, the world of the *Edinburgh Review*. He was indeed the authentic, self-conscious carrier of Scottish intellectual values and, as his biographer observes, 'At the age of thirty-three Stenhouse had become the sort of intellectual needed in the colonial environment — widely read, yet scholarly, discriminating yet encouraging, practical and generous.'[74] But most Scots, though they were literate were, unlike Stenhouse, far from intellectual.

In the period 1860-1919 the Australian colonies mounted various programmes of immigration, often in competition for people with North America, and between themselves. F.K. Crowley, in a large sample of Government assisted immigrants, found that 13.1 per cent (57,686) came from Scotland. Of this number Queensland took the lion's share (33,116), followed by New South Wales (8,636), Victoria (5,247), South Australia (4,820), Western Australia (4,817) and Tasmania (1,053). Of these assisted immigrants most came from the central belt of Scotland — Lanarkshire, Edinburgh, Midlothian, followed by Aberdeenshire, Forfarshire and Ayrshire. The previous disproportion of destitute Highlanders had diminished. Those Scots who came to Australia without assistance, as far as the evidence permits any certainty, appear to have accorded with the proportions within the British population. The Scottish element in the British contribution to the Australian population was well sustained, as census evidence shows in Table 5.1.

Table 5.1: Origin of UK-born Australian Residents (Percentage Distribution at Census Dates)

	Percentage of Australians resident in Australia and born in parts of the United Kingdom						
	1861	1871	1881	1891	1901	1911	1921
England & Wales	56.33	53.92	54.93	57.28	57.93	60.61	68.24
Scotland	15.48	14.65	14.25	15.08	14.97	15.76	16.15
Ireland	28.19	31.43	30.82	27.64	27.10	23.63	15.61

In part this reflected the continuing inflow of Scots, in part the relative decline of the Irish after 1881.[75]

The actual destination of the Scots immigrants is not clear, but it is likely that, increasingly, they entered the urban labour forces. During the years 1860-90 Australia had become the most urbanised of all the countries of recent settlement, and a diminishing proportion of its people settled on the land, despite recurrent rural labour shortages.

The effect of large-scale Scottish immigration was to create local patriotisms, sometimes expressed in the mushrooming of Scottish institutions. Emigré Scots communities — as, for instance, in London, Canada, the United States — typically maintained a pronounced Highland element, as if to emphasise a distinctiveness. The St Andrews Society was formed in Melbourne in 1846, but the greatest growth occurred in the aftermath of the gold rushes — there sprang into being the Geelong Commun Na Fienne in 1856, the Maryborough Highland Society in 1857, and Caledonian Societies at Ballarat in 1858, and Bendigo in 1859.[76]

The Scottish societies continued to emerge in the following decades, but rose to a peak in the years 1906-10 when, in Victoria alone, 17 new societies were formed. In 1905 it was necessary to create a federal body, the Scottish Union, to give order to the multiplication. These societies were, in several respects, the counterparts of Irish bodies in Australia and elsewhere. They were designed specifically to counteract the apparent and growing dominance of English influences in Australia. They had many of the same priorities as their Irish equivalents: their three aims were to regulate and control Scottish sports; to establish scholarships for children of Scottish descent; and to attack the tendency for the word 'English' to serve for matters which concerned the whole of Britain. They were an expression of Scottish identity, symbolic of Scottish culture and fraternity, and given further visibility by the erection of an extraordinary number of Burns statues throughout the land. It was all done in an effort to resist the homogenisation of the Scots into a society which was being dominated by what were identified as specifically English forms.

VIII

Much of the Scottish story in Australia in the half century up to the First World War was related to the expansion of the Scottish interest in the Australian capital market. By 1850 Scotland had become a large participant in the now fully articulated system of economic relations associated with the *Pax Britannica*. In this system there were simultaneous flows of capital, labour and expertise to the new world; capital called up in Glasgow and Edinburgh offered serious alternatives to London within the general framework of the British capital market. And, as A.R. Hall observes, 'it is wrong to discuss the story of British capital inflows simply in terms of the initiative of Australian borrowers and conversely to regard the activity of Australian borrowers as passive.'[77] There appears to have been equal vigour and enthusiasm at both ends of the chain of capital: Scotland was particularly well equipped to supply capital, and Australia was fully geared to attract capital through a wide range of commercial links and institutions. It became an alliance of economic interests, and one freely entered into: on both sides there was sharp practice (especially in advertising and in funding arrangements) but it was essentially a reciprocal connection formed between participants in the international world of capital.

Australian economic development was by no means exclusively limited to pastoral or primary industry development, and indeed, in the 1870s and 1880s, some of the largest capital outlays were in the heady expansion of Melbourne and the other cities. Nevertheless it was the great pastoral boom which achieved most prominence in the investor's mind; millions of pounds of British investment were directed to the grazier through the wool merchants and banks. Some capital was channelled through direct investment in Australian companies, but a large part of the story is contained in the operations of specialised pastoral companies which were notably successful in attracting Scottish funds. As J.D. Bailey points out, these institutions were 'a significant feature of the financial web of British imperialism. The pastoral finance companies were . . . the instrument through which British capital helped develop the farflung empire.'[78] In this the Scots not only provided a surprisingly large part of the capital, but also the expertise in management and, as well, part of the banking structure. By 1852 there were reports that Scottish stock exchanges (especially Aberdeen) had become obsessed with Australian gold speculation and, by extension and more lastingly, by Australian investment companies. Despite recurrent setbacks (for example, the collapse of the Glasgow financial boom in 1857) the land company emerged as the favoured Scots investment, and it provided opportunities for all sorts of investors, including those of a speculative turn of mind. The great success of the Scottish Australian Company had a continuing demonstration effect.[79] So did other spectacular successes — Charles Tennant, principal founder of the multinational Tharsis enterprise, graduated from speculations in the British railway mania of the 1840s, to a series of Australian land ventures in which he scored a cool reward of £80,000, which formed the foundation of further gains in his widely spread activities in chemicals and mining.[80]

The record of a single pastoral company may exemplify the mechanisms which facilitated the development of the export base of the Australian economy. Gibbs Ronald and Company, founded in the 1850s, was the precursor of what became the Australian Mercantile and Finance Company. Essentially an alliance of expatriate Scots, it became expert in the provision of capital to the pastoral industry. Robert Bruce Ronald, from an Ayrshire family with connections in the Liverpool wool trade, emigrated to the Barwon River district in 1854. A splendid example of the Calvinist temperament, Ronald was shocked by the *mores* of Australian society; townsmen were, he said, 'generally speaking a low mushroom underbred race', for whom he had little respect. He complained, 'Business, business is the only thing, money making the only pursuit and the people have no other pleasure.' In fact, like most others, he became much devoted to commerce, notably in his partnership with Gibbs.[81] The company developed its connections with Scotland further in 1865 when Richard Gibbs visited the homeland to raise funds. There he was able to tap into the embryonic network of capital connections which relied on the services of local solicitors, who for decades had in Scotland advised clients on investment, as well as legal, matters. Gibbs organised several solicitors to advertise for funds on behalf of the Company, offering high-yielding securities. It was able to slot into the Scottish system which had already accustomed the Scottish investing public to the idea of debentures secured on uncalled capital and assets.

In 1865-6 the Gibbs Ronald enterprise already raised 10 per cent of its capital in Scotland and its successor was dependent almost entirely on Scottish and English capital by 1877. It continued to make sorties into the Scottish market which, despite apparent risks, was not deterred from investment in Australia. Much of the capital was secured on illiquid pastoral advances. The collapse of the City of Glasgow Bank in 1870 inevitably damaged business confidence, particularly since the Bank had been dabbling in land transactions, and Australian securities were heavily implicated in the collapse;[82] but Scottish investors, perhaps because of the constricted character of the home capital market, continued to look outwards, especially in the 1880s.

> This was the era of promotions of Scottish investment trusts special- ising in overseas securities . . . and of Australian finance and banking companies which issued terminable debentures similar to those of the Scottish heritable security companies and banks.[83]

The formation of land mortgage companies was particularly vigorous in the years 1878 to 1884, reflecting the rising Australian demand for funds and a readiness to pay 10 per cent on invested capital. Since finance could be raised in Britain at 4 per cent or 5 per cent there was obviously great scope for financial enterprise to link the markets. A.R. Hall has expressed surprise at the prominence of Scotland and its partic- ular ease of raising subscriptions; he offers two general reasons: first, the efficacy of the sales techniques of company agents; and second, the confidence which was accorded by Scots to Australian debentures at a time when there were few safe securities within Scotland which could yield comparable returns.[84]

Writing in *Blackwood's* in 1884, W.R. Lawson also expressed wonder at the extraordinary record of Scottish investment and enterprise abroad. In somewhat hyperbolic terms he said 'From an unknown inaccessible corner of the world [Scotland] has been transformed with- in the life of two generations into the favourite haunt of the tourist and the house of merchant princes.' He claimed that three quarters of foreign and colonial investment companies were of Scottish origin, or hatched by Scots on Scottish models. The Australian experience fitted the thesis, within which there was, however, a suggestion of folly – 'for a small country like Scotland to be able to spare, even for a time, tens of millions sterling, is one of the most striking paradoxes in the history of commerce'. Lawson argued that the small differential return on overseas investment was out of all proportion to the additional risk. Land companies in particular, were too adept at extracting Scots' savings: he feared the collapse of 'fancy stocks'. He advocated a greater consideration for domestic investment: 'it looks almost like mockery to ask if the extra 1 per cent or even 2 per cent interest which may be earned abroad, is worth the spasms of agony with which the distant harvest has to be gleaned'.[85]

These doctrines flew in the face of the prevailing collective psychology of Scottish investment, especially that relating to Australia. It was the high propensity to take risks which enabled the Scots to accumulate long-term colonial investments which yielded returns far into the future. There were periodic and sometimes appalling losses but, on the whole, the record was remarkably prosperous and stable and owed much to the institutional framework which connected Scottish savings with colonial enterprise. J.D. Bailey, who explored this mechanism in detail, credited the Scottish success in Australia to 'the willingness of Scottish solicitors to raise funds on behalf of overseas companies'. In the 1880s, on his estimate, 40 per cent of all Australian borrowing came from this source. Solicitors, and chartered accountants, generated funds and then remitted them through the appointed agent of an Australian company. It was said that Edinburgh in the 1880s was 'honeycombed' with such agencies which were exceedingly lucrative and much sought after by Scottish solicitors.[86] Some observers invoked as explanation the characteristic thriftiness of the Scots; their institutions were certainly remarkably well-geared to reap a small margin on overseas investment. The critical feature of the system was its broad base: it tapped savings even in the most remote parts of Scotland, and from the smallest investors. This system of capital mobilisation saved Australian enterprise from total dependence on London. The solicitors played an active part in diverting Scottish savings abroad, a tendency which Bailey (and other economic historians) attribute to the general deficiency of domestic outlets, and the existence of a pool of capital continuously surplus to the needs of the Scottish economy. Moreover the sustained decline of local interest rates 'increased investment by Scottish insurance companies in overseas rather than domestic securities'. If there is doubt about the reality of capital glut in Scotland, there is no doubt that the development of the Australian economy was accelerated by its easy access to the investible funds of the Scots.[87]

The principal borrowers were banks and finance companies involved in pastoral development. Usually they were strictly investment concerns: 'they rarely managed and operated pastoral properties on their own account, but most Australian woolgrowers were indebted to them in one way or another'. The banks generally worked with direct deposits, but the companies operated mainly by way of short-term debentures, often amounting to a large nominal capital of which perhaps only a fifth was actually paid up. The uncalled portion was then used as a security for the issue of debentures and deposits, high gearing ratios enabled the holders of equity capital to obtain large profits. It was a speculative and, ultimately, a fragile structure of capital transfer. By the 1880s it is probable that more than a third of all Australian pastoral, mortgage and investment company securities were owed to Scotland.

The network by which capital for Australia was raised in Scotland undoubtedly facilitated the process of credit transfer, even to the extent of 'determining the ability of the overseas companies to borrow'. In the late 1880s the overseas competition for British funds intensified and some Australian land companies felt that they were losing ground. Consequently 'they played the bold card of opening London offices with local professional directors and Scottish agencies, thereby hoping to attract depositors in the same way as the banks of issue'. Again the Scots seem to have responded more vigorously and, when the London capital market turned away from Australia, in the following decade, Scotland's role grew still larger. Bailey cites the example of D. Johnston Smith and Williamson which raised more than £5 million for five Australian banks in the years 1883 to 1893. Nearly all the banks advertised in Scottish newspapers for funds, they raised deposits of £50 or more on terms which allowed their creditors to make sudden withdrawals.[88] Thereby the vulnerability of the structure of capital was increased.

The scale and intensity of capital operations in Australia changed during the great land boom of the 1880s. The general criteria of investment almost certainly deteriorated, and the Scots were heavily involved in the frenetic expansion of credit. There was a shift towards investment in urban land mortgage, particularly for the building of 'Marvellous Melbourne'. Many urban land finance companies operated under the guise of 'banks' or 'building societies'; they eventually proved to be the weakest links in the chain of capital. The fact that insurance companies were now heavily committed to colonial outlets may have encouraged the illusion of security. The Scottish Widows' Fund and Scottish Provident, each of which invested £1 million in Australia in 1886-9, sent out special representatives to locate the best investments, in land and 'first class city property'. Their rectitude may have saved them in the coming 'Crash of '93'. A.R. Hall has judged that, for many other creditors, the conditions of capital investment were insecure. The earning power of Australian stock depended on the continued flow of funds, almost all of which was committed on a short-term basis. 'Once the flow dried up, however, as it did when the rottenness of many Australian financial institutions in the early nineties began to come to the surface, it was realised that they were a fundamental source of weakness.'[89] The in-built volatility of British (including Scottish) deposits in Australia eventually precipitated the banking crisis in 1893.

IX

Scotland, therefore, made a disproportionate contribution to capital foundation in Australia, and also exerted a formative influence on the evolution of the banking system and its practices. Taking the two elements together, it is not surprising that, in the blame apportioned for the financial catastrophe of 1893, the Scots have received a disproportionate share. After all, in the two decades after 1870 Scottish overseas investment grew ninefold, and in the year immediately prior to the crisis Scotland was the dominant source of loanable funds: 'the Scottish situation provided the key to the continued flow of British capital to the Australian colonies'.[90] The boom had been fuelled by 'a dizzy inflow of capital' increasingly fermented in Scotland. The indictment of the Scots creditors was even more specific: some observers (and historians) claimed that the crisis of 1893 was precipitated by the refusal of Scots investors to renew their terminable deposits and debentures due to mature on the Scottish Whitsun term day, 15th May — thus signalling the collapse of a large proportion of Australian banks and financial institutions.[91]

Contemporary explanations of the crash stressed the dependence of Australia on British, notably Scottish, investors: 'as Britain opens or closes her hand to lend, so the prosperity of these colonies advances or declines'. During the crisis 14 out of 25 Australian banks suspended payment. The revealed fragility of the Australian banks was regarded with astonishment because they were thought to run on 'the Scotch system' and were 'often staffed by Scotsmen'.[92] For many decades the Scottish influence in Australian banking circles had indeed been regarded as a guarantee of sobriety and professionalism. In 1880 Mortimer Franklyn had remarked that

> We should not be very far wrong perhaps in attributing the circumspection with which business on a large scale is conducted in Melbourne, to the fact that the Scottish element has always been influential in financial and mercantile circles.

Robert Ronald captured the general reputation of Scottish probity and efficiency in 1889 when he said, 'we require a Scotsman with good colonial experience or one who could acquire it soon'.[93]

The close associations between Scottish and Australian banks not only generated 'a good atmosphere for confident investment' but, it has been said, exerted a formative influence on Australian financial structures, most specifically in the development of branch banking. S.J. Butlin, historian of early Australian banking, somewhat deflated these claims. He pointed out that, in fact, Scots did not predominate and that the pressure of local financial needs (rather than imported Scottish ideas) caused banks to spread themselves into branch banking. Yet though the influence of Scots may not have been specific, it may have been pervasive. George Kinnear, the first general manager of the Bank of Australasia (in 1834), recruited most of its officers in his home city, Edinburgh.[94] The 'Scotch system' in banking may indeed have related more to matters of psychology and temperament than technique. In 1880 (only a decade or so before the system collapsed in disaster) the prominent banker, Henry Giles Turner, wrote a paean of praise to the Victorian banking system:

> We are to a great extent, removed from the influence of that increasing panic which is the marked characteristic of Englishmen in times of doubt and difficulty, and, by the long familiarity with the Scottish system of banking, have acquired that confidence in the depositories of our surplus cash that is the marked disposition of the North Briton.

During the crisis of 1893 the *Bankers' Magazine* cautioned Australians against radical, un-Scottish solutions to the problem.[95] There was probably too much automatic obeisance to Scottish practice. When, in 1887, the Scottish manager of the Colonial Bank of Australasia appeared before a Royal Commission on Banking Loans, he justified a policy of low liquidity ratios on the grounds that the Scottish banks, with their renowned care and prudence, set the correct example. As E.A. Boehm says, it was an opinion which made no allowance for the local peculiarities of banking in Australia. Too often the invocation of Scottish practice was the excuse for local conservatism, and sometimes inappropriate to Australian needs.[96]

Recent research has also diminished the opprobrium that contemporaries directed against the Scottish investors during the moment of crisis in 1893. Boehm (in opposition to Bailey) argues that the Scottish withdrawals were not decisive:

> The facts indicate that the banking crisis . . . would have occurred largely as it did whether British depositors had intended to withdraw or not. But it is still true that its large holdings of British deposits was a great inherent weakness of the banking system.

Nevertheless the implication was, in part, that the remarkable propensity of the British, especially the Scots, to invest in Australia in the 1880s, helped to create structural weakness in the economy. This was the other side of the coin which attributes great benefit to the overseas capital investment in Australian development. It also suggests that the criteria of investment adopted by Scottish investors, were over-optimistic. In the early twentieth century the Scots appear to have generally withdrawn their funds from the land mortgage and insurance companies. In many respects it was an end of an era.[97]

X

The crash of 1893 revealed more than the weakness of the Australian financial system. It exposed also several other strands of the Scottish story in Australia. It was not surprising that many Scots who came to Australia in the decade of the gold rushes eventually became prominent in the hazardous boom of the 1880s. The success, and subsequent failure, of some of the Scots in property finance caused a certain degree of malicious celebration among contemporary writers, especially those who had little sympathy for Presbyterian *mores*.

Two Scots of these years exemplify the story. James Munro, born in a Sutherlandshire village, migrated to Edinburgh where he became a printer, and in 1859, aged 20, he departed for Melbourne. He entered the property mortgage business, and founded the Victorian Permanent Building Society which he managed for 17 years. In the wild boom of 1887-9 he became a millionaire. He was a member of the Victorian Legislative Council by 1874 and served as Premier in 1890. He fell heavily in the crash and, like many fellow countrymen, fought vainly to recover his fortunes. James Balfour (1830-1913) followed a career not dissimilar, but he came to personify the most public and caricatured face of Scottish influence in Australia. The son of a sternly Calvinistic Edinburgh corn merchant, Balfour went to London at the age of 18 and four years later, in 1852, accepted a position with a projected Australian company with strong Scottish connections. His was then a relentless rise to affluence and power, and the accumulation of property during the boom. He was a member of the Victorian Legislative Council for most years from 1866 to 1913, a newspaper proprietor, company director and sheep station owner. He was also the most prominent Presbyterian layman of his day, the very personification of Presbyterian aspirations to godliness and property. He was one of a coterie of establishment figures in 'Marvellous Melbourne' who built extravagant coffee palaces to adorn the city, to lead the people to better ways, while they themselves got drunk on finance.

Contemporary writers were much intrigued by the likes of Munro and Balfour who seemed to combine extreme Scottish probity, Presbyterian temperance, and the highest moral tone, with the most rapacious speculative drive. Balfour was accused of sailing close to the wind of acceptable commercial practice; he narrowly escaped sequestration when his affairs collapsed in 1893. On his death he was vilified as 'the King-pin of Victorian Presbyterianism, a Top-Note of parritch piety, and the keystone of the whole Wowseristic edifice'.[98] It was a taunt levelled at many successful Scots in late nineteenth-century Australia. Another, whose reputation was similarly tarnished, was Sir Thomas McIlwraith, the energetic entrepreneur who eventually became Premier of Queensland. It has been said that

> McIlwraith's ethics displayed the harsh double standards of many Calvinists. He once reproached a politician for reading a newspaper on Sunday although he himself drank to excess, fathered an illegitimate daughter in Victoria and did not emerge blameless from the three largest financial scandals in Queensland history.[99]

The role of the Scots as social controllers, as muscular capitalists, as prime ministers, journalists, scientists, artists, educators and benefactors,[100] must all remain indeterminate. The common wisdom, and the caricature, is that they were disproportionately prosperous, pious and practical, but there is no systematic knowledge to verify such propositions. It is perfectly possible that their national drink contributed as much to Australian morality as their cultural values.

Notes

1. This essay is primarily a commentary on the existing literature on the Scots in Australia, and is written mainly with non-Australian readers in mind. I wish to thank Dr C.W. Munn of Glasgow University and Mrs Joan Hancock of the Flinders University for their help, and to acknowledge my special debt to the published works of D.S. Macmillan and J.D. Bailey, whose analyses of Scottish investment in Australia have been indispensable to this study.

2. C.M.H. Clark, *A Discovery of Australia* (Sydney, 1976), p. 47.

3. See James Scott, 'The Scottish Martyrs Farms', *Journal of the Royal Australian Historical Society* (hereafter *JRAHS)*, vol. 46 (August 1960).

4. A.G.L. Shaw, *Convicts and the Colonies* (London, 1966), pp. 164-5.

5. Quoted in L.C. Robson, *The Convict Settlers of Australia* (Melbourne, 1976), p. 10.

6. A. Majoribanks, quoted in Lloyd Evans and Paul Nicholls, *Convicts and Colonial Society 1788-1853* (Sydney, 1976), p. 132.

7. Archibald Alison, quoted in Evans and Nicholls, *Convicts and Colonial Society*, p. 133.

8. Ibid.

9. Robson, *Convict Settlers*, pp. 44-5, 76, 78, 130; see also L. Robson, 'Origins of the Women Convicts sent to Australia 1787-1852', *Historical Studies*, VII (1963).

10. On the career of a successful ex-convict from Scotland see Andrew Thompson (1733?-1810) in *Australian Dictionary of Biography* (hereafter *ADB*), vol. 2, p. 519.

11. See J.V. Barry, 'Captain Alexander Maconochie R.N., K.H., *Victorian Historical Magazine*, Vol. XXVII (June 1957).

12. See for instance the career of Charles Cameron (1779-1827) in *ADB*, vol. I, pp. 196-7.

13. M.H. Ellis, 'British Military Regiments in Australia', *JRAHS*, vol. XXXVII (1951).

14. Cf. the career of William Douglas Campbell (1770-1827) in *ADB*, vol. I, pp. 208-9.

15. See Margaret Steven, 'Robert Steven – His Scottish Background', *JRAHS*, Vol. 46 (1960); *Merchant Campbell* (Melbourne, 1965); David S. Macmillan, 'Scottish Enterprise in Australia 1798-1879', in Peter L. Payne, *Studies in Scottish Business History* (London, 1967).

16. D.S. Macmillan, *Scotland and Australia, 1788-1850: Emigration, Commerce and Investment* (Oxford, 1967), pp. 61-3.

17. Ibid., p. 74.

18. Cf. J.M. Bumsted, *The People's Clearance* (Edinburgh, 1982).

19. See Thomas Francis Bride, *Letters from Victorian Pioneers* (Melbourne, 1969), pp. 146-150; Alexander Henderson, *Early Pioneers of Victoria and Riverina* (Melbourne, 1936); James Dixon, *Narrative of a Voyage to New South Wales and Van Diemen's Land in the Ship Skelton during the year 1820* (Edin-

burgh, 1922). See also G.H. Crawford, 'The Scotts: Thomas, George and James', *Tasmanian Historical Research Association*, vol. 14 (1956).

20. La Trobe Library, Melbourne, Papers of the Wilson Family, MF940.

21. Mitchell Library, Sydney, Wentworth Papers, D'Arcy Wentworth Correspondence 1821-7, A754-1, p. 181, R.L. Murray to Wentworth, 15 May 1823.

22. Mitchell Library, Sydney, Waugh Papers, A827. David Waugh to John Waugh, 28 September 1834.

23. D.S. Macmillan, *Scotland and Australia*, p. 153.

24. Ibid., p. 164.

25. Waugh Papers, David Waugh to Miss Eliza Waugh, 25 September 1837. See also Mitchell Library, Despatches to the Governor of New South Wales (A1275), John Dunmore Lang, 11 March 1837; Christine Dobbin, 'Dr John Dunmore Lang and the Challenge of the Colonial Environment' (unpublished History Honours thesis, University of Sydney, 1961); J.D. Lang, *Transportation and Colonization* (1837), p. vi.

26. See for instance G.F. Davidson, quoted in R.B. Ward, *The Australian Legend* (Melbourne, 1958), p. 49. For successful Highland immigrants see, for example, Victor Feehan, *Alexander Cameron, King of Penola. A Biographical Sketch* (Doncaster, Victoria, 1979); *ADB*, vol. V, p. 165 (John Mackintosh). See also J.A. Maher, *Kilmore 1837-1937* (Lowden, Kilmore, 1938), which has miscellaneous material about some of these immigrants.

27. George Dunderdale, *The Book of the Bush* (c. 1870; reprinted Melbourne, 1973), p. 165. See also Nehemiah Bartley, *Australian Pioneers and Reminiscences* (1896; reprinted Brisbane 1978), p. 44.

28. William Kelly, *Life in Victoria* (London, 1859), I, pp. 108, 369. William Howitt, *Land, Labour and Gold* (London, 1855), p. 67. See also Geoffrey Serle, *The Golden Age* (Melbourne, 1963), p. 2.

29. Quoted in Paul De Serville, *Port Phillip Gentlemen and Good Society in Melbourne before the Gold Rushes* (Melbourne, 1980), p. 41.

30. Records of the Port Phillip Association, La Trobe Library, Melbourne.

31. Ibid.

32. Stephen Roberts, *The Squatting Age in Australia* (Melbourne, 1935), p. 307.

33. Margaret Kiddle, *Men of Yesterday: A Social History of the Western District of Victoria 1834-1890* (Melbourne, 1961), pp. 14, 24, 39.

34. See D.S. Macmillan, *The Debtor's War* (Melbourne, 1960), p. 24.

35. See Paul De Serville, *Tubbo: the Great Peter's Run* (Melbourne, 1982), p. 20.

36. *Comfort for the Poor. Meat Three Times a Day. Voluntary Information from the people of New South Wales collected in that Colony by Mrs Chisholm in 1845-46* (London, 1847), Statement no. 29, p. 10. See also, Robert Sutherland, *The History of the Presbyterian Church of Victoria* (London, 1877), pp. 24-5.

37. John E.P. Bushby, *Saltbush Country. A History of the Deniliquin District* (Sydney, 1980), p. 38. See also C. Stuart Ross, 'Some of the Murray Pioneers and their services to the State', *Victorian Historical Magazine*, vol. III (1913-14), pp. 84-5.

38. See Joseph Anderson, *Recollections of a Peninsula Veteran* (London, 1913).

39. J.G. Johnston, *The Truth: Consisting of Letters from Emigrants to the Australian Colonies* (Edinburgh, 1839), p. x. Cf. [Thomas Walker], *A Month in the Bush of Australia* (London, 1838), p. 7.

40. La Trobe Library, MF151, Papers of the Hunter Family of Kalangadoo.

41. Kiddle, *Men of Yesterday*, pp. 33, 44.

42. La Trobe Library, Melbourne, Black Papers, Letterbooks, Outwards, Black

to Gladstone, 16 August 1841.

43. Dunderdale, *Book of the Bush*, pp. 223-5; Roberts, *The Squatting Age*, p. 305. See also De Serville, *Port Phillip Gentlemen*, p. 39.

44. Hal Porter, *Bairnsdale. Portrait of an Australian Country Town* (Sydney, 1977), p. 118. Roberts, *The Squatting Age*, p. 305.

45. Kiddle, *Men of Yesterday*, p. 14.

46. Based on De Serville, *Port Phillip Gentlemen*, pp. 43, 49, 60, 85, 143-9, 169, and Appendices.

47. See A.T. Yarwood and M.J. Knowling, *Race Relations in Australia. A History* (Melbourne, 1982), pp. 174-5. See also Peter Cunningham, *Two Years in New South Wales* (1827; reprinted Sydney 1966, edited by David S. MacMillan).

48. See Graham Abbott and Geoffrey Little (eds.), *A Respectable Sydney Merchant: A.B. Spark of Tempe* (Sydney, 1976).

49. R.C. Michie, *Money, Mania and Markets* (Edinburgh, 1981), pp. 61-2.

50. Macmillan, *Scotland and Australia*, p. 221.

51. This section is based on the work of D.S. Macmillan.

52. Macmillan, *Scotland and Australia*, p. 352.

53. Quoted in Macmillan, *Scotland and Australia*, p. 357.

54. See S.G. Foster, *Colonial Improver. Edward Dea Thomson 1800-1879* (Melbourne, 1978).

55. Based on entries in the *Australian Dictionary of Biography*, vols. I and II.

56. Anthony Trollope, *Australia* (1873, reprinted 1967), p. 420.

57. Quoted in Donna Hellier, 'The Humblies: Scottish Highland Emigration to and Settlement in Victoria, 1850-1900', *Australia 1888*, Bulletin, no. 10 (1982), pp. 64-5.

58. William Kelly, *Life in Victoria* (London, 1859), vol. I, p. 309.

59. Ibid., vol. II, p. 105.

60. See the Hobart Gaelic newspaper, *An Teachdaire Gaidhealach*, 1 August 1857.

61. *Book of the Bush*, p. 199.

62. William Craig, *My Adventures on the Australian Goldfields* (London, 1903), quoted in *Gold Fever*, edited by Nancy Keesing (Sydney, 1967), p. 164.

63. Howitt, *Land, Labour and Gold*, p. 67.

64. A.W. Greig, 'Letters from Australian Pioneers', *Victorian Historical Magazine*, vol. XII (1927), pp. 70-104.

65. Some shepherds were paid wages, but (in various parts of Australia) they chose to work for a share in the increase of the flocks. A successful and thrifty shepherd could thereby rapidly build up his own flock – and eventually compete with his previous employer as a squatter in his own right. See Rica Erickson, *The Victorian Plains* (Osborne Park, 1971), p. 12. Several career paths of emigrant Scots are traced in Maher, *Kilmore 1837-1937*, passim.

66. B.C. Cameron and J.C. McLennan, *Scots' Corner. A Local History* (Armidale, 1971), passim. See also the story of George Fairbairn, in Michael Cannon, *Life in the Country* (Melbourne, 1974), p. 14.

67. This is based on D.B. Waterson, *Squatter, Selector and Storekeeper. A History of the Darling Downs 1859-93* (Sydney, 1968).

68. Trollope, *Australia*, pp. 442-3.

69. There is some evidence. For example in the Victorian Parliament, from 1859 to 1900 something like 30 per cent of the 691 members were born in Scotland. Kathleen Thomson and Geoffrey Serle, *A Biographical Register of the Victorian Parliament, 1859-1900* (Canberra, 1972). Cf. R.B. Ward, *The Australian Legend* (Melbourne, 1958), pp. 48-9. Ward seems to argue that the Scots were too successful, middle class, educated and Presbyterian to add much to popular culture in Australia.

70. T.C. Smout, 'Scotland and England: Is Dependency a Symptom or a Cause of Underdevelopment?' *Review*, vol. III (Spring, 1980), pp. 601-30.

71. Waterson, *Squatter, Selector and Storekeeper*, pp. 134-6.

72. See Derek Whitelock, *The Great Tradition. A History of Adult Education in Australia* (St Lucia, 1974); C. Turney, 'Henry Carmichael – His Advanced Educational Thoughts and Practice', in C. Turney (ed.), *Pioneers of Australian Education* (Sydney, 1969); and Geoffrey Serle, *From the Desert the Prophets Come* (Melbourne, 1973), p. 23.

73. See, for example, K. Elford, 'Church, State, Education and Society: an Analysis of Aspects of Eastern Australian Society, 1856-1872', unpublished PhD thesis, Sydney University, 1971; Keith R. Campbell, 'Presbyterian Conflicts in New South Wales, 1837-1865', *Journal of Religious History*, V (1968-9).

74. See Ann-Marie Jordens, *The Stenhouse Circle* (Melbourne, 1979).

75. F.K. Crowley, 'The British Contribution to the Australian Population 1860-1919', *University Studies in History and Economics*, II (1954).

76. A.H. Chisholm, *Scots Wha Haè. History of the Royal Caledonian Society of Melbourne* (Sydney, 1950), p. 2.

77. A.R. Hall, *The Export of Capital from Britain 1870-1914* (London, 1968), pp. 151-2.

78. J.D. Bailey, *A Hundred Years of Pastoral Banking. A History of the Australian Mercantile and Finance Company, 1863-1963* (Oxford, 1966).

79. Michie, *Money, Mania and Markets*.

80. S.G. Checkland, *The Mines of Tharsis* (London, 1967), p. 97.

81. Based on Bailey, *Pastoral Banking*.

82. Bailey, *Pastoral Banking*, pp. 55 *et seq.*; A.R. Hall, *The London Capital Market and Australia 1870-1914* (ANU, Canberra, 1963), p. 109-10, 167.

83. Bailey, *Pastoral Banking*, pp. 65-6.

84. See Hall, *London Capital Market*, pp. 109-10, 167.

85. W.R. Lawson, 'Scottish Capital Abroad', *Blackwoods Edinburgh Magazine*, CXXXVI (1884).

86. Baxter, quoted in A.S.J. Bastier, *The Imperial Banks* (London, 1929).

87. J.D. Bailey, 'Australian Borrowing in Scotland in the 19th Century', *Economic History Review*, 2nd series, vol. XII, p. 279; Macmillan, 'Scottish Enterprise'; A.R. Hall, *London Capital Market*, p. 112.

88. E.A. Boehm, *Prosperity and Depression in Australia 1887-1897* (Oxford, 1971), p. 257; Bailey, 'Australian Borrowing in Scotland', p. 269; A.S.J. Bastier, *The Imperial Banks*, p. 153.

89. Hall, *London Capital Market*, p. 117. *The Bankers' Magazine*, vol. LVII (1894), p. 805.

90. Bailey, *Pastoral Banking*, p. 142.

91. Michie, *Money, Mania and Markets*, p. 133.

92. A.G.V. Peel, *The Australian Crisis of 1893* (London, 1893), p. 3.

93. Quoted in Bailey, *Pastoral Banking*, p. 130.

94. S.J. Butlin, *Foundations of the Australian Monetary System 1788-1851* (Melbourne, 1953), pp. 262, 287.

95. Quoted in Crawford D.W. Goodwin, *Economic Enquiry in Australia* (Durham, NC, 1966), pp. 188-9, 191.

96. See Boehm, *Property and Depression*, p. 236.

97. Ibid., p. 302. See also N.G. Butlin, *Investment in Australian Economic Development 1861-1900* (Cambridge, 1966); Hall, *London Capital Market*, p. 119

98. Quoted in Andrew Lemon, *The Young Man at Home. James Balfour 1830-1913* (Melbourne, 1982), p. 1. See also Michael Cannon, *The Land Boomers*

(Melbourne, 1966), pp. 35, 124-5.

    99. *ADB*, vol. 5, p. 161.

    100. There is an able summary of prominent 'Scots in Australia' by A.H. Chisholm in *The Australian Encyclopaedia* (Sydney, 1958), vol. 8, pp. 32-7.

6 'TAM McCANNY AND KITTY CLYDESIDE' – THE SCOTS IN NEW ZEALAND

Tom Brooking

There is a popularly held belief among New Zealanders that a dour puritanism and canniness were the characteristics which most distinguished nineteenth-century immigrants from Scotland. The stern faces of the founders of Otago glaring down from the walls of Dunedin's Early Settlers' Museum would make even as determined a reprobate as Robbie Burns think twice before engaging in further ribaldry. Likewise, stories concerning the parsimony of Harry Lauder on his visits to New Zealand are legend. Folklore suggests that unrelenting Presbyterian rigour and watching the pennies combined to make New Zealand a more sober, thrifty and respectable country than Australia. The character of our trans-Tasman neighbour was rather shaped by the more colourful and rumbustious southern Irish. Because the Irish were the dominant minority Australia became more American and therefore, inferior. Because the Scots were the dominant minority in New Zealand, the country became more British and therefore, superior. Wakefield's notion that New Zealand was stocked by a more genteel group than Australia lingers on in the minds of most New Zealanders.

Historians, in attempting to discern what is distinctive about New Zealand, have conceded that there might be a grain of truth in this mythology.[1] But it is a begrudging acknowledgement. Generally ethnic differences within New Zealand's European heritage have been played down. Most historians imply that the Scots joined forces with the English hegemony to combat the celtic challenge. Others have stressed the Scots contribution to education,[2] farming,[3] and distilling.[4] The input of Scots capital, especially in relation to the New Zealand and Australian Land Company, has received some attention.[5] Biographies have also been written about several leading entrepreneurs who were born in Scotland.[6] But no one has ventured further than this except for G.L. Pearce in a very lightweight general study.[7] Overall New Zealand historians, unlike their American counterparts, have shown little interest in the role played in national development by ethnic groups.[8]

This chapter can be little more than an exploratory essay. There is nothing like an adequate data base for an authoritative assessment of the Scots' contribution to economic or social or political development in New Zealand. We also need similar studies on English and Irish immigrants if we are to have an adequate framework for comparison. In the meantime the brand of economic history to be reported upon is nearer Robbie Burns than Adam Smith.

An initial assessment of the Scots' contribution to economic development in nineteenth-century New Zealand confirmed the prevailing historical orthodoxy. Nearly all findings appeared negative and there seemed to be little that was distinctive about the Scots. With the exception of the leaders of the Otago Settlers and the Highlanders of Waipu the Scots were typical pioneers caught up in the 'rush to be rich'. The ascetic ideals of William Cargill and Norman McLeod were soon exchanged for the crass and comfortable materialism of all white settler spin-off societies.[9] Furthermore, even though a smaller proportion of Scots than English came from the higher levels of British society, they nevertheless represented the full range of nineteenth-century immigrants to New Zealand. Furthermore, the colonial experience of Scots was much the same as any other group. Some were outstanding successes, the majority achieved modest improvement or stayed roughly the same, and a few worsened their lot. A Scottish background seemed to have little bearing on economic behaviour in New Zealand.

Upon further reflection, however, such negative conclusions and a desire to flirt with outmoded Weberian notions concerning protestantism and capitalism, were rejected. The Scots did make important and distinctive contributions in the areas of capital formation, entrepreneurship, and labour. But this conclusion did not become apparent until the author realised that such supposedly social and political contributions as education and land reform had profound economic ramifications. The desire for improvements in education tells as much about the aspirations brought by immigrants, while setting up educational institutions involved major investment decisions. Scots-born entrepreneurs who promoted the establishment of universities and secondary schools were investing in the nation's future as well as enhancing their personal kudos. Similarly, Scots-born politicians held equally clear ideas on the pattern of economic development which the country should follow. Somehow there was a distinctive Scots approach to national development.

Wealthy Scots were not only acting out of a sense of *noblesse oblige* and a desire for quick profit in committing themselves to community and nation building. They genuinely seemed enthusiastic about the participation in community affairs, and local government committees were preferred to prestigious clubs. Possibly this trait was related to the tradition of sharing out responsibility for parochial affairs among a relatively large number of people.[10] Their life style was also distinctive in that it was usually less ostentatious than that of the rich and powerful English-born merchants and estate owners. Probably this relative modesty and understatement reflected the more egalitarian nature of Scots society,[11] as well as the humbler social origins of well-to-do colonials born in Scotland. But even more important than commitment to democratic institutions and the adoption of a more modest style was the fact that some wealthy Scottish-born landowners, such as Donald Reid, believed fervently in closer settlement. It seemed that rich and poor Scots immigrants alike shared a burning desire to do away with the abuses of landlordism and to create a more just and equitable society. Reid's views in fact were little different from the Scots born and less wealthy political radicals John McKenzie and Robert Stout. Some English-born estate owners, particularly William Rolleston,[12] also supported radical schemes for land reform. But Rolleston was acquiescing to the inevitability of change. This view was essentially negative and stoic whereas that of Reid, McKenzie and Stout was positive and dynamic.

Politicians and entrepreneurs born in Scotland led New Zealand to become a nation of smallholders. Many other groups in the new society, especially the English non-conformist agricultural labourers and the Irish,[13] shared this vision of rough economic and political equality. Market forces also encouraged the move towards intensive farming. But it was the Scots-born politicians who rallied the forces of egalitarianism to win for New Zealand even more progressive land laws than those of Australia.[14] As a result of those laws and the efforts of the Scots-born pioneers of the refrigeration industry, the power of the big landowners was broken earlier than would have otherwise been the case; they made the implementation of McKenzie's land reforms possible.

Yet there was an irony involved. Even though an equality was achieved in New Zealand which would have been impossible of realisation in the old country, it was achieved at the cost of both New Zealand and Scottish independence. The growth of the frozen meat and dairy industries severed almost all financial links with Glasgow and Edinburgh, and shifted the centre of financial control to London. As a result the Scots became as dependent upon English colonialism in their new country as they had been in their old; a point realised by several witnesses to the 1905 Land Commission.[15]

Origins and Destinations

The geographical origins of the immigrants who came from Scotland to New Zealand in the nineteenth century can be established with some degree of certainty, at least in regional terms. Their social origins are also discernable. Likewise their destinations in New Zealand are reasonably easy to establish and the proportion of the colonial population they represented can be calculated precisely. But what is less clear is their detailed reasons for emigrating to such a distant land and undertaking such an arduous and uncomfortable voyage. The subsequent experience of Scottish immigrants after arrival in the new colony is also largely unresearched. Some information has been collated to help fill this gap, but it is only a small beginning.

It is generally assumed that most Scots who travelled to New Zealand went to the colony's most distinctively Scottish settlement – Otago. But in fact Scots came to New Zealand long before the Otago settlement was established in 1848. Scots were represented amongst the sealers, whalers and adventurers who visited New Zealand's shores before the country was annexed by the British in 1840.[16] Several of Auckland's early prominent businessmen were also Scots. Indeed there was frequent complaint of the unfair advantages gained by the 'Scotch Clique' in the early Auckland press. Then in 1842, 500 Scots labourers and artisans came from Renfrewshire and other Lowland areas to help develop the capital city's hinterland.[17] Scots were also sprinkled around the early New Zealand Company settlements of Wellington (1840), Wanganui (1840), New Plymouth (1841), and Nelson (1842).[18] A few settled in Canterbury before the area was colonised in 1850, when more of their countrymen came to join them.[19] But in each case the Scots represented rather insignificant minorities. The Free Church settlement of Otago was quite different in that it was predominantly Scottish.

Although the Otago settlement was never as exclusively Scottish as its promoters would have liked, Maxwell's exhaustive study of the immigrants who came to the province between 1848 and 1860 reveals that 80 per cent were born in Scotland. Most of the remainder, dubbed the 'Little Enemy' by the Scottish establishment, were English. There were very few Irish and no Welsh.

Maxwell has been able to locate the origins of 2,535 of the 4,978 Scots who came to Otago before 1861.[20] The majority came from the small industrial towns situated around the edges of Glasgow and Edinburgh. (Some 28 per cent: nearly 19 per cent from Midlothian and ten per cent from Lanarkshire.) The over-representation of Midlothian

reflected the promotion and initiation of the Otago scheme in Edinburgh. The other major sources of migrants were the small towns and
rural areas of several Lowland counties, in both central and eastern
Scotland, especially Perthshire. By way of contrast only nine per cent
came from the Highlands (excluding Caithness which rather belonged to
the Lowlands in both the geographical and cultural sense). But it seems
likely that there was a considerable degree of second-step migration to
New Zealand. Many of these so-called Lowlanders had probably left the
Highlands only a generation or two before migrating to New Zealand.
Very few came directly from areas worst affected by the clearances
because those areas had been cleared well before Otago was settled. In
sum, all parts of Scotland were represented with the exception of the
Hebrides. A more narrowly focused study by McLean confirms the
numerical dominance and over-representation of Midlothian and Perthshire and the under-representation of Lanarkshire, Scotland's most
populous county.[21]

Maxwell and McLean also agree that the great majority of Scots who
came to Otago were hewers of wood and drawers of water. The capitalists were nearly all English. Some certainly inflated their occupation
upon departure to avoid stigmatism, and the leaders of the new community complained bitterly of the drunken lumpen proletariat whom
they disowned as sassenachs.[22] But generally, despite distortions caused
by misleading occupational labelling and the blatant behaviour of the
bottom social layer, the respectable working class who held rudi-
mentary educational qualifications, were predominant. There were a
few artisans, but they were under represented despite the efforts of the
immigration agents. Even so this shortage did not create too many
problems as the semi-skilled were often more flexible and therefore
better able to cope with the demands of pioneering. Married couples
with small families predominated at first, reflecting the desire of the
settlement's promoters to establish a stable, concentrated community
built around the nuclear family. But single men soon became more
numerous as the reality of the settlement deviated sharply from Wakefield's ideal.

Migration dried to a trickle in the early 1850s and did not revive
until 1858 when a modest recovery based on the development of
pastoralism persuaded more to come between 1858 and 1860. The
dynamic immigration agent – James Adam – also played a part in
reactivating the flow of migrants for his personal success made him the
best of all possible advertisements. Then something happened which

dramatically altered the pattern of immigration as well as the development of Otago and New Zealand; gold was discovered at Gabriel's Gully in August 1861.

Thousands of gold miners flocked to Otago from Victoria. A significant proportion, perhaps a quarter, were Scots. But this new influx was different in that the miners, whether Scots, Irish or English, were products of the New World, fiercely egalitarian and set on the achievement of material gain. They were not particularly interested in the ethnic exclusiveness, nor the religious ideals of the leaders of the Otago settlement. They belonged to a new international brotherhood of individualistic capitalists and despised Wakefieldian notions of a class settlement. The miners were dubbed the 'new iniquity' by Otago's founding fathers and transformed the character of the settlement. With their arrival the religious experiment came to an end.

Most of the miners seem to have been fairly well educated, with Scots miners being prominent in the establishment of Aethenaeums and Miners' Institutes. Once the easily mineable gold ran out in Otago, some moved on to the West Coast rushes, but many stayed behind and became storekeepers, farmers and agricultural labourers. A few switched to coal mining or continued on as employees of the quartz mining companies. Some of this latter group moved to the Thames area where they became prominent at the managerial level in the quartz mining companies. Although the general outlines are fairly obvious, the details have yet to be collated.[23]

The next major influx of Scots immigrants came in the 1870s, as part of the Vogel Government's immigration drive. John Morris has estimated that 19.5 per cent of the 100,000 assisted immigrants came from Scotland as against 45.5 per cent from England and 29.5 per cent from Ireland. Europeans (3.7 per cent), Scandinavians (2.87 per cent) and Welsh (2.1 per cent) made up the remainder. For the first time Irish immigrants outnumbered Scots. The New Zealand government preferred Scots, and in an effort to attract them, employed 73 immigration agents in Scotland and placed advertisements in 288 Scottish newspapers. But the USA and Canada proved more popular destinations. It seems that economic hardship in Ireland was greater, and this persuaded more people to make the longer and more arduous voyage to New Zealand. This factor is also borne out by the presence of a significant number of Highlanders for the first time (19.5 per cent of the Scots immigrants). This group were not concentrated in any one county, but were scattered evenly. Only the Hebrides was not represented. Otherwise the geographical origins of the Scots migrants were much the same as before, except that Glasgow was a more important source of supply and Midlothian less important.

The great majority of Scottish assisted immigrants were agricultural labourers (31 per cent) and domestics (19 per cent), as was the case with the English and Irish immigrants. But artisans (20 per cent) and general labourers (10 per cent) were also represented in significant numbers. It seems that the New Zealand government achieved the kind of occupational profile it wanted, with more precision in the case of Scottish immigrants than with English or Irish immigrants. City dwellers were obviously present, but they were by no means as predominant as the mythology, promoted by settlers who came before 1870, would have it. Like the English agricultural labourers studied by Rollo Arnold, the assisted immigrants who came from Scotland were generally hard working settlers who made a real contribution to the development of farming. On the other hand the experience of urban and town life brought by some of the Scots, especially those from Glasgow and Edinburgh, proved helpful in improving the quality of urban life style in New Zealand.

The majority of the Scots immigrants (62 per cent) went to Otago. Although the provincial government obviously preferred Scots, this concentration suggests that there was some degree of chain migration. As a result, the total number of Scots-born nearly doubled, and Otago became entrenched in its position as New Zealand's most Scottish province. Canterbury (18 per cent) and then Wellington (10 per cent) were the next most popular destinations.

In most other respects the Scottish immigrants of the 1870s were typical of the assisted immigrants in that they were predominantly young, male and single. Young, single women also came in large numbers for the first time, but there were far more Irish single women than Scots. The Highlanders were nearly all single young men, whereas married couples with small families tended to come from Edinburgh, Glasgow and other towns in the industrial heartland.[24]

This was the last major wave of British migration to New Zealand. But Scots continued to trickle into New Zealand from the late 1890s, as the New Zealand economy recovered from depression. A small peak of migration occurred in the first decade of the twentieth century, but little is known about this group.

Popular mythology and impressionistic literary evidence has grossly inflated the numbers and importance of the Highlanders who came to

New Zealand. James Adam and the Revd James Begg, for example, both claimed that Highlanders were numerous and successful.[25] This claim seems odd when it has been long known that Presbyterians heavily outnumbered Catholics among Scots immigrants who came to New Zealand and that most Highlanders went, in fact, to Nova Scotia, the USA and Australia.[26] Apart from the 4,000 or so Highlanders who came in the 1870s (the group encountered by Begg), the Otago and New Zealand governments, despite some considerable effort, failed to persuade a disproportionate number to come to the new Edinburgh in the antipodes. Yet the myth persists, and probably refers to second-step migration. Many of the Highlanders who talked to Begg were referring to their ancestral home rather than the place where they were living before they left for New Zealand.

There is, of course, one other group who have not received mention, the third-step migrants. Many Scotsmen moved into England, especially London, throughout the nineteenth century. This group are naturally more difficult to trace but some undoubtedly came to New Zealand, as all the professional groups examined contained members with unambiguously Scottish names who were born in London, Manchester, and Kent. Some of this group were the sons of earlier Scottish migrants, while others came to New Zealand via England.

Table 6.1: Ethnic Composition of New Zealand's Population, by Percentage

	1871	1881	1891	1901	1911
Scotland	14.38	10.77	8.30	6.20	5.13
England	26.15	24.33	18.71	14.50	13.28
Ireland	11.60	10.08	7.61	6.20	4.06
New Zealand	36.46	45.60	58.61	66.83	69.74
Australia	4.85	3.53	2.55	3.52	5.03

Source: New Zealand Census.

Tables 6.1 and 6.2 show quite clearly that Scots who came to New Zealand made up a significant but declining minority who were concentrated in Otago. Their proportional and numerical superiority was never as great as folklore suggests. In fact after the large influx of Irish in the 1870s, Otago was the only province where Scots outnumbered Irish. But in the early twentieth century, Scots became more numerous in Wellington. It appears, therefore, that the relatively well-educated Scots benefited from the rapid expansion of the state bureau-

Table 6.2: Numbers and Percentage of Scots Living in New Zealand, by Province

	1871	(%)	1881	(%)	1891	(%)	1901	(%)	1911	(%)
Auckland	5,546	15.04	6,216	11.78	6,770	13.04	6,803	14.21	9,762	18.88
Taranaki	419	1.14	711	1.35	946	1.82	1,216	2.54	1,514	2.93
Hawkes Bay	656	1.78	1,189	2.25	1,662	3.20	1,722	3.56	2,182	4.22
Wellington	2,079	5.64	3,849	7.30	5,425	10.45	6,122	12.77	8,077	15.62
Nelson	1,814	4.92	1,664	3.15	1,939	3.74	1,673	3.50	2,121	4.10
Marlborough	498	1.35	535	1.01	576	1.11	434	0.90	490	0.95
Westland	1,828	4.96	1,081	2.05	947	1.82	690	1.44	579	1.12
Canterbury	4,433	12.02	8,499	16.11	7,897	15.21	6,848	14.31	7,532	14.57
Otago	17,032	46.19	28,992	54.96	25,739	49.58	22,352	46.70	14,326	27.71

Source: New Zealand Census.

cracy which occurred at this time. The fact that Scots crept ahead of the Irish in Hawkes Bay and came to equal the Irish in Taranaki also suggests that Scots joined the northward drift of New Zealanders in general.[27] The small proportional increase of the Scots over the Irish in the first decade of the twentieth century was the result of a minor immigration boom in that period.

Overall the Scots were scattered around the whole of New Zealand, but concentrated in one province, and represented in significant numbers in three others, Auckland, Wellington, and Canterbury. Although they were a significant minority, they were not nearly as large a group as say the Irish in Australia, who represented between a third and a quarter of the population. The other key feature in New Zealand before World War One was the dominance of the English compared with either celtic group. If the Scots influence was as great as mythology suggests, then it was out of all proportion to their numbers.

Capital

Scots investors in the nineteenth century made significant contributions to capital accumulation in several new world countries. New Zealand was one of those recipients. But as was the case with migrants, Scottish capital supplemented the major input of capital from England. Scotland was easily the most important source of capital after England, with Australia being the third biggest supplier. Ireland and Wales by way of contrast contributed insignificant amounts (see Table 6.3).

Table 6.3: Country of Origin of Direct Borrowing (Percentages by Value)

	1866	1891	1896	1901
England, Wales & Ireland	72.90	72.06	62.66	80.73
Scotland	21.31	20.16	12.11	7.74
Victoria	0.75	1.28	7.10	0.22
New South Wales	0.34	0.43	5.36	0.31
Other	4.17	4.38	5.97	3.74
Unknown	0.53	1.70	6.81	7.25

Source: M. Arnold, 'The Market for Finance in Late Nineteenth Century New Zealand', p. 78.

Scottish capitalists also made the Otago settlement possible, and contributed an as yet uncalculated share of provincial and central government loans.[28] More is known about the extent of the Scots contribution to the private sector, however, thanks to the work of Margaret Arnold. From her study of mortgages and finance company records she has calculated that for the later part of the nineteenth century Scots made up 11.67 per cent of the lenders and contributed 16.91 per cent of the value of private overseas loans.[29]

Scottish investment in the private sector was characterised by two outstanding features: it was concentrated in the region where Scots were most numerous, Otago/Southland; it was mainly directed towards the pastoral industry. Woolgrowing, as Scots investors had already discovered in Australia, produced a substantial and fast return on capital. Dividends between 10 and 25 per cent were common. Table 6.4 reveals that most Scottish investment in New Zealand was speculative, short-term, and focused on pastoralism. The money for these ventures was usually raised through the issuing of debentures rather than shares and contained, therefore, an element of risk. But the huge profits (frequently in excess of £2,000 per annum) made from runholding, generally persuaded investors to take the risk. Financing the runholders and big estate owners through the medium of banks and stock and station agencies (a nineteenth-century Australasian term for mortgage companies often based in Britain but domiciled in the antipodes) rather than engaging in runholding directly also secured lucrative returns and attracted Scottish investors. Supplying the pastoralists with goods was equally profitable, as was shipping wool. Scots capitalists were quick to seize their opportunity in these activities, especially as they could be readily combined in a single operation. The other major spin-off from the pastoral industry was obviously textile production, and Scots capitalists were again prominent in floating woollen mills. These related activities became inextricably entwined and the same Scots businessmen kept appearing on the boards of directors of banks, stock and station agencies, shipping companies and woollen milling companies. In contrast extractive activities such as mining did not attract much Scots capital.[30]

Scottish capital came via Australia as well as direct from Scotland. The Bank of New South Wales, for example, which had great success in New Zealand, maintained direct links with the Scots money market.[31] Various industrial ventures promoted in Otago, such as the Oomaru and Milton Woollen mills, also drew on finance supplied by Scots living in Australia.[32] Furthermore, informal contacts within the

Table 6.4: Scots Based Companies Floated for the Development of Pastoralism in Otago and Southland

	Founded	Wound Up	Shares	Paid Up Capital (£)
Assets Company Ltd	1883	1955-6	500,000	1,028,825
North British and NZ Investment Co	1886	1901-3	20,000	80,000
Northern Investment Co of NZ	1880	1905-7	100,000	368,839
Otago and Southland Investment Co	1864	1906	250,000	783,098
Scottish and NZ Investment Co	1877	1900-7	117,000	383,021
NZ and Australian Land Co	1877	196?	uncertain	1,028,825
Other Major Companies Involving Scots Entrepreneurs				
British and NZ Mortgage Agency Co (Cargills, Gibbs and NMA)	1881	1889-98	342,822	87,006
Robert Campbell & Son	1881	1917-20	420,000	over 120,000

Source: H.J. Hanham in R. Chapman and K. Sinclair (eds.), *Studies of a Small Democracy*, pp. 60-1.

Australian banking world proved useful. Ross and Glendinning, woollen merchants and manufacturers of Dunedin, for example, benefited from the fact that most members of the London branch of the Bank of New South Wales came from Caithness, home of John Ross, founder of the company.[33]

Most of the major Scots-backed promotions were floated in the early 1870s, before the collapse of the City of Glasgow Bank in 1878. When that crash came the recklessness associated with Scottish banking practice caused hardship in New Zealand as well as Scotland. Yet through perseverance, more careful management and mergers, most of these pastoral companies survived into the 1890s. By that time it was obvious that the heyday of the great estates and extensive pastoralism was over and that agriculture and intensive farming held the key to economic development. Also the New Zealand economy, like most colonial economies in process of maturation, was generating its own capital. Declining returns on investments, better opportunities elsewhere and a dwindling demand for overseas capital combined to reduce the flow of Scottish capital to a trickle.[34]

The most important, successful and closely studied of the pastoral development operations backed by Scottish capital was the New Zealand and Australian Land Company. It grew, as did most of its smaller counterparts, out of Scottish participation in the development of the Australian pastoral industry. In 1859 Mathew Holmes, an Irishman with experience in wool-broking in Australia, persuaded the prominent Glasgow financiers, James Morton and J. and A. Dennistoun, to help him purchase first the leasehold and later the freehold of several large estates in New Zealand. Holmes was so successful that in 1866 he formed an incorporated company, the Canterbury and Otago Association, with the support of Morton and the Clydeside shipping magnate, Lewis Potter. This company's assets included 28,000 acres of freehold land and over 200,000 acres of leasehold property. Holmes and his successor, William Soltau Davidson, were astute managers and expert buyers of quality land. Between them they managed to increase the company's freehold holdings to over 100,000 acres by 1877. The Otago Agricultural and Land Investment Association Limited, another Scottish enterprise, was also absorbed in 1869, increasing the company's total holdings to over half a million acres.

In the same year as Holmes formed the Canterbury and Otago Association (1866), James Morton incorporated another company known as the New Zealand and Australian Land Company Limited. This company held 186,000 acres of freehold and 1.2 million acres of leasehold land. Most of the freehold properties were in New Zealand and most of the leasehold properties in Australia. The New Zealand properties were not as valuable, nor as well situated as those held by the Canterbury and Otago Association. Consequently they tended to absorb large amounts of funds in improvements. The Australian operation began to flounder and Morton decided to try and salvage the situation by merging the weaker company with the stronger. Despite Davidson's opposition the merger went through and Davidson faced the challenge of managing the new New Zealand and Australian Land Company which owned 15 estates in New Zealand, comprising more than 324,000 acres valued at £2.8 million. The Australian leasehold of 1.2 million acres was also kept under the Company's control. Under Davidson's expert management the company flourished. The Company also made three crucial contributions to New Zealand's economic development.

The colony's first dual-purpose sheep capable of producing quality wool and meat was developed on the Company's Corriedale estate in the 1870s. The breed still carries the estate's name and is found in several countries throughout the world. It should also be noted that it was developed by a Scots farm manager, James Little.

Davidson's key role in organising the first shipment of frozen meat to the British market in 1882 was of much greater importance. With the help of Holmes and another Scot, Thomas Brydone, he arranged for a consignment of meat to be sent from the Company's Totara estate. Davidson's efficiency and his contacts with the Scottish-based Albion Line helped him steal a march on the New Zealand Refrigeration Company. As a result of this initiative Davidson and Brydone were both asked to join the board of directors of the New Zealand Refrigeration Company, where they played a vital role, especially in organising the distribution of frozen meat within the British market.

The New Zealand and Australian Land Company's third major contribution took the form of New Zealand's first dairy factory, established on the Edendale estate, again in the portentous year of 1882. Davidson and Brydone both realised that dairying held enormous potential if quality butter and cheese could be produced in New Zealand. Their success meant they were content to write the experiment off as a loss.

None of the other Scottish backed pastoral companies were as successful for they lacked the expert management and vast financial resources of the New Zealand and Australian Land Company. The other companies, particularly the notorious New Zealand Agricultural Company in which Scots investors and Scots-born politicians were involved,[35] also tended to be seeking more rapid returns. Consequently, their input was much smaller and their contribution less significant.

None of the major stock and station agencies had direct links with Scotland. The National Mortgage Agency was essentially a London-based operation, Dalgety's was primarily an Anglo-Australian concern and Wright Stephenson's was a Dunedin-based operation backed by the Bank of New South Wales.[36] Even the major Otago based provincial stock and station agency, Donald Reid, drew its capital from NMA and the Colonial Bank. But NMA included the Royal Bank of Scotland among its backers and its on the spot manager, John McFarlane Ritchie, came from a well-known Glaswegian banking family. Two of NMA's brokers were also based in Scotland and one of its directors, John Morrison, was a director of the Bank of Scotland. NMA's close association with the New Zealand and Australian Land Company, and Ritchie's background ensured that links with Scots investors were maintained, but only to supplement the contributions of English investors.[37]

There were two other major financial companies which serviced the pastoral industry. One, the New Zealand Loan and Mercantile Agency, was based in Auckland and controlled by the Irish-born entrepreneur, Thomas Russell. It was backed by the Bank of New Zealand and English capital.[38] The other, Murray, Roberts and Co., based in Dunedin, had access to large amounts of Scottish capital. The founder and manager of the firm was John Roberts, sons of a Selkirk woollen manufacturer. He drew on his Selkirk connections to help his firm secure the leasehold of several large runs in Hawkes Bay as well as Otago, and was active in promoting the New Zealand Refrigeration Company, the Mosgiel Woollen Company and the Colonial Bank (1874-95).[39] When Margaret Arnold tracked the sources of loans in Scotland she found a concentration in Selkirk, resulting from Roberts' enterprise.[40] His firm seems to have drawn on Scottish capital more directly than any other provider of rural credit.

Scots bankers had considerable success throughout the nineteenth century in establishing subsidiary operations in many parts of the world. But this was not the case in New Zealand. No bank was able to utilise Scots capital as effectively as the New Zealand and Australian Land Company or Murray, Roberts and Co. Dunedin promoters floated two banks supported in part by Scottish capital – the Bank of Otago (1864-72) and the Colonial Bank. But neither was particularly successful. Russell's Bank of New Zealand and the Bank of New South Wales, gained a head start on the Bank of Otago as they commenced operations in 1861. The southern bank never seemed able to close the gap, and Auckland investors benefited as much, if not more, from the Otago gold rushes than their Dunedin counterparts. The Colonial Bank was also unable to challenge the monopoly exerted by the Bank of New Zealand and the Bank of New South Wales. It was backed by John Roberts and secured the services of the experienced and influential banker, William Larnach, but it always suffered from under-capitalisation and its late start. The Australian banking crisis of 1893 finally proved too much and the Colonial Bank was absorbed by the Bank of New Zealand between 1894 and 1895.[41]

The pattern associated with the development of banking in New Zealand was similar to that of insurance companies. Russell once again stole a march on his southern competitors by founding the New Zealand Insurance Company in 1859 and the South British Insurance Company in 1872. The market was thereby monopolised until the population was substantially increased by large-scale immigration. Then in 1873 Scots-born promoters in Dunedin formed the National Insurance Company, backed by the National Bank, the Bank of NSW and NMA. Although it proved a successful venture the newer company was never able to secure as large a share of the market as its northern rivals.[42]

Shipping was the other major activity which attracted Scottish capital. Scottish lines clearly benefited from the settlement of New Zealand,[43] and the appearance of indigenous coastal shipping companies soon attracted investors. The most important of these operations was the Union Steamship Company, founded in 1875. Its parent company, the Harbour Steam Company, although only small and loosely organised, had already caught the attention of the Clydeside shipping magnate, Peter Denny, partly because of the involvement of the Scots-born promoter and politician, James MacAndrew. Denny supplied the bulk of the capital which floated the Union Company in 1875. This enterprise later developed into an oligopoly and New Zealand's first equivalent of a multinational company. Its founder and director, James Mills, was an Englishman, but Scottish capital gave him his start. Denny supplied the company with ships, and John McFarlane Ritchie remained as one of the most important directors.[44]

Scots capital played a significant part in the development of nineteenth-century New Zealand, but a more important contribution was made by Scots-born financiers, managers and merchants based in Dunedin. It was these men who channelled capital in certain directions, who made the key 'on-the-spot' decisions and persuaded the capitalists of Glasgow, Edinburgh and Selkirk to follow their directives; they put money to work. In combination the contribution of Ritchie, Roberts, George Grey Russell (of National Insurance and NMA) and Edward Bowes Cargill (seventh son of the founder of the Otago settlement, director of the New Zealand Refrigeration Company and the Union Steamship Company, financier, runholder and general promoter) was as considerable as that of the more colourful Thomas Russell in Auckland. Furthermore, the greater attention to detail of this group prevented disasters such as the catastrophic collapse of the New Zealand Loan and Mercantile Company. Care did not of course prevent them experiencing some failures, but their overall contribution was positive and important.[45] Although staunch allies of the big landowners for most of the nineteenth century, they soon turned their attention to helping smaller farmers when it became clear that the country's destiny lay with this group. Consequently, investment flowed from the estates and runs of the South Island to the dairying districts of Auckland and the North Island. Higher returns proved more attractive to Scots financiers living in New Zealand than ethnic loyalties. Whether based in Dunedin or Glasgow, Scots financiers were businessmen first and Scotsmen second. The key role of the Dunedin directorate, both in the development of pastoralism and in underpinning the shift of the economic dynamic northwards, has been ignored for too long by New Zealand historians.

Entrepreneurship

Entrepreneurs born in Scotland, both individually and collectively, made a proportionately greater contribution to the economic development of nineteenth-century New Zealand than did Scottish capital or labour. The inputs of capital and labour were roughly equal to the numbers of migrants who came from Scotland, whereas the endeavour of Scottish farmers, manufacturers and businessmen outweighed their numbers. The entrepreneurial contribution of the Scots was certainly proportionately greater than that of the more numerous English. Capital and labour were essential for development, but entrepreneurial skill was required to convert the potential for progress into material advancement. By taking risks, seizing initiatives and employing labour, Scots and English entrepreneurs assisted by the state helped transform a virtually underdeveloped colony into a prosperous capitalist nation.

Colonies in their pioneer phase encourage men to take risks in pursuit of material rewards. Scots seemed to take up that challenge more readily in nineteenth-century New Zealand than did any other major ethnic group. They also were better able to turn their experience in farming, industry and commerce to advantage. Jews were the only group of European migrants who were more successful as entrepreneurs.

Separation of entrepreneurs in rural and urban categories is somewhat arbitrary because the two sectors were interdependent. But it is convenient as most entrepreneurs lived in the area where they made their livelihood. Furthermore, the export orientation of the producers of wool, gold and timber, and later meat and milk, locked them into the international economy. Promoters of industries which processed these raw materials also shared a concern with international markets. By way of contrast manufacturers were more concerned with the local market and the internal economy. Merchants and other middlemen usually lived in the main towns, but their control of capital in-flows and imports meant that they serviced the needs of both primary and secondary producers, rural and urban sectors; they too require separate examination. Scots were evenly spread through all three of these interdependent groupings.

Division by scale of operation is convenient and logical, as size affected both the organisation and capital requirements of business operations. But it must be remembered that the great majority of entrepreneurs were engaged in small-scale operations. In sum small businessmen made a far greater, but less spectacular contribution to development than the few large-scale enterprises which tend to catch the historian's eye.

Rural entrepreneurs can be readily differentiated into three main groupings: operators of large runs and owners of big estates; farmers and farm managers; a miscellaneous group of contractors, storekeepers, middlemen, transport operators and small town promoters. Scots were prominent in all three categories.

Runholding was most important in the early period of New Zealand's development and was later confined to high country areas. Individual Scots as well as companies established by Scots were over-represented among the runholders. There were three reasons for that over-representation. The crucial role played by Scots capitalists in promoting pastoralism has already been noted, but the fact that the Scots were the first group to arrive in the Otago/Southland region was equally important, as was Scottish experience in sheep farming.

The great majority of New Zealand runholders who migrated from Scotland lived on their properties or worked them from a nearby residence, although there were a few absentees domiciled in Scotland who employed managers. These runs ranged in size from vast holdings such as the 315,400 acre Morven Hills run operated by John and Allan McLean, to small runs of a few hundred acres which provided summer grazing for lowland farms.

Scots runholders were naturally enough most numerous in Otago/Southland. Marilyn Campbell in her study of runholding in that region estimates that approximately half the runholders were Scotsmen. Several members of this group also had experience of squatting in Australia, but central and provincial government regulations made squatting in New Zealand virtually impossible. Pastoral licences had to be obtained by the time the pastoralists began their operations in the early 1850s. George Gammie, for example, had owned runs on the Darling Downs, while Donald McLean had engaged in runholding in New South Wales. Others, such as James Wilson, invested money made in the Victorian gold-rushes in acquiring the lease of a run. Whether they came via Australia or direct from Scotland, these men represented a considerable range of occupational backgrounds. Persons with commercial experience were the most numerous, as they obviously had ready access to capital. Cuthbert Cowan of Ayrshire and James Robert Cuthbertson, for example, were both bankers. Professionals, especially doctors such as Andrew Buchanan and James Menzies, were also well represented. Lawyers and military men were present, and sons and relations of men in prominent places had a high profile. John and E. B. Cargill, along with their brother-in-law John Hyde Harris, were the most notorious examples of this group. There were also a few farmers' sons, such as Donald Reid, and the occasional shepherd or crofter. Donald McLean, for example, was the son of a displaced tacksman, and Allan and John McLean were sons of a crofter. But such instances of spectacular upward social mobility were rare. Highlanders, because of their expertise as stockmen, were in great demand as shepherds. Many became station managers as a result, but relatively few became runholders.[46]

Acland's and Pinney's studies of Canterbury runholding reveal a similar pattern. Nearly a fifth of the 237 prominent runholders mentioned by Acland[47] were Scotsmen, when Scots represented a mere 9 per cent of Canterbury's population. Pinney also found that most of the Scots in the MacKenzie Country were Highlanders, several of whom started their careers in New Zealand as shepherds.[48] Furthermore, nearly all the managers mentioned by Acland were Scots. Although station managers were not entrepreneurs in the strict sense of the word, they were so respected by the run owners that many of them were given first option on the sale of runs. Several of them took advantage of that offer according to Acland.

M. D. N. Campbell's study of runholding and the big estates in Hawkes Bay also reveals that Scots were over-represented in that region. Slightly more than a quarter of the runholders and big estate owners were Scots, yet they only represented 11 per cent of the population in 1871. Once more Highlanders do not appear to have been well represented, even though two of the most important runholding families had Highland names, McLean and Campbell. Commercial backgrounds still predominated, but in this area more of the runholders seem to have come from farming backgrounds.[49]

Scots were as keen on buying freehold estates as their English counterparts. Stevan Eldred-Grigg has calculated that in 1866, 23 per cent of owners of estates over 5,000 acres in extent were born in Scotland. The over-representation of Scots seems to have remained constant throughout the nineteenth century. The 1882 Freeholders List records that 12 of the 33 holders of estates valued over £100,000 had unambiguous Scots names. In 1892 a list of estates of over 10,000 acres was compiled to assist the introduction of a land tax. Some 92 of the 219 individuals listed and nine of the 25 owners of the biggest estates had unambiguous Scots names. Scots were also more heavily represented amongst the absentee owners as seven out of 13 absentee owners of over 10,000 acres lived in Scotland. By the time the next comprehensive list was compiled in 1903, Scots were slightly less numerous with only 54 unambiguous Scots names appearing amongst the 159 total.[50] In Otago in 1892, Scots were even more heavily represented. Eleven out of 17 owners of estates over 20,000 acres were definitely Scotsmen. We also know something about the Scottish backgrounds of these men: five had been merchants or bankers, three had been farmers, two had been small businessmen and one was a surveyor by training; at least three had experience of pastoralism in Australia.[51] In other words the social background and previous experience of these men was similar to that associated with Otago runholders.

Most of the Scots estate owners were good farmers who considerably improved their properties and kept abreast of advances in methods and machinery. Several became successful stock breeders, and they were active leaders of the Otago, Canterbury and Hawkes Bay A.&P. Societies. In general the Scots estate owners of the South Island co-operated with the government in the break-up of their properties, although there was more opposition amongst the Hawkes Bay group. At one extreme was Donald Reid, advocating radical land reform programmes, even though he owned large areas of land himself. He was by no means an exception.[52] Then there was another group, represented by men like John Douglas, who encouraged the state to purchase the less profitable estates.[53] At the other extreme were the Campbells and McLeans, who tried to block closer settlement. This group were very much in the minority, however, as most Scots estate owners shared William Soltau Davidson's realisation that New Zealand's future lay with more intensive farming. Furthermore, they were primarily businessmen who viewed land in economic rather than sentimental terms. Like their English counterparts, they also usually divided their properties among their children, so undermining the possibility of evolving into a colonial gentry. Even if estates continued to be farmed as one unit, kin rivalries tended to tear them asunder.

In sum, the contribution of Scots estate owners was greater than that of the New Zealand and Australian Land Company and the other pastoral companies floated by Scots capitalists. By developing vast tracts of country they helped make the Liberal land reform programme a success, especially as they tended to hasten rather than delay the implementation of that programme.

Scots represented the entire range of New Zealand farmers in terms of specialisation and size of operation; they were characterised by several distinctive features. The most obvious was the predominance of mixed and stock farmers and farmers operating middling sized units of middling value. This reflects the concentration of Scots in Otago, where mixed and sheep farming was supreme and where larger units were common. There is also a suggestion that the Scottish background of these men orientated them more towards stock farming and open tussock country. Certainly they seem to have been under-represented among dairy farmers, and obviously preferred working open country to breaking in the bush. Farmers of Scots descent seem little different from other Otago and South Island farmers in general in their relative satisfaction with leasehold tenures. Often the leasehold proved more suitable on improved open country, at least as a stepping stone to ownership.[54] John McKenzie knew this, and his policies tended to reflect his South Island as well as his Scottish experience.

The Scottish origins of farmers suggest that Highlanders were more successful in the rural sector than the urban. Even so the eastern Lowland counties, especially Perthshire, are prominent again, as is Ayrshire in the southwest. The relatively high proportion emanating from

Glasgow provides another hint that second-step migration was more common than the national figures indicate. A background in Scottish farming helped rather than hindered a man's progress in New Zealand farming, especially in areas like Otago and Southland, where conditions and specialisations were similar to those of Scotland.

Farmers of Scottish descent made their most obvious contribution through developing a thriving oats trade with Victoria. This trade was an important export earner between the 1870s and the First World War. At its peak in 1901 nearly £1 million was earned, representing around 7 per cent of total export earnings. Nearly half those oats were produced in Otago/Southland, and oats have remained an important part of crop rotations in that region despite the decline in demand induced by the demise of the horse.

Scots were probably more flexible farmers than the English once they realised that traditional methods would not work particularly well in the new environment. The original Otago settlers attempted to follow a traditional approach in the early days of the Dunedin settlement, but were quick to change their ways when it became obvious that changes paid handsome profits. They were prominent in developing the dairy industry from the early 1880s in Otago/Southland, and firms like Reid and Gray of Oamaru led the country in developing agricultural machinery to meet the demands of New Zealand farming.[55] Some were also leading advocates of a more scientific approach to farming. They were prominent in A. & P. Societies and progressive farmers' clubs, such as the much acclaimed club at Waitahuna.[56] One man, however, stood out above the others.

James Glenny Wilson, a well educated Scot from Roxburghshire, was a large landowner in the Manawatu. He devoted his life to encouraging New Zealand farmers to follow a more scientific approach, first through the A.&P. Societies and later as president of the New Zealand Farmers' Union. One of his life-long dreams was realised in concrete form when Massey Agricultural College was established in 1926. He also played a key role in persuading the government to improve its collection of agricultural statistics and in introducing agricultural instruction into the school curriculum.[57]

Special mention should also be made of John McKenzie's role in establishing the Department of Agriculture in 1892. McKenzie set up this important wing of the state bureaucracy almost single handed and always considered it his greatest achievement. Without this agency his land laws would not have been nearly so effective. The Department of Agriculture helped the man on the land through providing practical advice and regulating both production and marketing. Its officers introduced the quality control so essential in making New Zealand a competitive exporter of agricultural products. Such an agency would have been established sooner or later, but McKenzie's drive and experience as a practical farmer ensured that it came sooner, that it worked in a beneficial way, and that it had sufficient administrative power to be effective.[58]

Unfortunately, the Scots contribution to New Zealand farming was not entirely positive. On the debit side of the ledger it should be noted that Scots who came to Otago did not have the same love of trees as the English in Canterbury. The open and treeless tussock country of inland Otago undoubtedly reminded many Scots of home. They seemed content to leave it treeless. As a consequence, lack of shelter has been a problem in rural Otago ever since, and the natural grandeur of the scenery has not been enhanced as it might. The aesthetic sensibility revealed by Dunedin's founding fathers in establishing a reserved green belt was unable to challenge the ascendency of the utilitarian approach to rural land use.

Scots were also represented among the phlethora of small town businessmen and middlemen who made up the rest of the middling group of rural society. Some worked as storekeepers, butchers and hoteliers (although not as frequently as the Irish) on their way to becoming farmers. Others undertook those entrepreneurial roles for life or became grain merchants, country solicitors, mail contractors, real estate agents, newspaper proprietors, blacksmiths, land valuers and transport operators.

The merchant princes of Dunedin and Auckland were the urban equivalent of the big estate owners. Although Scots were not quite as prominent within this group as they were within the rural entrepreneurial elite, they were still represented in significant numbers. The most conspicuous Scottish merchant princes were William Larnach and John Logan Campbell, neither of whom was a member of the Dunedin directorate, although they had intermittent dealings with that key group.

Larnach was the son of a Caithness man, who became a run overseer in Australia, and the nephew of the manager of the London branch of the Bank of New South Wales. He was an archetypal nineteenth-century optimist who seemed to live ten feet off the ground and did everything on a grand scale. His land speculation ventures were widespread and involved enormous risks. The complexities of his dealings in this area have not yet been unentangled, but they obviously concerned financiers in

Scotland, England, New Zealand and Australia. Sometimes the provincial government had to come to his rescue, as was the case with the sale of the Moa Flat estate to Big Clarke in 1871.[59] Occasionally, even the central government became entwined, as was the case with the New Zealand Agricultural Company in 1884.[60] Larnach's intermittent forays into politics were desperate attempts to undo his financial tangles.

Larnach also set up a major importing business with another Scot, Henry Guthrie. It had assets of over £400,000 at its peak in the mid-1870s. Furthermore, he was a major shareholder in the Westport Coal Company, the Bank of New Zealand, the Colonial Bank and the National Insurance Company. Although his financial troubles were not as spectacular as those of some of the Auckland merchant princes, he seemed unable to recover as effectively as his northern counterparts, and his misfortunes caused him so much anguish that he committed suicide in 1896.

Dr John Logan Campbell left less to chance and was not as unlucky as Larnach. As a result he was just as influential but far wealthier. The son of an Edinburgh doctor, he came to New Zealand to make a quick fortune which would enable him to retire in comfort in Scotland. Like several of the more successful Scottish merchants, he also had connections with the East India Company and contemplated trying his luck in India. These Indian mercantile links proved helpful in getting his business operations underway. Initially he supplied basic commodities to both Maoris and settlers, but he soon became involved in land speculation, the promotion of the Bank of New Zealand and the New Zealand and South British Insurance Companies. Later he added liquor wholesaling to his business activities. He tried to return to Europe but ran into a series of misfortunes and so came back to Auckland. A man of sturdier physique and greater mental stability than Larnach, he lived to a ripe old age. Logan Campbell, even more than Larnach, turned the unregulated nature of colonial economic life to considerable personal advantage by circumventing or even making the rules.[61]

Immediately below the big merchants was another group engaged in a more modest scale of operations. Scotsmen dominated this level of commercial and banking life in Dunedin and Invercargill and were well represented in other parts of New Zealand, especially Wellington and Auckland. Several smaller stock and station agencies were established by Scots such as Tothill, Watson and Co. or Carswell, White and Co., both of which were based in Invercargill. Some became timber and coal merchants, as did William Jardine in Dunedin. Others followed specialised lines, such as tea importing; for example William Balk and Co. of Dunedin. Scots were also importers (McKerras and Hazlett, Dunedin), exporters (W. R. Cameron and Co., Dunedin), real estate agents (Macrorie and Cuthbertson, Invercargill), shipping agents (John Mill, Port Chalmers), auctioneers (James MacIndoe, Dunedin) and seed merchants (Nimmo and Blair, Dunedin). Naturally Scots joined Jewish and English entrepreneurs in setting up general stores. J. H. Smith of Invercargill and Ballantynes of Christchurch were two of the most successful.

Scots were particularly prominent at the management level of banks and major firms. During the 1890s the Dunedin branch managers of the BNZ, the Bank of New South Wales, the National Bank, the Union Bank of Australia, the Loan and Mercantile Agency Co., and Turnbull Martin and Co. (Australian shippers), were all Scots. Then there was another group who held national managerial positions in the Commercial Union Assurance Company; Trustees, Executors and Agency Co.; the Government Life Insurance Department; Perpetual Trustees Estate and Agency Co.; the National Mortgage Agency; the National Bank and the Westport Coal Company. Peter Barr, the progressive Dunedin accountant who helped overhaul business organisation in the city, was also of Scottish descent.[62]

Manufacturers were the other major group of urban entrepreneurs and Scots were again prominent in this group. They were especially active in establishing foundries and engineering works, woollen mills, papermills, flourmills and breweries. In 1900, 14 of New Zealand's 65 foundries were located in Dunedin, Invercargill and Oamaru. Half of these enterprises had been founded and developed by Scotsmen. A. and T. Burt was the biggest and best known of Dunedin's engineering works. Cossens and Black, John McGregor and Co., Kincaid and Co., and J. and T. Christie were Dunedin's other well-known engineering firms founded by Scottish migrants. Scots also founded engineering works in the other major centres, while many of the metallurgists and battery managers in the Thames gold mining industry were Scotsmen.[63]

Scots were to the fore in promoting the Mosgiel, Roslyn, Milton, Oamaru and Timaru woollen mils. The Mosgiel Mill which employed some 276 hands by 1910 was floated by the Scots-born Dunedin business directorate in association with the Jewish manufacturer and merchant, Bendix Hallinstein.[64] Ross and Glendinning, who founded the much bigger Roslyn Mill which employed 1,000 hands in 1910, were both Scots. This Highlander/Lowlander partnership also owned the Shag Point Coal mine and several very large runs.[65] The Milton,

Oamaru and Timaru mills were much smaller and probably more typical of colonial capitalism. All three mills were heavily dependent on the local capital market and struggled for survival. They had few connections with Scots capital, but Scotsmen dominated their management and directorates.[66] By way of contrast the Kaiapoi and Onehunga mills were established by English-born entrepreneurs backed by English and Australian capital. But Scots were once again prominent at the managerial level.[67]

Two Scotsmen pioneered paper making in New Zealand. Edward McGlasghan set up New Zealand's first paper mill at Woodhaugh, Dunedin in May, 1876. Edward Bain of Invercargill set up the Mataura Mill a month later. McGlasghan came from a well-to-do Edinburgh family and was trained as a merchant. He was a brother of John McGlasghan, secretary of the Otago Association, which promoted the settlement of the province. Edward McGlasghan put his capital to good effect in runholding, flourmilling and promoting several companies.

Finally, brewing in Dunedin was essentially a Scottish concern. The Speights and Wilson families intermarried and by the 1920s controlled McGavin's, Strachanans and the Caversham brewery, which were also founded by Scots. Several smaller breweries were also established by Scotsmen in other parts of New Zealand. One well-known example was the Tui Brewery founded by the Fraser family at Eketahuna. New Zealand's short-lived distilling industry which only lasted from the late 1860s until the mid 1870s, was entirely a Scots affair, dominated by the Wilson family of Dunedin.

Labour

Scots could be found in a wide range of labouring jobs with general labourers predominant. But the old specialisations of Scotland did not entirely disappear. Some Scots became coal miners or worked for the quartz mining companies at the lower level.[68] At the higher level skills were well represented in places like the Hillside workshops. Scots carpenters, wrights, smiths, fitters, brass moulders, etc. fared well in New Zealand. Probably the top end of this group infiltrated the engineering profession, and this might explain the heavy over-representation of Scots in that part of the work force. A background in, say, a Clydeside foundry obviously proved advantageous in securing work and rapid promotion in New Zealand.

The contribution of Scottish labourers has been underplayed for three main reasons. First, the founder myth, which has shaped the writing of most local history in New Zealand, tends to concentrate on the so-called pioneer successes, rather than people who laboured with their hands and did not become farmers or businessmen. Second, it is very difficult to find out much about this group. Labouring men and women have left little behind them in the way of written evidence, while oral history is still very much in its infancy in New Zealand. Furthermore, they do not appear in publications like the *Cyclopedia* and are seldom recorded in the archives of genealogical societies. Finally, in New Zealand the Scots adopted a relatively low profile in the trade union and labour movement, although they were represented in proportion to their numbers. Generally the activists belonged to the so-called moderate wing, whereas the most prominent militants were Australian-Irish. This is not completely true as one of the leading Red Feds and New Zealand's second Labour Prime Minister was a Scot. Peter Fraser was born in Ross-shire in 1884 and came to New Zealand in 1910, where he soon became a leading organiser of waterside workers.[69] But Fraser was something of an exception, as most of the Scots who constituted 12 per cent of the leaders of the early movement were moderates. This preference was undoubtedly related to the fact that the majority of Scots were Presbyterian, a religion much concerned with respectability. Agnostic and Catholic Scots generally found revolutionary socialism a more attractive doctrine, although the Presbyterian Fraser was yet again an exception in this respect. Presbyterianism inclined, however, to promoting egalitarianism and reform of abuses. This helps explain why Scots tended to support evolutionary moderate socialism and political rather than industrial action. It should also be remembered that some of these so-called moderates were quite radical when it came to the matter of land reform and were ardent advocates of land nationalisation.[70]

Women of Scottish descent are an even more difficult group to investigate. Nearly all sources relating to them are anecdotal.[71] Many cases of individual achievement could be cited, but the formulation of generalisations concerning their economic and social role is next to impossible. Wills, school records, property titles, letters and diaries need to be searched in systematic fashion and combined with an intensive interviewing programme if we are to understand more of this apparently 'hidden' group. In the interim some interesting information can be gleaned from an examination of the 1882 Freeholders List.

Wives (who were not necessarily Scottish) and daughters of men with Scottish names owned property of similar value to their men folk.

Low value properties were slightly more numerous, suggesting that women owned land for purposes of speculation and security. Until the Married Woman's Property Act was passed in 1884 it was not legally possible for a married woman to own property in her own name, unless she went to a lot of trouble to circumvent the law. Probably, therefore, most of the married women who owned property were widows. Overall though, the percentage of women with Scottish names who owned properties represented a minority. It would seem that other ethnic groups were more interested in acquiring property for all family members, especially in cities.

The number of women with Scottish names who held paid employment seems very low. None the less, Scots women probably did take work or work in a part-time capacity. Even if they did not do so most of the women who stayed home laboured hard for no financial reward. Like most pioneer women they bore and raised large families in adverse conditions, undertook strenuous physical tasks, found time to participate in school committees and community activities and worked longer hours than anyone else. It is interesting to note, however, that the lot of some women of Scottish descent was eased relative to other groups because Presbyterians were controlling their fertility by the early 1900s, whereas Catholics were not.[72] On the other hand women of Scottish descent were subjected to abuses such as wife desertion. Perhaps, once again, the popularity of temperance amongst Presbyterians eased their women's lot, especially as these women far outnumbered male adherents. But it should be noted that few unskilled labourers belonged to the Presbyterian church.[73] Overall the immense contribution made by Scottish women has been played down like that of all colonial women. They were unsung heroines who helped build a nation. But there seems little that was distinctive other than the fact that women of Scottish descent were among the first to control their fertility and were more inclined to encourage their daughters to receive secondary and tertiary education. They were also active participants in the temperance movement. Otherwise sex was a far more important determinant of behaviour than ethnicity.

Conclusion

A proper assessment of the Scottish contribution to New Zealand's economic development obviously needs to move into areas generally regarded as preserves of political and social historians. It must be noted that Scots were significantly over-represented among members of the Legislative Council and the House of Representatives before 1914. They were almost certainly over-represented on such local government bodies as county councils and road boards. This impression is gained by reading the 1905 Land Commission where most local body representatives were Scots. There is no doubt, however, that Scots were leaders in the urban improvement movement which began in Dunedin. Inspiration and guidance came direct from the Cockburn Association of Edinburgh, and Scots were more numerous than any other group in the Dunedin Amenities Society. This pioneering body became something of a model for other New Zealand cities.[74]

Educational development in New Zealand also undoubtedly received greater assistance from the Scots than any other immigrant group. Otago was quite justified in boasting that it provided the best educational facilities in the provincial period.[75] Furthermore, the Otago Scots also founded New Zealand's first university in 1869, first girls' secondary school in 1871 and were prominent in establishing, administrating and staffing the University of New Zealand and Victoria University of Wellington.[76] Scots also played a key part in founding several other outstanding boys' state secondary schools including Otago Boys High, Christchurch Boys High, Waitaki Boys High and Nelson College, which were modelled in part on Scottish grammar schools rather than English public schools.[77] Oddly enough the private Presbyterian schools were generally not as successful as the state schools; the essential problem was inadequate funding.[78] The realisation that the Scots community could not pay for its own education was a key factor in deciding Scots educational leaders to push for the introduction of compulsory state education in 1877. These same advocates, in association with several prominent Scots-born politicians and the non-conformist English also ensured that the new system was secular.[79]

Scots were almost certainly represented in disproportionate numbers on education boards, boards of governors and school committees. No one has yet calculated the precise representation, but there is no doubt that the Scots belief in scholarly excellence and equality of educational opportunity had a very beneficial influence on the development of the New Zealand education system. Probably their efforts helped New Zealanders reach high rates of literacy and educational achievement earlier than would otherwise have been the case. Unfortunately less enlightened opinions also operated, lowering the quality of education and limiting the opportunities available to the nation's children. The efforts of Scots and others saw the introduction of free places in secondary schools in 1903, but secondary education was not made compulsory until 1944. It was fitting, however, that the Minister of Education responsible for that innovation, Peter Fraser, was a Scot. Had the nation as a whole given education as high a priority in terms of government spending and investment as the Scots migrants of the nineteenth century, there is little doubt that New Zealand could have developed an excellent rather than adequate, education system.

It seems that the Scottish subculture was absorbed with relative speed by the English majority culture, except in the areas of religion and education. This did not mean that the ethnic contribution of the Scots was unimportant, however. A complex dialogue between the class background of the Scottish migrants and their ethnic character encouraged the promotion of reforms to ensure greater equality in the areas of land ownership and education. Most of these migrants were persons of modest origin, who like the majority of New Zealand immigrants wanted to better their material lot and win greater independence. Because they were Scots they were prepared to support slightly more radical policies than the English to ensure that the inequality of the British landowning system was not reduplicated. As a people they had suffered more from the abuses of landlordism than the English. Even if they lived in the industrial heartland, the injustice of the clearances and the iniquity of the Scottish rural social order was still felt with some keenness. Indeed the notion that the Scots had been oppressed by Scottish landlords in the control of their more powerful neighbour was an important ingredient in emerging Scottish nationalism.[80] Furthermore, Scotland was far smaller than England and a more cohesive cultural unit despite the Highlander/Lowlander division. Somehow Scots migrants believed even more fervently than the English that the evils of the old world should not be reproduced in the new. There was some kind of loose consensus between many of the colonial *nouveau riche* and the migrant poor that the order of things should be improved. It was no accident that the outcry against sweating and a whole range of related social evils which erupted in Dunedin in 1890 should have been orchestrated and led by middle-class Scots. This same group, backed by rural parliamentarians and social engineers born in Scotland, then proceeded to enact the most radical land laws in the world and introduce a series of progressive welfare and labour measures. But these actions stopped well short of revolution. The reform of abuses and the removal of fetters was their major objective. Very few wanted to do away with the capitalist system. Most Scots seemed content with helping people to help themselves and with encouraging national efficiency.[81]

By the outbreak of the First World War, New Zealand was a more equitable and democratic society than Scotland. Geography, historical accident, 'newness', economic forces and other ethnic groups had all played their part in ensuring that this was so. But the Scots migrants also played a key role in the formative period of the late nineteenth century when latifundia was replaced by small farming and oligarchy gave way to democracy. Thereafter the contribution of the Scots assumed only minor importance as the flow of migrants and capital dried up. Yet the early Scots settlers had established a tradition on which later generations of New Zealanders could draw as they struggled to find New Zealand solutions to New Zealand problems.

Notes

1. Stevan Eldred-Grigg, *A New History of Canterbury* (Dunedin, 1982), pp. 20-1. Jeanine Graham, 'Settler Society', and Erik Olssen, 'Towards A New Society' in W.H. Oliver and B.R. Williams (eds.), *The Oxford History of New Zealand* (Wellington, 1981), pp. 116 and 264-5. W.H. Oliver, *The Story of New Zealand* (London, 1960), pp. 268-88. Angus Ross, 'Scots in the South' in *New Zealand's Heritage*, no. 19 (Wellington, 1971), pp. 522-7. K. Sinclair, *A History of New Zealand*, 1st edn (London, 1959), pp. 195-301.

2. Rollow Arnold, *A New Educational History for New Zealand* (Wellington, 1973); and 'The Village and the Globe: Aspects of the Social Origins of Schooling in Victorian New Zealand', *Australian and New Zealand History of Education Society Journal*, vol. 6, no. 2 (1977), pp. 1-12. Ian and Alan Cumming, *History of State Education in New Zealand, 1840-1975* (Wellington, 1975). W.J. Gardner, *Colonial Cap and Gown: Studies in the mid-Victorian Universities of Australasia* (Christchurch, 1979).

3. G.T. Alley and D.O.W. Hall, *The Farmer in New Zealand* (Wellington, 1941). B.L. Evans, *A History of Agricultural Production and Marketing in New Zealand* (Palmerston North, 1969). P.R. Stephens, 'Innovation on the Farm' in *N.Z. Heritage*, no. 81, pp. 2260-4. L.J. Wild, *The Life and Times of Sir James Wilson of Bulls* (Christchurch, 1953).

4. Stuart Perry, *The New Zealand Whiskey Book* (Auckland, 1980).

5. H.J. Hanham, 'New Zealand Promoters and British Investors, 1860-95', R.M. Chapman and K. Sinclair (eds.), *Studies of a Small Democracy: Essays in Honour of Willis T. Airey* (Auckland, 1963), pp. 56-77.

6. E.g. John H. Angus, *Donald Reid Otago Farmers' Limited: A History of Service to the Farming Community of Otago* (Dunedin, 1978). R.C.J. Stone, *Young Logan Campbell* (Auckland, 1982).

7. G.L. Pearce, *The Scots of New Zealand* (Dundee, 1976).

8. Both Graham and Peter Gibbons talk in terms of cultural homogeneity in the *Oxford History of New Zealand*, pp. 116 and 302-3. But this view is slowly being challenged. Geographers and historians have combined to research more into immigrants of different nationalities, e.g. Rollow Arnold, *The Farthest Promised Land: English Villagers, New Zealand Immigrants of the 1870s*

(Wellington, 1981). Ng Bickleen Fong, *The Chinese in New Zealand: A Study in Assimilation* (London, 1959). K.W. Thomson and A.D. Trlin (eds.), *Immigrants in New Zealand* (Palmerston North, 1970).

9. The phrase the 'rush to be rich' is taken from Geoffrey Serle, *The Rush to be Rich: A History of the Colony of Victoria, 1883-1889* (Melbourne, 1971). On the Otago Settlement see A.H. McLintock, *The History of Otago. The Origins and Growth of a Wakefield Class Settlement* (Dunedin, 1949). On the Highlanders of Waipu see Pearce, *N.Z. Scots*, pp. 65-76.

10. T.C. Smout, *A History of the Scottish People, 1560-1830* (London, 1969), pp. 280-92, 361-79, 440-8 and 449-79; and 'The Social Condition of Scotland in the 1840s', *The Dow Lecture* (Dundee, 1980).

11. Ibid.

12. William Downie Stewart, *William Rolleston, A New Zealand Statesman* (Christchurch, 1940), pp. 137-52.

13. Arnold, *Farthest Promised Land*; and 'English Rural Unionism and Taranaki Immigration, 1871-76', *NZJH*, vol. 6, no. 1 (1972), pp. 20-41. R.P. Davis, *Irish Issues in New Zealand Politics, 1868-1922* (Dunedin, 1974).

14. W.P. Reeves, *State Experiments Australia and New Zealand* (Melbourne, 1969), vol. 1, pp. 274-82, points out that no state government in the Australian federation ever won the power of compulsory repurchase.

15. 'Report of the Royal Commission on Land Settlement and Tenure', *Appendices to the Journal of the House of Representatives*, 1905, C-4 and C-4A. Several witnesses argued that now New Zealanders were beholden to the money lenders of London rather than to the big runholders.

16. J.S. Marais, *The Colonisation of New Zealand*, 2nd edn (London, 1968). Harry A. Morton, *The Whales Wake* (Dunedin, 1982). Pearce, *N.Z. Scots*. pp. 35-50.

17. Stone, *Logan Campbell*, pp. 103-14 and 108-9.

18. See Ruth Allan, *Nelson: A History of Early Settlement* (Wellington, 1965). Marais, *Colonisation*.

19. W.H. Scotter, *A History of Canterbury*, vol. 1 (Christchurch, 1965).

20. V. Maxwell, 'Scots Migration to Otago', PhD in progress, University of Otago.

21. Roslyn McLean, 'Class, Family and Church: A Case Study of Interpretation. Otago, 1848-1852', unpublished BA Hons Research Essay, University of Otago, 1980; and Maxwell, 'Scots Migration', Appendices.

22. McLintock, *History of Otago*, and D.G. Herron, 'Alsatia or Utopia? New Zealand Society and Politics in the Eighteen-fifties', *Landfall*, vol. 13, no. 4 (1959), pp. 324-41.

23. See J.H.M. Salmon, *A History of Goldmining in New Zealand* (Wellington, 1963), pp. 57-123. Biographies compiled by Philip Ross May, *The West Coast Goldrushes* (Christchurch, 1962).

24. John Morris, 'The Assisted Immigrants to New Zealand, 1871-1879: A Statistical Study', unpublished MA thesis, University of Auckland, 1973.

25. James Adam, *Twenty-five Years of Emigrant Life in the South of New Zealand* (Edinburgh, 1874). Hocken Pamphlet Collection, 40/18. Hocken Library, Dunedin. James Begg, 'A Visit to New Zealand', An Address Delivered at a meeting in the Edinburgh Literary Institute, 26th February 1874. Hocken Pamphlet Collection 17/14.

26. Michael Flinn *et al.*, *Scottish Population History from the 17th Century to the 1930s* (Cambridge, 1977), pp. 441-55; and David S. Macmillan, *Scotland and Australia, 1788-1850, Emigration, Commerce and Investment* (London, 1967), pp. 71-131.

27. See Arnold, *A New Educational History*. A.G. Bagnall, *Wairarapa, An*

Historical Excursion (Hedley's Bookshop for the Masterton Trust Lands Trust, 1976), pp. 364-76. T. Brooking, 'Economic Transformation', Oliver and Williams, *Oxford History of N.Z.*, p. 230.

28. There has been considerable work on internal investment, e.g. J.A. Dowie, 'Studies in New Zealand Investment, 1871-1900', unpublished PhD thesis, Australian National University, 1965. But little work has been carried out on sourcing of Government loans.

29. M.N. Arnold, 'The Market for Finance in Late Nineteenth Century New Zealand with Special Reference to Rural Mortgages', unpublished MA thesis, Victoria University of Wellington, 1981, pp. 77-81.

30. Angus, 'City and Country: Change and Continuity. Electoral Politics and Society in Otago, 1877-1893', unpublished PhD thesis, University of Otago, 1976, pp. 19-120. Gavin McLean, 'The Union Steamship Company', PhD in progress, University of Otago. Gordon Parry, *N.M.A. The Story of the First Hundred Years: the National Mortgage and Agency Company of New Zealand, Ltd., 1864-1964* (Dunedin, 1964).

31. Sinclair and W.P. Mandle, *Open Account: A History of the Bank of New South Wales in New Zealand, 1861-1961* (Wellington, 1961).

32. G.J. McLean, *Spinning Yarns: A Centennial History of Alliance Textile Ltd and its Predecessors, 1881-1981* (Dunedin, 1981).

33. Norah Ross, *The March of Time: Ross and Glendinning* (Dunedin, 1967), p. 10.

34. M. Arnold, 'Finance Markets', pp. 80-2 and 210-16.

35. D.A. Hamer, 'The Agricultural Company and New Zealand Politics, 1877-1886', *Historical Studies Australia and New Zealand*, vol. 10, no. 38 (1962), pp. 141-64.

36. Parry, *N.M.A.*, Gardner, 'A Colonial Economy', Oliver and Williams, *Oxford History*, pp. 68-70.

37. Angus, *Donald Reid*. Parry, *N.M.A.*

38. Gardner in Oliver and Williams, *Oxford History*, pp. 67-70.

39. Harraway, 'John Roberts'.

40. M. Arnold, 'Finance Markets', p. 77.

41. N.M. Chappell, *New Zealand Banker's Hundred: A History of the Bank of New Zealand, 1861-1961* (Wellington, 1961). Hardwicke Knight, *The Ordeal of William Larnach*, (Dunedin, 1981).

42. Gardner, in Oliver and Williams, *Oxford History*, p. 69.

43. E.g. the Albion Shipping Company.

44. G. McLean, 'Union Steamship Company'. The Northern Steamship Company was also founded by a Scot, Captain Alexander McGregor, in 1881.

45. Gardner gives this group a begrudging acknowledgement but they deserve greater recognition.

46. R.H. Beatties, *Early Runholding in Otago* (Dunedin, 1974). Robert Pinney, *Early South Canterbury Runs* (Wellington, 1971).

47. L.G.D. Acland, *The Early Canterbury Runs*, 4th edn (Christchurch, 1975).

48. Allan McLean was the most spectacular example of a shepherd who became a runholder, and later a big estate owner. He arrived with nothing in Australia where he made money from mercantile activity. When he died in 1907 he left an estate valued at £600,000. Ken Coates, *Otago Daily Times*, 9 April 1983, p. 18.

49. M.D.N. Campbell, 'The Evolution of Hawke's Bay Landed Society, 1850-1914', unpublished PhD thesis, Victoria University of Wellington, 1972, Appendix A.

50. 'Land and Income Department Further Report', *AJHR*, 1892, B-20A and *AJHR*, 1903, B-20.

51. Taken from Volume Four of the *Cyclopedia* and *A Dictionary of New Zealand Biography*, G.H. Scholefield (ed.), 2 vols. (Wellington, 1940).

52. Angus, *Donald Reid*. A paper by T. Brooking, G. Kearsley, and T.J. Hearn on 'Land Settlement and Voting Patterns in the Otago Provincial Council, New Zealand, 1863-1872', to be published in *NZJH*, shows that a few runholders joined Reid's land reform faction which was dominated by farmers.

53. P.C.F. James, 'The Price of Pomohaka Downs: The Purchase, Subdivision and Settlement of a South Otago Estate, 1893-1905', unpublished BA Hons Research Essay, University of Otago, 1982.

54. This point was reiterated by witnesses to the 1905 Land Commission. See R.L. Bailey, 'Agrarian Aspirations and Demands as Illustrated by the 1905 Royal Commission on Land Tenure', unpublished MA thesis Massey University, 1972. T. Brooking, 'Agrarian Businessmen Organise', pp. 25-30.

55. Evans, *A History of Farm Implements*. H.G. Philpott, *A History of the New Zealand Dairy Industry* (Wellington, 1937).

56. Brooking, 'Agrarian Businessmen Organise', pp. 252-324.

57. Wild, *The Life and Times of Sir James Wilson*. T. Brooking, *Massey, its early years: A History of the Development of Massey Agricultural College to 1943* (Palmerston North, 1977).

58. Brooking, 'Sir John McKenzie and the Origins and Growth of the Department of Agriculture, 1891-1900', unpublished MA thesis, Massey University, 1972.

59. Michael Clarke, *'Big' Clarke* (Carlton, 1980), pp. 246-54.

60. Hamer, 'N.Z. Agricultural Company'.

61. Stone, *Young Logan Campbell*.

62. A.S. Paterson and Co., general merchants, for example, had branches in Auckland and Wellington. This whole section is based on the *Cyclopedia*.

63. See Angus, *Donald Reid*, pp. 64-5.

64. This section is based on the *Cyclopedia, Statistics of New Zealand*, and Salmon, *Goldmining in New Zealand*.

65. Peter J. Stewart, *Patterns on the Plain: A Centennial History of Mosgiel Woollens Ltd.* (Dunedin, 1975).

66. Norah Ross, *March of Time*.

67. Gavin McLean, *Spinning Yarns*.

68. Tony Bamford, 'Black Diamond City: A History of Kaitangata Mines, Miners and Community, 1860-1912', unpublished BA Hons Research Essay, University of Otago, 1982. J.B. McAra, *Gold Mining at Waihi, 1878-1952* (Christchurch, 1978), pp. 305-9.

69. Barry Gustafson, *Labour's Path to Political Independence: The Origins and Establishment of the New Zealand Labour Party, 1900-1919* (Auckland, 1980), p. 156.

70. E.g. George Fowlds and Alexander W. Hogg. Gustafson, *Labour's Path*, pp. 156-8.

71. E.g. Miriam Florence MacGregor, *Petticoat Pioneers: North Island Women of the Colonial Era* (Wellington, 1973).

72. Susan Sheehan, 'A Social and Demographic Study of Devonport, 1850', MA Research Essay, University of Auckland, 1980.

73. Jill Farrell, 'The Caversham Presbyterian Church, 1880-1920', unpublished fourth year class essay, University of Otago, 1979.

74. Geoffrey Vine, 'The Dunedin Amenities Society: Origins and Early Development', BA Hons Research Essay in progress, University of Otago, 1983.

75. Ian Breward, *Godless Schools? A Study of Protestant Reactions to the Education Act of 1877* (Christchurch, 1967). A.G. Butchers, *Education in New Zealand: An Historical Survey of Educational Progress Among the Europeans*

and Maoris since 1878 (Dunedin, 1930).

76. J.C. Beaglehole, *The University of New Zealand: An Historical Study* (Wellington, 1937). Gardner, *Colonial Cap and Gown*.

77. Burnard, 'A Colonial Elite'. Donaldson, *The Scots Overseas*, pp. 167-80. Pearce, *N.Z. Scots*, pp. 60, 93 and 162.

78. Lucy Duncan, 'What Katy did at School: Changes in the Curriculum of Girls Secondary Schools in Dunedin, 1900-1920' unpublished BA Hons Research Essay, University of Otago, 1982.

79. Arnold, *A New Educational History*. Breward, *Godless Schools*.

80. Smout, *Scottish People*, pp. 480-515. G. Donaldson, *Scotland: The Shaping of a Nation* (Newton Abbot, 1974).

81. Smout, 'The Social Condition of Scotland in the 1840s'.

7 SCOTTISH ENTERPRISE IN INDIA, 1750-1914

James G. Parker

The economic development of India in the period 1750-1914 can be seen as falling into two phases. The first involved the victory of private enterprise over the East India Company and its monopoly of British trade with India and the East. The second witnessed the emergence of India in the second half of the nineteenth century, both as a major producer of raw materials for British industry and of cash crops such as tea and jute, and as a market for British products. The dominant role played by British capital in this process prevented the development of an industrialised economy on European lines. It was as a client economy that India's future under the British lay. Thus the country remained in 1914 as it had been in 1750 — predominantly agricultural. However, within these limitations progress was made in a number of fields, and in these the Scottish contribution was significant. By the end of the Victorian era Scots firms had attained a controlling position in key sectors of the economy of British India. This ascendency was in great measure attributable to the success of their predecessors in firstly establishing a foothold in the East and secondly in contributing to the defeat of the East India Company. It is therefore to these pioneers of Scottish enterprise in India that any study of the period as a whole must first turn.

Scottish Interests in the East India Company

The East India Company was first granted its exclusive right to conduct English trade with India and the East by a charter of Elizabeth I in 1600. Though compelled thereafter to petition parliament for periodic renewal of its charter in return for a share of its profits, the Company successfully defended its monopoly for over two centuries. From the earliest years it was a London-based body dominated by members of the small and interconnected group of families who controlled the great financial and mercantile institutions of the City. The executive powers of the Company were vested in 24 directors elected annually by proprietors of £500 stock who met in a General Court. By the early years of the eighteenth century the Court of Directors had become an almost self-perpetuating body encountering little or no opposition from a quiescent General Court. Occasionally, when parliamentary opposition parties united with those sections of the City's mercantile community excluded from the Eastern trade, the directors could rely on the government for protection of their charter. It was a reciprocal relationship: no eighteenth-century administration could hope to raise the loans in the City that were so vital to its finance without the support of such institutions as the Company, the Bank of England and the South Sea Company. Within the Company itself the directors were able to defeat periodic challenges from hostile elements among the stockholders by relying on several powerful parties, or interests, representing such subsidiary areas of the Company's business as the ownership of shipping, the supply of broad cloth and other merchandise for sale in India, and the purchase of imported spices, saltpetre, tea, silks, etc., from whose ranks many of the directors were drawn.

In the last decade of the seventeenth century efforts to break the Company's monopoly came close to achieving success. However, the threat posed by a 'New' East India Company, launched with considerable backing in the City, was effectively neutralised when the upstart body was absorbed into the existing Company, forming from 1709 a stronger 'United Company of Merchants trading to the East' whose monopolistic position became more entrenched than ever. It was in this period also that Scottish merchants, eager to participate in the lucrative Eastern trade, combined with elements of the Company's City opposition to float a 'Company of Scotland Trading to Africa and the Indies' which, with the backing of a still independent Scots parliament, received a royal charter in 1695. Initially, the new venture had ten promoters, or suppliers of capital, from Scotland and an equal number drawn mainly from the Scottish expatriate community in London. However, a fundamental disagreement over policy among the promoters led to the London-based members dropping out. They had seen the enterprise as a means of challenging the East India Company's trade monopoly, while the home-based Scots were primarily concerned with establishing a colony abroad. With the withdrawal of the London capital the threat to the East India Company evaporated. In search of a colonial settlement the Scots looked west rather than east, and their hard-raised funds were dissipated in the disastrous Darien adventure.[1]

With the failure of the Scottish Company those Scots wishing to engage in commerce with India had to find other ways round the East India Company's monopoly. One method was to join forces with the

Company's rivals on the Continent. Scots merchant communities in such commercial centres as Rouen, Ostend, Gothenberg and Copenhagen provided the capital and personnel for a number of European ventures into Eastern trade. Often, it seems, it was a case of making the best of an enforced exile as many had strong Jacobite connections. The Edinburgh-born brothers, Colin and Hugh Campbell, who had been supercargoes with the Ostend Company until its collapse in the 1730s, moved to Gothenberg where, with fellow exiles including Thomas Erskine, later Earl of Mar and Kellie, and George Carnegie, a refugee from Culloden, were instrumental in launching the Swedish East India Company. In Denmark the East Indian Asiatic Company, which was founded in 1732, provided opportunities for other Jacobite Scots such as the Browns of Colstoun, one of whose number became governor of the Danish Company's Indian settlement in 1773.[2]

But for those Scots who remained at home the key to future success lay in the establishment of a foothold within the East India Company itself. In the decades immediately following the Act of Union there are signs that a growing Scottish business community in London, drawn to the city as the political and economic centre of the United Kingdom, was beginning to penetrate the Company's innermost circles. Though the Company's agreement with the government in 1698 for the renewal of its charter stipulated that directors should be 'natural-born subjects of England',[3] the London-based Scots merchant Sir William Stewart (d. 1723) entered the Direction of the rival 'New' Company in that year and went on to be a director of the United Company, as well as Lord Mayor of London.[4] Scottish banking families with continental connections, such as the Hopes and Drummonds, were finding places in the Company's Direction by the 1720s and 1730s. The surviving papers of a member of the latter family, John Drummond of Quarrell (1676-1742), who was a director from 1722 to 1734, show that even at this early stage of development of the Company's settlements in India the patronage that was the perquisite of each director was being eagerly sought by relatives and friends in his native Stirlingshire.[5]

Less discernible, but no less significant, progress was being made within the most powerful of the 'interests' in the Company's General Court — that representing the provision of its shipping. From the early seventeenth century the Company had found it more convenient to hire, rather than own, the vessels required to carry on its overseas business. To encourage shipbuilders, owners and managers, the last known to contemporaries as 'husbands', to provide the specialised ships necessary for its long-distance trade certain groups were favoured with contracts and came to monopolise the supply of the Company's shipping. This shipping interest retained sufficient representation on the Direction not only to satisfy its patronage needs, but also to ensure that its ships continued to be taken on and that the rates of hire remained high.

By the middle of the eighteenth century, when faint stirrings of activity in the General Court associated with the Company's early attempts to grapple with newly-won political and territorial responsibilities in India were beginning to be noticeable, a number of Scots can be identified among the ranks of the most influential managers and owners. Some, such as Charles Foulis (d. 1783), a scion of the Foulis family of Colinton and manager of twelve East Indiamen between 1762 and 1783, were former commanders in the Company's maritime service. Like Foulis, the Scots husband Andrew Moffatt could boast strong maritime connections through his brother Captain James Moffatt (C. 1733-90) who represented the family's interests in the Direction from 1774, while the Moffatts' kinship with the Earl of Mansfield gave them an influential ally in government circles.[6] Some, such as the brothers Alexander (C. 1693-1765) and Abraham Hume (1703-72), began in the service of the Company's continental rivals before moving to London shipping circles; others, like the parliamentary borough-monger Sir Lawrence Dundas (C. 1710-81), invested in Company shipping as they did in Company stock — to secure as large a share as possible of Indian patronage for political purposes.[7]

Growing Scottish influence at East India House, the Company's home in Leadenhall Street, led to more opportunities in the Company's service in India for young relatives and connections north of the border. Employment with the Company had always been attractive, not because of the salaries paid by the directors which were small, but because of the opportunities open to the Company's servants to participate on their own accounts in the internal trade of India or in the 'country' trade carried on between the Company's settlements and other parts of south-eastern Asia. To these commercial openings the further inducement of profits from an expanding political power on the Indian mainland was added from the 1760s.

The directors had traditionally eschewed any involvement in internal Indian affairs, contenting themselves with a trade based on agreements with the 'nawabs', local representatives of the great Mogul. By the middle of the eighteenth century, however, the Mogul empire was in decline and in the ensuing disarray the Company's servants found themselves drawn into local struggles for political power. In Bengal, where the Company's main settlement lay, hostilities broke out with the local nawab in the 1750s and led to the Company's forces under Robert Clive setting up a puppet nawab. Victory over the French in the Seven Years War soon followed and so eliminated the Company's main European rival. The first steps on the road to political power had been taken.

As one nawab was deposed for another in return for huge gifts of money, and the Company's new power was exploited to the full by its employees in Bengal, a stream of enriched 'nabobs' returned home. Appointments in India became more sought after than ever. Already by 1750 Scots were able to claim three of the eight junior appointments made that year to India,[8] and in the next 20 years when opportunities for gain were at their highest this proportion was maintained if not increased. As in other parts of the world Scots who had established themselves in lucrative niches gave helping hands to their countrymen who had just arrived. The close ties of kinship and sense of national identity of the Scots were particularly valuable for those in India. Company employees needed friends to represent their interests at East India House and to handle the remittance home of their fortunes, which was usually done through bills on the Company. Another feature of the Company's Scots Employees at this time was the relatively high proportion of men of titled or landed rank, younger sons of the peerage and gentry of Scotland where a tradition of social mobility, combined with a lack of opportunities for employment at home, overcame any prejudice against the pursuit of a mercantile career in the East.

Typical of the young Scot of good connection arriving in Bengal in this period was Stair Dalrymple, younger brother of Sir Hew Dalrymple, Baronet of North Berwick. Appointed in 1752 he expected to have to spend some 15 or 20 years in India, during which time he told his brother, 'I may be made Governour if not that, I may make a Fortune which will make me live like a Gentleman'. In the early years he would serve the Company 'for little or nothing recompence, but that dont signifie much for we have the Liberty to Trade as much as we please and at the end of five years we may be great men of good Interest'. He was soon taken under the wing of one John Brown, 'a Scotch Gentleman of distinguished veracity and Honour', who invited him 'to come and stay at his House untill I had got lodgings without the least Knowledge of me, or without the least Knowledge of my friends in Scotland'.[9] Unfortunately, Dalrymple did not live long enough to amass his 'fortune', perishing in the hostilities between the Company and the Nawab Siraj-ud-Daula five years later.

By 1773 another Company servant, Thomas Graham of Airth, could write to his brother that his countrymen grew so numerous in Bengal 'that I am afraid that I shall not be able to enumerate them with that exactness I have hitherto done'.[10] Some Scots directors such as John Michie,[11] who sat in the Direction from 1770 until his death in 1788, built up personal followings in India by providing for young relatives and connections. Michie's nephew Jonathan Duncan (1756-1811), later Governor of Bombay, described to him how on a Sunday 'Lumsden, Elliot, Burnet and Forbes are generally with me in the country, as we in some Measure consider ourselves as a family Connection, of which you are of course the Benefactor, who has been the making of all of us'.[12]

The turbulent events in Bengal in the 1760s were reflected in developments within the Company in London. Various parties struggled for power in the Courts of Directors and Proprietors, some concerned with extracting the highest possible dividend from the Company, others to protect the interests of friends still in India. The great shipping magnates like Sir Lawrence Dundas and Andrew Moffatt were courted by all the main groups and were plied with promises of patronage, the hire of extra ships and increases in the rates of hire. One such party, of interest here because of the wide range of Scottish connections in the City's East Indian circles it could call on for support, was that organised by the Johnstone family of Westerhall. Three members of the family, the brothers John, Patrick and Gideon Johnstone, had received Company appointments in Bengal in the 1750s through the influence of their uncle, Lord Elibank, a prominent East India stockholder. The most successful of the three, John, had benefited from the struggles with the Bengal nawabs, but fell foul of Robert Clive who was sent out to reform the abuses in the Company's administration. In its struggles in the mid-1760s to secure John's reinstatement and the remittance of his huge fortune, the Johnstone party could mobilise large amounts of Scottish-owned stock at election times which would be 'split' into £500 voting qualifications and divided among its followers in support of whichever faction in the Company the family happened to be allied with at the time.[13]

The financial straits the Company found itself in by the end of the 1760s, coupled with the public outcry against the excesses of its servants in India, led to intervention in its affairs by the government of the day in the shape of the Regulating Act of 1773. This made certain changes in the Company's constitution designed to reduce the power of the great interests at election times, including the extension of each director's term of office to four years and the reduction to six of the number of directors seeking re-election in any one year. Further intervention by Pitt's ministry eleven years later led to the establishment of a Board of Control to supervise the Company's affairs. With the reforming legislation came a new generation of governors-general, such as Warren Hastings and Lord Cornwallis, who greatly reduced the opportunities for private gain and laid the foundations of the Indian civil service. The Board of Control ushered in a new era in Company relations with the State and provided the means by which one man, Henry Dundas, was to dominate Indian affairs for the next two decades.[14]

The origins of Dundas's interest in the Company's affairs are obscure, but he seems early to have developed a genuine concern for Indian matters over and above the obvious potential value of the Company's patronage to his political control of Scotland for Pitt. He was a prominent member of the parliamentary secret committee set up in 1781 to investigate a war the Company had been waging in southeast India against the local native powers. As a commissioner (1784-93) and later president (1793-1801) of the Board of Control he took much of the new body's work on his own shoulders. He saw the way to a better regulation of the Company's administration through ministerial control of the directors. By the end of the 1780s he had built up government influence at East India House to the point where prospective candidates for the Direction had first to gain his support for any real chance of success.

However, while Dundas undoubtedly achieved a position of hitherto unparalleled government ascendency in the Company, the extent of his personal Indian patronage has been over-estimated both by contemporaries and later historians. By the time of the Dundas era, as has been seen, Scots were finding employment in the Company's civil, military and maritime services in some numbers. But their success was attributable to the steady growth in Scottish influence within the Company over the previous century, and not to Dundas's munificence. Though his surviving papers overflow with applications for Indian appointments, he was in a position to oblige only a limited number, as he replied to one applicant soon after leaving the Board:

From the contents of your letter, I perceive that you are under great misapprehension on the subject of Writers to India, and it is necessary to put you right on the subject. The whole appointments belong exclusively to the Individual Directors except two which they annually give to the President of the Board of Control. In addition to these two I reckon that on an average, while I was at the head of

India affairs, I received two more from individual Directors, whom I had occasion to oblige in the course of my Patronage in other Departments.[15]

Aware of the popular misconceptions about the extent of his power to favour fellow Scots, Dundas was careful also in his choice of candidates for support at the elections of Company directors. He wrote in 1787 of one Scottish applicant:

> I refused this year to support on my Interest a very good Man who had proposed himself to me as a Candidate for the Direction. I told him fairly that, as Captain [William Fullerton] Elphinstone, the last chosen was my Country man, I could not furnish the handle . . . of raising any Objections . . . amongst the Proprietors.[16]

However, one aspect of Dundas's involvement in Company affairs did have major significance for the future of Scottish participation in Indian trade and investment. This was the part he played in bringing into the Direction an increasing number of 'free merchants', private traders who were permitted to set up in business in India and to engage in the local coastal trade of the Company's settlements. As the expansionist policies of a series of energetic governors-general in India forced the Company further and further into debt, demands from the free merchants for an opening of the Company's trade to private enterprise found a ready ear among home-based merchants and manufacturers who saw in India a potential source of raw materials and a vast new market for their products. It is the role played by the Scottish elements in this private trading interest that must now be considered.

Scottish Free Merchants and Houses of Agency

For those who lacked the influence at East India House necessary to secure an appointment with the Company in India there was the possibility of becoming a free merchant, based usually at one of its three main settlements at Fort William (Calcutta), Madras and Bombay. Such merchants were permitted, under licence from the Company, to participate in local trade but not in the Company's commerce with the United Kingdom. However, the system proved difficult to regulate. The directors found it hard to limit the number of adventurers setting themselves up in business, particularly as many were closely involved with Company employees in commercial ventures.

Until the last quarter of the eighteenth century a free merchant's license was regarded as a second best to a Company appointment. A few free merchants returned to the United Kingdom with large fortunes, but they were the exceptions. Most rose no higher than the level of shopkeepers in one or other of the Company's settlements with little chance of acquiring the competency necessary to live the life of a gentleman on their return home. However, as the reforms of Hastings and Cornwallis prevented Company servants engaging in private trade more opportunities opened up for the free merchants. By the 1770s certain merchants were beginning to accept on deposit the salaries of Company employees to whom other avenues of private gain were now closed. The employees received interest on their capital which the merchants, or houses of agency as they were becoming known, used to finance new and increasingly diverse ventures. The more successful firms established partners in the main Company settlements and at ports such as Canton and Bencoolen, so constructing a network of business contacts throughout south-east Asia.

It was in Bengal that the most pronounced growth of the agency houses took place. The existing inland trade of the region was supplemented by Calcutta's importance in the Company's commerce with the United Kingdom. In a normal year by the middle of the century 60 per cent of British imports from India came from Bengal.[17] The thriving country trade based on Calcutta provided opportunities for investment in such areas as the ownership of local shipping and marine insurance with which the Company did not concern itself. As new territories in north-east India were brought under British control the agencies eagerly put their money into early ventures in commercial agriculture and mining. By 1790 15 firms were registered at Calcutta, a total which rose to a maximum of 23 in 1803 before tailing off towards the early 1830s.[18] A small group of about half a dozen of the more enterprising agencies were soon dominating the Bengal economy. With such names as Fergusson, Fairlie and Co., Cruttenden, Mackillop and Co., Colvin, Bazett and Co., Alexander and Co., Palmer and Co., Mackintosh and Co., and Lambert, Ross and Co., the high proportion of Scots in their number is unmistakable.

A typical Scots agency house of the period was that of William Fairlie who had left home in the early 1780s to set up as a free merchant in Bengal with his fellow Ayrshireman, John Fergusson. The firm's name underwent a series of changes as old partners withdrew their capital in preparation for retirement in Scotland and younger members of the

Fergusson and Fairlie families were brought out to India. Thus the house was known successively as Fairlie, Fergusson and Co., Fairlie, Reid and Co., Fairlie, Gilmore and Co. and eventually as Fergusson, Clark and Co. The firm illustrates the diversity of interests maintained by the Bengal agencies of the period. Fairlie accepted cash from Company employees, handled work on a commission basis for firms in other Company settlements and later in the United Kingdom, traded on his own account and invested in various inland projects. His firm enjoyed a monopoly of contracts to supply the East India Company's Bengal army with elephants, bullocks and victuals. Fairlie was one of the two largest owners of shipping in Calcutta and invested heavily in shipbuilding, thus contributing to an increase in Bengal-built ships from around 6,000 tons in the years 1807-9 to almost 25,000 tons between 1810 and 1813. In insurance too he was active, setting up the Calcutta Insurance Office and the Calcutta Life Insurance Company.[19] Under the able management of Fairlie and Fergusson the firm became one of the most prosperous in the country. On his arrival in London in 1790 Fergusson was described by Dundas as the 'greatest European merchant, I suppose, ever came from India'.[20] Fairlie was also held in high esteem. A fellow merchant wrote of him, 'I suppose no English House in India has such extensive concerns as Mr Fairlie's . . . His fortune is very large and his credit almost unbounded'.[21]

In Bombay an even smaller oligarchy of agencies had by the end of the century gained a stranglehold over the economy. Of the five controlling firms, at least three, run by David Scott (1746-1805), Charles Forbes (1774-1849) and Alexander Adamson, were Scottish, and to these may possibly be added the agency founded by James Tate. Their economic power was largely based on their ability to corner Bombay's flourishing export trade in raw cotton to China. To this was added a political influence unequalled by their fellows in Bengal or Madras, and they have been described by one historian as the 'real rulers' of Bombay.[22] The Company authorities in Bombay were dependent on financial support from Calcutta to pay for their civil and military administration. When the necessary cash was not available, or when communications were broken in time of hostilities, the Company had to fall back on loans from the great firms. Forbes told a parliamentary committee how, during the Company's war with local native powers in the years 1803-5, he had helped supply 'their wants, and relieved their difficulties, to the extent of nearly two million and a half sterling'.[23]

Various factors contributed to the success of the Scottish free merchants and to the dominant position they attained in the local economies of the Company's settlements. Not least of these was the advantages they derived from their strong ties of kinship. The Scots agencies were almost entirely family concerns. When much of their trade was based on credit and conducted over long distances it was vital to have trustworthy representatives in every port. The Bombay merchant David Scott found places in his firm for a succession of nephews sent out from Fife to make their fortunes. Failing this, he would try to find them junior partnerships in other Scottish houses with which he was associated. Thus he described to William Fairlie the advantages both to himself and to his nephew Alexander Shank if a place could be found for the youngster in Canton with Hamilton, Reid and Co.:

> Mr Shank would certainly increase the connection of the House at China, as having you and all my Indian friends. The Houses of most consequence at Bombay at Madras and at Bengal I flatter myself would be happy to establish Mr Shank's interest. Credit we could give him as much as they pleased, so upon the whole I think Mr Hamilton would have the *quid pro quo*. The above if it could be brought about would serve my nephew essentially, and of course serve me.
>
> This is taking it in a private point of view but I look to it in a different and more extended view. In every appointment, or rather arrangement, of this sort I look to the House. To secure a broad bottom to the House we should never lose sight of bringing forward attached friends in the most consequential Houses of the three Presidencies and China . . . I shall write to Messrs Tate and Adamson to co-operate with you in this, and I hope through my letters from here and our friends in India that this will take place.[24]

However, even to the Scots kinship was not in itself sufficient to guarantee acceptance into the family firm. Junior partners had to be of proven ability. David Scott was prepared to recommend Shank to Hamilton and Reid only if 'his capacity suited'. William Jardine, co-founder of the great China house of Jardine Matheson, wrote to a nephew who was seeking a position with the firm:

> . . . impress this on the minds of your young cousins . . . [that] I can never consent to assist idle and dissipated characters however nearly connected with me, but am prepared to go to any reasonable extent in supporting such of my relatives as conduct themselves prudently and industriously.[25]

A nephew of one of the firm's early partners, though professedly 'willing, well-disposed and desirous of making himself useful', was packed off home by Jardine on the grounds that 'Bell's *Life of London* was oftener in his hands than the books'.[26] Successful merchants like Jardine who had found their way to India and China as little more than adventurers made sure that the next generation coming out from Scotland received a thorough education. Jardine's young partner James Matheson attended Edinburgh University, followed by two years in a London counting house before joining his uncle's firm of Mackintosh and Co. in Calcutta. Similarly Charles Forbes, who transformed his uncle's Bombay house into a firm of international standing, and David Scott were graduates of Aberdeen and St Andrews universities respectively.[27]

Perhaps the most important factor behind the success of the agencies was their indispensability to the East India Company's system of trade and finance. In subsidiary settlements such as Bombay they provided the short-term cash necessary to keep the Company's local administration functioning in time of difficulties, as has been seen. By the early years of the nineteenth century they were also playing a key role in the Company's international trade, particularly that with China which remained the one profitable area of its business. Despite early attempts by the Company to bar all but its own employees from Canton, two firms, Hamilton and Reid and Dent and Co., had succeeded in gaining a foothold. The former was founded by John Reid, a Scots adventurer who arrived in 1779 with credentials as consul of the Emperor of Austria which placed him technically beyond the Company's jurisdiction. The firm was eventually superseded by the better-known house of Jardine Matheson. Dent and Co., until its collapse in 1860 Jardine Matheson's greatest rival, was established by yet another Scot, Alexander Davidson, who circumvented the Company's monopoly by assuming Portuguese nationality.[28]

Hamilton and Reid, and Dents based their prosperity on the import of raw cotton and opium from fellow agencies in India which found a ready market in China. The profits from this trade, which in the case of opium was carried on against the wishes of the Chinese authorities, were paid into the Company's treasury at Canton in return for bills on London or one of the Company's principal Indian settlements. The cash could then be used by the Company's supercargoes to purchase the tea and other commodities which composed its China trade. The system was of immense value both to the agencies in providing a means of remitting home their profits, and to the Company which did not have to export valuable bullion from England, a facet of its trade which had long given ammunition to its enemies at home.

The area of business for which the agencies are best known and which had the most significance for the future direction of British investment in India was indigo production. This crop had long been grown for dye to some extent in north-east India but had never been able to challenge the dominant position in the world market of the more efficiently produced indigo dyes of North America and the West Indies. Following the Treaty of Paris of 1763 and the decline of production in the defeated French colonies, the West Indian process was introduced to Bengal under the aegis of the Company. The climate proved conducive and, encouraged by demand from British cotton manufacturers, production increased rapidly.

The Bengal agency houses, ever alert to new areas of investment, were quick to enter the field. A wave of speculators descended on the Bengal region to open up new plantations using capital borrowed from the agencies. Restrictions on European land ownership led to a convoluted and financially unsound system of growth and production, with the agents at one end providing capital and later handling the sale of the finished product, and native landholders at the other working under contract to the planters. Notwithstanding, indigo soon became the country's chief export and maintained this position until replaced by opium in the 1830s. Alexander and Co., one of the firms most heavily committed to indigo, reckoned in 1828 that the agencies controlled a total of over a million acres under cultivation, and around 300 factories providing work for half a million native families.[29]

By 1830 a slump had set in. The combined effects of a new process of producing artificial dye on the Continent and a severe credit crisis which struck the agencies in the years 1830-3 led to many bankruptcies among planters and agencies alike. Indigo production survived on a smaller scale and remained a valuable export commodity throughout the nineteenth century. By 1911 there were still some 120 plantations in operation.[30] In its attraction of large amounts of British capital to an area of cash crop production it set the trend for future-nineteenth-century investment.

The End of the East India Company Monopoly

As the agency houses became more prosperous and ambitious for new markets it was inevitable that they should look beyond the confines of their commerce in Indian and Chinese waters and towards securing a foothold in the East India Company's trade with the United Kingdom. The Company's inability to conduct a profitable trade with India and its dependence on the agencies in the East for finance made its mono- polistic position more and more untenable. At home, too, there was support for opening the Eastern trade from the Company's traditional enemies in the outports and also from the newer manufacturing areas of England and Scotland where entrepreneurs were eager to import raw materials direct from India and to exploit the East's apparent potential as a vast untried market for their goods.

Before the Company's charter came up for renewal in 1793 merchants from Glasgow joined those from other commercial centres south of the border in petitioning parliament for a reduction in the Company's trading monopoly and for permission to import raw materials from India in their own ships. The strength of protest grew in succeeding years and by 1812, when the charter was again considered for renewal, other parts of Scotland were becoming involved. Merchants of Paisley, Kirkcaldy and Kilmarnock argued for the infusion of new capital into the Eastern trade as the Company clearly lacked the necessary resources. The Edinburgh Chamber of Commerce sought access to both Indian and Far Eastern markets. By the end of 1812, a total of 130 petitions had reached parliament from all over the British Isles and a standing deputation with representatives from all the impor- tant manufacturing and trading areas had been established in London. It included prominent figures from Liverpool, Bristol, Birmingham, Edinburgh and Glasgow.[31]

The 1793 agitation succeeded only in achieving an increase in the private trading allowance of the commanders of the Company's East Indiamen which could be put at the disposal of private merchants. The 1813 charter, however, opened the Company's Indian commerce to private enterprise, leaving it only its profitable China trade. Success on this occasion was due not only to the groundswell of opinion in the country against the Company, but also to the growing influence in the Company's Court of Directors of the agencies and the support for their cause of Henry Dundas.

Dundas found himself in agreement with the arguments being used by the free merchants in favour of opening the Eastern trade, and, as has been noted already, found reliable supporters in the persons of those agency representatives he helped on to the Direction. Of most importance in this respect was the Bombay merchant David Scott who had left India in 1786 to act for his firm in London. With ministerial assistance he entered the Court of Directors in 1788 and was soon on the closest terms with Dundas, who came to rely heavily on Scott's knowledge of the Company's trade in the East. By the election of April 1789 Scott was also assuming much of the responsibility for ensuring government control of the Court. He produced schemes for Dundas whereby the Company's debts in India could be transferred to England using his many powerful Scottish agency connections in the East. Monopolies of any sort were anathema to him and he took a prominent part in the movement to open the Company's system of hiring ships to free tender. He remained the agencies' most influential spokesman as well as Dundas's most zealous follower until ill health brought on by over work at East India House forced him into retirement in 1802.

The opening of the India trade in 1813 gave a great boost to the influence of the agencies, both in the City in general, and in the Company in particular. Under Dundas a nucleus of directors representing the private trading interest grew up round Scott. But from the second decade of the nineteenth century the free traders developed from an influential minority into the most powerful party at East India House. The great Scottish houses of Bengal, Bombay and Canton were represented by such directors as Robert Campbell, Robert Cutler Fergusson, John Forbes, Thomas Reid, David Scott junior, Henry Shank and John Inglis. Like the City families of the previous century who had dominated the Company, the private traders continued the hereditary traditions of the Direction, David Scott himself being followed by his son of the same name and by his nephew Henry Shank. One estimate has put the number of private trading directors at 17 out of a possible 30 in 1831, with Alexander and Co. enjoying the reputation of 'having put the majority of the Directors in their seats'.[32]

When the time approached for parliamentary renewal of the Company's remaining monopoly – its China trade – in 1833, pressure both inside and outside East India House proved irresistible. The agencies were by this date getting round the restrictions on their trading directly between the United Kingdom and China by using Singapore as an entrepôt. Home-based firms who had been quick to take advantage of the opening of the India trade in 1813 now clamoured for access to China. At the forefront were merchants like Kirkman Finlay (1772-1842), who were deserting traditional areas of business such as cotton manufacture for new investments in India. Finlay had represented Glasgow in the outports' delegation in London in 1812. His ship the *Duke of Buckinghamshire* had been the first to clear the Clyde for India in 1816, and in the following year the two partners he sent out to India had established a branch at Bombay. By 1822 Finlay was exporting bleached calicoes to Canton via Singapore through the agency of Jardine Matheson, and other merchants in the west of Scotland and Lancashire were finding the Chinese receptive to their cotton piece goods.[33]

Twice as many petitions descended on Westminster in the years 1829-30 as in 1812-13, and an outport delegation took up residence in London four years before the charter came before parliament. A trade depression added weight to the demands for new markets in the East and with the Charter Act of 1833 parliament duly obliged by relieving the Company of its trading functions. It was to live out the last quarter century of its existence to 1857 concerned only with the administration of its territorial responsibilities in India, and even in these the Board of Control was steadily encroaching on the traditional powers of the directors.

Having contributed to such a large extent to the breaking of the Company monopoly it was ironic that the agencies should not survive long to enjoy the fruits of their labours. The years 1830-3 witnessed the collapse of a number of the most important Calcutta houses – Palmers, Mackintoshs, Alexanders, Fergussons, Colvins, and Cruttenden and Mackillop. The reasons were not hard to find. The most immediate was over production of indigo, followed by a drop in prices in the world market associated with competition with the new 'Prussian blue'. Contemporaries also pointed to aspects of the agency system, such as the periodic large-scale withdrawals of capital by retiring partners and the interdependence of the agencies and the Company in its pre-1833 form, as contributory factors.

Some of the firms which had diversified their investments and which were operating on an international scale by the 1830s survived into the new era in a modified form. Also some of the family names closely associated with the agency system in its years of ascendency reappear in the later period. But the age of the eighteenth century agencies was over. They had helped to alter the whole nature of India's export trade. Under the Company Indian-made piece goods manufactured at local village level on traditional lines had constituted an important part of British imports from the East. However, in the period 1790-1830, mainly due to agency investment in such areas as indigo production, there was a three- to fourfold increase in the export of cash crops and a corresponding decline in demand for Indian manufactures which faced discriminatory tariffs in the United Kingdom. Writing in 1837 Captain Robert Grindlay, a pioneer of steam navigation to the

East, summed up how British investors and entrepreneurs saw the future Indian economy:

> India can never again be a great manufacturing country, but by culti-
> vating her connexion with England she may be one of the greatest
> agricultural nations . . . England will gain a double advantage by
> securing in India, at once a field for raising the raw material, and a
> market for the consumption of manufactured goods.[34]

Managing Agents and Particular Areas of Scottish Investment

In the decades following the credit crisis of 1830-3 a fresh system of private capital investment rose from the ashes of the old houses of agency. A new generation of men – to be known as managing agents – appeared who were better equipped to cater for the needs of an Indian economy freed from the shackles of the East India Company. Like the old mercantile houses they drew much of their capital, in the early days at least, from civil servants, soldiers, planters and other private investors in India who, on returning home, found it convenient to leave their concerns in the safe hands of an agent. As the century progressed and new fields of business opened up, individuals and companies in the United Kingdom with money to invest would entrust their holdings to the agents in return for commission.

As a small number of managing agents achieved an international reputation for reliability and sound business practice, capital was drawn to India which might not otherwise have been forthcoming given the attraction to investors in the late-Victorian period of other areas of the Empire, such as Australia, Canada and South Africa. Though the opening of the Suez Canal in 1869 and the extension of steam communication to India by the second half of the century considerably shortened the distances and travelling time between the United Kingdom and the East, Indian investments continued to be regarded with some suspicion by the Victorian middle classes. Spectacular business failures in the early 1830s and again in 1847, followed by the great jolt given to imperial self-confidence by the Mutiny of 1857 served only to confirm doubts about the wisdom of taking on financial commitments in India. With the exception of investment in railway building which, as will be seen, was underwritten by the Government of India, it was left to the managing agents to raise and direct capital into new enterprises.

By the end of the century a fairly small group of agents were in control of the major sectors of the economy of British India, comprising principally the production of cash crops such as tea, coffee, jute, and indigo. Less important areas of industrial development proper, such as steel production and coal mining, and the related fields of banking, insurance and shipping also came under their sway. The members of this ruling elite had progressed from acting on behalf of others to promoting new enterprises with their own capital. The leading firms might be registered variously in London, Glasgow and Calcutta but, as their names indicate, their origins were predominantly Scottish. They included Andrew Yule and Co., Burn and Co., Jardine, Skinner and Co., Jardine Matheson, Octavius Steel and Co., Begg, Dunlop and Co., Duncan Brothers and Co., James Finlay and Co., George Henderson and Co., and Shaw, Wallace and Co.

Burn and Co. and Jardine Matheson represented the nucleus of firms whose roots lay in the Company era and who had come through the financial difficulties of the 1830s unscathed and ideally situated to fill the vacuum left by the collapse of the agency house system. Burn and Co.'s pedigree stretched back as far as Jardine Matheson's having been founded in 1781 by Colonel Archibald Swinton who was later joined by his countryman Alexander Burn. Others of Indian background had arrived more recently. David Jardine began as a general merchant in the 1840s and by the end of the century his firm of Jardine, Skinner and Co. had investments in jute, tea, timber and coal, as well as interests in shipping and insurance. There were still opportunities for enterprising individuals lacking the normal commercial training and background. Dr David Begg came out to India in the early 1830s and with Charles Mackinnon, physician to the planters of Bihar, acquired huge interests in indigo plantations. Unlike his fellow investors, Begg had the foresight to move into sugar, and later into tea and jute, before the bottom dropped out of the indigo market, leaving Begg, Dunlop and Co. as one of the most powerful firms of managing agents in the country.[35]

The most important newcomers to the ranks of the managing agents from outside the country were a number of firms whose traditional interests lay in domestic British manufacturing and commerce, but whose business contacts with the East encouraged them to pursue new investments in India. Firms such as James Finlay and Co. and Duncan Brothers and Co., whose main concerns had been in Lanarkshire cotton, first of all sent junior partners to Bombay or Calcutta to better conduct their export trade, and eventually shifted the main part of their business from the west of Scotland to the tea and jute producing areas of India. Perhaps the biggest of the Scottish firms from this sort of background was Andrew Yule and Co.

Andrew Yule (1834-1902), son of a Stonehaven linen and woollen draper, was a partner with his brother George in a prosperous Manchester textile business by the late 1850s. Attracted by the possibilities for new investments in India, Andrew went out to Calcutta in 1863 and began work as an agent for insurance companies and British textile exporters. Under the vigorous management of Andrew Yule, and later of his nephew Sir David Yule, 1st Baronet (1858-1928), the firm invested heavily in jute and tea, buying up bankrupt mills and plantations as they came on the market and putting up capital for new ventures. The need for coal for the drying process in tea production and the importance of having efficient transport on the Ganges, Bengal's main commercial artery, led to further investment in coal mining and inland shipping. By 1911 Yules' combined capital in these fields was unsurpassed by any other firm in the country.[36]

As the spearhead of British investment in Victorian India there were few areas of the economy with which the managing agents were not concerned. For the purposes of the present study, however, it will be necessary to concentrate on those areas in which Scottish involvement was most marked.

Jute

As early as 1835 the East India Company had sent samples of raw jute from Bengal to the flax manufacturing centres of the United Kingdom in the hope that it might be developed for cordage. However, the jute in its natural state proved so coarse as to be unworkable until experiments in Dundee led, by the 1830s, to the 'batching', or softening, process by the application of a mixture of water and whale oil provided by the town's own whaling industry. Demand for the raw jute soon increased as Dundee and its surrounding area became a centre for the manufacture of carpets in the 1830s, and in the next decade for sacking for East Indian coffee, South American guana, etc.

Firms such as Nairns of Kirkcaldy, founded in 1847 to manufacture floor coverings from flax, now turned to jute. The industry received a tremendous boost during the Crimean War when the normal Baltic sources of flax and hemp were cut off, only to be struck by bankruptcies as the inevitable slump followed the end of hostilities. However, the American Civil War ushered in a further halcyon period for the Dundee manufacturers as they sold in vast quantities to both sides. Jute had established itself as Dundee's biggest manufactured product.

But this very success rebounded on the town as enterprising individuals realised that the production process perfected there could be transferred to the source of the raw jute in Bengal.[37]

Thanks to the ever-increasing demands of the Dundee jute manufacturers Bengal established itself by the middle of the century as the major source of the raw fibre. The next step, to the manufacture of jute in situ, was taken in 1854 when a former coffee planter, George Acland, imported a mill and staff from Dundee. Significantly Acland was financed by the managing agents, Jardine, Skinner and Co.[38] Early success soon attracted other managing agents who began to finance similar ventures in the Calcutta area. George Henderson, managing agent for the Glasgow-financed Borneo Co., which was founded in 1856 to trade with Sarawak, persuaded his principals to invest the firm's surplus capital in a jute mill which opened five years after Acland's venture. Once again overseers from Dundee were brought in to run the mill.[39]

By 1870 there were five jute mills in Bengal and local demand was no longer able to absorb production. Inevitably the Calcutta mills began to compete in the international market with the Dundonian ones, though in the early years at least Bengal concentrated more on courser products, leaving Dundee to monopolise the upper end of the market. Like its Scottish parent, the Bengal industry experienced alternating periods of boom and slump. The recurrent cycle served to strengthen the grip of the leading firms of managing agents who swallowed up the weaker and more speculative enterprises during the periods of depression.

The Dundee and Calcutta manufacturers periodically came to blows in their competition for the same markets. In 1894 the introduction of 24-hour shift working in Calcutta, associated with the threat of Indian jute products to traditional Scottish markets in the United States, led to protests from Dundee about the exploitation of Calcutta mill workers and to an enquiry by the Indian Government. However, the Bengal industry was too dependent on its Scottish parent for the continuance of any serious division. The Calcutta firms recruited their overseers and technicians almost exclusively from the Dundee area throughout this period and the tradition continued well into the present century with many examples of generations of family involvement with the same mills. Machinery, too, came largely from Tayside foundries.

There was also investment by Dundonian jute interests in the ownership of Calcutta mills, but this is less easy to chart. One example was the highly successful Samnugger Co. floated in 1873 by J. J. Barrie of

Dundee in conjunction with Thomas Duff, formerly of the Borneo Co. The firm led the Indian challenge to Scottish jute manufacturers on the international stage, making considerable inroads into the San Francisco hessian wheat sack and Australian corn bag markets.[40] One estimate has put Dundonian ownership in Bengal at 10 per cent in the last two decades of the century, and this figure was probably exceeded by the Calcutta interests of the other areas of Scotland such as Glasgow.[41]

The real power lay with the oligarchy of managing agents based in Calcutta. By the end of the century the majority of plantations and mills were either owned or controlled by them. They dominated every stage of production. They ran the inland shipping concerns which transported the raw jute to the mills and the labour force from areas of high population density to the plantations, and acted for the international shipping lines which carried their exports. Their partners sat on the bodies representing the various parts of the industry – the Jute Dealers Association, the Jute Fabric Shippers Association and the powerful Indian Jute Mills Association. This, combined with the strength of the Scottish elements in the industry, helped secure a remarkable degree of co-operation among all those involved. In times of market depression the IJMA's members could be relied upon to present a united front in pricing and in limiting production when the future of the industry as a whole was at stake. By 1914 the Scottish contribution to the development of the industry in terms of the provision of capital, management skills and technical expertise had made it one of the country's two greatest manufacturing industries, rivalled only by cotton which was largely Indian financed and free of British involvement.

Tea

The development of tea production in India shows many of the same features as jute. The East India Company's trade in this commodity had been based almost entirely on China tea. However, following experiments with imported and indigenous plants in north-east India, several nurseries were established by the end of the 1830s. The new field of investment proved particularly attractive to British-based firms who had a traditional connection with the East India Company's tea trade. Scottish firms in close touch with their countrymen in the East were quick to take advantage of the ending of the Company monopoly in 1833 to import direct to their places of business. The Edinburgh dealer Andrew Melrose was one of several Scots importers organising the first shipment of tea to Leith in 1835 through the agency of Jardine Matheson.[42] Two of the most successful firms to switch the bulk of their capital to tea in the course of the century were Duncan Brothers and James Finlay and Co.

The Glasgow firm of Playfair, Bryce and Co. sent out to Calcutta in 1859 a junior partner, one Walter Duncan, to handle its sale of cotton piece goods. By the 1870s the firm, now Walter Duncan and Co. in Glasgow and Duncan Brothers in Bengal, was withdrawing from its former business in cotton exports and taking on agency work for owners of tea gardens. A succession of young and enthusiastic members of the Duncan family went out to run the Calcutta branch and pursued an aggressive policy of tea investment. When Walter Duncan died in 1899 the firm either owned or managed 25 estates in north-east India with nearly 19,000 acres under cultivation, rising to 38 estates by 1911, as well as maintaining interests in other areas such as jute and shipping. Throughout this period the firm retained strong connections with Scotland. Despite the increasing concentration of their business in India, Duncans' head office remained in Glasgow until after the First World War when the international scale of their operations necessitated a move to London. Similarly, when the firm floated the Anglo-India Jute Mill Co. in 1895 as its first venture into jute manufacturing the new subsidiary was registered in Scotland.[43]

The connection of James Finlay and Co. with India pre-dated that of Duncans' and was largely attributable to the policies of Kirkman Finlay, son of the founder, whose part in the victory of private enterprise over the East India Company has already been noted. Under his direction the firm gradually forsook its business commitments in the west of Scotland for fresh pastures in India. This trend was continued under later partners, most notably Sir John Muir, 1st Baronet (1828-1903) who married into the firm and was sole proprietory partner from 1883. While retaining Finlays' headquarters in Glasgow, he opened up branches all over India and was responsible for a programme of extensive investment in existing regions of tea growing in the north-east of the country as well as in new areas such as south-central India, where a depression forced many coffee planters to sell out to his subsidiaries, the North and South Sylhet Tea Companies. By 1896 over two-thirds of the area planted out with tea in the rich Kanan Devan Hills region of the south belonged to the Finlay Group making it 'almost a James Finlay preserve'.[44] At the time of Muir's death the firm controlled 74,000 acres under tea and employed a work force of some 70,000.[45]

As in the jute industry managing agents like Duncans and Finlays involved themselves at every level of production. When problems arose in the 1880s over the supply of an adequate work force for the tea gardens in north-east India the agents formed the Tea Districts Labour

Supply Association with branches in neighbouring regions to recruit greater numbers of native workers. But difficulties could normally be ironed out by organisations like the Indian Tea Association representing the interest of those agents with the biggest stakes in tea production. Like its equivalent, the Indian Jute Mills Association, it was closely affiliated to the Bengal Chamber of Commerce whose influence extended to every sector of the region's economy. The Scottish connection with tea in India is also evident in terms of contributions to improved techniques of production. The Glasgow-born Claud Bald (1853-1924), who spent 26 years as manager of a plantation at Darjeeling, was author of *India Tea*, one of the best-known technical works on tea growing and preparation.[46] Also important was William Jackson (1849-1915), who returned to his native Aberdeen after working on one of the Scottish Assam Company's gardens, and developed new machinery for the tea drying process.[47]

As a result of the vigorous investment policies of firms like Finlays, Duncans, Yules and Begg, Dunlop and Co., India overtook China during the 1880s as the world's greatest exporter of tea, and opened up new markets in such areas as Australia and the United States. In conjunction with Octavius Steel and Co., Shaw, Wallace and Co., Williamson, Magor and Co., and Bird and Co. the above-mentioned firms controlled over 60 per cent of Indian tea production in the first decade of the new century.[48] Tea had become one of India's largest sources of foreign revenue and employers of labour, with an invested capital in 1900 of £20 millions and with half a million acres under cultivation.[49]

Shipping and Railways

The opening up of India and China to private enterprise and the subsequent increase in the number of firms participating in trade and investment there led to demands for faster and more efficient means of communication. In the period before the appearance of the Suez Canal firms such as Alexander Hall and Co. of Aberdeen and Robert Steele and Co. of Greenock led the field in the design and construction of fast oceangoing clippers whose races to be first home with the season's tea during the 1860s became legendary. But the real future of communications with India by sea rested with steam. Best placed to take advantage of the ending of the East India Company's monopoly were well established firms such as Jardine Matheson, who were already in control of an extensive fleet for the Eastern coastal trade, or the Burma Steam Navigation Co., set up by Robert Mackenzie of Calcutta's Scots mercantile community in partnership with William Mackinnon (1823-93) from

Glasgow. The firm began by acquiring the East India Company's contract to carry the mails between Bengal and Burma. With a combined capital raised through the respective connections of the two men in the west of Scotland and Calcutta the firm became the British India Steam Navigation Co. Under the management of Mackinnon, created a baronet in 1889, the company extended its passenger and carrying trade to East Africa and the British Isles, emerging as one of the foremost shipping lines in the East.[50]

Stimulated by the success of Mackinnon and of the managing agents' shipping ventures, British-based lines began to look East. Those firms specialising in trade with India by the third quarter of the nineteenth century included the Blue Funnel, Shire, Peninsular and Orient, Glen and Castle lines, the last three of which were Scottish-based or run. The largest of these, the P & O, had been part founded by an Orcadian, Arthur Anderson (1792-1868). The firm's early interests were in trade with Spain and Portugal. When the carrying of the Indian mails was put out to tender in 1840 by the East India Company, the P & O won the contract to carry them as far as Egypt from where they were taken over land to the Persian Gulf for collection by Company ships from Bombay. Soon Anderson was providing staging posts on the Nile and was able to carry both passengers and cargo through to the Gulf and on to India.

The opening of the Suez Canal ushered in a period of cutthroat competition. From a rate of £10 to £12 a ton from Calcutta in 1869 freight charges dropped to 20s. to 30s. by 1887.[51] Attempts were made to fix rates charged by the established lines in 1879 but the entry of new firms, such as the Glasgow-based Ben Line, in the last two decades of the century made regulation difficult and led to some companies, like the Castle Line, going out of business. Larger enterprises were able to swallow up less profitable ones. The P & O merged with Mackinnon's BISNC in 1914 producing a combined tonnage of one and a quarter million and capital of £15 million.[52] Under the management of James Mackay, 1st Earl of Inchcape (1852-1932), who had come out from Scotland to join Mackinnon in 1874, the new firm embarked on a policy of absorbing its smaller competitors. Thus, while the provision of an efficient and modern system of steam communication undoubtedly served as a stimulus to the Indian economy, it also helped render this area of British investment in the East almost as monopolistic as the managing agents' control of mainland crop production and industry.

Despite the obvious advantages accruing to the Indian Government from improved communications with the United Kingdom, the real drive for investment in this quarter came not from the East India Company, but from private enterprise with the managing agents at the forefront. As has been seen, Jardine Matheson's shipping interests sprang directly from their mercantile pursuits. Shipping magnates such as Mackinnon and Mackay had intimate connections with the Calcutta agents. Thus Mackay was a senior partner in Macneill and Co. and was chairman of the Bengal Chamber of Commerce and Sir James Matheson was chairman of the P & O up to 1858. In the same way the early pressure for the introduction of railways to India came from the Bengal and Bombay managing agents. As various schemes were submitted to the East India Company for approval it soon became clear that the directors were concerned primarily with the strategic importance of the proposed rail links and not with their potential value to the Indian economy. However, private investment found support in the person of Lord Dalhousie, Governor-General, 1848-55, who actively campaigned for the victory of private over public interests because of the 'tendency of English rule to paralyze initiative in India'.[53]

Early ventures such as the East India Railway Co., set up in 1845 to press for East India Company permission to build a rail link between Calcutta and Mirzipur, and representatives from a number of the main firms of managing agents on its board.[54] But the huge amounts of capital required for the planning and construction of a rail system, and for the purchase from the United Kingdom of locomotives and rolling stock, could not be raised in India alone. The managing agents had to attract British investment to a continent which, as has been seen, compared unfavourably with other parts of the Empire. Following protracted negotiations in the late 1840s an agreement was reached whereby the Government of India agreed to guarantee a 5 per cent dividend for investors in the railways, the ownership of which would revert to the Government after 99 years.[55] With such safeguards railway development in India became much more of an attractive proposition to private British capital and the way was clear for the construction of a national network of railways.

Banking

The key position the agency houses and their successor the managing agents had built up as the major suppliers of capital in nineteenth-century India left few opportunities for the growth of a proper banking system. The East India Company had also shown little enthusiasm for the emergence of an independent banking establishment which might challenge its lucrative exchange business between India and London.

The Company had permitted the setting up of three banks in Bengal, Bombay and Madras in 1806, 1840, and 1843 respectively to handle the banking of its local administrations but it retained a say in the choice of directors and subscribed much of the capital.[56]

By the 1840s there was pressure on the Indian Government to allow the establishment of chartered banks, which enjoyed limited liability status. One of the first schemes for such a bank was put forward by the Hawick-born James Wilson (1805-60), who entered politics after a successful career as a London hat maker. As joint-secretary to the Board of Control he became involved with Indian affairs. In 1852 he produced a plan for a Bank of India, Australia and China to provide 'legitimate facilities of Banking to the vast and rapidly extending trading between the Australian colonies, British India, China, and other parts of the Eastern archipelago'.[57] To attract British investors who were ever wary of speculative ventures in the East the Bank's first prospectus prohibited it from making advances where cash crops were the only security and from involving itself in any form of mercantile activity. To secure a firm footing for the new bank in India he brought in representatives of a number of the great Calcutta managing agents.

In the next 20 years branches were established all over the eastern hemisphere. By 1870 the rapid growth in tea and jute production proved too much for the bank to resist, and the restrictions on its investment policy set out in the first prospectus were overturned and a tea garden financed in 1878. As other chartered banks were set up only to collapse in the periodic credit crises of the period, Wilson's bank went from strength to strength and was the most powerful bank in the East by the turn of the century. All the time close connections were maintained with the managing agents who controlled so much of the Indian economy, with powerful figures such as Lord Inchcape serving on the board. A tradition of Scottish management of the bank was carried on into the next century. Wilson himself was succeeded on the board by his countryman William Nicol (1790-1879), founder of the Bombay firm of managing agents of that name.

While this study has been concerned primarily with the positive aspects of Scottish involvement in the economic development of India, something has also to be said on the debit side. The Scots who played a major part in determining the areas into which British investment was directed must bear some of the responsibility for India's failure to realise her full industrial potential. India remained subservient to the needs of the British economy both in her development as a producer of cash crops and raw materials, and as a market for British manufactures. The tight control exercised by the managing agents and the exclusion of Indian capital and personnel from all but a few areas of investment prevented the emergence of a more independent and truly Indian-run economy.

A common feature of the whole period was the inability of the British to identify wholeheartedly with Indian interests. Neither the free merchant of the East India Company era nor the Victorian managing agent saw his residence in India as anything more than a temporary exile. Having made his fortune or fulfilled his contract, he would return home to enjoy his retirement. Though firms such as Duncans and Finlays might move the whole scope of their operations to India the continuous two-way stream of young hopefuls coming out and older men going home, the long traditions of family involvement in business enterprise and a strong sense of national identity meant that their Scottishness was never under threat.

Notes

1. See John Prebble, *The Darien Disaster* (London, 1968).

2. For Scots Jacobites serving with continental East India companies, see A.A. Cormack, *The Carnegie Family in Gothenburg* (Montrose, 1947); P.T.S.E. Hauch-Fausboll, *Records of the Browns of Colstoun House* (Copenhagen, 1930); G. Chaussinand-Nogaret, 'Religion et Societé Une elite insulaire au service de l'Europe: les Jacobites au XVIIIe siecle' in *Annales*, vol. 28 (1973), pp. 1097-122.

3. Peter Auber, *An Analysis of the Constitution of the East India Company* (London, 1826), pp. 204-5.

4. For Stewart, see A.B. Beaven, *The Aldermen of the City of London*, 2 vols. (London, 1908, 1913), vol. 1, pp. 134, 344, 350; vol. 2, p. 122.

5. For Drummond, see Romney Sedgwick, *The House of Commons, 1715-1754*, vol. 1 , pp. 622-4; his papers are in the Scottish Record Office, GD 24/1/464/C.

6. For Foulis and the Moffatts, see J.G. Parker, 'The Directors of the East India Company, 1754-1790', unpublished PhD thesis, Edinburgh University, 1977, pp. 182-6 and passim.

7. For the Humes and Dundas, see Sir L.B. Namier and John Brooke, *The House of Commons, 1754-1790*, 3 vols. (London, 1964), vol. 1, pp. 357-61; vol. 2, pp. 652-3.

8. P.J. Marshall, *East Indian Fortunes, The British in Bengal in the Eighteenth Century* (Oxford, 1976), p. 12.

9. Scottish Record Office, GD 110/1021/6, 13: Stair Dalrymple to Sir Hew Dalrymple, 1 November 1752, 3 January 1754.

10. Scottish Record Office, GD 29/2136: Thomas Graham to John Graham, 28 January 1773.

11. For Michie, see Parker, pp. 175-8.

12. Guildhall Library, MS 5881, file 2: Jonathan Duncan to John Michie, 22 February 1784.

13. For the Johnstone party in the Company, see L.S. Sutherland, *The East India Company in Eighteenth Century Politics*, 2nd edn (Oxford, 1962), pp. 116-55; M.M. Stuart, 'Lying under the Company's Displeasure' in *South Asian Review*, vol. 8, no. 1 (October 1974), pp. 48-52.

. 14. For Dundas, see Cyril Matheson, *The Life of Henry Dundas First Viscount Melville* (London, 1933); Barun De, 'Henry Dundas and the Government of India (1773-1801). A Study in Constitutional Ideas', unpublished DPhil thesis, Oxford University, 1961.

15. Scottish Record Office, GD 224/30/4/25/3 (1-2): Henry Dundas to John Rutherford, 31 October 1804. I am indebted to David Brown of the Scottish History Department, Edinburgh University for drawing my attention to this letter. Quoted with the kind permission of His Grace the Duke of Buccleuch.

16. Scottish Record Office, GD 51/17/69, f 4: Henry Dundas to Sir Archibald Campbell, 23 March 1787.

17. Marshall, *Indian Fortunes*, p. 29.

18. S.B. Singh, *European Agency Houses in Bengal, 1783-1833* (Calcutta, 1966), pp. 9-10.

19. Ibid, pp. 11, 20; Amales Tripathi, *Trade and Finance in the Bengal Presidency, 1793-1833* (Bombay, 1956), pp. 88, 118, 143.

20. Henry Dundas to W.W. Grenville, 30 May 1790, quoted in Historical Manuscripts Commission, Thirteenth Report, Appendix (London, 1892), vol. 1, p. 588.

21. David Scott to 1st Earl of Mornington, 2 January 1798, quoted in C.H. Philips (ed.), *The Correspondence of David Scott*, 2 vols. (London, 1951), Camden Third Series, vol. 75, p. 122.

22. Holden Furber, *John Company at Work. A Study of European Expansion in India in the late Eighteenth Century* (Harvard, 1948), vol. 60, p. 221.

23. Quoted in K.N. Chaudhuri (ed.), *the Economic Development of India under the East India Company, 1814-58* (Cambridge, 1971), p. 297n.

24. David Scott to William Fairlie, 30 March 1795, quoted in Philips, *Correspondence of David Scott*, vol. 75, p. 29.

25. William Jardine to Andrew Johnstone, 21 March 1830, quoted in W.E. Cheong, *Mandarins and Merchants, Jardine Matheson & Co., a China agency of the early nineteenth century* (London, 1979), p. 208.

26. Quoted in Michael Greenberg, *British Trade and the Opening of China, 1800-1842* (Cambridge, 1951), p. 39n.

27. For Matheson, see Alexander Mackenzie, *History of the Mathesons* (Inverness, 1882), pp. 59-72; for Forbes, see his entry in the *Dictionary of National Biography*.

28. For Hamilton & Reid and Dent & Co., see Greenberg, *British Trade*, pp. 23-33.

29. Ibid., p. 34.

30. D.H. Buchanan, *The Development of Capitalistic Enterprise in India* 2nd edn (London, 1966), p. 40.

31. Tripathi, *Trade and Finance*, pp. 124-7; C.H. Philips, *The East India Company, 1784-1834*, 3rd edn (Manchester, 1968), p. 184.

32. Quoted in Philips, *East India Company*, p. 243n.

33. Colm Brogan, *James Finlay & Company Limited, Manufacturers and East India Merchants, 1750-1950* (Glasgow, 1951), pp. 10-11; Greenberg, *British Trade*, p. 101

34. Quoted in Daniel Thorner, *Investment in Empire: British railway and steam shipping enterprise in India, 1825-49* (Philadelphia, 1950), p. 6.

35. For the background to these firms, see Somerset Playne and Arnold Wright (eds.), *Bengal and Assam, Behar and Orissa. Their History, People,*

Commerce and Industrial Relations (London, 1917), pp. 91, 128; A.K. Bagchi, *Private Investment in India, 1900-1939* (Cambridge, 1972), pp. 188, 363.

36. For a history of the firm, see *Andrew Yule & Co. Ltd., 1863-1963* (Privately printed, 1963). A copy of this work was kindly made available by the present firm, Yule Catto and Co.

37. See Bruce Lenman, Charlotte Lythe and Enid Gauldie, *Dundee and its Textile Industry, 1850-1914* (Dundee, 1969), publication no. 14.

38. D.R. Wallace, *The Romance of Jute. A short history of the Calcutta Jute Mill Industry, 1855-1927* 2nd edn (London, 1928), pp. 7-14; Buchanan, *Capitalistic Enterprise*, p. 152.

39. H.C. Longhurst, *The Borneo Story, The History of the First 200 Years of Trading in the Far East by the Borneo Company Limited* (London, 1956), p. 17; Wallace, *Jute*, p. 15.

40. Wallace, *Jute*, pp. 36-7.

41. Lenman, Lythe and Gauldie, *Dundee*, p. 34.

42. Hoh-Cheung Mui and Lorna H. Mui, 'Andrew Melrose Tea Dealer and Grocer of Edinburgh, 1812-1853' in *Business History*, vol. 9, no. 1 (January 1967), pp. 35-6.

43. See *The Duncan Group, Being a short history of Duncan Brothers, 1859-1959* (London, 1959).

44. Sir P.J. Griffiths, *The History of the Indian Tea Industry* (London, 1967), p. 159.

45. Brogan, *James Finlay*, p. 47.

46. W.H. Ukers, *All About Tea*, 2 vols. (New York, 1935), pp. 160-1.

47. Bruce Lenman, *An Economic History of Scotland, 1660-1976* (London, 1977), p. 192.

48. Bagchi, *Private Investment*, p. 176.

49. Griffiths, *India Tea*, p. 140.

50. See Boyd Cable, *A Hundred Year History of the P & O 1837-1937* (London, 1937).

51. Ibid., p. 183.

52. Ibid., p. 207.

53. Quoted in L.H. Jenks, *The Migration of British Capital to 1875*, 2nd edn (London, 1963), p. 212.

54. Thorner, *Investment in Empire*, p. 61.

55. Ibid., p. 169.

56. T.B. Desai, *Economic History of India under the British* (Bombay, 1968), p. 207.

57. Quoted in Compton Mackenzie, *Realms of Silver. One Hundred Years of Banking in the East. A history of the Chartered Bank of India, Australia and China* (London, 1954), p. 5.

8 THE SCOTS IN LATIN AMERICA: A SURVEY

Manuel A. Fernandez

The routes to Latin America were not among those most frequented by wandering Scotsmen during the nineteenth century. They showed greater interest in other areas that either were, or had been, parts of the British Empire. For many reasons the southern half of the New World proved to be somewhat inaccessible to Scotsmen, and the dreams of grandeur that the continent evoked in the minds of the most intrepid and enterprising — as in the unfortunate Darien Scheme — were often fatefully crushed by a combination of the hostile environment and the zeal with which the Spaniards guarded their own empire. Indeed the fact that Latin America had been a part of the Spanish and Portuguese empires for more than 300 years prior to the nineteenth century was the main obstacle to the formation of a nucleus of British settlements that could be built upon later, when the industrial revolution in Britain demanded an integration of markets on a world-wide scale.

The hostility of the Latin American environment therefore was not simply a question of wild jungles, rivers, swamps, yellow fever or small pox. There was also the problem of cultural differences that were inimical to prospective Protestant and English speaking settlers. Besides, Latin America was a continent in turmoil during the first three decades of the nineteenth century, as the old colonial yoke was broken in most Spanish possessions and the resulting republics proved unable to generate stable political and social institutions that would guarantee a degree of economic success, let alone safety of life, to European immigrants, however welcome these were made by the factions or caudillos in power at the time. Yet, notwithstanding many difficulties, there are visible signs of a significant Scottish presence in Latin America, even during the period when the sub-continent was still under the aegis of Spain and Portugal. If we are to believe the account of the French Jesuit historian Charlevoix, Father Thomas Field, a Catholic missionary, was probably the first Scot to settle in South America, as early as 1586.[1] Father Field was a member of a party of five Jesuit missionaries (two Portuguese, one Spaniard, one Italian and Field) who set sail from Brazil, heading towards the Guarani lands in modern Paraguay. They had the misfortune of meeting an English pirate ship at sea whose captain 's'emporta contr'eux d'une maniere indecente' giving full expression to the ardent reformist feelings so prevalent at the time. Having endured fierce deprecations against popery, the five Jesuits were put into a boat, without provisions or oars and left to die in the high seas. Fortunately, however, they were placed in a shore-bound stream and drifted toward Buenos Aires, which they reached alive, and where they were able to find comfort and provisions in order to recommence their journey. They settled in Asuncion, where they were the pioneers of the most successful Jesuit enterprise in Latin America. Their arrival there coincided with the outbreak of an epidemic, and they were faced with the toilsome operation of assisting the suffering Indians.[2] Field later became a devoted preacher in fluent Guarani language, and as the director of the Jesuit school founded in the settlement, made a major contribution to the conversion of over 200,000 Guaranies. In 1625, having spent nearly 40 years in Paraguay, Field died 'at a very advanced age and plentiful in virtue'.[3]

Other Scotsmen who went to Latin America before the nineteenth century were generally involved in more mundane affairs than Field. One such case was the buccaneer Wallace, who is usually associated with the foundation of Belize, or British Honduras, which he accomplished by forming alliances with the local Indians, defying the Spaniards and successfully establishing a British colony of logwood settlers during the first part of the seventeenth century.[4]

There must have been other instances of Scottish connections with Latin America in previous centuries, but this section aims to survey the various ways in which Scotland carved a place for herself in Latin American history during the nineteenth century. Naturally, being such an extensive area and because of the lack of previous work on the topic, this survey on Latin America must be selective and to a large extent circumscribed to the southernmost cone of the continent involving mainly Uruguay, Paraguay, Argentina and Chile.[5]

Looking at the expansion of British interests in Latin America, the first impression one receives is that Scotland was almost absent from this process. It is only through a careful scrutiny of the sources that a distinctive Scottish component can be detected. There are various reasons for such a false first impression. Two in particular must be mentioned. One, of course, was the widespread use in all specialist literature of the words 'England' and 'English' as synonymous with 'Britain' and 'British' respectively, which, applied indistinctively to settlers, merchants, investors and others resulted in an unwitting concealment of the non-English component of British expansion overseas.

Even Michael Mulhall, an Irishman very conscious of his nationality and author of the best study on British interests in Latin America during the 1870s, gave his account the misleading title *The English in South America*. This custom persisted well beyond the turn of the nineteenth century. For instance, a correspondent of *The Economist* visiting the nitrate establishments in northern Chile in 1909, reported to London as follows:

> The machinery was all made in England, chiefly in Glasgow, and as a proof of the value of English workmanship, it may be stated that the refuse from English machinery only contains two or three percent of nitrate.[6]

Another more important factor that disguised the Scottish presence in Latin America was that many enterprises founded by Scotsmen were not in fact launched in Scotland, but rather emerged from very simple origins in Latin America, using the experience acquired in menial jobs and achieving economic success the hard way. This meant that such enterprises are not mentioned in standard sources such as the *Stock Exchange Yearbook*, *Company Register Office*, or other financial literature. This aspect raises the issue of assimilation into the host economy and questions the legitimacy of us referring to 'Scottish' enterprises, when they had in fact already become part of another country's economy.

Nevertheless, it can be argued that, in as much as the Scots concerned remained Scots, that their profits were remitted at least partially to Scotland, and that the individuals concerned eventually returned to Scotland, as generally seems to be the case, it is still legitimate to treat such cases as forming part of the Scottish enterprises abroad. It is in this context that a distinction can be drawn between the English, Scottish, and Irish presence in Latin America. They differed in the first place in the numbers of individuals concerned, and in the case of Argentina, the country where by far the largest number of Britons settled during the nineteenth century, shows that the Irish constituted the largest sector with the Scottish and the English a long way behind. The British consul in Buenos Aires reported in 1865: 'the British population is calculated at 32,000, of which number 28,000 are Irish'.[7] The remaining 4,000 were equally divided between Scots and English.

Another more significant difference was found in the degree of integration into the host country. The impression left by all accounts is that the attitudes of Scotsmen towards integration lay midway between the tendency towards total assimilation shown by the Irish and the attitude of the English, more determined to remain aloof with regard to the local society. In the case of the Irish, despite the many institutions that tended to preserve their cultural identity, their social and economic status and their religion helped to draw them closer towards the local communities.

Scots, on the other hand, kept a balance between an allegiance to their cultural heritage and a sense of responsibility towards the country that had received them. In the words of an outstanding Scottish entrepreneur in Argentina, the duty of a pioneer in the new lands of a vast country did not 'necessarily mean the making of great fortunes. . . but the cultivation of every thousand acres of land produce the greatest amount of comfort for the maximum number of people'.[8]

The 'Scottishness' of the expatriate community in Latin America manifested itself in many ways, be it in the commemoration of significant dates, in the persistent loyalty to the Presbyterian faith, in the organisation of Scottish societies, and on particular occasions, the wearing of their typical costumes. As for their commitment towards the local communities, this varied according to the particular nature of the activities in which they were engaged in nineteenth-century Latin America.

Scotland in the Struggle for Latin American Independence

Very few British merchants ventured into Latin America prior to the period of struggle for independence from Spain, since the establishment of full economic relations between Britain and Latin America necessitated the breaking of the commercial monopoly enforced by Spain on her American colonies.

By the end of the eighteenth century the British government had already realised that there was much to be gained from a Latin America independent from Spain. When British forces captured Trinidad in 1797, the government saw that the newly acquired territory could be used as a bridgehead for the liberation of the Spanish colonies from the 'oppressive authority of the peninsular crown', and the first governor appointed in Trinidad was instructed to act accordingly.[9] Moreover, in those years young Latin Americans like Francisco Miranda and Bernardo O'Higgins had begun to promote actively their continent's independence in Britain. In fact it was partly due to the persuasive arguments that Miranda brought to bear upon the Foreign Office that the expedition led by Commodore Sir Home Popham was despatched in 1806. The original objective of the mission was to attack Spanish positions in Venezuela, Miranda's native country, but Popham, on his own initiative, decided to direct the attack against the River Plate, with disastrous results. Buenos Aires rose in arms in defence of the Spanish Crown and successfully defeated Popham in 1806, as also the reinforcements led by Whitelocke in 1807.[10]

The failed expedition had a favourable impact on the independence movement in the sense that it demonstrated the capability of the local 'criollo' army to resist an invasion from Europe. The same capability was later to be used against the forces of King Ferdinand of Spain, in whose name the English had been defeated. On the other hand the failed expedition also raised the hopes of a large number of merchants in Britain who foresaw the possibility of making a fortune in the liberated territory of Latin America.

John Parish Robertson — that remarkable Scottish merchant, then only 14 years old — was present in Rio de la Plata during the later stage of the attempted British invasion of Buenos Aires, and in his *Letters from Paraguay* has left a beautiful account of the early vicissitudes of British merchants in Argentina. With many others, Robertson had sailed from Greenock in 1806 in a fine ship called *Enterprise*, in the wake of the Rio de la Plata expedition. In his words,

> British commerce, ever on the wings for foreign lands, soon unfurled the sails of her ships for South America. The rich, the poor, the needy, the speculative and the ambitious all looked to the making or mending of their fortunes in those favoured regions.[11]

The Buenos Aires defeat, however, was a catastrophe that shattered the illusions of the hopeful merchants. Two hundred and fifty ships had to hastily leave the River Plate with the mortification of seeing the Spanish colours flying in the citadel of Buenos Aires. The failed experience of 1806-7 reinforced the conviction in Britain that the independence of Spanish America was a necessary prerequisite to the full penetration of British trade into the area. The reality prompted army and navy men from Britain, many of them redundant after the Napoleonic wars in Europe, to go to Latin America and help eradicate Spanish rule from the continent. Although few of them went there purely for idealistic reasons, the fact remains that they were materially important in the final defeat of Spanish power, and the Scots featured prominently among those who went; their role was crucially important, whether as officers or rank and file, admirals, or privateers.

By and large the most outstanding British figure in the struggle for Latin American independence was Lord Thomas Cochrane, a man from Lanarkshire who vindicated his reputation in the seas of Chile, Brazil and Greece. Cochrane's astounding naval career has been amply documented and we need only sketch the main features of his participation in the struggle for the independence of Chile and Peru.[12] Perhaps it was providential that an invitation by the nascent Chilean republic in 1817 reached Cochrane at a moment when he had fallen in disgrace at the House of Commons, from which he was expelled, despite his forceful claims of innocence and the reputation he had established during his naval career. Having accepted the invitation, he found himself in Chile, entrusted with the formidable task of strengthening the precarious independence from Spain by checking the powerful peninsular navy based in the Spanish stronghold of Callao, when Peru still was under Spanish power. Given the poverty of resources that prevailed in Chile, the limited number of ships put under his command and the total lack of naval traditions and sailors with which to accomplish such a daunting task, Cochrane could only rely on his ingenuity, his ability to attack by surprise, and the sheer gallantry of his crew. Cochrane made several incursions into the coastal waters of Peru, captured several enemy ships and defeated the Spaniards in Valdivia, a port deemed impregnable by the Spaniards. He also achieved a hard-earned success in Callao by defeating the largest proportion of the Spanish fleet in the Pacific. His campaign resulted in the capture or destruction of 11 Spanish war vessels and 17 gunboats. The inhabitants of Valparaiso, the main Chilean port, took to the harbour and the streets to give Cochrane a rapturous welcome when the triumphant Chilean fleet returned.

It was unfortunate that having served both Chile and Peru in the struggle against Spain, Cochrane's glorious naval achievements were not matched with similar success in his relations with the new Latin American leaders ruling the emerging republics. Cochrane's independent style conflicted with the natural aims of a new authority anxious to assert its central control over the newly independent states. Antagonism concerning power and money developed between the Latin American authorities and Cochrane, leading the latter to resign his post of vice-admiral in the Chilean navy and to accept a subsequent invitation to render his valuable services to Brazil in 1823. Lord Cochrane's contribution to Latin America's independence, however, has been universally acknowledged by all historians of the new republics, and one of them has gone to the extent of asserting that Cochrane, 'in English hearts is second only to Nelson, and in Chilean hearts, second to none'.[13]

During his campaign in the Pacific, Cochrane always took pride in his Scottish origins, a fact frequently remarked upon by his contemporaries, even in minor details. For instance, on special occasions he would not only dress in the full costume of a Scottish chief, but also once persuaded the Chileans at a dinner he offered on St Andrew's day to declare the latter as the patron saint for the liberating campaign which was about to start.[14] In this he was not alone, since there is every indication that a number of Scots followed him in his campaign and his compatriot MacFarlane, whom Cochrane appointed farm manager of the hacienda received from the Chilean government, seems to have been the vice-admiral's right hand man in Chile.[15]

Sir Gregor MacGregor, a Highlander, was another remarkable man of arms who became involved in Latin America's struggle for independence. He went to Venezuela in 1811, married a lady from Caracas, Dona Josefa Lovera, and engaged in a succession of both military and economic activities. The great honours he achieved in battle contrasted sharply with the disastrous results of MacGregor's financial endeavours. On his arrival at the beginning of the independence wars, he enlisted in the Venezuelan army, soon becoming a colonel at the service of General Miranda. Two years later he served under Simon Bolivar, until he was appointed the commander of a division, even replacing Bolivar on certain occasions. His military campaign resulted in the capture of Maracaibo, Quebrada Honda and Alacran, and his participation was also decisive in the battle of Juncal, which secured the independence of a major part of Venezuela in 1816.[16] MacGregor's most successful military tactics, which allowed him to defeat larger numbers of Spaniards, consisted of gaining the support of various Indian tribes which agreed to fight under his command. MacGregor might well have been a source of wonder to his troops, dressed in his full Highland regalia and with bagpipes resounding in the plains of Venezuela, about to enter military engagement.[17] In 1817, when Venezuela's independence had been secured and MacGregor had been duly decorated with the Medal of the Order of Libertadores awarded by Bolivar, he left Caracas and occupied himself with less worthy enterprises until 1822, the year in which he conceived his ill-judged Poyais scheme, to which we shall refer later.

Besides Cochrane and MacGregor, a good many Scotsmen took part in Latin America's struggles for independence. At least two other names deserve mention. One was Captain Robertson, a Scot who served under the Chilean navy in 1822, not against the Spaniards in Peru, where

Cochrane was then fighting, but in southern Chile, where some penin-sular forces were attempting to foment an Indian uprising against the emerging Chilean republic. Captain Robertson was granted the Island of Mocha in Chile in recognition of his services to the Chilean govern-ment. He settled there with his Chilean wife and was joined later by a brother from Scotland.[18] The second name is that of a privateer, 'the famous MacKay, a daring Scot who took by assault the Spanish ship *Minerva* . . . under the most extraordinary circumstances'.[19] Indeed the *Minerva*, a major ship in the Spanish Armada, was captured by MacKay with only 24 comrades in a successful assault carefully planned in Val-paraiso in the early 1810s.

Apart from the personal desire for honour and money the partici-pation by Scots in the independence wars was regarded by contemp-oraries as necessary for securing the development of economic inter-course between Britain and the new republics. It was natural that by 1815 a war-weary Europe should look upon the territories then being freed from Spain and Portugal as a land of promise. In Britain the trans-ition from illegal to legal trade with Latin America which developed against the background of the Napoleonic wars, undoubtedly helped to weather the harsh depression then prevailing by providing a substantial outlet for British exports. Indeed, more than one-third of all British ex-ports were diverted to Latin America during the Napoleonic wars.[20] British merchants anxiously followed the development of the indepen-dence wars and from 1815 onwards insistently lobbied the government, calling for Britain's official recognition of the new republics, or at least, the negotiation of a new treaty with Spain that would include trade regulations more liberal than those prevailing in the eighteenth century.[21]

It is interesting to note that the inroads made by the British mercen-aries into Spanish and Portuguese domination in Latin America were quickly followed up by eager merchants and mine surveyors from Britain. John Parish Robertson, the merchant from Kelso already mentioned, was closely associated with General Miller, a remarkable English campaigner who fought hand in hand with San Martin and O'Higgins for the independence of Chile and Peru. The Scotsman was quick to engage in commercial pursuits in the liberated zones, and it is likely that he supported financially the armed side of British presence in Chile and Peru.[22] On the other hand Lord Cochrane had some eco-nomic designs of his own. Knowing that the country he was invited to serve in 1817 was rich in copper ores, he invited John Miers, a minera-logist from London, to join him in the development of Chile's mineral resources.[23]

Perhaps the clearest example of the association between economic interests and Latin America's independence wars can be seen in the unusual step taken by some Scottish and English merchants in Santiago when the decisive battle of Maipu was about to start in April 1818. The battle entailed a head-on clash between the Spanish army and the armies for independence; the outcome was by no means certain. The merchants concerned 'armed themselves, joined the patriot cavalry as volunteers and participated in the brilliant charges [that] decided the fate of the country'.[24]

Scottish Settlements in Latin America

By the early 1820s the process of Latin American independence was irreversible. The rapid growth of British trade with the region and the prospect of further expansion created a favourable climate for emigration from the British Isles into the new American republics. It was by no means a massive outflow, but sufficient to establish a nucleus of British settlers almost everywhere in Latin America. As regards Scotland, there are very few instances of purely Scottish settlements. The two most notable cases were the failed Poyais scheme in Central America and the half-successful Monte Grande colony in Buenos Aires, both during the early 1820s.

The Poyais scheme originated with Sir Gregor MacGregor in the aftermath of his successful military role in Venezuela. Somehow the ghost of the earlier Darien Scheme was present in MacGregor's project. He conceived the ill-fated plan of establishing a Scottish settlement in his 'Kingdom of Poyais', possibly because by 1821 the Spanish threat was no longer a hindrance to a new attempt at a Darien-type expedition, or perhaps because certain areas in Central America already had a well established British presence.

The territory of Poyais was situated in the area surrounding the western border between Honduras and Nicaragua on the Mosquito shore. During the eighteenth century there had been a British garrison in the area which remained stationed there until 1782, when they were expelled by the Spaniards and, four years later, Britain officially relinquished her hold over the territory and handed it over to the Spanish crown, an act that 'at the time was considered by the British people a most prodigate surrender'.[25] The Indians in the Mosquito country, however, preserved all the external traces of the strong alliance they had developed with the British from the times of Wallace, the Scottish buccaneer of the seventeenth century. The Indian king usually assumed the name of whoever was currently reigning in Britain and in his tropical court there were Mosquito counterparts to the Duke of York and the rest of the British nobility. It was from one of these Indian chiefs, King George Frederick, that Gregor MacGregor obtained the concession of the territory of the Poyers which was to be the base of his illusory Kingdom of Poyais. The grant of land comprised about two-thirds of the Indian territory and was

> drawn up in the usual technical style of phraseology and conferred to the grantee little less than absolute sovereignity over the extensive region which it comprised, [it was signed] George Frederick, his mark; the mark being a sort of scratch. The King not knowing how to write.[26]

In April 1821 MacGregor travelled back to Britain, set up a London Poyaisian Legation at 1 Dowgate Hill and appointed his fellow Scotsman W.J. Richardson as the official representative of 'His Highness, Sir Gregor MacGregor, the Cazique of Poyais'.[27] He also issued a proclamation 'to his subjects' in which he mentioned the schools, banks, farms and other institutions existing in his kingdom and expressed the necessity of taking honest and industrious settlers who would assist in the development of those healthiest and most productive parts of Central America. The appeal for immigrants to his kingdom was directed specifically to the Scottish people. In 1822 a loan was raised on the London money market for £200,000, the bonds of which rose only one point above the issue price, and when it became apparent that neither principal nor interests were to be recovered, their price on the Stock Exchange appropriately became nil, thus provoking big losses for many gullible investors who believed in the scheme.[28]

But there was worse to come. Many Scots believed in the scheme to the extent of leaving their own land and settling in MacGregor's fabulous Kingdom of Poyais. In accordance with the requirements of labour mentioned in MacGregor's proclamation, it was not only humble folk that responded to the appeal but also clerks, teachers and other qualified personnel. Three vessels with emigrants sailed from Scottish ports in 1823. Early that year, probably February or March, the *Honduras Packet* sailed from Greenock followed by the *Kinnesley Castle* from Leith. The largest shipment was made in the *Skeen*, which also sailed from Leith in June. The total number of prospective settlers is unknown, but we do know that shortly after their arrival in Poyais, the first two ships had landed '131 men and lads, 25 women, 37 children' plus 9 dead and 1 person unaccounted for, thus making a total of 203 Scots.[29] On their arrival the settlers found a distressing scene. The accounts told of a harsh voyage, arriving at a place where no kingdom was to be seen, but only a dense jungle 'on the margins of a wilderness. . . exposed to the scorching rigours of the climate'. They were met by a self-styled Colonel Hall, MacGregor's appointed governor, who requested the settlers to make an oath of allegiance or otherwise quit the territory.[30] The settlers, realising that they had been deceived beyond belief, took desperate actions: some put to sea in small boats heading towards Belize, thereby suffering losses; some committed suicide; others were killed by fever; those who remained were rescued by Mark Bennert, the senior magistrate from Belize, who found them 'almost dying and scarcely able to stand'.[31]

An official inquiry was made after the disastrous end of the scheme and much blame fell on MacGregor. In disgrace, he lived for some years in Paris, where his wife died. Then in 1839, he wrote a memorandum to the Venezuelan government requesting his naturalisation in the republic, which was granted in recognition of services rendered to Venezuela's independence. The naturalisation decree provided that MacGregor would be reinstated to his rank of General of Division and that an appropriate sum of money be paid to him. He spent his last years in Caracas, where he died in 1845.

Another attempted Scottish settlement in Latin America, if not totally successful, enjoyed better fortune and was conducted on sounder principles than that of Poyais. This was the Monte Grande Colony in Argentina, projected and financed by John and William Parish Robertson, the two brothers from Kelso.

Monte Grande was a rural district about 30 km from Buenos Aires and contained rich land for agriculture and cattle raising. Buenos Aires was a growing town where already in 1824 there was a strong Scottish commercial and landed community. Indeed, between 1806 and 1824, 29 Scottish merchants had established themselves in Buenos Aires and twelve of them also owned important tracts of land.[32] The colony was planned at a very appropriate time, because 1825 was the year when Britain granted recognition to Argentina and established treaty relations with the young republic.

The Robertson brothers signed a colonisation contract with the Argentine government early in 1824, in which they committed themselves to introduce not less than 200 European families, whilst for its part, the Argentine government undertook to grant lands which would be occupied by the colonists in perpetuity, to advance a sum of money, and to provide 'implements and other necessaries' to be agreed upon. The contract also stipulated the right to exercise the Protestant religion.[33] Armed with the contract that bore the signature of President Bernardino Rivadavia, the Robertsons began to recruit the prospective Scottish settlers from 'the banks and braes o'bonnie Doon, the dales of the sweet-winding Nith, the Annan, the Teviot, Ettrick's bonnie birken shaws, the dowie dens o'Yarrow' and other rural districts with strong farming traditions. In May 1825 the colonists gathered in Edinburgh and were conveyed to Leith, where they boarded the *Symmetry* that would convey them to Buenos Aires. The party was made up of 43 married couples, 42 single men, 14 single women and 78 children, a total of 220 passengers accommodated in what space was left amid the impressive load of bridles, reins, harnesses, ploughs, saddles, breechings, belly and back bands, scythes, sickles, shovels, turnip hoes, sheep shears, harrows, cart wheels and axles, churning machines, and other agricultural implements. Whether on account of travelling with so large a volume of much appreciated implements on board, or because of having received a full half-year's pay in advance (at the rate of £17 10s. for ploughmen and £10 for labourers), or simply because such was the healthy nature of farming folk, the 78-days passage was pleasant and not devoid of merriment and frolic. At the moment of leaving the ship, 'with a glass in hand and head uncovered, each pledged the other, singing the immortal "Auld Lang Syne" in full chorus, with "three times three" for their gallant captain and his officers and another "three" for the good ship *Symmetry* that had borne them safely over the "waste of waters'".[34] Once established in Monte Grande the colonists soon cleared the vast fields, built their houses, and in due course, reaped the rewards of their skill and hard labour.[35] The colony put into practice very sophisticated farming methods hitherto unknown in Argentina, with 16,000 acres of wasteland brought into full production. Over 2,000 acres were formed into enclosures, properly fenced and cultivated, 1,000 acres devoted to peaches and other crops and the remaining 13,000 acres left to the rearing of 3,000 head of cattle and 1,000 head of sheep. One crop alone, maize, yielded a harvest of 800 tons in one year, which left plenty to be marketed in town. Moreover, Monte Grande's butter and cheeses also became familiar products in the capital's market. The colonists also made bricks and used lime they found in their fields to build 31 new houses and 47 ranchos. The houses, a witness said, are generally neat and substantial, of from six to seven apartments each. . . the industry and activity which prevail in all over the colony are truly praiseworthy, and it cannot but be gratifying to see at this distance from home the members of a little community like this, preserving all the sober and moral habits acquired in their own country.[36]

The most remarkable fact was that all this was achieved in the first three years following the arrival of the colonists. Returning from his successful military campaign in Chile and Peru, General Miller visited the colony in 1826 on the occasion of the baptism of 15 children born since the arrival of the party from Scotland. At its peak in 1828 the colony had grown to 399 adults and 115 children. A young minister recently ordained by the presbytery of Glasgow joined the colonists in 1827, followed shortly afterwards by a schoolmaster.[37] The success was, however, short lived. A number of factors combined to put the colony into disarray. One was its heavy reliance on the resources and efforts of one man alone, John Parish Robertson, the promoter of the scheme, and, when the assistance promised by the Rivadavia government in the original contract failed to materialise, the fate of the colony depended entirely upon the commercial fortunes of its creator. The emerging internal unrest of Argentina, another crucial factor, was aggravated by the secessionist movement in the Banda Oriental, the eastern side of the River Plate. Soon Brazil also became involved in the conflict, intervening to assist the Banda Oriental and support the formation of a Latin American 'Switzerland' that was to be called Uruguay. Brazil's blockade of the River Plate spelt ruin to the Robertsons' commercial career and left them unable to support the Monte Grande colony in which they had already invested £60,000. As for the Argentine government, the promised colonisation subsidy was never forthcoming. On the contrary when General Lavalle took office, the Monte Grande contract was cancelled, because the government did not have the money to pay fares and settlement grants to the colonists.[38]

The internal unrest of 1825-8 plunged Argentina into open civil war in 1829, and on various occasions the opposing factions of Lavalle and Rosas raided Monte Grande in search of provisions. Nevertheless, personal security was not the main obstacle to the progress of the colony; both Lavalle and Rosas punished the assailants and offered the settlers guarantees of personal safety. The main problem was the total disruption of economic life in the nascent nation, where an internal market barely existed and where commerce was heavily hindered by an ever depreciating currency and rising inflation.[39] Many settlers also felt that their fortunes could improve through commercial or farming exploits outside the colony. Accordingly, they decided to leave for Buenos Aires or go further inland to rural districts where they put their skills to good use as bricklayers, blacksmiths, or farmers and laid the foundation of many successful enterprises that were to prove so crucial in the development of further Scottish interests in Argentina.

Other Scottish settlements were either negligible in terms of numbers, or have left no trace of their fortunes in Latin America. There was, for instance, the case of the emigration of Clydeside miners in 1854, consisting of about 39 families and a few bachelors. Their destination was Vancouver Island, but having crossed the Strait of Magellan to Chilean shores, they were hired *en route* by Matias Cousino, a coal magnate in the Lota region. They settled in the coal mines and formed the basis of an expatriate community that continued to grow in later years.[40] The Falkland Islands was another place that attracted a strong Scottish contingent, particularly from the Western Islands. Indeed, with regard to the Falklands the main purpose of the Colonial Land and Emigration Commissioners during the 1840s was to direct 'a number of distressed Scotch islanders' to the Falklands because

no class of persons could be so eligible as early settlers in that colony as the inhabitants of the islands and western coast of Scotland. They are a seafaring people, hardy and industrious; they are inured to a rigorous climate and have for some time past, we fear, been in a very distressed condition.[41]

It is difficult to know exactly how many Scots actually went to the Falklands, but the indications are that a substantial proportion of the settlers were Scottish. The 1881 census of the Falklands does not give an indication of the origins of settlers, but it does give a breakdown of figures in respect of their religion which indicate that there were 782 Anglicans, 420 Presbyterians, 251 Roman Catholics and 100 from other denominations. It is likely that over one-third of the settlers came from Scotland, particularly to work as shepherds.[42]

In the second half of the nineteenth century there was a noticeable flow of Scottish emigrants who settled in different parts of Latin America, and travellers discovered the Scots to be so ubiquitous that they were found in the middle of a desert in northern Chile, on the top of the Andes in Bolivia and in dense jungles in Brazil.[43] Their presence in Latin America was neither the result of an organised immigration policy of the host nations, nor the product of carefully planned emigration from Scotland. As was to be expected, the fortunes of those settlers varied considerably in accordance with their skills, capital resources and the degree of assistance provided by the various governments concerned. It is not surprising, therefore, to find some Scots requesting the Foreign Office 'to assist us leaving this wretched place', and others writing home saying:

> I have so much to say about this beautiful country. . . my efforts have been successful. . . my brother Andrew is now working his farm, Young works with me at the mill. . . the Hornsbys are settled at Traiguen in a fine piece of land [ready to] establish a hotel as they had at Gairloch. I wonder why you yourself do not come here.[44]

Latin American governments usually resorted to immigration agents who were paid a sum of money for each European colonist they managed to persuade to emigrate. What the prospective settler found on arrival to the promised land was not of concern to the agent, and the experience of the numerous British consuls in Latin America shows that official action had to be taken in order to prevent British subjects from going to new republics which were unprepared to receive them. Although British subjects were requested not to act as immigration agents for foreign countries, nothing prevented other Europeans from doing so in Britain, and it is of interest to note that these individuals had more success in Scotland than in other parts of Britain. For instance, the British headquarters of the Belgian firm De Llanos y Keats and Co., immigration contractors to the Chilean and Argentine governments during the 1880s and 1890s, was in Glasgow, with agents in Dundee, Aberdeen, Inverness, Paisley, Dublin and Grimsby.

Scottish Economic Enterprises in Latin America

It is interesting to note that despite the acute conditions of civil unrest prevailing in Argentina during the early two-thirds of the nineteenth century, the country maintained its pre-eminence as the favourite destination for Scottish settlers. Undoubtedly, it was the immense untapped resources Argentina had to offer that attracted the Scots to her shores, particularly to those areas of activity requiring developments which had already successfully been tried at home. One such example was the livestock enterprises pioneered by the Scots in the River Plate republics. In this respect the failed Scottish settlement at Monte Grande nevertheless achieved a degree of success in providing its colonists with experience that proved invaluable when they were scattered throughout the republic. Monte Grande taught them how to deal with the local people and their quarrelsome authorities and how to adapt the skills and technology they brought from Scotland to the new environment in the Argentine estancias. The scheme had also shown that cattle and sheep raising were viable enterprises with considerable economic potential. The almost permanent conditions of internal unrest were but a nuisance at times and called for special measures to be taken, but they never prevented the rapid development of Scottish farmers in several parts of Argentina and Uruguay.

One remarkable characteristic of the Scottish estancias in Argentina and Uruguay is their generally humble beginnings. An enterprising spirit permitted a notable increase in productivity on such farms. Young and Sterling, for instance, two young joiners who are regarded as the first estancieros in Uruguay, raised their initial capital by working at their original trade at Buenos Aires, and then later bought lands on the banks of Rio Negro, Uruguay, in 1823. By the mid-century their estate was exceedingly prosperous and was further expanded during the 1880s and 1890s.[45] Similar examples of self-made Scotsmen abound. Anderson, another pioneer in Paysandu, Uruguay, during the 1840s, invested all of his savings in sheep and land and accompanied only by a staunch 'gaucho' – the cowboy of the pampas – 'slept on his saddle under the stars. The house was to come later, when the wool of the sheep and the beef and hides of the cattle would have justified it.'[46] John Hanna was another shrewd Ayrshire farmer who, though originally employed as manager at an Argentine estancia in 1828, bought his own farm in 1837, from which he reaped the rewards of toilsome endeavours that raised him to a baronial life style, becoming 'an honest man closebuttoned to the chin; broad-cloth without and warm heart within'.[47] Similar cases can be seen in the fine estancias developed by Thomas Fair, White and MacClymont, George Bells and sons, Lawrie, Dodds and Brown, John Davidson, the Gibson brothers and many more Scottish landowners in the River Plate countries.[48]

The achievements of Scottish estancieros were not simply limited to turning low-lying and marshy lands into flourishing productive enterprises. Such men must also be credited for the remarkable improvements they introduced, which almost amounted to an independent economic movement that established the preconditions for the substantial export expansion in Argentina during 1880-1914. In some areas, for example, the combination of investment and work provided by Scottish settlers developed elaborate systems of drainage that brought into production large tracks of formerly inhospitable lands.[49] Once established in their estancias, such men were also the first to develop new breeds of sheep, cattle and horses that adapted magnificently to the new environment and greatly increased productivity, allowing them to compete successfully in international markets against producers from other areas. John Hanna was the first to experiment in cross breeding in the late 1820s, and he successfully developed a new breed of sheep by crossing the mestizo with the Negretti breed.[50] The Gibson brothers were also actively developing new breeds in the 1830s, and their 'Ingleses Estancia' was a show piece, where they adapted the Merino and Lincoln breeds and developed the Lincoln cross to improve the native sheep.[51] In mid-century the wool trade declined with production hindered by labour scarcity during the shearing season, and woollen manufactures gradually displaced by cotton. Meat provided an alternative economic outlet of considerable potential, but its perishability meant that it could only be transported to distant markets on the hoof or salted and dried. The Gibson brothers devoted themselves to the task of transforming meat into a more durable merchandise. They failed to develop a process whereby they could export preserved meat, but they did achieve a substantial improvement in marketing conditions in Argentina's domestic economy by setting up a boiling-down factory on their estancia in the mid-1850s, which allowed them to sell processed meat in urban areas, leading to a brisk rise in prices in the then depressed Argentine livestock trade.[52]

The Scottish tradition of sheep breeding and cattle raising, well established during the first half of the nineteenth century, was followed by a second, more industrialised generation of farmers at the time when meat extracts were developed in the 1860s and refrigerated processes in the 1870s. Some of the early Scottish pioneers retired to their native land, most to spend old age in peaceful opulence. Others died on their estancias. In general, however, their successors were also men from Scotland. The most remarkable case during the second half of the century was that of George Corbett, a native of Edinburgh who owned a total of 741,000 acres of land distributed in five provinces of Argentina in the 1860s. Prompted by the shift in market demand from wool to meat, he developed further breeds that suited the prevailing market trends. In sheep farming he opted for the Lincoln variety and favoured transferring more production from the Merino area to Patagonia, which became the land specialising in wool. In cattle raising he crossed the Shorthorn with the Aberdeen Angus breed, proving that the resulting variety gave the best meat.[53]

In the mercantile field a good many British merchants in Latin America during the nineteenth century originally came from Scotland, and this Scottish presence was noticeable from the very beginning of the century. As in the case of farming enterprises, the River Plate area became the stronghold for the Scottish mercantile community. The merchants Thomas Fair, David Spalding, Alexander Wilson, John Miller, John Carter and the brothers John and William Parish Robertson were already established there prior to 1810, and as the war of independence progressed, they were joined in the following decade by George MacFarlane, Duncan Stewart, Henry Hoker, Stewart Campbell, Duncan and many others whose commercial pursuits were to make them familiar names in the progressively intense trade between Britain and Latin America as the century advanced.

Among the multifarious enterprises undertaken by John and William Parish Robertson in Latin America, their role as merchants was pre-eminent. They provided the most remarkable example of initiative, innovation and imagination during the unstable first three decades of the century. Their activities merit special mention for several reasons: they were the first to develop an active interregional trade within Latin America; they transformed the mercantile patterns prevailing among Argentine producers; through their Monte Grande scheme, they effectively transferred new technology and skills from Scotland to Argentina. They achieved all this by integrating themselves in the local community, for which they always showed respect and affection not devoid of a sense of personal attachment. The geographical scope of their mercantile endeavours comprised Paraguay, Uruguay, Argentina, Peru and Chile, and they dealt in both domestic and international trade.[54] By 1811 John Parish Robertson had already settled in Asuncion after an expedition that took three months to cover the 1,200 miles up stream on the Parana River. A ship load of British goods was sold at considerable profit in Asuncion and the proceeds invested in 1500 bales of 'yerba mate', the much appreciated Paraguayian tea which, sold at Corrientes and Buenos Aires, brought the Robertsons further bountiful profits. The smoothness of trading in Paraguay was not to last. Already troubled by the uncertainties of a war-ridden continent during the 1810s, the situation in Paraguay was aggravated when the country fell under the aegis of Francia, a notorious dictator. He expelled the Robertsons from Asuncion when an arms shipment consigned to him was confiscated by General Artigas in the Banda Oriental. Almost ruined, the two Scottish brothers settled once more in Argentina in 1818, where they soon made up the money lost in the Paraguayian adventure. Established at Corrientes, they set out to transform the whole system of commercial practice in the country by destroying the widespread 'habilitaciones system'. The latter was a speculative commercial operation consisting of money advances granted by merchants to producers, which could only be recovered when the product concerned, such as wheat, hide, mineral ores, wool and tobacco was delivered to the merchants in repayment of the debt. The deal was extremely risky for the merchant and utterly unfair for the producers who received very low prices for their goods. The local producer was additionally affected by high prices demanded by merchants for imported goods. The Robertsons brought about radical change:

> We reversed the plan of the old Spaniards: we gave high prices for hides, and took low ones for goods. This new feature brought men of respectability into play: we looked upon well to whom we trusted: we had the vigilant, active, and powerful 'Don Pedro' Campbell to 'cut the camp', and see that we had fair play. We ourselves superintended the working of the machinery; and our 'habilitados', or agents, got rich on our bargains, they had an additional stimulus to fulfil their engagements, and to repeat and augment their operations.[55]

Their sounder commercial approach brought the two brothers corresponding economic success and allowed them to make the huge investment of £60,000 in 1824 in the Monte Grande Colony (see pp. 230-233). The acute depression, the state of war with Brazil, and the internal strife that broke apart the newly independent 'Provincias Unidas' during 1828-30 also destroyed this second venture of the two brothers. They attempted another pioneering enterprise in Chile and Peru, but this also collapsed due to similar reasons. In the 1830s the two brothers returned to Britain almost as they had left in 1807, when young John had sailed to Latin America from Greenock, 'with two guineas in his pocket'.

John Wylie was a Glasgow merchant firmly established in San Luis Potosi, Mexico, from the very beginning of the nineteenth century, with an extensive network of agents throughout Mexico and in Bahia, Rio de Janeiro and Buenos Aires. Wylie dealt mainly in textiles, furniture, and tea, and his relative success in risky Latin American markets was to a large extent due to his canny approach to credit operations in economies chronically affected by inflation and ruled by a very volatile currency. The soundness of his approach can be grasped by the following typical instruction he issued to his agents:

> You are not to sell to any person or persons on credit who reside out of town of San Luis Potosi, nor must you sell upon credit to any person or persons in San Luis but such as you know to be safe and good men. Nor will you give any person a longer credit than four months, and stipulate that the goods must be paid for in hard dollars.[56]

Tea was a commodity successfully introduced by Wylie into Mexico and the east coast of South America, but the process required several decades of persistent effort. In 1818 Miers found that the locals in Buenos Aires 'displayed much anxiety to accommodate their meals to our taste, and provided for us at morning and evening tea and coffee, which they never were in the habit of taking themselves'.[57] By the same year and on the other side of the Andes people were even less aware of the potion so popular in Britain. By the mid-nineteenth century, however, the market for the formerly exotic infusion had expanded beyond the bounds of the British expatriate community in Chile, and expanded even further in 1856, when the Glasgow house of Weir Scott and Co. was established in Valparaiso. By applying modern marketing techniques, i.e. widespread advertising and promotion, attractive packing and flexible price policies, Weir Scott was soon in control of the tea market throughout Chile. By 1874 the house could boast that of the 304,768 pounds of tea imported into Chile, the house had cleared 134, 490 pounds, which was 'nearly equal to all the other importers together'.[58] Weir Scott not only specialised in the wholesale distribution of tea, but also dealt in large volumes of foodstuffs and groceries, china-ware, cutlery, etc. Later in the century it was one of the first merchant companies in Chile to enter the industrial sector, when they established a large condensed milk factory at Graneros, whose output practically met the whole domestic demand.[59]

It is of interest to remark upon the fact that most Scottish mercantile enterprises in Latin America either raised their capital on the spot or invested modest outlays raised at home. Rather than looking for openings in which to invest idle fortunes, the Scottish merchants entered commerce in order to acquire one, and the examples of this abound. Duncan Wright and James Parlane, for instance, the founders of the House of Parlane MacAlister in Argentina, initially invested nothing more than the savings they had gathered in their employment as clerks.[60] Other merchants relied on very generous credits granted by Scottish producers at home. The textile firm of Sloan of Glasgow, an important poncho and poncho-cloth supplier to the River Plate in the 1830s, shipped the goods on receiving only one-third of the total price; the remainder was to be remitted after the goods had been sold.[61]

On occasions there were Scottish merchants who combined their ability to raise capital on the spot with the security of having, however modest, a financial backer in the mother country. The most typical example here is the case of the mercantile enterprises that were developed on the west coast of South America by three young Scotsmen: Alexander Balfour from Levenbank, Stephen Williamson from Anstruther, and David Duncan from Alyth. In 1850, when they were 26, 23, and 20 years respectively, they decided to form a partnership to start business in Latin America. They had met in Liverpool, a place to which they had emigrated in search of better fortune. Unable to raise the initial capital required for their enterprise, the trio sought the assistance of Alexander Lawson, a linen manufacturer from King's Kettle in Fife, who was Stephen Williamson's uncle. Lawson assisted the young men 'in the confidence of [your] honourable conduct and unrelaxing industry' and offered them 'that amount of pecuniary assistance which I deem amply sufficient to enable you to make a fair start'.[62] The sum advanced amounted to £5,000, which allowed the young partners to start business in Valparaiso in 1852 under the name Williamson, Duncan and Co., and set up an office in Liverpool, which they registered as S. Williamson and Co. In their first years the house dealt mainly in Scottish exports to the Chilean markets, and their most important consignors were John Duncan and F. Molison and Co. of Dundee and, obviously, uncle Alexander Lawson.[63]

After many ups and downs, the partners gradually became well acquainted with their markets, and the firm steadily prospered and became involved in the successful shipping of Chilean goods for the British market. By the end of the century, the house was well established in Chile and Peru, with nearly 30 branches on the west coast and had even abandoned the narrow role of commission agents to become heavily committed in the emerging Chilean and Peruvian industrial sectors. They had flour mills in Chile and Peru, a linseed oil mill at Valparaiso, a smelting establishment for silver, lead and copper in northern Chile, and also owned a sizeable shipping fleet, which in the 1870s had 14 vessels. Moreover, the partners sat on the boards of important railway companies, banks and insurance companies in the emerging joint-stock sector in Chile.[64] The humble £5,000 advanced by Lawson progressively multiplied and their net capital, not counting all the assets, amounted to £500,500 in 1875, £538,419 in 1885, and £1,292,526 in 1899.[65] As to the geographical scope of their operations, by the late 1860s they had even established a house at San Francisco, California, where they successfully developed oilfields that were later taken over by the Shell Co. on the eve of the Great War.[66]

One of the partners, David Duncan, left the firm in 1863 and joined Henry F. Fox, the surviving partner of Ravenscroft Fox and Co., a well-established house in Valparaiso, and formed Duncan, Fox and Co. the same year.[67] The new firm also thrived in the eventful years of the late nineteenth century in Chile. Besides their role as merchants they entered the fields of copper mining, nitrate processing, flour milling, and even sheep farming in Patagonia. They also established branches and associated houses in Peru and Bolivia. In Chile, the base of their operations, Valparaiso had ceased being their only establishment in 1886, when the house expanded to all areas of Chile, establishing eleven branches in the country.[68]

Undoubtedly the parallel expansion of Weir Scott, Balfour Williamson and Duncan Fox on the west coast of South America leads to the conclusion that the Scottish houses jointly controlled the largest proportion of business among the foreign houses established in the area.

Other Scottish mercantile houses were not so significant for their size, but rather for the substantial change they introduced in commodity trade on a world-wide scale. Two cases can be mentioned. One concerns that of Duncan MacNab and Duncan Stewart, who were pioneers in the development of industrially based farming enterprises. As early as 1832, they established the basis for meat packing and drying in Argentina. By the mid-century, more than 50 British houses had entered the business and transformed Argentina into one of the major meat producers.

The second case is that of two Glasgow merchants, Peter and Thomson Aikman. According to a Chilean historian who quotes some files of the Aikman house in Latin America, the Scottish merchants are credited with the introduction of nitrates into the European market in 1830. In that year one of the house's vessels anchored at Iquique, in the nitrate region, requiring some ballast for the return voyage to Britain. The captain was offered 50 tons of nitrate at a very convenient price. The nitrate was loaded, and the ship sailed back to Britain. On arrival in Liverpool the port authorities refused to allow the landing of the cargo on the grounds that it appeared to be a highly explosive substance. Peter Aikman, who was then at Liverpool, ordered the cargo to be thrown overboard but reserved 10 sacks which were brought to

Glasgow, where the house chemist made an assay on the substance and suggested that it be tested as a fertilizer. The nitrate was distributed among farmers in the Glasgow area, and given favourable results, the house continued to import modest quantities until a higher demand developed in Germany.[69] The nitrate trade was to develop into one of the most voluminous transfers of merchandise from South America to Europe and other parts of the world. From the year of its inception to the eve of the First World War around 50 million tons of nitrate were produced on the west coast of South America. The nitrate trade even helped to give the dwindling sailing vessels another lease of life that allowed them to sail into nitrate ports well after the beginning of the twentieth century.

Scotland, as can be expected, made a substantial contribution to Latin American countries in the field of shipbuilding and ship-related enterprises. In the nineteenth century this contribution was connected with the development of steam navigation. The first steamer to enter Latin American waters was the *Rising Star*, which arrived in Valparaiso in 1818, brought there under the auspices of Lord Cochrane.[70] In 1824 John Parish Robertson also aroused the expectations of sea-side dwellers when his steamer entered the River Plate.[71] In Brazil steamer services in inland waters were introduced by John Proudfoot, a Glaswegian who settled in Buenos Aires in 1835 and later moved to Rio Grande do Sul. His enterprises ranged from cotton growing, farming, submarine cable contracting and shipbuilding. He had extensive estates on Clydeside, and the steamers used in his Rio Grande-Porto Alegre line were all built in his Clyde yards.[72] From mid-century onwards Clydeside steamers were found at most major Latin American ports.

In other cases, even though the steamer lines were not Scottish enterprises, they were unable to operate efficiently without the assistance of Scottish technology. Such was the case of the Pacific Steam Navigation Company, organised in 1840 by the American William Wheelwright with capital raised in Britain and subsidies from the Chilean government. A succession of steamers were built in Port Glasgow for the Company during the 1850s, combining the designs of J.R. Napier with the engine power built by John Elder. The new ships resulted in savings of 30 to 40 per cent of coal previously burned by similar steamers. In 1870, a year after John Elder died, the Board of the Pacific Steam Navigation Company recalled that their connection with Elder had begun in 1856, on the occasion of the *Valparaiso* being fitted with a set of compound engines. The Board added:

The Company have built no fewer than 22 steam-ships in that yard and have been supplied with 30 pairs of double-cylindered engines. In fact, on account of the advantages in the saving of fuel, which, according to our experience reaches 30 to 35 per cent, we would not think of any other type of machinery.[73]

Scottish shipbuilding is also associated with the introduction of steam navigation of Lake Titicaca. Such an undertaking posed a formidable challenge to technology and ingenuity. Titicaca is located in the Upper Andes, at 3,660 metres above sea-level covering an area of about 6,500 square kilometres, separated from the nearest coast by 400 kilometres of steep mountains and a coastal desert completely devoid of either water or railroad communication. No wonder that the first steamers took about nine years from their arrival on the coast in 1862 to their launching on the Titicaca in 1871 and 1872. The *Yapura* and the *Yavary* were built in Britain and sent to Arica, in Peru, from where all the pieces were carried across the Andes by mule and then assembled at the Titicaca port of Puno, on the Peruvian side. The two steamers are said to have been built in Glasgow, and after the heroic journey to Puno 'reassembled there by Indians under the direction of a dour Scottish engineer who knew no Spanish or Aymara'. There are, however, other versions concerning the origin of these ships and conclusive evidence to settle the issue has not been found.[74] The building of the third Titicaca steamer, *Aurora del Titicaca*, was beyond doubt built by Alexander Stephens and Sons at their Kelvinhaugh yard in 1869, and subsequently underwent the epic journey from the Scottish yard to the port of Puno.

Other shipbuilding related works in Latin America also originated in Scotland. The first plate-iron floating dock, for instance, patented by John Elder in 1863, was built in his yard in the same year, its 3,000 tons being transported to Callao where it was assembled.[75] Another example can be seen in the way that many a river in Latin America was rendered navigable by using dredges mainly from Renfrew.[76]

Before leaving the subject of transport it should at least be mentioned that the establishment of the railway in Latin America must undoubtedly have had a Scottish connection. It is likely that there were more cases similar to that of the Chilean-Scottish brothers John and Mathew Clark. In the 1870s they set out to pierce the Andes with a gigantic railway scheme destined to link the Atlantic and the Pacific by a railroad that entailed the construction of 38 bridges and 15 tunnels.[77]

It should be said that not all Scottish enterprises in Latin America met with success. The cases of failures were frequently ambitious schemes that did not take proper account of the peculiarities of each particular market. One such failure was that of MacFarlane, the Scot who, perhaps concerned that civilisation had not yet arrived in Chile in 1820, decided to offer his own contribution by establishing the first brewery in that country. The business proved shortlived, probably because the market was already saturated with the popular home-made (or rather wigwam-made) 'chicha', a beverage brewed by the Indians and universally consumed at that time.[78]

Another failure was that of Hugh Dallas, a merchant on the east coast of South America, who was moderately successful so long as he restricted his activities to those market areas he knew well: Buenos Aires, Montevideo, and Rio de Janeiro. When he tried to expand to the west coast, however, dealing with commodities he had not touched before, his enterprise encountered risks that it was finally unable to withstand.[79]

The most resounding failure was that of P. Henderson and Co. from Glasgow, a firm that invested over £1 million in trying to gain control of coastal shipping on the River Plate in 1886. They organised 'La Platense Co. Lt.', a shipping concern that engaged in a costly freight competition with a French rival. Showing considerable tenacity it finally bought over the French undertaking at a very high price and found itself burdened by an enormous fleet of 58 steamers, 16 sailing vessels, and 22 other minor boats, plus two large yards. This was at a time of acute depression in both coastal and overseas trade in Argentina during 1889-90. The high running costs and the depreciation of local currency turned this giant enterprise into a non-viable concern. The Baring crisis of 1890 inflicted the final blow and forced 'La Platense' to go into liquidation.[80]

All the enterprises discussed so far refer to what may be termed as direct investment, i.e. undertakings whose capital was not publicly raised on the stock exchange in the form of shares. This direct investment and economic activity on the part of the Scots seems to have been particularly strong in the River Plate area, and there is every indication that Scottish portfolio investment also had a preference for Argentina and Uruguay. Charles Jones recently carried out a survey involving the major British investors in those two countries and found that in 1895 seven out of the 68 largest investors in the River Plate joint-stock companies were Scottish (see Table 8.1).

Table 8.1: Major Scottish Shareholders in River Plate Companies,
c. 1895

	No. of Companies in which shares held	Total Value of portfolio
Bank of Scotland	9	97,331
Bruce, John (Edinburgh)	4	25,944
Bunten, James E. (Glasgow)	4	75,180
National Bank of Scotland	7	112,155
Stewart, James Reid (Glasgow)	2	92,830
Scottish Investment Trust Company Ltd. (Edinburgh)	4	46,827
Union Bank of Scotland	10	114,665
	Total:	564,932

Source: Charles Jones, 'Who Invested in Argentina and Uruguay?' *Business Archives*, no. 48, November 1982.

Conclusions

During the nineteenth century Latin America was only of marginal importance as a destination for Scottish emigrants and capital. What outflow that did take place tended to concentrate on the River Plate area. Given the limitations of the scope of this survey on what is still an unexplored field, we have referred only to the most salient features of Scottish enterprise in Latin America. There are, however, many other areas of interest in which the Scottish presence made itself felt in Latin America. We may identify just a few as a way of suggesting topics for further research.

A major theme concerns the vicissitudes of the churches the Scots zealously helped to found and develop in Latin America. This enterprise met not only with natural problems of survival in the midst of strong catholic societies, but also those resulting from conflicts with the Foreign Office which preferred to recognise and assist the Episcopal Church. Additional research needs to be done on the Scots' stubborn defence of their Presbyterian faith, the foundation of the various 'rancho kirks' in the Argentine pampas, and Stephen Williamson's public debates in Chile against catholicism and favouring freedom of cults. There were also Scottish naturalists and mineralogists connected with Latin America, such as J. Tweedie, Captain Hall and Dr Gardner, and a number of Scots who reached prominent positions in public service in Latin American governments. In a field so specialised as photography, for instance, there was the case of William Letts Oliver, a pioneer in the art, who built his own camera in 1857, when he was 13 years old, and whilst still an adolescent, became a successful photographer in Chile from 1860 onwards.[81] There must be many other similar cases calling for further research.

In an overall assessment of the pursuits that have been discussed in this chapter there emerge several distinctive features concerning the Scottish presence in Latin America. Firstly, the number of Scots who went to that sub-continent obviously did not compare with the numbers going to Canada, the United States, Australia, or even India. The initial capital they brought with them was also negligible, and in most cases all their financial resources were raised in the host country itself. Quite naturally, their most successful spheres of activity were those in which Scotland herself already possessed a rich and long-standing tradition and experience, such as farming, stock raising, shipbuilding, and mercantile activities. What is remarkable though is the fact that Scotsmen were always prepared to build upon such traditions, using the imagination that was required to adapt their trades and skills to an environment utterly unknown to them at the beginning, but cherished by them once they got to know it.

Notes

1. Pierre François Xavier de Charlevoix, *Histoire du Paraguay* 3 vols. (Paris, 1756), vol. 1, pp. 175-6. The authority of Charlevoix regarding Father Field's Scottish origin is challenged in the *Dictionary of National Biography* where it is stated that he was an Irish priest. The earliest account of Scottish presence further north from South America is that of the merchant Thomas Blake, established in Mexico during 1554-85. King's College Library in Aberdeen hold copies of three volumes of Blake's papers.

2. Michael G. Mulhall, *The English in South America* (Buenos Aires, 1878), p. 70.

3. Charlevoix, *Histoire*, vol. 1, pp. 200, 333.

4. Parliamentary Papers, *Commercial Tariffs and Regulations of the Several States of Europe and America, Together with the Commercial Treaties between England and Foreign Countries*. Parts xvii, xviii, and xix: 'Spanish American Republics' (by John MacGregor), 1847 [769] LXIV, p. 13.

5. To our knowledge, there is not a single historical account of the Scottish presence in Latin America and the topic deserves further extensive research.

6. *The Economist*, 29 May 1909, p. 1128.

7. Parliamentary Papers, *Report for the Consular District of Buenos Aires* (by Clive Ford), 1867 [3791] LXIX.

8. Speech by Herbert Gibson to the St Andrew Society in Buenos Aires in

1872. Quoted in James Dodds, *Records of the Scottish Settlers in the River Plate and Their Churches* (Buenos Aires, 1897), p. 336.

9. See Ricardo Levene, *A History of Argentina* (Durham, USA, 1937), pp. 192-4.

10. George Peddle, *A History of Latin America* (London, 1971), pp. 90-1.

11. John Parish Robertson and William Parish Robertson, *Letters on Paraguay*, 3 vols. (London, 1838), vol. 1, p. 97.

12. Cochrane's very remarkable naval career is described in minute detail in his *Autobiography of a Seaman*, 2 vols. (London, 1859-60). On his contribution towards Latin America's independence see also his *Narrative of Services in the Liberation of Chile, Peru and Brazil from Spanish and Portuguese Domination*, 2 vols. (London, 1858-9).

13. Benjamin Vicuna MacKenna, *The First Britons in Valparaiso* (Valparaiso, 1884), p. 29.

14. See J. Miller, *Memoirs of General Miller in the Service of the Republic of Peru*, 2 vols. (London, 1828), vol. 1, p. 33.

15. MacKenna, *The First Britons*, p. 34.

16. On Sir Gregor MacGregor's services to the independence of Venezuela see his *Exposicion documentada que el General Gregor MacGregor dirigio al Gobierno de Venezuela y resolucion que en ella recayo* (Caracas, 1839). See also Mulhall, *The English in South America*, pp. 274-8.

17. Mulhall, *The English in South America*, p. 277.

18. Ibid., p. 250.

19. MacKenna, *The First Britons*, p. 30.

20. Manuel A. Fernandez, 'The Chilean Economy and its British Connections', unpublished PhD thesis, University of Glasgow, 1978, p. 54.

21. See Arthur Redford, *Manchester Merchants and Foreign Trade* (Manchester, 1934), pp. 97-100.

22. While staying at the household of John Robertson in Buenos Aires in 1817, General Miller was persuaded to abandon his commercial endeavours and not to change his 'profession of arms for one of mere money-making'. Later, during the military campaign against the Spaniards, Robertson was always present to say farewell to Miller's expeditions and, occasionally, offered a magnificent ball to the General and his officers. See Mulhall, *The English in South America*, pp. 218-22.

23. J. Miers, *South American Exploits in his Travels in Chile and La Plata*, 2 vols. (London, 1826).

24. Miller, *Memoirs*, vol. 2, p. 222.

25. Parliamentary Papers, *Commercial Tariffs and Regulations*, part xvii, p. 36.

26. Ibid., p. 37.

27. *The Times*, 14 June and 26 August 1823.

28. J. Fred Rippy, *British Investments in Latin America, 1822-1949* (Minneapolis, 1966), p. 21. The 1822 loan was never repaid, but despite this, MacGregor made further attempts to raise two more loans in 1823 and 1825. See Poyais, *Loan of Two Hundred Thousand Pounds Sterling for the Service of the State and the Government of Poyais* (London, 1823). The copy of this prospectus held by the British Library is attached to a single sheet headed 'Take Care of Your Pocket. Another Poyais Humbug.' See also Poyais, *Prospectus of a Loan of £300,000 Sterling, Contracted with the Government of Poyais for the Purpose of Consolidating the Same: For Working the Gold Mines, and for Promoting the Growth of Indigo, Sugar, Tobacco, etc.* (Lothbury, 1825).

29. *The Times*, 2 September 1823.

30. *Greenock Advertiser* (as quoted in *The Times*, 26 August 1823).

31. *The Times*, 26 August and 1 September 1823.

32. Dodds, *Records of the Scottish Settlers*. Dodd's comments and collection of documents relating to early Scottish settlers in Argentina have proved invaluable for our account of the Monte Grande Colony. Dodds himself was for most of the second half of the century one of the settlers and an active member of the Presbyterian Church.

33. Ibid., pp. 22-3.

34. Ibid., p. 13.

35. It was perhaps an irony that the first task for the settlers consisted of clearing the land of thistles which grew in such profusion in Monte Grande that one of the colonists had to invent an ingenious machine for eradicating them. Ibid., p. 35.

36. *British Packet* (Buenos Aires), 23 August 1828, quoted by Dodds, *Records of the Scottish Settlers*, pp. 32-5.

37. Ibid., pp. 31 and 202-10. The minister in question was Dr William Brown who served the Scottish community in Buenos Aires for 20 years and later became Professor of Divinity and Biblical Criticism at St Andrews University.

38. See Jose Luis Busaniche's Prologue to John and William Parish Robertson, *Cartas de Sud-America*, 3 vols. (Buenos Aires, 1950), vol. 1, pp. 37-44.

39. Dodds, *Records of the Scottish Settlers*, p. 57.

40. *Chilean Times*, 23 November 1878, cited by John Mayo, 'British Interest in Chile and Their Influence, 1851-1886', unpublished PhD thesis, Oxford University, 1977, p. 26.

41. Parliamentary Papers, *Report of the Colonial Land and Emigration Commissioners*, 1841 [3] III.

42. Parliamentary Papers, *Falkland Islands: Governor's Report for 1881*, 1884 [c. 4015] LIV. On another occasion, reporting on the success of the Government Savings Bank, opened in 1888, the Falklands Governor informed that, taking the population to be 1900 persons, 'the majority of the depositors are shepherds employed on the farms, thrifty, true to the traditions of Scotland, from which country most of them have emigrated'. *Governor's Report for 1890*, 1892 [c. 6563].

43. Bryce did not find only the Scots to be everywhere in Latin America in 1912, but the Aberdonians in particular. See James Bryce, *South America: Observations and Impressions* (New York, 1912), p. 190.

44. The first quotation is from distressed settlers at Chiloe, Chile, seeking the assistance of the Foreign Office to supplement the public subscription opened by the *Glasgow Weekly Mail* in 1901 to remove them from their failed settlement. (See D. Greenhalgh to Foreign Office, 18 June 1901, FO 16/334.) The second quotation is taken from one of the letters written by British settlers also in Chile and published as a pamphlet in the late 1880s. (See Chile, *Letters from Settlers*, n/d, p. 8.)

45. Mulhall, *The English in South America*, p. 337.

46. Cited by Koebel, *British Exploits in South America, A History of British Activities in Exploration, Military Adventure, Diplomacy, Science and Trade in Latin America* (New York, 1917), pp. 503-4.

47. Mulhall, *The English in South America*, pp. 408-9.

48. Dodds, *Records of the Scottish Settlers*, pp. 265-71. The account of the rise to prominence of Scottish estancieros in Argentina is also found in Mulhall's *The English in South America*, pp. 407-12.

49. Dodds, *Records of the Scottish Settlers*, p. 271.

50. Ibid., p. 266.

51. Herbert Gibson, *The History and Present State of Sheep Breeding in the*

Argentine Republic (Edinburgh, 1893), passim.

52. Koebel, *British Exploits*, p. 499.

53. Walter Feldwick (ed.), *Commercial Encyclopedia: South America* (London, 1924), p. 218.

54. In 1842 the two brothers reminisced about their 'best five and twenty years' in their lives as follows: 'We ranged alternatively from England to Paraguay, from Corrientes to Buenos Aires, and from Buenos Aires to England . . . while the peregrinations of one were limited to those places, the other crossed the Andes, stretched along the shores of the Pacific, from Concepcion in Chile to Trujillo in Peru, and so, vice versa.' See John and William Parish Robertson, *Letters on South America*, 3 vols. (London, 1843), vol. 1, p. 3.

55. Ibid., pp. 176-7.

56. John Wylie to Sinclair Taylor, 20 November 1835 in 'Letter Books of John Wylie and Wylie Cooke and Co.', MSS, Department of Economic History, University of Glasgow.

57. Miers, *Travels in Chile and La Plata*, vol. 1, p. 6.

58. The wide acceptance of Weir Scott's tea sold in Chile, the house explained, was largely the result of careful selection by 'our House in Glasgow made personally by our senior partner, Mr A.G. Scott'. *Valparaiso and West Coast Mail*, 3 April and 6 November 1875.

59. Feldwick (ed.), *Commercial Encyclopedia*, p. 863.

60. Reber, *British Mercantile Houses in Buenos Aires, 1810-1880* (Cambridge, Massachusetts, 1979), p. 58.

61. Ibid., p. 59.

62. Alexander Lawson to Alexander Balfour, 6 February 1850, in 'Archive of Balfour Williamson & Co.', MSS, University College, London.

63. Wallis Hunt, *Heirs of Great Adventure: the History of Balfour Williamson & Co. Ltd.*, 2 vols. (Norwich, 1951), vol. 1, p. 25.

64. See M.A. Fernandez, 'Merchants and Bankers: British Direct and Portfolio Investment in Chile during the Nineteenth Century', forthcoming in *Ibero-Amerikanisches Archiv*.

65. Stephen Williamson to J.W. Hobblethwaite, 13 March 1876; S. Williamson to Alexander Balfour, 10 April 1886, and 'memo on responsible capital', Liverpool, 22 July 1900, in 'Archive of Balfour Williamson & Co.'.

66. Lord Archibald Williamson, *Balfour Williamson & Co. and Allied Firms: Memoirs of a Merchant House* (London, 1929), pp. 37-55.

67. See Eric E. Davies, 'History of Duncan Fox & Co., Limited'. Typescript, Santiago, 1956. (I am grateful to Mr T.A.A. Elliott from Ravenscroft Shipping Ltd., who kindly allowed me to consult this work.)

68. Ibid., passim.

69. Oscar Bermudez, *Historia del salitre desde sus origenes hasta la Guerra del Pacifico* (Santiago, 1963), pp. 104-5.

70. Arthur C. Wardle, *Steam Conquers the Pacific: A History of the Pacific Steam Navigation Company* (London, 1940), pp. 14-15. Lord Cochrane was so interested in steam-powered ships that even at the height of the independence war he devoted some time to test the coals in southern Chile for steam purposes. See Roland E. Duncan, 'Chilean Coal and British Steamers: the Origin of a South American Industry' in *Mariner's Mirror*, LXI, 1975, p. 271.

71. Mulhall, *The English in South America*, p. 511.

72. Ibid., pp. 345-6 and 513.

73. W.J. Macquorn Rankine, *A Memoir of John Elder, Engineer and Shipbuilder* (Edinburgh, 1870), pp. 65-7.

74. I am grateful to Ms Meriel Larken, London, who is currently doing research on this topic and drew my attention to various conflicting accounts

concerning the origin of the steamers *Yaravi* and *Yapura*. A detailed account of the assembly and launching of the two ships at the Port of Puno can be found in the 'Archive of Alexander Stephens & Sons, Ltd.', MSS, file UCS 3/1/227, Glasgow University.

75. Rankine, *A Memoir of John Elder*, pp. 36-7, and Mulhall, *The English in South America*, p. 524.

76. Mulhall, *The English in South America*, p. 351.

77. There is a biography of the Clark brothers published in Chile. See Santiago Marin Vicuna, *Los Hermanos Clark* (Santiago, 1929). The Transandine Expedition, carried out in 1871-2 by a team of British engineers (among which were many Scotsmen) is recounted by Robert Crawford in *Across the Pampas and the Andes* (London, 1884).

78. It is said that the development of MacFarlane's brewery was also hindered by heavy taxation levied by the Chilean government. See Mulhall, *The English in South America*, p. 357.

79. Reber, *British Mercantile Houses*, p. 103.

80. See Dorothy Laird, *Paddy Henderson. A History of the Scottish Shipping Firm P. Henderson & Company and Other Enterprises which Sprang from Their Initiative and Spirit of Maritime Adventure, 1834-1961* (Glasgow, 1961), pp. 158-71.

81. Dodd's *Records of the Scottish Settlers* is an invaluable source for the history of the Presbyterian Church in Argentina. Other Scottish pursuits are mentioned in Mulhall's *The English in South America*. Oliver's collection of photographs is held by the Bancroft Library, University of California, and his role as a pioneer in photography is discussed in Alvaro Jara's *Chile en 1860: William L. Oliver: un precursor de la fotografia* (Santiago, 1973).

9 THE SCOTS IN MEIJI JAPAN, 1868-1912

Olive Checkland

I

There were few foreigners of any description in Japan until the end of the 1850s. Commander Perry of the United States navy breached the traditional Japanese policy of seclusion when in 1853 he demanded in the name of his government that Japan should open up some of her ports to foreign trade. This dramatic intervention reflected the foreign search for more markets where the manufactured products of the industrial nations could be sold as well as their search for raw materials to feed their demanding machines.

But even in the pre-Perry period Japan had not been cut off entirely from the rest of the world. During the long isolation (since 1603) the Tycoon's government had permitted the Dutch to maintain a 'factory' on the small artificial island of Deshima in Nagasaki harbour. There a trickle of goods and, perhaps more importantly, books had been allowed to enter Japan from the West. Even this extraordinarily restricted access to Western ideas was enough to infect some of the local princes and their young Samurai with curiosity about the West and its achievements. This disaffection was conveyed to the Japanese government, which already by the 1830s was worried and confused by the threatening behaviour of western powers in China and, fearing for the future, responded arbitrarily, sometimes encouraging and sometimes rebuffing initiatives from the outside world.[1]

Because of the need to defend Nagasaki, which was remote from the centres of power in Japan, but perilously close to Korea and China where the Western powers were established, the government encouraged the Prince of Hizen, the local overlord, to send his men to learn the art of iron cannon founding from the Dutch. Other industrial developments sanctioned under the old regime included the spinning mill (set up by Platt Brothers of Oldham) at Kagoshima, the Satsuma capital, and naval dockyards and workshops set up by the French at Yokosuka (Yokohama) and Nagasaki. There is little doubt that there was growing dissatisfaction with the policy of seclusion. Some believed it necessary to make contact with the West, either to discover more of the new learning or to explore the possibilities of profitable trade.

The Japanese government signed a treaty with the United States on 29 July 1858, and quickly upon its heels came a British mission. The objectives were diplomatic, although amply backed up by the 'gun-boats in the bay'. The British treaty with Japan was signed on 26 August 1858, heralding a decade of lively trading. There was a strong Scottish presence. But the old government in Japan had been undermined and was demoralised, and in 1868 the Emperor was restored to his throne by young activists from the clans of the south west, thus toppling the Tycoon and the old guard from power.

The change of government in 1868 with the accession of the Meiji emperor heralded a period of quite extraordinary change, during which many Scots played a part in bringing to Japan their skills and expertise. It is hoped here to show how effective the Scots were in helping to create the new Japan. For this purpose the term Scots is taken to mean those who were born and educated in Scotland. Usually their professional training was also undertaken in their country of origin. But Scotland was not a political entity and for the Japanese (and many others) the term Scots is rarely used. Scots of that period were accustomed then as now to being called English or at best British. Nor do the official records of the Japanese government help, for the English and the Scots, and indeed the Australians and the New Zealanders working in Japan, were all, for official purposes, lumped together as British. It should perhaps be noted that some Scots, after service in Japan, proceeded to Australia or New Zealand and settled there. Other Scots already from these countries were attracted to Japan and there was a similar reciprocal movement around the Pacific Ocean, between Japan and California and Canada. From the Japanese records which remain it is not possible to discover how many Scots went to Japan. While from Scottish sources it is possible to follow up the careers of those Scots who held important posts in Japan and who often left papers, books and other writings as a record of their achievement, there may have been many more lesser men whose careers cannot be traced.

For the Scots and other expatriates, jobs in Japan were similar to those elsewhere in the colonial empire, where the environment could be difficult and challenging, but where the terms and conditions of employment were understood and where the rewards did much to compensate for the sacrifice of working away from home. On these matters there was an enormous gap of comprehension between the Westerners and the Japanese.

For the Japanese the foreigners, however rare their skills and advanced their technology, were hired employees.[2] As such they were clearly subject to superior Japanese authority. Although many foreigners were treated with enormous respect by the Japanese, all of them, however distinguished, had to understand where the ultimate power lay.

The unwillingness of the Japanese to delegate and pass authority to foreign experts is a reflection of the structure of Japanese society as well as of national characteristics. Feudalism was not abolished in Japan until 1871. Inevitably the feudal attitudes persisted.[3] Although upward social mobility was possible, it was the exception rather than the rule. Most lived in a strictly hierarchical society subject to many checks and restraints. Highly skilled foreigners had to fit into the structure; they could not expect to remain uncontrolled outside the system. In addition Japanese pride often prevented them from admitting ignorance and accepting tutelage. Even with goodwill, the gap in comprehension between the two groups remained wide.

The retention by the Japanese of ultimate authority, even in the early days of Meiji when they had a great deal to learn, is one of the most notable features of their industrialising process.[4] It sets Japan apart from the generally expected behaviour of developing nations. The Japanese interpretation of the power structure must have come as a shock to many British employees accustomed as they were to the pattern of imperialistic employment. Elsewhere in colonial and quasi-colonial countries senior management posts were reserved for the British, 'natives' being restricted to menial jobs, rarely progressing above the bottom rung of the managerial ladder.

The 'success' or 'failure' of those in Japanese employ depended partly on their technical competence but ultimately on their ability to co-operate with Japanese officials. Those who arrived with a strong sense of self-importance determined to shoulder the 'White Man's Burden' were hardly likely to succeed. On the Japanese side there were without doubt, especially in the early years of Meiji, some Japanese officials who were bitterly resentful not only of the foreign intruders, but also of the whole heady pace of change. These men do seem to have caused problems, behaving obstructively in their frustration and resentment. Foreigners, including Scots, varied greatly in their ability to handle this sort of interference. It is only fair to say that some Scots, whose careers are known in detail, seemed to have no difficulties. To balance the resentful Japanese official, there were probably ten others keen to advance the project in hand. Some life-long friendships between foreign experts and their Japanese mentors resulted from fruitful joint co-operation.

Most foreign employees were young, hired for service in Japan immediately upon becoming qualified. They were in their mid-twenties, few were over 30 years of age when first employed. By appointing such young men Japan obtained the services of enthusiasts, well trained, but flexible enough to work happily under general Japanese supervision. As Marquis Okuma had opined, 'Experience was not a criterion for office, dedicated effort was the prime consideration' in early Meiji Japan.[5] Most foreigners appreciated and entered fully into the spirit of the enterprise.

Foreign experts were carefully selected. The vetting process involved was slow and thorough, perhaps relying ultimately on personal recommendation. In the case of the Imperial College of Engineering in Tokyo (see below) the staff of which was British, with a strong Scots bias, a remarkably effective and dedicated team was brought together.

Where recruitment was done by advertisement, interviews were conducted by foreigners authorised by the Japanese government. In the case of the Japanese Lighthouse Service the Board of Trade in London passed the job to David and Thomas Stevenson of Edinburgh, who were to be the contractors. But even when the interviewing system was used, personal recommendation was also taken into account. Numbers of Scots lighthouse keepers were employed in Japan on the direct recommendation of Stevensons of Edinburgh. Although mistakes were sometimes made, by and large the Japanese recruitment system worked remarkably well and provided them with a range of loyal and devoted foreign staff.

Foreign employees were usually well paid. Salaries were in Mexican dollars, sometimes causing exchange problems. Salaries varied of course depending on the skills of the employee. The Japanese government had no difficulty in recruiting the men they wanted because adequate and perhaps generous salaries were paid. Salaries varied from under $50 a month to $2,000 a month, although only one foreigner (a distinguished railway engineer and administrator)[6] was ever employed at the latter figure. Between 1868 and 1900, 74 per cent of all foreign employees were hired at rates of $200 a month or less, some 19 per cent earned between $300 and $400, and 7 per cent earned over $500 a month.[7]

Scots were to be found in Japan serving in many capacities. Some were diplomats whose presence in Japan set the scene for the future. Others were merchants and traders working for a variety of British firms primarily concerned with trade with Japan. Journalists and doctors were other professions represented, the former producing eagerly read

English language newspapers and the latter offering Western medicine. There were teachers and educators (with a wide variety of skills), engineers, bankers and lawyers, most employed by the Japanese government.

Many more humble men, clerks and assistants, as well as technicians, lighthouse keepers and engine drivers came to pass on their skills. Some arrived in Japan for one purpose and were diverted to another as new opportunities offered. Others tempted by larger financial rewards shouldered greater responsibilities than would ever have been possible had they remained at home. Some few Scots were offered long-term employment by private firms and so attained a rare intimacy with Japanese society. Some Scots found Japanese society congenial and remained there.

In addition there were Scots travellers, who tempted by a country so recently closed to them, quickly added Japan to their itineraries.[8]

II

It was trade which attracted the Scots to Japan, and Scots merchants who, whether in London or the Far East, applied pressure, vigorous in pursuit of their objectives and clamant against those who sought to restrain them. The British diplomatic presence brought to Japan to legitimise trade, found the tactics of some merchants distasteful. The lack of sympathy between the two groups, which may have reflected both the hazards of life and the risks of trade in early Meiji Japan, had no particular reference to the Scots, although many merchants were Scots and most diplomats English.

Exceptionally, the first British diplomatic plenipotentiary sent to Japan was a Scot, the 8th Earl of Elgin.[9] His role was to negotiate a treaty with the Japanese which would allow the British similar rights as those already agreed with America, the Netherlands and Russia. As a result of the preliminary work done by other governments' agents, Elgin was able to arrive at Nagasaki on 3 August 1858, moving on to Tokyo, where speedy negotiations allowed the Treaty to be signed on 26 August, prior to his departure on 30 August 1858.

Lord Elgin's personal private secretary, Laurence Oliphant,[10] of a Scottish family, was a gifted, cultivated Victorian, who wrote with grace and skill of his world-wide travels. These two men, each distinguished in his own way, seem to have been two of the few Scots in the diplomatic service in Meiji Japan.

After the signing of the treaty Scots merchants waited impatiently for the diplomatic formalities to be completed. Some did not wait. The Dutch Minister wrote to Townsend Harris, the American Minister, from Nagasaki remarking that 'On February 18, 1859, a number of men had arrived from Shanghai among them K.R. MacKenzie.'[11] The naming of Kenneth Ross MacKenzie, a Scot who spent a lifetime in the Far East, reflects his importance as an associate of Jardine Matheson.[12]

1 July 1859, when the Treaty ports of Nagasaki, Hakodate, Yokohama opened, found K.R. MacKenzie in Nagasaki and William Keswick in Yokohama, the latter on Jardine Matheson's business. Hakodate (in the north on the island of Hokkaido) was primarily important for fishermen and those involved in ancillary industries, and had no special interest for the big traders.

William Keswick discovered that at Yokohama the Japanese, nervous of the coming invasion, had attempted to box up the foreign barbarians by isolating them on a 'seaward facing stretch of shore backed up by a swamp with rivers on either side'.[13] While Rutherford Alcock, the British Minister, was attempting to negotiate a better position, Keswick came ashore with his trading cargo. The Minister was annoyed, but as the Foreign Office advised, Jardines had achieved such a 'reputation in the East that trade would probably settle where they did'. Foreigners were allocated lots at Yokohama, and Keswick bought Lot No. 1, 'Ei Ichi-ban', No. 1 House, as well as Lots 22 and 23 behind it.

Trade was difficult. The Japanese, unhappy with the threatened depredations of the ever demanding foreigners, imposed currency restrictions, which temporarily halted trade. The merchants, frustrated by the obstructiveness of the Japanese, started buying up Japanese gold coins (*cobangs*) with silver *ichibu* and exporting them to China. Rutherford Alcock was furious and castigated the merchant community as 'the scum of the earth'.[14]

When the dust had settled it was clear that more orthodox trading was taking place. By November Keswick managed to get together 'a really worth-while shipment, of silk, copper, abalone, lacquer, porcelain, shark's fins, sea slugs and *cobangs*'.[15] Jardine Matheson's were convinced that the trade would develop.

The establishment of the merchant community in Yokohama and Nagasaki marks the beginning of modern relations between Britain and Japan. Later (1 January 1868) other ports were opened, including Kobe (known in early days as Hyogo), Osaka and Niigata. The latter place, rather isolated on the north west coast of the main island Honshu, was of little significance although Kobe and Osaka had much greater potential. Once Yokohama, Kobe and Osaka were established as Treaty ports, Nagasaki lost its earlier supremacy.

It is clear that trade (usually paying a nominal duty of 5 per cent) was growing. Exports to the West were primarily silk, tea, lacquer, and fancy goods. There was also a local trade in the form of dried seaweed, fish, and other assorted sea products, which were sent to China and other eastern ports. British manufactured goods, including wools and cottons, were acceptable as imports. Later when Japan was being modernised, rails, railway material, telegraph equipment, as well as machinery of all kinds found a ready market in Japan.

There was a strong contingent of Scots trading in Japan. The famous house of Jardine Matheson, which operated from Shanghai and Hong Kong, and had close connections with Mathesons in London, was founded and run by Scots.

Perhaps the best examplar is William Keswick (1834-1912), who had been educated at Merchistons School in Edinburgh, and thereafter served in Mathesons' London office until 1855, when at the age of 21, he took up employment in China. During his 27 years in the Far East he served in 16 stations including Yokohama, Osaka and Nagasaki in Japan, being taipan from 1874. By 1886 he was back in England where he took over Mathesons in London. He had worked closely with Sir Robert Jardine (1825-1905), who spent eleven years in China from 1849, before returning home. Sir Robert, a baronet with vast Scottish estates, became an MP and lived the life of the landed aristocracy while still taking an interest in business affairs. Hugh Matheson (1821-98),[16] who commanded Mathesons' London office until 1886, had not served in the Far East, either for health reasons or because he, being strongly evangelical, declined to countenance the opium trade. He also had been born and educated in Edinburgh and was then sent to Glasgow (where he attended some courses at the University) for office training, before being transferred to the London office. Hugh Matheson like the others, maintained a Scottish home, spending summer vacations and finally retiring there.

But the great houses of the East also did business with a variety of lesser men, not directly employed, but who sometimes acted for them. Thomas Blake Glover[17] (1838-1911) was born at Fraserburgh, but educated and based at Aberdeen during his formative years. Glover arrived at Nagasaki as a young man of 21 in 1859, recommended to Kenneth Ross MacKenzie. Although originally employed by MacKenzie as a clerk, Glover soon set up his own firm. The decade before the Meiji Restoration was hectic in Nagasaki, where retainers of disaffected princes negotiated with foreign merchants over a wide range of products. Glover, funded both by Jardine Matheson and later by the Netherlands Trading Society, was into everything, buying and selling ships to various clan chiefs, importing a slip dock (for the repair of ships), running the first small railway ever seen in Japan, and rigging up the first primitive telegraph line. He was also doing dangerous business, buying and selling arms and ammunition for sale to both government and the restless clans. Although he juggled successfully with inadequate funding for several years, he was brought down in August 1870 by a petty creditor and became bankrupt. Glover stayed in Japan and worked to bring the Takashima Coal Mine, which had earlier been one of his ventures, into profitability. He succeeded in paying off his creditors in 1875.

But despite his difficulties, Glover was well regarded by those young Japanese with whom he had associated in Nagasaki, and who were now emerging as the leaders of the new Japan. Glover was offered work, as adviser and consultant, by Iwasaki Yataro (1835-84), the founder of Mitsubishi. In this capacity, employed in both Nagasaki and Tokyo, Glover spent the rest of his career. He died in 1911 at Shiba Park in Tokyo, a legendary figure and one who was regarded by both Japanese and British as one of the makers of the new Japan.

At a less exalted level Scots merchant houses regularly recruited young Scots to clerkships. The 'lad o' pairts', perhaps having some 'far cousinly' connection with a senior member of the firm, was presented by anxious relatives as worthy of employ. Many were posted to stations in India, Siam, Malaya, China or Japan. A few became agents, attaining senior positions of authority and respect, and occasionally one might break away and make good as an independent merchant. Most remained, trusted and confidential, but clerks none the less, for their whole careers.

In the early days merchant houses provided their own ancillary services, handling for themselves matters which related to banking and insurance. Dealing in currency, manipulating imperfect markets and exchange arrangements could be profitable. Later, branches of foreign banks, established elsewhere in the Far East, opened in the Japanese treaty ports.

The Japanese were anxious to establish their own modern banks. They decided to adopt the American banking system. The government authorised two great merchant houses Mitsuigumi and Onogumi to set up the First National Bank of Japan in 1872. Despite the preference for American practices, it was a Scot who was credited with exerting a strong influence on Japanese banking in the early 1870s.

Alexander Allan Shand (1844-1930)[18] was apparently trained in a bank in Scotland.[19] He arrived in Japan in the late 1860s and in 1870 became acting manager of the Yokohama branch of the Mercantile Bank of India, London and China. Within a year or so he was recruited by the Ministry of Finance. In the next few years Shand succeeded in 'establishing a school of banking administration where he trained employees of the Ministry in Western methods of bookkeeping and prepared many of Japan's most important bankers for their future work'.[20]

Within two years of the establishment of the First National Bank, Onogumi, the great trading house, went bankrupt and the Ministry of Finance called in Shand to make an inspection of the bank. As a result of this, the first bank inspection in Japan, Shand discovered that large and small loans had been granted without security, the currency reserve was insufficient to cope with a run on the bank, and that there had been a general slackness. Matters were subsequently put on a proper footing, Shand remaining the chief foreign adviser (until he left for London in 1878) to the Bank's president, Shibusawa Eichi.

It was part of Japanese general policy to remain as independent of the foreigner as possible, so that although foreign banks were willing to lend, the Japanese government was reluctant to borrow. It is believed that some foreign loans were negotiated by men like Shand for the Japanese government, but they have always proved difficult to trace.

III

Scottish teachers and educators were employed in early Meiji Japan in many capacities. In some senses they brought a distinctive Scottish view of education, although this may not have been apparent to the Japanese. Scottish education was closer to that of Europe and based on a broader grouping of subjects than that of England. Although Latin and Greek were competently taught, the Classics did not, as in England, dominate the syllabus. Moral and Natural Philosophy (Physics) were taught, which together with Chemistry and Mathematics brought a broad spectrum of knowledge to the student.[21] As the Japanese were looking particularly to Britain for applied scientific and technical education it was not inappropriate that they should be attracted to Scotland.

In general terms Japanese school education was widely influenced by American practice. Medical education and some science teaching was based on ideas which came from Germany. It should perhaps be noted that in Japan most Scots were appointed as individual teachers and therefore had little opportunity of influencing the school or college in any particularly Scottish direction. There was one example, however, of a more noticeable Scottish presence.

The Imperial College of Engineering was set up by the Ministry of Public Works in Tokyo in 1872.[22] It was not part of the educational network established by the Ministry of Education. Those responsible for the Public Works Ministry, which was given responsibility for 'the railway, the mining, the lighthouse, the telegraph and the manufacturing departments which are all the property of the government', knew that it was essential to have some efficient training arrangements for young Japanese intending to pursue a career in engineering.

In selecting staff for the Imperial College of Engineering there seems little doubt that influential Scots consulted in London did advise the Japanese to look to Scotland and perhaps in particular to the University of Glasgow. Like the other ancient Scottish universities, Glasgow had remained small, but by the late eighteenth century had achieved considerable renown in a diversity of fields. Adam Smith, as professor of Moral Philosophy, William Cullen and William Hunter as professors of Medicine, and Joseph Black as professor of Chemistry had brought distinction to its learning.[23] Indeed at Joseph Black's request James Watt, the University's instrument maker, had worked on steam power, and eventually produced a practical steam engine which heralded the industrial revolution. Thanks to the Crown, which had established the first chair of Engineering at the University of Glasgow in 1840, engineering became a university subject bringing together theoretical training in engineering and scientific subjects and marrying them to practical work experience as well as laboratory work.[24]

When Ito Hirubumi asked Hugh Matheson, his first mentor in London, to recommend staff for the Imperial College of Engineering, Matheson thought of these Scottish achievements. He[25] spoke to his relative, Lewis Gordon, then an engineering consultant in London, who advised contact with McQuorn Rankine.[26] Professor Rankine, then professor of Engineering at Glasgow, recommended his best senior student, Henry Dyer. Dyer (MA, BSc, CE, Glasgow, 1848-1918) was appointed Principal of the Imperial College of Engineering at the age of 24, before he had finished his final diet of examinations.

Other Scottish staff appointed included David H. Marshall (MA, Edinburgh, 1869), professor of Mathematics, William Craigie (MA, Aberdeen), professor of English Language and Literature and Secretary to the College. Craigie left Japan a sick man and died shortly after in Scotland. His successor was William Gray Dixon (MA, Glasgow).[27] In later years other Scottish staff included Thomas Alexander (1848-1933, CE, Glasgow) assistant professor of Engineering, Thomas Gray (CE, BSc, Glasgow) as instructor of Telegraph Engineering, and James Main Dixon (MA, St Andrews) who replaced his brother W.G. Dixon.

Two other distinguished professors, not Scots, who had attended Kelvin's[28] lectures in Glasgow and worked in his laboratories, were W.E. Ayrton (1847-1908) professor of Natural Philosophy, and John Perry (1850-1920), professor of Engineering.

Others who were on the staff, but with no known Scottish connection included John Milne (1850-1913), professor of Mining and Geology, Edward Divers (MD, Queen's, Belfast, 1860), professor of Chemistry, and Edmund F. Mundy (Associate of the Royal School of Mines), professor of Engineering Drawing. Both Milne and Divers remained in Japan until the end of the century.

The College remained an independent unit for 13 years; it was then amalgamated with the Imperial University of Tokyo. Dyer remained as principal for ten years, before returning to Scotland,[29] for the remaining four years, Edward Divers, formerly professor of Chemistry became principal. Over the 13 years there was a steady turnover of staff. Where possible Japanese were appointed to replace the British whose contracts expired or who obtained posts elsewhere.

The course at the College lasted for six years, with two years general scientific training, two years for the study of technical subjects and two years of practical work. All the teaching was in English. During the first and second years the course consisted of classes in English, Geography, Elementary Mathematics, Mechanics and Physics, Chemistry and Engineering Drawing. Thereafter students were to choose from one of the six options of Civil Engineering, Mechanical Engineering, Telegraph Engineering, Architecture, Chemistry, and Metallurgy and Mining Engineering.

In the final two years the students were to be engaged in applying the theory they had learnt to practical application. For this purpose they could work in factories, or engineering workshops, or other suitable industrial concerns (where these existed in Japan), or at Akabane. There a whole new workshop complex was established in Tokyo, north of the college, where fine engineering workshops were set up. At Akabane two types of men (in addition to foreign instructors) worked. There were the student members of the College and also hundreds of technicians. The creation of a corps of engineering technicians was in itself an important contribution to Japan's industrialisation process.

The use of the combined techniques of pure and applied science and technology is of great importance. For most Japanese students, almost all of Samurai class, the idea of handling machines and making things from dirty metal, must have been difficult to accept. It was a completely strange and outlandish concept. But Dyer, the practical engineer with a full workshop apprenticeship behind him, was a stickler for the practical application of the theory. It seems certain that it was Dyer's ambition to create in Japan the sort of engineering workshop involving close co-operation between engineers and craftsmen, with which he had been so familiar in Glasgow. This emphasis on heuristic education, which is most simply explained by the phrase 'learning by doing', insisting on marrying theory and practice, may have been Dyer's greatest achievement in Japan.

During the life of the College 211 students graduated, of these 59 gained first and 145 second class certificates, the remainder failed to complete because of ill health. The first graduating graduates were sent under government sponsorship to study abroad. The most successful candidates were financed by the Japanese government, others had to rely on wealthy parents. It is possible that government sponsored students were sent to Glasgow, although students sometimes worked at more than one centre of learning.

The students who graduated from the Imperial College of Engineering went into a variety of occupations. Several became educators themselves. Some became practical engineers, distinguishing themselves in building Japanese railways, telegraphs, roads, bridges and modern buildings, as well as bringing canals and water supply to the towns.

The Akabane Works[30] remained as a government engineering workshop eventually servicing the army.

Some of the experimental educational work done during these early Meiji years when Japan was in transition, has been criticised in Japan because the education proffered was so strange that the Japanese failed to understand it or its relevance. It is perhaps the greatest tribute which can be paid to Dyer's College[31] that from 1873-86, it did provide an elite of Japanese students, as well as their technical assistants, with an entrée into the modern world of nineteenth-century technology.

The organisation of the College was based on that of the Polytechnic of Zurich. Both Hugh Matheson and Ito Hirobumi agreed that this was so. Yamao Yozo, later Minister of Works, also insisted that the inspiration came from Zurich. It is suggested here that while accepting that the original syllabus and timetable originated in Zurich, the practical application of such a scheme owed much to Glasgow practice.

The two men responsible for the setting up of the College, Yamao and Dyer were both Glasgow products. Yamao, the oldest of the original Choshu Five, who had come to Britain in 1863, had worked and studied in London and Glasgow. Between 1866-8 Yamao had worked at Robert Napier's shipyard on the Clyde during the day and attended evening classes at the Andersonian College.[32] Dyer, incidentally a fellow evening student of Yamao's, was solely Glasgow educated and only visited Zurich on his journey home from Japan in 1882.

Others who worked in Japan may have brought to their jobs qualities which were typical of Scots teachers, but these were difficult to define as in any special way Scottish. The Imperial College of Engineering is the only education institution which with its students wearing distinctive Glasgow caps, might be said to have been Scottish based.

IV

The Scots engineer who worked in Japan usually belonged to one of four professional categories. Mechanical engineers were employed in factories, workshops and shipyards and other industrial concerns. Civil engineers were involved with railways, bridges, roads, water supply and sewers. Men, who would later be classed as specialist electrical engineers, worked on telegraph installation. In addition there were ships' engineers who were employed by Japanese shipping companies. All these men were backed up by a corps of technical workers, who brought a variety of expertise to their tasks. Some individuals, highly regarded by their Japanese employers, were offered greater responsibilities than would have been available at home. If such men responded successfully to these challenges, they qualified themselves for greater prestige and rewards.

Technicians as a category (whether Scots or not) cannot usually be identified. Such men, although vital to the success of all the engineering projects, remain invisible to the historian. Only by chance are details of foreign lighthouse keepers,[33] telegraph operators, railway men, and shipbuilding craftsmen available. It is tantalising to know so little of those who by the nature of their duties associated so closely with, and therefore did a great deal to effect the basic technological transfer to, their Japanese counterparts.

Construction engineers were most often trained by apprenticeship rather than in the universities of the time. Scots were distinguishable from other English speaking engineers by their accent, as well as by their national pride which soon convinced observers that there was indeed a characteristic Scotch engineer.

Richard Henry Brunton (1838-1901) was appointed as lighthouse engineer to the Japanese government on 24 February 1868.[34] By training he was a railway engineer and although born, educated and trained in Aberdeenshire he had sought employment in 1864 in London with W.R. Galbraith, engineer to the London and South Western Railway.

The appointment of a Scot may have reflected the Scottish initiative behind the Japanese lighthouse building project. When the Board of Trade was approached by the British Minister in Japan on this matter they referred to the lighthouse builders, D. and T. Stevenson of Edinburgh who were lighthouse engineers to the Commissioners for Northern Lights in Scotland.[35] David and Thomas Stevenson were at that time at the height of their powers, demonstrating, first in Scotland around the dangerous craggy coasts there, and then to the world, their technical prowess in mastering storm-tossed sites on the edge of dangerous seas.

The Japanese project was one of many overseas commitments, making Stevensons and Edinburgh the centre of an important and unexpected industry. All the plans were made in Edinburgh, and apart from the basic raw material of the lighthouse tower which was usually fashioned from local materials, all other components were manufactured and test assembled in Edinburgh before being packed and crated for despatch overseas. The only item manufactured elsewhere was the glass, most of which was supplied by Chance Brothers of Birmingham.

Neither Brunton nor his two assistants were lighthouse engineers. They were therefore employed for two to three months in Edinburgh to learn as much as they could from D. and T. Stevenson before proceeding to Japan, arriving there in August 1868.

For the next eight years Brunton established lighthouses, lights, and lightships on a variety of sites around the perilous and indented Japanese coasts. These have come to be known as the Japan Lights. It was a task both demanding and dangerous. For Brunton had to organise everything, chart the coasts (Japanese ships had normally anchored during the hours of darkness), decide on lighthouse sites (British ship captains were clamouring for guiding lights), survey the sites, note the problems, plan the structure, draw up plans, decide on basic raw material, whether available locally or not, and order equipment for the light and the structure to support it from Edinburgh. Once these preliminaries had been done he had to marshal the local labour, negotiate with the local authority, select native craftsmen and start the hazardous work of building the basic structure. In order to travel to the various lighthouse sites he had the service of the lighthouse tender, a small boat ably skippered by Captain A.R. Brown.[36] Brunton also had to co-operate with Japanese officials at all stages of his work and with all levels of authority.

As Brunton notes, 'On the completion of my term of service, the lighthouse department had established, or had in hand, thirty seven ocean lights, nine harbour lights, three light vessels, fifteen buoys and eight beacons.'[37]

But there were difficulties, although Brunton was a clever and versatile engineer he was irascible and bitterly resented the intrusion of the Japanese into what he regarded as his proper authority. In his *Pioneering Engineering in Japan* he did not attempt to excuse or explain his highly critical and intolerant remarks on Japanese officials.

Much later Charles Scott Meik (1853-1923) spent a period of service as harbour engineer with the Japanese government in 1887.[38] Meik was born in Edinburgh and educated at the High School before being apprenticed to Hawthorn's Civil Engineering Company for three years. Thereafter he moved to the Tyne and worked for two years with Armstrong Whitworth's at the Elswick works. Meik later (1881) became chief assistant to Thomas Meik and Sons, M.M. Inst. CE,[39] building many harbours in Scotland and the north of England. In 1887 he was invited to take up the position of Chief Engineer for Harbours and Rivers of Japan. His task in Japan concerned the north island Hokkaido, requiring him to report on the development of harbours and rivers there. The island had been occupied only by the primitive Ainu, but the Japanese, fearful of possible Russian aggression determined to develop and colonise it themselves. To this end they had encouraged families, including those of Samurai displaced by the modernisation programme, to move to Hokkaido on the promise of land for farming. Meik's reports were part of this development plan. He remained there for three years and submitted a series of competent and well judged plans, some of which were later adopted.

In the last resort it was for shipbuilding and naval architecture skills for which the Japanese continued to look to the west of Scotland until after the First World War. There were two groups of men associated with this long continued endeavour.

The first and most numerous were those whose technical competence took them to Japan and who remained there working for a life time in Japanese shipyards. It is in fact the foreign graveyards of Nagasaki, Kobe and Yokohama which reveal the existence of these men.[40] At Nagasaki John Hill, 'a native of Scotland and for many years an employee of the Mitsubishi Company' (who were and are the major shipbuilding company there) died in 1900, aged 58 years. James Fowler Mitchell (1829-1903) of Aberdeen, Scotland, 'Master Shipbuilder, for 44 years a resident of Japan, formerly of Nagasaki', died at Kobe. Mitchell had apparently moved from the Mitsubishi Shipbuilding works at Nagasaki to a similar job in Kobe. And John Hope Macdonald, a native of Stornoway, Scotland, 1st Officer of Nippon Yusen Kaisha (NYK), the largest Japanese shipping line, who died in Yokohama in 1903, aged 48 years.

At another level it is noteworthy that the holders of the Chair of Naval Architecture at the University of Glasgow were usually invited to Japan as consultants. The chair was founded in 1883 and the occupants until after the First World War were: 1883 — Francis Elgar, LLD; 1886 — Philip Jenkins; 1891-1921 — Sir John Harvard Biles, DSc, LLD. Francis Elgar referred to his 'lengthened visit to Japan when he was employed in Japan as adviser to the Japanese navy' between 1880-1.[41] Jenkins was there also, although he suffered from poor health, and Sir John Biles was a familiar figure in Japan. The only example of work done relates to an enquiry which Biles made for the Japanese with regard to a Clyde built ship the *Chiyoda*.[42] None of these men were Scots.

V

There were two groups of Scots working in Japan at any one time, those employed by the Japanese, either by the government or privately, and those working for British or other foreign businesses. Those in the latter group could, if they wished, remain in Japan encapsulated in the foreign settlements. The former group working directly with and under the authority of Japanese employers were much more likely to build up real relationships and indeed friendships with Japanese. Those Scots who went to Japan as instructors almost certainly had the opportunity to develop warm teacher/pupil relations with their Japanese students.

The Scots and the Japanese had much in common. The pride of the Scot in his educational tradition and his professional competence drew a sympathetic response from the Japanese.

With the appointment of Henry Dyer as principal, and other Scots graduates as professors, at the Imperial College of Engineering it seems likely that a particularly Scottish outlook of hard work, earnestness and endeavour, was present there. In the early days the Japanese lighthouse service, with Richard Henry Brunton in charge and Stevenson's in Edinburgh recruiting Scots lighthouse keepers for service in Japan, may also have had a special Scottish flavour.

But the foreign settlements remained the centre of life for most of the Scots residents. In Yokohama the bluff to the south of the town and in Kobe and Nagasaki the hills behind the town became pleasant residential areas. In accordance with the treaty rights (1859-94) small foreign municipalities were created to provide water, sewage, roads, drainage, and other services. The foreigners quickly developed their own sense of community, organising not only the basic amenities of life, but also leisure activities in the form of sports, games and picnics. As temporary exiles they spent their free time doing the things they might have enjoyed at home.

The Scots were very active. Through the St Andrew's Clubs they arranged Scottish country dancing, organised ceilidhs and the 'Go as you please'. This last requires everyone to participate, by singing a song, reciting a poem or making some other appropriate contribution to the general entertainment. Scottish groups founded Freemason's lodges in Yokohama, Kobe and Nagasaki.[43] These were social gatherings, but also involved members in arcane rituals and overflowed into business. The Burns Clubs brought other occasions for poetry and conviviality culminating on 25 January with the celebration of Robert Burns' birthday. These occasions were accompanied not only with such ceremonies of 'addressing the haggis' and 'toasting the lassies', but also with ample libations of Scotch whisky.

Some Japanese were involved with these manifestations of Scottish solidarity. No doubt the convivial spirit did much to counter the mystification which some of the rituals must have created.[44]

The many Scots visitors who came to Japan, either for business or pleasure, were good excuses for further parties and visits. Indeed from the contemporary travel books written by Scots a pleasant picture of life emerges. Visitors from Scotland, armed with introductions seemed to pass easily from one Scots family to the next. Indeed in summer the itinerary was extended for Hakone, in the mountains, and Chiba, by the sea, both removed from the heat of Tokyo, were favourite resorts and many Scots extolled both the beauty of Japan and the hospitality of their fellow countrymen.

The Scots were also active in organising various sports. Because of the large numbers of young Scots working in early Meiji Japan it was usually possible to present a Scottish team for almost any popular sport. Rowing and similar river and water sports were popular. Above all cricket was a popular summer pastime. The *Daily Advertiser* of Yokohama of 13 September 1875, announced the forthcoming cricket match: 'Scotland against the World at 1 p.m. today'.

After the 'exports decade' (1872-82) when the Japanese programme of importing skills slackened, a reverse process was encouraged. Young Japanese, already qualified in Japan, were sent on study programmes abroad. Those who were government sponsored had their expenses paid, others were sent and paid for by their families. Students were sent to many places and many countries. The nexus between Scotland and Japan remained very strong. Between 1886 and 1914 some 60 students from Japan were registered for long or short study programmes at the University of Glasgow. Simultaneously some served in the shipyards on the Clyde as apprentices, others worked in engineering workshops. The availability of Dr Henry Dyer in Glasgow after his service in Japan provided a valuable continuum. Japan's continued dependence on western technology, especially for skills associated with the shipbuilding and naval architecture, ensured a strong Japanese presence. Indeed, in 1889 a Japanese consulate was set up in Glasgow. This reflected the strong Japanese naval presence required to supervise the steady stream of vessels being built on the Clyde for the Japanese navy.

The presence in Scotland of so many Japanese in the later Meiji years can be taken as a compliment to those Scots who had earlier served with distinction in Japan.

Notes

1. For general introduction see W.G. Beasley, *A Modern History of Japan* (London, 1963), *The Meiji Restoration* (London, 1973), and Grace Fox, *Britain and Japan, 1858-1885* (London, 1969).

2. See H.J. Jones, *Live Machines: Hired Foreigners in Meiji Japan* (University of British Columbia, 1980).

3. Ishii, R., *A History of Political Institutions in Japan* (English translation, Japan Foundation, 1980), Chapter 5.

4. See Ian Inkster's work 'Meiji Economic Development in Perspective: Revisionist Comments upon the Industrial Revolution in Japan' in *The Developing Economies*,. XVII-I (March, 1979), pp. 45-68, and *Japan as a Development Model: Relative Backwardness and Technological Transfer* (Studienverlag Dr. N. Brockmeyer, Bochum, 1980).

5. Jones, *Live Machines*, p. 14.

6. Ibid., p. 90.

7. Ibid., p. 152.

8. I. Bird, *Unbeaten Tracks in Japan* (London, 1880) C.F. Gordon Cumming, *Memories* (Edinburgh, 1904).

9. T. Walrond, *Letters and Journals of James, 8th Earl of Elgin* (London, 1872). J.L. Morison, *The Eighth Earl of Elgin* (London, 1928).

10. L. Oliphant, *Narrative of the Earl of Elgin's Mission to China and Japan in the Years 1857, 58, and 59*, vols. I and II (Edinburgh, 1859). M.O.W. Oliphant, *Memoir of the Life of Laurence Oliphant and of Alice Oliphant his Wife*, vol. I and II (Edinburgh, 1891). P.P. Henderson, *The Life of L. Oliphant, Traveller, Diplomat and Mystic* (London, 1956). A. Taylor, *Laurence Oliphant* (London, 1982).

11. M.E. Cosenza, *The Complete Journal of Townsend Harris, First American Consul and Minister to Japan* (Rutland, Vermont and Tokyo, 1959), p. 74, n. 4.

12. The Jardine Matheson Archives are held in Cambridge University Library. See also J. McMaster, *Jardines in Japan, 1859-1967* (Groningen, 1967). M. Keşwick (ed.), *The Thistle and the Jade: a Celebration of 150 Years of Jardine Matheson & Co.* (London, 1982).

13. Keswick, *Thistle and Jade*, p. 155.

14. The official Notification which Alcock issued on this occasion was very severe and named both Mr Keswick and Mr Barker, who were acting for Jardine Matheson in Yokohama.

15. Keswick, *Thistle and Jade*, p. 157.

16. H.M. Matheson, *Memorials of Hugh M. Matheson*, edited by his wife (London, 1899).

17. See S. Sugiyama, 'Thomas B. Glover: A British Merchant in Japan, 1861-1870' in *Business History*, July 1984 and Algemeen Rijksarchief, The Hague, Netherlands, see Tweede Afdeling, Nederlandische, Handelmaatschappij, Nr. 5935.

18. Umetani, N., *Foreigners in the Service of the Japanese Government* (Tokyo, 1965), pp. 119-23 and 202-4. I am grateful to Professor Tamaki of Keio University, Tokyo for this translation. Obituary of A.A. Shand in *The Times*, 16 April 1930.

19. Scottish trained bankers were highly regarded, see G.M. Bell, *The Philosophy of Joint Stock Banking* (London, 1855), pp. 161-2.

20. G. Fox, *Britain and Japan*, p. 395.

21. See G.E. Davie, *The Democratic Intellect, Scotland and her Universities in the Nineteenth Century* (Edinburgh, 1961). L. Saunders, *Scottish Democracy, 1815-1840* (Edinburgh, 1950) and M. Sanderson, *The Universities and British Industry, 1850-1970* (London, 1972).

22. Material on the Imperial College of Engineering is held mainly by the Mitchell Library, Glasgow, and in Tokyo at the Unit of the history of the University of Tokyo, Japan. See also W.H. Brock, 'The Japanese Connexion: Engineering in Tokyo, London, and Glasgow at the end of the nineteenth century, Presidential Address, 1980' in *The British Journal for the History of Science*, vol. 14, no. 48, 1981, pp. 227-43. Professor Kita's help with Japanese material on ICE has been much appreciated.

23. J.D. Mackie, *The University of Glasgow* (Glasgow, 1954). Andrew Kent (ed.), *An Eighteenth Century Lectureship in Chemistry. Essays and Bicentenary addresses relating to the Chemistry Department (1747) of Glasgow University (1451)* (Glasgow, 1950).

24. C.A. Oakley, *A History of a Faculty Engineering at Glasgow University* (Glasgow, 1973). See also *Engineering in the British Dominions* (London, 1891).

25. H.M. Matheson, *Memorials* (London, 1899). pp. 202-8.

26. H.B. Sutherland, 'Rankine and his Times', Rankine Centenary Lecture, The Institution of Civil Engineers (London, 1972).

27. W.G. Dixon, *The Land of the Morning, an Account of Japan and its People Based on a Four Years Residence in That Country* (Edinburgh, 1882).

28. William Thomson, later Lord Kelvin, was the seminal figure who acted as a magnet attracting a generation of scientists and engineers to Glasgow.

29. Material on Henry Dyer and ICE, including annual reports giving details of courses and staff is held at the Mitchell Library, Glasgow, Glasgow University Library and Glasgow University Archives. In Japan Dyer wrote *The Education of Engineers: The Imperial College of Engineering* (Tokyo, 1879), *Valedictory Address* (Tokyo, 1882). In Glasgow he wrote many works on technical education and also *Dai Nippon: Britain of the East, a study of National Evolution* (London, 1904), *Japan in World Politics: A Study in International Dynamics* (Glasgow and London, 1909), and *Evolution of Industry* (London, 1895).

30. The Diet Library, Tokyo, Japan holds a copy of the catalogue of the Akabane Engineering Works (1880). I am grateful to Professor Kenji Imatzu of Kobe University for a xerox copy of this.

31. See Isabella Bird, *Unbeaten Tracks, pp. 189-91,* who refers to 'Dyers College' as being a common name for the ICE, she also refers to Dyer as 'intensely a Scotchman and not only very able in his own profession but a man of singular force, energy and power of concentration, with a resolute and indomitable will. He is felt in the details of every department of the College and combines practical sagacity with a large amount of well directed enthusiasm. It is said that of the foreign teachers in Japanese employment he is the one whose resolute independence and determination to carry out his own plans in his own way have been respected by the government.'

32. Glasgow University Library and Anderson's Library, the University of Strathclyde hold annual reports giving details of courses.

33. See David and Thomas Stevenson papers, National Library of Scotland, Out Letter Book, letter to R.H. Brunton, 30 March 1869. 'The three workmen who have been engaged to go to Japan leave on April 3. Their names are John Russel who was foreman of Joiners at Messrs. Milne, Thomas Wallace also from Messrs. Milne's, who is an iron worker and has been chiefly employed in Lighthouse Apparatus and John Mitchell who is a mason and understands granite dressing etc. We hope you find them all intelligent and useful in their different departments.'

34. Richard Henry Brunton's papers on 'Pioneering Engineering in Japan' were bought by William Elliott Griffis shortly after Brunton's death in London in 1901. They were intended for publication but in the end remained in a typed form. They are held in W.E. Griffis papers, Rutgers University Library, New Brunswick, New Jersey, USA.

35. See Craign Mair, *A Star for Seamen* (London, 1978).

36. Captain Albert Richard Brown's papers are held in Glasgow University Archives.

37. Brunton 'Pioneering Engineering in Japan', Chapter XXIV, p. 152.

38. Charles Scott Meik, C.E., 'Around the Hokkaido', *Transactions of the Asiatic Society of Japan* (Yokohama, 1889). Copies of C.S. Meik's reports on rivers and harbours in Hokkaido are available at the Library of the University of Hokkaido and the Prefecture Library, Sapporo, Japan.

39. Obituary of C.S. Meik, *Scotsman*, 14 July 1923.

40. The foreign graveyards at Nagasaki, Kobe and Yokohama are well-cared for and an important source of information about the foreign communities. Professor Kita's photographic record has been most useful.

41. Testimonials in favour of Thomas Gray, BSc, FRSE as a candidate for the Cavendish Professorship of Physics of the Yorkshire College, Leeds (1885). Letter of Francis Elgar, p. 17, GUL.

42. Sir John Harvard Biles (1854-1933) was perhaps the most distinguished

Naval Architect of his generation widely involved as government adviser and consultant. Some of the problems of tendering for ships to be built for the Japanese are explained in J.H. Biles, 'Memo on Visit to Japan and China', October 1895, in J. and G. Thomson papers in John Brown and Co. Papers, Glasgow University Archives.

43. C. Haffner, *The Craft in the East*, district lodge of Hong Kong and the Far East, Hong Kong, 1977.

44. In November 1874 the editor of the *Japan Punch* enjoyed himself at the expense of the Scots under the heading of 'St Andrews Day, the banquet wi' neeps'. The editor concluded his remarks, 'in the words of Burns, "The Taties was gran', the neeps was fine an' we a' got fou" '. This would be translated as, 'The potatoes were grand, the turnips were fine and we all got drunk.'

SELECT BIBLIOGRAPHY

Adam, M.I. 'The Causes of the Highland Emigrations of 1783-1803', *Scottish Historical Review*, XVII (January, 1920)

Bailey, J.D. 'Australian Borrowing in Scotland in the Nineteenth Century', *Economic History Review*, vol. 12 (1959-60), pp. 268-79

Black, G.F. *Scotland's Mark on America* (New York, 1921)

Brander, M. *The Emigrant Scots* (London, 1982)

Brock, W.H. 'The Japanese Connexion: Engineering in Tokyo, London and Glasgow at the end of the 19th century, presidential address 1980', *British Journal for the History of Science*, vol. 14, no. 48 (1981), pp. 227-43.

Brock, W.R. *Scotus Americanus: A Survey of the Sources For Links Between Scotland and America in the Eighteenth Century* (Edinburgh, 1982)

Buchana, D.H. *The Development of Capitalistic Enterprise in India*, 2nd edn (London, 1966)

Burton, J.H. *The Scot Abroad* (Edinburgh, 1881)

Chaudhuri, K.N. (ed.). *The Economc Development of India under the East India Company, 1814-58* (Cambridge, 1971)

Cheong, W.E. *Mandarins and Merchants, Jardine Matheson & Co., A China Agency of the Early Nineteenth Century* (London, 1979).

Clow, A. and N.L. *The Chemical Revolution* (London, 1952)

Cumming, C.F. *Memories* (Edinburgh, 1904)

Davis, G.E. *The Democratic Intellect, Scotland and Her Universities in the nineteenth century* (Edinburgh, 1961)

Devine, T.M. *The Tobacco Lords: A Study of the Tobacco Merchants of Glasgow and Their Trading Activities, c. 1740-90* (Edinburgh, 1975)

Dixon, W.G. *The Land of the Morning: An Account of Japan and its People Based on a Four Years Residence in that Country* (Edinburgh, 1882)

Dodds, J. *Records of the Scottish Settlers in the River Plate and Their Churches* (Buenos Aires, 1897)

Donaldson, G. *The Scots Overseas* (London, 1966)

Drysdale, J.M. *A Hundred Years in Buenos Aires, 1829-1929* (Buenos Aires, 1929)

Erickson, C.J. 'Who were the English and Scots Immigrants to the United States in the late Nineteenth Century?', D.V. Glass and Roger Revelle (eds.), *Population and Social Change* (London, 1972), pp. 347-81

Ferns, H. *Britain and Argentina in the Nineteenth Century* (Oxford, 1960)

Fischer, T.A. *The Scots in Germany* (Edinburgh, 1902)

Fox, G. *Britain and Japan, 1858-1885* (Oxford, 1969)

Gibbon, J.M. *The Scots in Canada* (London, 1911)

Graham, C.J. *Colonists from Scotland: Emigration to North America, 1707-1783* (Ithaca, 1956)

Greenberg, M. *British Trade and the Opening of China, 1800-1842* (Cambridge, 1951)

Harrison, J.R.C. *Robert Owen and the Owenites in Britain and America: The Quest for the New Moral World* (London, 1969)

Henderson, P.P. *The Life of Laurence Oliphant, Traveller, Diplomat and Mystic* (London, 1956)

Hook, A. *Scotland and America: A Study of Cultural Relations, 1750-1835* (Glasgow, 1975)

Hunt, W. *Heirs of Great Adventure. The History of Balfour Williamson & Company Limited*, 2 pts. (Norwich, 1951, 1960)

Insh, G.P. *Scottish Colonial Schemes* (Glasgow, 1922)

Jackson, W.T. *The Enterprising Scot: Scottish Investment in the West, after 1873* (Edinburgh, 1968)

Jones, C. 'Who Invested in Argentina and Uruguay', *Business Archives*, no. 48 (November 1982), pp. 1-24

Jones, H.J. *Live Machines, Hired Foreigners in Meiji Japan* (Tenterden, 1980)

Kerr, W.G. *Scottish Capital on the American Credit Frontier* (Austin, 1976)

Kerr, W.G. 'Scottish Investment and Enterprise in Texas', P.L. Payne, *Studies in Scottish Business History* (London, 1967)

Keswick, M. *The Thistle and the Jade, a Celebration of 150 Years of Jardine, Matheson & Co.* (London, 1982)

Koebel, W.H. *British Exploits in South America* (New York, 1917)

Lee, C.H. *A Cotton Enterprise* (Manchester, 1972)

McCulloch, J.H. *The Scots in England* (London, 1935)

McMaster, J. *Jardines in Japan, 1859-1967* (Groningen, 1967)

Macmillan, D.S. *Scotland and Australia, 1788-1850: Emigration, Commerce and Investment* (Oxford, 1967)

Marshall, R.J. *East Indian Fortunes. The British in Bengal in the Eighteenth Century* (Oxford, 1976)

Mulhall, M.G. *The English in South America* (Buenos Aires, 1878)

Musson, A.E. and E. Robinson, *Science and Technology* (Manchester, 1969)

Oliphant, L. *Narrative of the Earl of Elgin's Mission to China and Japan in the years 1857, 58 and 59*, vol. I. and II (Edinburgh, 1859)

Oliver, W.H. and B.R. Williams (eds.) *The Oxford History of New Zealand* (Wellington, 1981)

Parker, J.G. 'The Directors of the East India Company, 1754-1790', unpublished PhD thesis, Edinburgh University, 1977

Pearce, G.L. *The Scots of New Zealand* (Dundee, 1976)

Philips, C.H. *The East India Company, 1784-1834*, 3rd edn (Manchester, 1968)

Price, J.M. 'The Rise of Glasgow in the Chesapeake Tobacco Trade, 1707-1775', *William & Mary College Quarterly*, 3rd series, XI (April 1954), pp. 179-99

Pryde, G.S. *The Scottish Universities and the Colleges of Colonial America* (Glasgow, 1957)

Rattray, W.J. *The Scot in British North America*, 4 vols., (Edinburgh, 1880)

Reber, V.B. *British Mercantile Houses in Buenos Aires, 1810-1880* (Cambridge, Massachusetts, 1979)

Redford, A. *Labour Migration in England*, 3rd edn (Manchester, 1976)

Reid, W. Stanford (ed.), *The Scottish Tradition in Canada* (Ontario, 1976)

Rice, D. *The Scottish Abolitionists* (Baton Rouge, 1981)

Soltow, J.H. 'Scottish Traders in Virginia, 1750-1775', *Economic History Review*, vol. XII (1959-60), pp. 83-98

Thorner, D. *Investment in Empire: British Railway and Steam Shipping Enterprise in India, 1825-49* (Philadelphia, 1950)

Tyson, R.E. 'Scottish Investment in American Railways: the Case of the City of Glasgow Bank, 1856-1881', P.L. Payne, *Scottish Business History* (London, 1967)

Umetani, N. *Foreigners in the Service of the Japanese Government* (Tokyo, 1965)

Webster, S. *Emigration to the River Plate, Success of British Subjects in Buenos Aires, List of Landowners, Description of the City and Province of Buenos Aires* (London, 1871)

Williamson, A. *Lord Forres Balfour Williamson & Co. and allied firms* (London, 1929)

Wilson, Charles and William Reader. *Men and Machines: A History of D. Napier and Son, Engineers, Ltd., 1808-1958* (London, 1958)

Wilson, Gordon, M. *Alexander McDonald: Leader of the Miners*, (Aberdeen, 1982)

Young, James D. 'Changing Images of American Democracy and the Labour Movement', *International Review of Social Studies*, vol. 13 (1973), pp. 69-89

NOTES ON CONTRIBUTORS

Bernard Aspinwall. Lecturer, Modern History, the University of Glasgow. Presently writing a book on 'Scotland and America, 1820-1920'; 'Glasgow Trams and American Politics, 1894-1914', in *Scottish Historical Review*, 56, 1977, pp. 64-84; 'The Scottish Religious Identity in the Atlantic World, 1880-1914', in S. Mews (ed.), *Studies in Church History: Religion and National Identity*, vol. 18 (Oxford, 1982), pp. 505-18.

Tom Brooking. Lecturer, History, University of Otago, New Zealand. *A History of Dentistry in New Zealand* (Dunedin, 1981); contributor to the *Oxford History of New Zealand*. Presently writing a biography of Capt. William Cargill.

R.A. Cage. Senior Lecturer, Economic History, University of New England, New South Wales. *The Scottish Poor Law, 1745-1845* (Edinburgh, 1981); 'The Standard of Living Debate: Glasgow, A Case Study, 1800-1850', in *Journal of Economic History*, March, 1982, pp. 175-82; presently editing a volume on the condition of the working classes in Glasgow, 1750-1914.

R.H. Campbell, formerly Professor of Economic History, Stirling University. *Scotland Since 1707* (Oxford, 1965); *Scottish Industrial History: A Miscellany* (Edinburgh, 1978); *Rise and Fall of Scottish Industry, 1707-1939* (Edinburgh, 1980); with A.S. Skinner, *Adam Smith* (London, 1982); with A.S. Skinner, *Origins and Nature of the Enlightenment in Scotland* (Edinburgh, 1982).

Olive Checkland. Research Fellow, Scottish History, the University of Glasgow. *Philanthropy in Victorian Scotland* (Edinburgh, 1980); edited with Margaret Lamb, *Health Care as Social History: The Glasgow Case* (Aberdeen, 1982). Presently working on a history of Scottish activities in Japan.

Manuel A. Fernandez. Lecturer, United World College of the Adriatic, Italy. 'Merchants and Bankers: British Direct and Portfolio Investment in Chile during the Nineteenth Century', forthcoming, *Ibero-Amerikanisches Archiv*.

David S. Macmillan. Professor of History, Trent University, Ontario, Canada. With Alan Birch, *The Sydney Scene, 1788-1960* (Sydney, 1982); 'Problems in the Scottish Trade with Russia in the Eighteenth Century: A Study in Mercantile Frustration', in A.G. Cross (ed.),

Great Britain and Russia in the Eighteenth Century: Contacts and Comparisons (Boston, 1979); 'The Neglected Aspect of the Scottish Diaspora, 1650-1850: The Role of the Entrepreneur in Promoting and Effecting Emigration', in *Collected Seminar Papers No. 31*, Institute of Commonwealth Studies, London, 1982.

James G. Parker, Historical Manuscripts Commission, London.

Eric Richards. Professor of History, the Flinders University of South Australia. *The Leviathan of Wealth: The Sutherland Fortune in the Industrial Revolution* (London, 1973); *A History of the Highland Clearances* (London, 1982).

INDEX

Abernathy, John 43
Acheson, T.W. 64
Acland, George 210
Acland, L.G.D. 174-5
Adam, James 160, 163
Adamson, Alexander 200
administrators, Scottish, in Australia 116-17, 134
agriculture: New Zealand 156, 168, 172, 173-9; Scottish 42-3 *see also* pastoralism
Aikman, Peter and Thomas 241-2
Ailsa, Marquis of 128
Airlie, Earl of 100
Albion, R.G. 67-8
Albion Line 21
Alcock, Rutherford 256
Alexander, John 95
Alexander, Sir William 46, 50, 83
Alexander, Thomas 261
Alexander and Co. 199, 203, 205, 206
Alison, Archibald 115-16
Alison, Francis 86
Allan, Capt Alexander 55
Allan, Stewart and Co. 58
Allan Line 20, 55, 84
Anchor Line 20, 84
Anderson, Arthur 214
Anderson, Joseph 127
Anderson and Co. 75
Andrew Thomson and Co., Messrs 52, 67
Andrew Yule and Co. 208, 209
Anglo-American relations 101
Anglo-Indian Jute Mill Co. 212
Appleton, Nathan 96
Argentina 230-3, 234-8, 244-5
Arnold, M. 166, 170
Arnold, R. 162
Arthur and Company 99
Atcheson, Nathaniel 52-3
Audubon, James J. 92
Australia 15, 111-55, 252; aborigines 124, 131; bounty schemes 122-3; concentrations of Scots in 131, 140; convicts in 114-16; English

influences in 142; land policy 118-19, 121-2, 127; Scottish institutions in 141-2; Scottish investment in 142-7; shipping and 21
Australian Company of Edinburgh and Leith 46-7, 120-1
Australian Gas Company 132
Australian Mercantile and Finance Company 143
automobile industry 101
Ayrton, W.E. 261

Bache, Alexander D. 89
Bailey, J.D. 143, 145
Bain, Edward 181
bakeries 32
Bald, Claud 213
Balfour, Alexander 240
Balfour, James 150
Balk, William and Co. 180
Ballantynes store 180
Bank of Australasia 132
Bank of England 35
Bank of India, Australia and China 216
Bank of Montreal 62
Bank of New Brunswick 74
Bank of New South Wales 166, 170-71, 180
Bank of New Zealand 170-1, 179
Bank of Otago 170
Bank of Scotland 35
banks: Australian 134, 147-9, 171; Canadian 62, 74, 75; English 32-7; Indian 208, 215-17; Japanese 258-9; New Zealand 170-1, 180; Scottish, in England 33-7
Banks, Sir Joseph 118
Barr, Peter 180
Barrie, J.J. 210-11
Batman, John 123-4
Begg, David 208
Begg, Dunlop and Co. 208
Begg, Revd James 163
Bell, Charles 43

277